Crime and Justice

Crime and Justice
A Review of Research
Edited by Michael Tonry

VOLUME 20

The University of Chicago Press, Chicago and London

This volume was prepared under Grant Number 92-IJ-CX-K044 awarded to the Castine Research Corporation by the National Institute of Justice, U.S. Department of Justice, under the Omnibus Crime Control and Safe Streets Act of 1968 as amended. Points of view or opinions expressed in this volume are those of the editors or authors and do not necessarily represent the official position or policies of the U.S. Department of Justice.

The University of Chicago Press, Chicago 60637
The University of Chicago Press, Ltd., London

© 1996 by The University of Chicago
All rights reserved. Published 1996
Printed in the United States of America

99 98 97 96   4   3   2   1

ISSN: 0192-3234

ISBN: 0-226-80826-2

LCN: 80-642217

Contents

Foreword

The milestone of the twentieth volume in the *Crime and Justice* series offers an opportunity to reflect on its purpose and progress. When the National Institute of Justice and *Crime and Justice* editors Norval Morris and Michael Tonry launched this venture in 1977, no annual review in criminal justice existed for integrating the growing knowledge emerging from an ever-widening number of disciplines. The editors set themselves the ambitious task of looking beyond the domain of any one discipline to produce a broad overview of research on crime and responses to it written by outstanding scholars in the field. For its part, the National Institute of Justice envisioned a mechanism for distilling knowledge about the state of the art in a way that is rigorous and useful for policy makers and practitioners as well as the scholarly community.

Although I was not present at the creation of *Crime and Justice*, I welcome this occasion to take stock of this partnership between the National Institute of Justice and the nation's foremost scholars. In thinking about how well our mutual goals have been realized, several indices come to mind. One gauge is the influence of *Crime and Justice* in the world of research: the series is among the most frequently cited journals in the criminological literature. Boldness and innovation are certainly other measures of success. The editors and editorial boards of *Crime and Justice* were among the first to think seriously about the value of sharing perspectives on the organization and conduct of research in other countries and the insights to be gained through cross-national research on the increasingly global problem of crime. And in the world of policy, one need only look at the spectrum of topics and themes represented in the twenty volumes to recognize the relevance of this body of work for public policy debate. Path-breaking essays on biology and crime, family factors as correlates and predictors of delinquency, co-offending and criminal careers; state-of-the-knowledge summaries on gangs, police crackdowns, fines and day fines; major theme volumes on family violence, drugs and crime, modern policing, and prediction and classification—the contents of the *Crime and Justice* volumes reflect, and often anticipate, the research and policy challenges that represent the continuing agenda for serious inquiry as the twentieth century draws to a close.

As the principal supporter of the series since its inception, the National Institute of Justice is proud of its role in initiating and sustaining *Crime and Justice*. One salient characteristic of this endeavor has been the independence of the series. While the institute is deeply involved in exploring ideas for topics and themes, the decisions as to what is written are solely within the purview of the editors and the editorial board. The result has been candid, thought-provoking analysis on issues that deserve the most wide-ranging and serious debate. We have every confidence that future volumes will uphold the high standards that are evident in this volume and its predecessors.

Jeremy Travis
Director
National Institute of Justice

Preface

Many Americans, ordinary citizens and elected officials alike, have strong views about crime. Often they are based on common sense uninformed by knowledge. Car owners know that their behavior is influenced by more vigilant parking enforcement and assume that prospective burglars, robbers, and drug dealers will respond in similar ways to increased penalties. Two decades of research in the United States and elsewhere inform us that the links between penalty changes and behavior are much more complex than that. Year in and year out, three-quarters or more of Americans tell pollsters they believe crime rates are increasing. Both police and victim data show much more complicated patterns but agree to the contrary that crime rates have been steady or declining for significant periods since 1980 and were lower for most crimes in 1995 than fifteen years earlier.

Crime and Justice's premise from its inception has been that better policy making and better research will be based on both common sense and knowledge. Its methodology has been to ask especially well informed researchers and others to write comprehensive, balanced summaries of current knowledge, prior experience, and promising future inquiries.

The savvy National Institute of Justice officials who established the series in 1977, and their successors who have supported it since, understand that knowledge from social research influences policy in diffuse and unpredictable ways. Few people expect that research results, however convincing, will often be followed in the short term by changes in established policies. Occasionally that happens, as when publication of the results of the Minneapolis Domestic Violence Experiment showing reduced levels of repeat domestic violence by arrested men was followed in many states by enactment of laws requiring that such arrests be made, but that is unusual and attributable more to broad-based, heightened concerns about domestic violence in the mid-1980s than to research findings. More typically, results are released and become additional ingredients in the melange of considerations that shape attitudes and policies. This is especially true concerning subjects like crime that implicate heated ideological differences and provoke powerful visceral reactions.

Research results, however, do influence policy. The common sense of many police officers long told them that patrolling police cars prevented crime and that rapid responses to calls solved crimes. Research carried out in the 1970s showed that neither of these commonsense beliefs was true, and by doing so this research opened minds to the fundamental reconsideration of policing that has led in the 1990s to widespread support for community-based and problem-solving innovations.

Likewise, research on sentencing and corrections has repeatedly over the past twenty years influenced subsequent developments. Studies showing, for example, that presumptive sentencing guidelines can reduce sentencing disparities and link punishment policies to corrections resources partly explain why twenty states by the mid-1990s had established, or were working on, such schemes.

This volume, like its predecessors, consists mostly of state-of-the-art review essays that summarize important bodies of knowledge. Some, like those on school success and delinquency, on measurement of drug use, and on intermediate sanctions, are on subjects in which policy relevance and topicality are self-evident. Others, on delinquency theories and punishment philosophies, assess scholarship on the theoretical and conceptual backdrops before which attitudes are shaped and policy is made. The essay by Ellen Cohn and David Farrington (who has contributed more essays to *Crime and Justice* than any other writer) uses citation analyses to examine the series' interactions with the criminal justice and criminology literatures.

This is the twentieth volume in the series. That round number seems to us to signal a significant milestone. Jeremy Travis, director of the National Institute of Justice, has kindly contributed a foreword. To help readers find their way through the twenty volumes' nearly 9,000 pages, this volume contains a series of indexes—by author, subject, title, and volume—to the contents of all the volumes.

Every volume in the series but one was supported by the National

Institute of Justice. It is common for the executors of projects supported by outside funding to express gratitude to their sponsors. We greatly appreciate the National Institute of Justice's support for this volume and its predecessors, but our debt is greater than that of many grant recipients. The idea for *Crime and Justice* and the initial planning came from within the National Institute of Justice and, but for the continuing support for the venture over twenty years from many former directors and acting directors (Blair Ewing, Harry Bratt, Bob Burkhart, Jim Underwood, Chips Stewart, Michael Russell, Chuck DeWitt, and Carol Petrie) and from Jeremy Travis, the current director, the series would long ago have ceased to exist. For this volume as for many others, Mary Graham has served as the bridge between the series and its sponsor, and as always we are grateful for her never-failing kindness and efficiency.

We do not believe that the books in this series, or any books, are likely directly to influence public policies, but we do believe that these books and the essays in them inform the policy-making process, influence future generations of policy-relevant research, and help provide the knowledge that tests prevailing common sense about crime and punishment. Readers will decide for themselves whether they agree.

Michael Tonry
Norval Morris

R. A. Duff

Penal Communications: Recent Work in the Philosophy of Punishment

ABSTRACT

Recent writing about punishment includes attempts to provide sophisticated consequentialist accounts of punishment, to develop plausible versions of retributivism that will explain the idea that criminals *deserve* punishment, and to develop "teleological" accounts that cannot be classified as either strictly consequentialist or purely retributivist. Consequentialist accounts, however sophisticated, remain open to some version of the general objection that they fail to respect the moral standing of those who are punished or threatened with punishment. Strict retributivist accounts still face serious problems in explaining the role of hard treatment in punishment. Accounts that portray punishment as communicative offer the most hopeful way forward. Hard treatment may then be portrayed as a prudential supplement, serving a limited deterrent role, or, more ambitiously, as itself part of a communicative process that aims to bring the criminal to repent his crime, reform himself, and thus reconcile himself with those he has wronged. The conflict between this ambitious account of punishment as penitential communication and the more modest account of punishment as censure plus supplementary deterrence is relevant to sentencing issues and reflects an underlying tension between liberal and communitarian conceptions of society.

Penal theory in the 1970s was marked by a retributivist revival, in reaction against the consequentialist orthodoxies that had dominated

R. A. Duff is professor in the Department of Philosophy, University of Stirling. Grateful thanks are due to Michael Davis, Sandra Marshall, Stephen Morse, Michael Tonry, and Andrew von Hirsch for helpful comments and criticisms.

penal thought in the postwar period.[1] The decline of consequentialist theory was due in part to the perceived failure of consequentialist strategies to achieve their declared goals of crime prevention. The optimistic belief that we could rely on the human sciences to build truly cost-effective systems of deterrent, rehabilitative, or incapacitative punishments gave way to the pessimistic belief that "nothing works": punishment was not, and could not be, an efficient method of crime prevention (see Cohen 1985, pp. 33–35).[2] One response was to argue that punishment, and the image of criminals as responsible agents on which it depends, should be abandoned in favor of more efficient systems of "treatment" that make better use of the resources of the human sciences (see Wootton 1963; Menninger 1968). Another response, however, which underlay the retributivist revival, was to argue that punishment must be understood and justified in other terms, as something other than a technique for preventing crime.

The revival of retributivism also, and crucially, flowed from the perceived *moral* failings of consequentialism and of the scientific belief in social engineering that so often typified consequentialist (and especially utilitarian) perspectives on social policy. Liberal theorists began to reassert the importance of justice over utility and of individual rights against the state (Nagel [1972] is a good example of this kind of reaction against the moral excesses of consequentialism; see notably Rawls 1972; Dworkin 1978). The picture of the state as a benevolent and competent authority that could be trusted (if guided by suitable experts) to find efficient ways of promoting social goods was replaced by a conception of the state as a dangerously oppressive set of institutions whose powers over the citizens must be strictly limited to protect individual freedom and rights; the ambitious aim of "doing more good" was replaced by one of "doing less harm," or of "doing justice" (see Cohen 1985, pp. 30–35, 245–54; von Hirsch 1976).

There had, of course, always been some concern about the possible moral costs of a purely consequentialist perspective: in particular, in

---

[1] Some major early contributions to this revival were H. Morris (1968), American Friends Service Committee (1971), Murphy (1973), N. Morris (1974), Twentieth Century Fund (1976), and von Hirsch (1976); its early stages are charted and discussed in Gardner (1976), Tonry and Morris (1978), Allen (1981), Galligan (1981), Radzinowicz and Hood (1981), von Hirsch (1985, chap. 1), and Hudson (1987, chaps. 1–2).

[2] To which some sociological theorists replied that the penal system does "work," but to serve functions quite other than that of crime prevention: see Cohen (1985, pp. 21–30), Garland (1990), and Abel (1991).

penal theory, about its moral cost for the *innocent*. The frequent charge against purely consequentialist justifications of punishment was that they would sanction the "punishment" of the innocent—the framing of innocent scapegoats for the sake of effective deterrence or the pre-emptive detention of those who had not yet broken the law.[3] Some consequentialists argued that, properly understood, a sophisticated consequentialism would not sanction such injustices.[4] Others, how-ever, recognized that our pursuit of the consequentialist goal of crime prevention must be subject to independent side constraints of justice that forbid the deliberate punishment of the innocent (see Hart 1968; Walker 1991, chap. 11), and perhaps the excessive punishment of the guilty (see Hart 1968, pp. 24–25)—although these latter were less powerful protections against consequentialist urges to impose exem-plary deterrent, or indefinite rehabilitative, sentences. One measure of the moral shift in penal theory in the 1970s, however, was a new focus on the moral standing of the *guilty*. A just system of punishment, it was argued, must respect the rights not only of the innocent but also of the guilty: but a system of purely deterrent, rehabilitative, or inca-pacitative punishments does not do that (see Lewis 1953; Morris 1968; Murphy 1973).

Three main trends have characterized philosophical thought about punishment in the last decade in response to such attacks on purely consequentialist modes of penal theory. Some have offered more so-phisticated consequentialist theories that aim to meet the objections. Others have developed versions of a "positive" retributivism, seeking the positive justification of punishment in its character as an intrinsi-cally appropriate response to crime. Still others have tried to transcend the traditional distinction between "consequentialism" and "nonconse-quentialism," by articulating theories that (unlike standard retributiv-isms) give punishment an end beyond itself but that (unlike standard forms of consequentialism) find in the nature of that end substantive constraints on the means by which it may be pursued. The main focus

[3] Those who brought this charge had to face the reply that any system of human punishment, being fallible, will sometimes punish innocents inadvertently (see Schedler 1980; Alexander 1983; Duff 1991a, pp. 435–41) or indirectly (see Walker 1991, chap. 13); and that we do, in other contexts, accept as justified the preemptive detention of those who have as yet committed no crime and done no harm—for quarantine, or for psychiatric protection or treatment (see Walker 1980, chap. 5; Duff 1986, pp. 172–77).

[4] See Rawls (1955) (on which see McCloskey 1972; and Duff 1986, pp. 162–64); and Hare (1981), chaps. 3, 9.7 (on which see Primoratz 1989a, pp. 129–37).

of this essay is on these three trends: this will also involve attending
to some deeper issues in political philosophy (what conceptions of the
state underpin different theories of punishment) and to the ever-present
problem of the relationship between the ideal (as sketched in a justifying theory of punishment) and the actual (as manifested in our existing penal practices). We must also, however, listen to the increasingly audible voices of abolitionist critics of the whole practice of state
punishment (something to which philosophers have paid insufficient
attention).

Section I of this essay discusses some general features of consequentialist and nonconsequentialist theories. Section II focuses on recent
developments in consequentialist theorizing about punishment: particularly on theories that argue that a sophisticated consequentialism does
respect the moral standing of the guilty as well as the innocent. Section
III turns to retributivist theories that rationalize punishment as an
appropriate or obligatory response to crime—a response that need have
no aim beyond itself. Section IV explores what we may call "teleological" but nonconsequentialist theories according to which punishment
does indeed have some further aim—but an aim that itself determines
the means by which it may be pursued: central to these theories is the
idea of punishment as communication. Section V says something about
sentencing: in particular about the principle of "proportionality" and
about the implications for sentencing of a communicative conception
of punishment. Section VI attends to some of the arguments of abolitionists and advocates of "informal justice." Finally, Section VII tries,
if not to draw any determinate conclusions, at least to draw some
threads together and to identify some fruitful directions for further
discussion.

I. Consequentialism and Nonconsequentialism

Consequentialists hold that the justification of any action, policy, or
practice depends solely on its expected overall consequences: it is right
if its consequences are good (at least as good as those of any available
alternative) and wrong if its consequences are bad (worse than those
of some available alternative).[5] To justify a system of punishment, we
must therefore show not only that it does good (and does more good
than harm) but also that no available alternative practice could be ex-

---

[5] An agent acts justifiably (reasonably) if the expected or reasonably expectable consequences of her action are good; her action is objectively right only if its actual consequences are good.

pected to bring about as much or more good, at lower (or no higher) cost. It is not enough to show that punishment prevents crime, by deterring, rehabilitating, or incapacitating actual or potential criminals: we must also show both that the costs of such prevention do not outweigh its benefits and that no other, more cost-effective, techniques of crime-prevention are available.

Consequentialist theories differ most obviously in their accounts of what makes consequences good or bad. Utilitarians posit (and must then define) happiness as the only intrinsic good and unhappiness as the only intrinsic evil. Others seek more subtle (and often less unitary) accounts of the good(s) at which all human action must aim; I attend to some such accounts of the goods at which punishment should aim later. Such differences among consequentialists might, however, seem scarcely relevant to penal theory: surely, however we characterize the final good, the prevention of crime must count as a central instrumental good, and that is the good that can most obviously be served by a system of punishment.

Now it is indeed true that a consequentialist system of criminal law will generally prohibit only conduct that is actually or potentially harmful, destructive of whatever is taken to be intrinsically good. The prevention of crime will therefore be a good, and it seems obvious that it is the primary good that punishment can achieve, the only good great enough to outweigh its costs (see Bentham 1970, chap. 13, sec. 2; Honderich 1984a, pp. 28–29, 42–44). We should, however, attend more carefully to the idea of "prevention." Is the goal simply that fewer crimes are committed, or does it matter *why* they are not committed: whether, for instance, people obey the law only through fear of punishment or because they see that crime is wrong? We should attend too to the costs of a penal system: not only the financial costs of administering punishments, but the harms caused by the processes of investigation, trial, and punishment to those who are investigated, tried, and punished and also to anyone on whom the criminal justice system has some direct or indirect impact. Different accounts of the goods that a state should pursue will generate different conceptions both of the precise goals of punishment and of its costs: they will thus also generate different accounts of how a system of punishment must be structured and function if it is to be justified.

The common feature of all "consequentialist" accounts (as I shall use that term), however, whatever their differing conceptions of the good, is that they justify punishment in terms of its *contingent* or instrumental contribution to an *independently identifiable* good. The good that punishment is to serve (happiness or crime prevention, for instance) can be identified and explained without reference to punishment as the means by which it is to be achieved. It is therefore a contingent question whether punishment is a cost-effective means of achieving that good or whether particular systems of punishment efficiently promote that good; and we may find that other techniques would promote it more efficiently. Consequentialism is also *aggregative:* any consequentialist, who aims to produce the greatest amount of good at the least cost, must suppose that we can in some way add up the benefits of a system of punishment, and its costs, and then weigh the two totals against each other.

The contingency of the relation between punishment and its consequentialist aims generates the most familiar objection to any purely consequentialist theory of punishment: that it would justify clearly unjust kinds of punishment (the deliberate punishment of an innocent scapegoat, the excessively harsh punishment of the guilty), if they would serve the system's aims. For, just as it is a contingent question whether punishment is an efficient means to those aims, it is a contingent question whether (what we would call) *unjust* punishments might sometimes be efficient means to such aims: but, critics argue, an unjust punishment is unjustified whether or not it is consequentially efficient. The aggregative character of consequentialism also bears on this kind of objection: if what matters is the total amount of good produced, it does not matter in itself how either that good, or the costs incurred in achieving it, are distributed; we should be willing to sacrifice some individuals for the sake of achieving some greater good for others. Hence the common charge that consequentialism (most obviously in its utilitarian form) does not take seriously the distinction between persons, or the moral status of individuals (see Rawls 1972, pp. 22–33, 187–90; Nozick 1974, pp. 33–35; on the other side, see Parfit 1984, pp. 329–42), or that it fails to recognize the importance of individual rights as "trumps" that should protect us from being sacrificed to social utility (see Dworkin 1978, chap. 4).

A nonconsequentialist insists that actions and practices may be right or wrong in virtue of their *intrinsic* character, independently of their consequences. Thus what unites retributivist conceptions of punishment, insofar as they are essentially nonconsequentialist, is their insistence that punishment must be justified, not (primarily) by reference to its contingently beneficial effects, but in terms of its intrinsic character as a response to past wrongdoing. Hence the central retributivist claim that punishment is justified if and only if it is deserved in virtue of a past crime; the different versions of retributivism (see Cottingham 1979) can be seen as different attempts to articulate and explain this claim.

Nonconsequentialist principles are often negative, rather than positive: they prohibit action rather than require it. So a nonconsequentialist requirement of honesty, for example, typically does not require us to tell all of the truth all of the time, but forbids us to lie. In the context of punishment, a "negative" retributivism that forbids the punishment of the innocent (and perhaps also the excessive punishment of the guilty) has been more common, and more readily accepted, than a "positive" retributivism that *demands* the punishment of the guilty, to the extent that they deserve. A merely negative retributivism, however, clearly provides no complete justification of punishment (see Dolinko 1991, pp. 539–43): for it tells us that we *may* punish the guilty (their punishment is not unjust), but not that or why we *should* punish them. Negative retributivism thus figures most commonly not as a positive justification of punishment, but as a side constraint on consequentialist accounts: the "general justifying aim" of punishment (see Hart 1968) is, for instance, the prevention of crime, but our pursuit of that aim is constrained by a requirement that we punish only the guilty.[6]

My concern here, however, is with positive forms of retributivism that portray criminal desert not merely as a *necessary* condition of justified punishment (as negative retributivists portray it) but as a *sufficient* condition: the guilty *ought* to be punished, not because this will do some consequential good, but because their punishment is intrinsically right, as inflicting on them what they deserve.[7]

The central problem for a retributivist, whether negative or positive, is to explain this idea of desert. Punishment is supposed to be justified as an intrinsically appropriate response to crime; the concept of "desert" is supposed to indicate that justificatory relationship between past

---

[6] Though such a constraint is not always founded on the retributivist slogan that only the guilty deserve punishment: some appeal instead to the importance of protecting individual freedom (Hart 1968) or to a Rawlsian notion of fairness (Walker 1991, chap. 11).

[7] The strictest form of positive retributivism requires the punishment of the guilty, come what may (as Kant appeared to; see Kant 1965, p. 102). More modest versions portray criminal guilt as a good, but not necessarily absolute or always overriding, reason for punishment (see Dolinko 1991, pp. 539–40).

crime and present punishment. But what is that relationship? How does crime call for punishment or make punishment appropriate (see Ardal 1984; Honderich 1984a, chap. 2; 1984b)? It is not enough simply to appeal to the supposedly shared intuition that the guilty deserve to suffer (see Davis 1972; Moore 1987), since such an intuition, however widely shared, needs explanation: *what* do they deserve to suffer, and *why?*

Consequentialists justify punishment as a contingently efficient technique for achieving some benefit; retributivists justify punishment as an intrinsically appropriate response to past crime. "Mixed" theories combine consequentialist and nonconsequentialist elements; they reflect the belief that "any morally tolerable account" of punishment "must exhibit it as a compromise between distinct and partly conflicting principles" (Hart 1968, p. 1). The most familiar kinds of mixed theory are those, like Hart's, that set nonconsequentialist side constraints on our pursuit of the penal system's consequentialist aims (on Hart, see Ten 1987, pp. 81–85; Lacey 1988, pp. 46–56; Morison 1988; Primoratz 1989a, pp. 137–43); others allow consequentialist considerations a more subordinate role within a primarily retributivist framework (see von Hirsch 1993; and Sec. IIIE below). One question about any such theory is that of how stable the mixture will be. Can we so rank the different principles that one will always take priority (by insisting, for example, that the requirements of justice must *always* override those of effective crime-prevention)? Or should we instead recognize that we can never achieve more than an unstable compromise—that we will always face conflicts, which cannot be confidently or readily resolved, between the demands of justice and those of crime prevention (see Goldman 1979; Robinson 1987; von Hirsch 1993, chap. 6; Tonry 1994, pp. 79–80)?

There are also, however, theories that we cannot classify either as instrumentally consequentialist, or as straightforwardly retributivist, or as "mixed." They give punishment a forward-looking goal (moral reform or education, for example) that it might or might not in fact achieve: they thus differ from purely retributivist theories that hold that the purpose of punishment is achieved in and by the punishment itself. But they also differ from purely consequentialist theories, in that the relation between punishment and its purpose is not contingent: punishment is portrayed as an intrinsically appropriate (not just contingently effective) means of pursuing that goal; the goal itself determines the means by which it can be pursued. The goal is such, indeed, that retributive punishment—punishment that seeks to inflict on or to induce in the wrongdoer the suffering she deserves—is the means by which it should appropriately be pursued: but the notion of deserved suffering is now explained by relating it to punishment's further goal (see Sec. IV below).

A further task faces any theory of punishment. We might show that punishment produces or constitutes some good: that it contingently achieves some good, or that it is in itself a good. But this is not yet an adequate justification of a system of state punishment (which is what such theories typically aim to justify). For we also need to show that that "good" is one which it is the state's proper task to pursue, and to pursue by means of so coercive a practice as this: a critic could accept that punishment does or can serve the specified good but then argue that it is not the state's job to pursue such a good, by such means (see Murphy 1985). A justification of state punishment thus depends on a political theory of the state: an account of what justifies its existence, of what ends it should pursue, of the means by which it can properly pursue them. Different theories of the state can be expected to generate different accounts of the proper aims and methods of state punishment (see Philips 1986; Lacey 1988; for a contrary argument that penal theory is relatively independent of political theory, see Davis 1989): in what follows we will need to attend in particular to the difference between liberal and communitarian conceptions of the state.

II. Consequentialism Refined

This is not the place for a detailed rehearsal of the objections brought against purely consequentialist penal theories in the 1970s. We should, however, briefly recall those objections, so that we can see whether recent, more sophisticated forms of consequentialism can meet them.

A. Objections to Consequentialism

A penal system based on a strictly consequentialist "general justifying aim" does not, critics argued, even if it is also subject to nonconsequentialist side constraints that protect the innocent, do justice to the guilty: it does not treat them with the respect that is their due as rational, responsible moral agents.

These objections were sometimes put in Kantian terms: such a system treats those whom it punishes "merely as means" to those further social ends (the prevention of crime) for the sake of which they are punished (see Kant 1948, pp. 90–93; 1965, pp. 99–100; Murphy 1973,

p. 94). The meaning and implications of this Kantian slogan are notoriously obscure (see Murphy 1979; Walker 1980, pp. 80–85; 1991, chap. 6; Honderich 1984*a*, pp. 60–61). It certainly precludes the deliberate punishment of the innocent. If we frame an innocent scapegoat to preserve the deterrent efficacy of the law, or preemptively detain someone who has not yet broken the law, our treatment of him does not depend on his choices or actions as a responsible agent but solely on our belief that this will secure some social benefit: we thus treat him "merely as a means" to that social benefit—as someone whose interests can be sacrificed whenever it is useful to do so rather than as a moral agent whose treatment by the state should depend on his own responsible choices. But it is less obvious that such a Kantian injunction precludes the punishment of the *guilty* for consequentialist ends. We do of course still use them "as means"; we punish them because it is useful to do so. But if their punishment also depends on their guilt (on their having voluntarily committed a crime), we surely do not use them "*merely* as means": they are now "found to be deserving of punishment before any consideration is given to the utility of [their] punishment" (Kant 1965, p. 100); their choices as responsible agents are respected, since they are punished only if they choose to break the law (see Benn 1958, p. 325; Walker 1980, pp. 80–85).

But there is still force to the objection that any system of punishment whose justifying aim is conceived in purely consequentialist terms of deterrence, rehabilitation, or incapacitation does not give the guilty the respect due to them as rational moral agents. It has most obvious force against a rehabilitative conception that allows offenders to be subjected to whatever kind and extent of "treatment" is thought necessary to "cure" or reform them. Such a view requires indeterminate sentences: since courts cannot be expected to tell in advance just what treatment will be necessary, the offender must be handed over to experts who can determine what she needs and how soon she can safely be released (see Wootton 1963; Walker and McCabe 1973, pp. 101–2, on "occasionalism"). It also precludes any necessary relationship between seriousness of crime and severity of punishment: the character and duration of the treatment that an offender is thought to need will not depend solely or even primarily on the seriousness of the crime for which she was convicted. But, critics objected, the mere fact of breaking the law should not make someone so completely vulnerable to the coercive attentions of the state, and it is unjust if the length and character of her punishment is thus detached from the nature and seriousness of her crime (see von Hirsch 1976, chap. 2; Allen 1981; von Hirsch and Ashworth 1992a, chap. 1).

There are two aspects to such criticism: one concerning ends, and one concerning means. As to ends, talk of "rehabilitation" suggests that the punishment aims not merely to benefit others, by preventing crime, but to benefit the criminal herself; but even if (which is by no means obvious) those ends are mutually consistent, liberals would insist that the state has no right to subject a citizen to treatment against her will for her own supposed benefit: "the only purpose for which power can be rightfully exercised over any member of a civilized community against his will, is to prevent harm to others" (Mill 1972, chap. 1, para. 9). As to means, the objection is that to treat any citizen, even if she has broken the law, as someone to be remolded or reformed by whatever efficient (even if humane) techniques we can find is in effect to treat her as an object to be manipulated, which is to deny her proper status as a responsible moral agent who should be left free to determine her own attitudes (and her own conceptions of her good) for herself (see Lewis 1953; Morris 1968). One could express this objection by saying that such rehabilitative punishment does not punish offenders *for* what they have done: although they are liable to punishment only because they have broken the law, the nature and extent of that punishment depends not on what they did, but on what is thought necessary to reform them. To respect an offender as a rational moral agent, however, requires us to base our response to her on what she has done (see Duff 1986, chap. 6).

A similar objection applies to purely incapacitative punishments, whose aim is simply to prevent the crimes that it is predicted the offender might well commit if left free, particularly to strategies of "selective incapacitation," which aim to identify for preventive detention those who are most likely to commit serious crimes. Quite apart from the problem of "false positives" (given the inaccuracy of our predictive techniques, we will detain as dangerous too many who are not actually dangerous), the objection is that such people are detained not for what they have done but because of what they might do if not detained; but if we are to treat citizens with the respect due to them as responsible moral agents, we must leave them free to choose whether to obey the law, and subject them to the coercive attentions of the law only if and when they choose to break it (see Floud and Young 1981;

Bottoms and Brownsword 1982; Honderich 1982; Lacey 1983; von Hirsch 1985; Duff 1986, pp. 170–78; von Hirsch and Ashworth 1992*a*, chap. 3).

So too with deterrent punishments, at least if sentencing is determined directly by the goal of deterrence: if the sentences imposed on particular offenses or offenders depend on the requirements of cost-effective deterrence. For this again means that the offender is not punished for what *she* has done, but for the sake of some future effect on others; the severity of her punishment depends not on the seriousness of her crime but on such factors as the current prevalence of that type of crime and what is needed to deter others from committing it.

Some have argued, however, that a suitably side-constrained system of deterrent punishments would fully respect the rights of those who are punished or threatened with punishment. It is to these theorists that I now turn.[8]

B. *Deterrence, Consent, and Self-Defense*

Why should we not say that a system of deterrent punishments does treat both criminals and potential criminals as rational agents, if it threatens punishment against, and inflicts it on, only those who voluntarily break the law? It offers the citizen prudential reasons to obey the law, thus treating him as a rational agent whose conduct can be guided by the provision of reasons; it respects his choices and makes his fate depend on his choices, since he is punished only if he nonetheless chooses to break the law (see Hart 1968, pp. 22–24).[9] Furthermore, even if such a rationale for punishment does not itself require any strict proportionality between seriousness of crime and severity of punishment, it does require that potential offenders be able to know in advance just what they would be liable to suffer if they broke the law: it thus precludes a system of wholly indeterminate sentencing, or one that allows the courts discretion to impose whatever sentence they think is required for deterrence.[10] Perhaps we cannot say that, under

---

[8] I will look later (in Sec. III*E* below) at theorists who allow deterrence a more limited role within a primarily retributivist system of punishment: my concern here is with those who understand the justifying aim of punishment in strictly consequentialist terms of deterrence.

[9] For doubts about the "choice" model of criminal liability to which this argument appeals, see Duff 1993.

[10] It need not preclude all judicial sentencing discretion. In particular, since offenders are not likely to complain if they are punished less severely than the law allows, the system need only set maximum sentences for each offense, allowing the courts to impose sentences below the maximum if this seems adequate to the needs of deterrence.

such a system, an offender *wills* his own punishment in choosing to break the law, since he would no doubt prefer to break the law without being punished.[11] But we could say that he *consents* to his own punishment, since he chooses to break the law in the knowledge that this makes him liable to punishment, and (unless we posit an implausibly inalienable right not to be punished) his punishment therefore does not infringe his rights.

This argument is as yet unpersuasive: a robber who threatens his victims with harm if they disobey his orders cannot justify inflicting that harm when they disobey by arguing that in choosing to do what they knew would make them liable to that harm, they consented to it. Nino (1983), however, offers a more sophisticated version of this argument, which seeks to distinguish a deterrent system of punishment from the robber. Given a just system of law, imposing justified obligations on its citizens (this already distinguishes the law from the robber), we might, for the sake of "social protection," attach "normative consequences" to breaches of the law: we make offenders liable to punishment. Now while an agent does not necessarily consent to all known *factual* consequences of her actions (I do not consent to being shot by the robber), she does consent to every necessary *normative* consequence of her actions: so an offender consents to becoming normatively liable to punishment, in which case its imposition does not infringe her rights.

Now *if* the state is justified in attaching such "normative consequences" (liability to punishment) to breaches of the law, it is no doubt justified in actualizing those consequences against anyone who nonetheless breaks the law (although given that prior justification, I am not clear why we must appeal to the agent's supposed consent to justify actualizing such consequences). But the crucial question, to which Nino pays inadequate attention, is that of what justifies the initial attachment of those normative consequences: what justifies a state in threatening punishments for breaches of the law? It is not enough to say that it does so to protect society against the harm of crime: for while we may agree that the protection of society by the prevention

[11] I leave aside here the possibility of arguing that since he would as a rational agent have agreed to a social contract that created such a system of punishment, in punishing him we thus respect his will as a rational agent. For apart from doubts about any such appeal to the agent's "rational will" (see Murphy 1973, pp. 101–2; Duff 1986, pp. 217–28), we would need to ask why such rational contractors would agree to a system of deterrent punishments, rather than a system of rehabilitative, incapacitative, or retributive punishments; which is, in effect, the question I am pursuing here.

of crime is a proper aim for the state, there remains the question of the means by which it can properly pursue that aim. Even if I am justified in demanding something from you, I am not thereby justified in using *any* means to secure your compliance:[12] what then justifies the state in using such threats to secure our compliance?

A just state is of course justified in demanding our obedience to its just laws and can (indeed should) seek to secure our compliance by offering us good reasons to obey: those moral reasons that justify its laws (see Duff 1986, chap. 3). But if, to secure compliance from those who are unimpressed by such moral reasons, it then creates new prudential reasons for compliance by threatening punishment, it must face Hegel's objection: that it then treats the citizen (any potential criminal) "like a dog instead of with the freedom and respect due to him as a man" (Hegel 1942, p. 246; see Duff 1986, pp. 178–86).

If I am to respect another as a rational moral agent, I need not refrain from trying to persuade her to modify her conduct: respect does not preclude attempted persuasion. Respect does, however, preclude manipulation or coercion, and requires what Bickenbach calls "transparent persuasion" (Bickenbach 1988, p. 770); that is, I should attempt to modify her conduct only by giving her *relevant* reasons to modify it herself. Now though there are complexities in the idea of "relevant reasons," I think at least this much is true: if what justifies me in trying to persuade someone to modify her conduct is (my belief) that she *ought* to do so, the relevant reasons I should offer her are precisely and only those moral reasons that justify my belief that she ought to do so and my attempt to persuade her to do so. If instead I offer her prudential reasons for behaving differently, and particularly if I *create* those prudential reasons by threatening to inflict harm on her if she remains unpersuaded, I cease to treat or to respect her as a rational moral agent; I am instead trying to manipulate or coerce her into obedience. But is the same not true of a state that seeks to induce its citizens to obey its laws, not by offering them the relevant moral reasons that supposedly justify its laws, but by a system of deterrent punishments that creates new and irrelevant prudential reasons for obedience (see Duff 1986, pp. 50–54, 178–86)?

---

[12] Compare the definition of "blackmail" in English law, as making "any unwarranted demand with menaces" (Theft Act 1968, sec. 21; see Smith and Hogan 1992, pp. 606–10): even if my demand is warranted, there is the further issue of whether (I believe that) "the use of the menaces is a proper means of reinforcing the demand."

Some have argued that we can justify threatening punishment as a deterrent by analogy with the use or threat of force in self-defense (see Alexander 1980; Farrell 1985; and Quinn 1985). We are justified in using force to ward off attacks on ourselves (or others). We are also, it is said, justified in *threatening* potential attackers with harm in order to deter them, and we are justified in *inflicting* that harm if they nonetheless attack us (as is supposedly shown, in part, by the fact that we would be justified in creating a mechanism that would automatically inflict that harm if they attacked). But this is just what a system of deterrent punishments involves: to defend members of the community against criminal attacks, the state threatens potential wrongdoers with harm if they engage in such attacks; that threat, and its implementation, are justified as a matter of social self-defense.

I am not sure that such an argument meets the Hegelian objection. The use of force in *direct* defense against an attack on which the person against whom I use the force has already embarked can clearly be justified as an appropriate defensive response to his attack: it aims not to modify (to coerce) his future conduct or choices but to prevent him carrying through a wrongful action that he has already initiated (see Duff 1986, p. 227). I may also warn a potential assailant that I will use such (necessary, defensive) force if he attacks. Even if I intend thus to give him prudential reason not to attack me (rather than simply appealing to the moral reasons against attacking me), at least I am not creating new and quite irrelevant reasons for him to desist: for I would be justified in using such force and can be seen simply as warning him of this. The deterrent threats posited by this argument, however, are a matter of *indirect* self-defense: we warn the potential assailant that if he attacks we will use against him a degree of force that might well exceed what would be justified as a matter of direct self-defense; force greater than would be necessary directly to ward off his attack. But do we not then treat him "like a dog instead of with the freedom and respect due to him as a man": as someone to be coerced by fear, instead of a rational moral agent whom we should try to persuade by appeal to the relevant kinds of moral reason?

But why should we observe such moral restraints when dealing with those who would attack us? If moral appeals will predictably fail to dissuade them (and these deterrent threats are directed only against those who will not be dissuaded by moral appeals), why should we not then offer them (create for them) prudential reasons to refrain from attacking us, or to obey the law—which is still to address them as rational agents, with reasons that will weigh with them (see Baker 1992)?

This issue poses a fundamental moral question about how we should conceive our relationships with our fellow citizens. The use of deterrent threats that this argument seeks to justify is morally most plausible between strangers (potential enemies) or against outlaws: it makes most moral sense either in situations in which there is no law to bind us (to bind us by obligations, or to bind us together as members of a community) or when the person threatened is, we think, deaf to the moral appeal of the law—he is in spirit, if not yet in action, an outlaw. But is this really how we should see our fellow citizens? It is worth noting that such justifications of punishment as a deterrent are often cast in the language of "us" and "them": *we* must use such threats to deter *them*, the potential criminals we fear (see Baker 1992, pp. 153–54: contrast von Hirsch 1993, pp. 12–14, 41–44, on which see Sec. III*E* below). I would suggest, however, that the proper question is not how *we* should prevent or dissuade *them* from breaking the law (which is to treat "them" already as outlaws) but how we as fallible moral beings should encourage *ourselves* to obey the law. We should, that is, still treat those who might commit or be tempted to commit even serious crimes as fellow members of the moral community; we should not be so ready to abandon the moral language in which the law should speak to its citizens, in favor of the brutally coercive language of deterrent threats. [13]

It might be said that this is naive idealism: we should recognize that there are those who are "outlaws" (which is why we need the coercive apparatus of the criminal law) and that we have the right to defend ourselves against them by deterrent threats. I say a bit more later about the relationship between philosophical ideals and empirical actualities (see Sec. IV*C* below); but I also discuss an alternative, morally less disturbing, way of building a deterrent dimension into a system of punishment (see Sec. III*E* below).

C. *The Ends of Consequentialism*

An alternative consequentialist strategy is to offer a more sophisticated account of the aims of punishment, of the goods at which a

---

[13] And see Oldenquist (1988) for an interesting argument that retributive punishment, understood as "ideally, putting someone in disgrace and the eliciting of repentance" (p. 468), is an essential way of marking the criminal's membership of our moral community; this connects with some of the communicative ideas explored in Sec. IV below.

system of punishment should aim, than is offered by the simple idea of crime prevention.

Goldman (1982), for example, sketches a theory of punishment that he thinks respects the kinds of limit that retributivism insists on, and that utilitarians cannot readily justify, but that will also ensure that the social benefits of punishment outweigh its costs—something that retributivism notoriously cannot offer. The rights of citizenship, he suggests, should be seen as a package that is normally acquired, along with the related duties of citizenship, at adulthood: but if a person breaks the law, flouting her duties as a citizen, her package of rights reverts in trusteeship to the community. She does not, however, *lose* those rights; nor therefore may she be subjected to whatever kind of punishment (or treatment) would be socially useful. Rather, the community that now holds her rights as trustee must seek to restore her as soon as possible to the full enjoyment of her rights, by restoring her to law-abiding membership of the community; it must also preserve and respect as many of those rights as is possible—as many as can be respected while preventing her from committing further crimes. On this view, Goldman argues, incapacitation and rehabilitation would be the proper particular goals of punishment; and such a system of punishment would serve the good of the community, without sacrificing individuals to that good.

This account is not of course strictly consequentialist, since it requires that the citizen have forfeited her rights, by breaking the law, before she can be justifiably punished. What makes it relevant here, however, is that it portrays the offender's restoration to the community as part of the aim of punishment, along with (indeed as an aspect of) a more sophisticated conception of "crime prevention" as the aim. Could it therefore claim to meet the objections to earlier, cruder consequentialist theories, by giving due weight to the moral standing of the guilty?

Goldman does not say much about what he takes "rehabilitation" to involve: in particular, whether it is to be simply a matter of using whatever humane techniques we can to induce law-abiding dispositions (which would hardly treat the guilty as responsible moral agents) or rather a matter of trying to persuade, and to help, the criminal to accept the moral demands of the law, which might still treat him as a responsible moral agent (see further below, Sec. IV). The goal is indeed to restore the criminal to the full rights and membership of the moral community, and we are to use the least restraint or force necessary to achieve that aim. But he also argues that we must do as *much* as is necessary to achieve it and to prevent the offender from committing further crimes. I cannot see either how this can set the retributivist limits to the severity of punishment that his account is meant to impose,[14] or how it treats the criminal as a responsible moral agent—rather than as someone whom we must remold into law-abiding conformity. The basic problem with his account, I think, is that he sees the criminal as forfeiting into trusteeship her *entire* package of civil rights: for how can we still claim to treat her as a responsible moral agent, if we see her as someone on whose behalf we must exercise such a trusteeship?

Lacey also seeks a richer account of the goods that state punishment can achieve (Lacey 1988). She rejects the liberal individualism implicit in much penal theorizing (although she preserves individual freedom or autonomy as a central value) in favor of a communitarian perspective that emphasizes the essentially social nature of human beings: their good can be found only within communities, whose existence and flourishing depend on shared values and public goods. This communitarian perspective, she argues, makes state punishment easier to justify as a means of protecting the community and its most basic values or interests. The Kantian objection that such punishment uses the individual "merely as a means" to some social good is undermined once we reject that sharp distinction between individual and community to which it appeals, and recognize that an individual's own good depends on that of the community (pp. 172–73; since, however, a Kantian respect for autonomy forbids using individuals as means even to *their own* good, infringing their autonomy even for the sake of their own future good, and since Lacey wants still to preserve autonomy as a central value, it is not clear how far she has dissolved the conflict between autonomy and coercive state punishment).

The function of the criminal law, on this account, is to protect the existence and security of the community, by protecting its basic values and interests; though these will vary between different communities, Lacey argues that "autonomy" and "welfare" must be central to them (pp. 103–5, 178–80). The function of state punishment is then to support the criminal law: this function has a symbolic dimension (punishment makes the law's demands real, and expresses and helps to main-

---

[14] Goldman (1982) himself (pp. 74–75) partly recognizes this problem and offers what he admits may not be wholly satisfactory responses to it.

tain commitment to its values) and a practical dimension (punishment prevents crime by such means as deterrence, incapacitation, and providing the opportunity for reform). Lacey thus hopes to find room for central aspects of both retributivist and utilitarian conceptions of punishment. Her account also, she argues, has important implications for the distribution and the forms of punishment. Since the aim is not merely the prevention of crime, but the protection of the central values of autonomy and welfare, we must look for distributions and modes of punishment that will serve those values: thus, for instance, we should favor purely symbolic punishments wherever possible (although she also allows extended incapacitative detention for persistent dangerous offenders; pp. 194–95), and we should respect the principle of "residual autonomy," that "no punishment should be so draconian as effectively to coerce compliance" (p. 119). Although there will need to be "trade-offs" between autonomy and other values such as welfare (autonomy is not to have *absolute* priority over all other values), she argues that it requires punishment to be limited to the truly guilty— those whose criminal acts "are hostile to and express rejection of fundamental community values": for "to punish those who have exhibited no such hostility would be to fly directly in the face of those values themselves" (pp. 187–89).

It is of course a general feature of consequentialism that, whatever account is given of the goods to be achieved or the evils to be averted by a system of criminal law and punishment, we should prefer distributions and kinds of punishment that themselves, as far as is possible, promote such goods or avoid such evils; a Benthamite utilitarian will look for a system that causes only as much pain as is absolutely necessary to achieve its ends. The provision of a richer account of good and evil will then have significant implications for the construction of a system of punishment: if we take autonomy and welfare as our central goods, we must look for ways in which punishments can be distributed and inflicted that will as far as possible respect the autonomy and welfare of those who are punished. But this raises questions, to which Lacey pays insufficient attention, about the appropriate aims and methods of punishment. How far do deterrent and incapacitative punishments, for example, respect the autonomy of those who are punished or threatened with punishment (see above, Sec. II*B*)? What modes of punishment can claim to respect autonomy (see below, Sec. III*E*, Sec. V)? Lacey is no doubt right to argue that a system of punishment serves its function by a variety of particular means, but we must look more carefully than she does at the relations between those means and the values that they are meant to serve.

It is also, however, a general feature of consequentialism that, whatever account is given of the "good" that is to be maximized, it cannot rule out means that are themselves destructive of that good: for it cannot rule out the possibility that such destruction will in the long run maximize that good. A Benthamite utilitarian justifies punishments that cause pain (itself an intrinsic evil) if they will avert greater pains in the future. So too, if we interpret the value of individual freedom (the citizen's capacity to plan and determine her own future; see Hart 1968) as a *consequential* value, so that our aim is to maximize such freedom, we might sometimes have to infringe the freedom of some (punish an innocent scapegoat; subject the predictably criminal to preventive detention), to increase the freedom of others. For crime is destructive of individual freedom; thus by preventing crime we protect freedom; and if such freedom-infringing punishments do prevent crime, they might be justified on the grounds that they do, on balance, maximize freedom. So too with autonomy and welfare. Even if we say (see Lacey 1988, p. 189) that one goal must be to maintain respect for these values, we cannot be sure that punishments that infringe such values might not also, in the end, protect them by preventing crime. Thus if we are to insist that a system of punishment must not "fly directly in the face of" the very values it is meant to protect, that is, that it must respect those values, we must (as Lacey tentatively acknowledges, p. 189) interpret those values as *non*consequentialist or not *purely* consequentialist values: that is, they must be taken not merely to set goals that we should strive to achieve (goods that we should strive to maximize) but also to constrain our pursuit of those goals. But once we interpret such values in this way, we must again ask more carefully which modes of punishment will indeed respect them.

The same problem arises for Braithwaite and Pettit's "republican" theory (Braithwaite and Pettit 1990; von Hirsch and Ashworth 1992*b*, 1993; Pettit and Braithwaite 1993). Like Lacey, they locate their account of punishment within a wider political theory and a larger account of the proper aims of the criminal law. They, however, argue for a strictly consequentialist theory of criminal justice (chap. 3), whose target should be "the maximization of the dominion of individual people" (p. 54): "dominion" is the "republican," rather than liberal, conception of liberty (which is still a strictly negative conception, however)—the assured and equal freedom of citizens living under the law. This target, they argue, will generate a secure allocation of the rights that may be problematic for other kinds of consequentialism (like the right of the innocent not to be punished). It also generates the "decrementalist" strategy of progressively reducing the scope, the power, and the activities of the criminal justice system, and favors nonpunitive over punitive responses to crime; when punishment is necessary, its aims should be "reprobation" (bringing offenders to recognize and be shamed by the wrongfulness of their conduct) and "reintegration" (restoring both victims and offenders to the community; see also Braithwaite [1989] on "reintegrative shaming").

Now liberals as well as "republicans" would agree that the powers and intrusiveness of the state must be strictly limited; some retributivists also argue that punishment should be understood as a form of "reprobation" or censure (see below, Sec. IIIC); nor is a principle of parsimony, and a related decrementalist strategy of reducing the extent and severity of punishment as far as we can without betraying or damaging the values that punishment should serve, peculiar to the "republican" perspective. But the particular framework within which Braithwaite and Pettit set these aims (and which helps to determine just what they mean) raises some questions: in particular, concerning its strictly consequentialist structure and its definition of "dominion" as the key good to be promoted (see von Hirsch and Ashworth [1992b] for some apposite criticisms).

We must ask first (though I cannot pursue this question in detail here) whether "dominion" as they define it is an end that can generate the principles, presumptions, and goals that they wish to derive from it. Can any single end be both broad enough to serve as *the* aim of the criminal justice system and yet substantive enough to generate determinate implications for the structure and operations of the system? More specifically, can an end defined strictly in terms of a *negative* concept of liberty carry the weight they want it to carry? The idea of citizenship, to which they appeal, invites a much richer interpretation, which would include certain kinds of *positive* right or liberty—notably, those concerned with participation in the community's governance, and with the citizen's standing in the criminal process as one who must be addressed and treated with respect. They do want to include such elements in their theory, but as derivations from the end of maximizing dominion, understood as negative liberty: but, quite apart from doubts about how we are supposed to calculate degrees or quanta of "dominion," I suspect that such elements can be securely founded only on a richer account of the end.

We must also ask whether they can both insist that dominion is a strictly consequentialist value (that we must aim to "maximize dominion") and yet set the kinds of constraint on the criminal justice system that they wish to set—constraints, for instance, forbidding the punishment of the innocent or the "excessive" punishment of the guilty. Measures that infringe dominion will of course be for that reason and to that degree undesirable, and we must remember too that dominion is impaired if people lose the *assurance* that their freedom is protected (if, for example, it is known that innocents are likely to be framed). Braithwaite and Pettit argue (pp. 72–76) that for these reasons the system's officials ought to "forswear the framing of the innocent," even if it seemed that such framing might be useful: for otherwise citizens will realize that they might "have their personal dominion invaded if that is for the best overall," which would lead to an overall *loss* of dominion. They also argue (pp. 78–80) that the goal of promoting dominion, unlike that of simple crime prevention, will not "motivate punishments that exceed uncontroversial limits in degree or kind": the "certain and grievous damage on dominion" that such punishments inflict "is unlikely to be offset by an appropriately large increase in . . . the level of overall dominion" by preventing crime. But we must also remember that preventing crime *protects* the dominion both of those who would otherwise be the direct victims of crime and of those who would otherwise be more fearful of becoming victims of crime (since such fear undermines their assurance of protection). While I am not clear how we are to carry out the calculus that weighs the dominion-infringing against the dominion-protecting effects of different penal policies or acts, I do not see how their confidence that that calculus will result in firm protection for the innocent against being framed, or for the guilty against punishments that we would regard as clearly excessive, is justified: they still face, I think, the familiar objection to any purely consequentialist theory, that it makes such protections for the individual contingent on the likely effects of particular policies in particular contexts and, thus, vulnerable to infringement when it would be useful to sacrifice the individual for some greater social good.

Braithwaite and Pettit's strict consequentialism also impinges on their accounts of reprobation and sentencing. Reprobation is valued instrumentally, as an effective means to the desired end; sentencing is also to be determined instrumentally, as are decisions about whom and when to prosecute in the first place. Thus while the legislature should specify maximum (sometimes heavy) penalties commensurate with the seriousness of the various crimes, so as to send the right kind of "reprobative message to the community" (see pp. 127–28, 176–77), the prosecuting authorities should ask themselves whether prosecuting in this (kind of) case would serve the dominion-enhancing goals of the system, and the courts should decide what actual penalty (if any) to impose with a view to those same goals, rather than try to impose "just deserts" on all offenders. Indeed, Braithwaite and Pettit vigorously criticize retributivism in general and the demand for "just deserts" and "proportionate punishments" in particular: among other objections, they argue that the project of inflicting "just deserts" on all offenders is (even if we could determine what they deserve) quite impractical, given the costs involved in trying to detect all offenders; that its pursuit would actually increase injustice, since it would be "blue-collar" or "street" criminals, rather than "white-collar" criminals, who suffered more; and that the proper goals of crime prevention, by persuasion, education, and cooperation, require (especially in the case of white-collar or corporate crime) a policy of highly selective prosecution and punishment that is inconsistent with any demand for just deserts.

Now the problems of selectivity in the detection and prosecution of offenders must indeed be faced by anyone who takes justice seriously, especially by retributivists who take justice and equality to be primary and nonconsequentialist values for a system of criminal justice. We cannot simply say that a penal system is just so long as it inflicts proportionate punishments on all those who are actually, and correctly, convicted: justice is not done if, for example, those who are prosecuted and convicted form only a small proportion, selected by unjustly discriminatory methods, of those who are actually guilty (this is one of the ways in which penal justice, the justice of convictions and punishments, cannot be separated from the justice of the system of criminal law as a whole; see further below, Sec. VI). Nor, however, can we sensibly demand that *every* effort must be made to detect, prosecute, and punish *every* offender; thus we need to ask just how decisions about investigation and prosecution, as well as sentencing decisions, should properly be made. But if such decisions were made on purely consequentialist grounds, even if those grounds concerned the maximization of dominion, the result would surely be kinds of injustice to which we should object. For to be told that I am to be prosecuted, while someone else who is known to have committed a more serious crime is not, simply because this is what will best serve the system's consequentialist goals; or that I am to be punished severely, while someone convicted last week for just the same crime received a much lighter sentence or no punishment at all, because only a few such severe sentences are needed to convey the appropriate moral message to the community (see pp. 128, 176–77): is to be told that justice is being manipulated, and the idea of punishment as justified reprobation is being distorted, to serve some social end.[15]

The idea of punishment as justified reprobation is distorted here because it is a moral distortion to see blame or reprobation simply as an instrumental technique for securing some desired end (see Duff 1986, chap. 2; von Hirsch and Ashworth 1992b). If I am to address another person as a responsible moral agent, I may (indeed, sometimes should) blame, or reprobate, her for what she has done: but that blame must be an honest response to her conduct, motivated and justified by the fact that she acted wrongfully; if it is simply a technique by which I hope to induce her to modify her conduct (a technique that I adopt because I think it most likely to be effective), I cease to treat or respect her as a rational moral agent. Likewise, if the criminal law is to address and treat its citizens as responsible moral agents, it should indeed censure them if they flout its justified demands: but the fact and the degree of that censure (and so also the severity of the punishment that expresses that censure) must be determined by the fact and the seriousness of their wrongdoing—not by a purely instrumental concern to maximize some good.

Of course, if we took dominion not (merely) as a consequentialist goal that we should seek to maximize but as a nonconsequentialist value that must be respected, we would get a different, and perhaps less morally disturbing, picture. We would then forbid practices and policies that failed to respect the dominion of those involved, and sanction only modes of punishment that were consistent with respect for the dominion of those punished. This might lead us to an account of punishment as essentially reprobative, on the grounds that being subject to the reprobation of my fellow citizens is not inconsistent with a

---

[15] To which it might be replied (see Davis 1982) that such a practice is unjust only if there is some alternative and practicable system that all rational people would prefer. But, apart from the question of why that is the appropriate criterion of justice, the point here is simply that justice makes categorical demands on a legal system that no purely consequentialist account can capture.

due respect for my dominion; what would then matter, however, would not be the instrumental efficacy of reprobation, but the fact that it (unlike a system of purely deterrent or incapacitative punishments) respects the dominion of the offender.

In a later article, Braithwaite and Pettit suggest a rather different picture (Pettit and Braithwaite 1993). A criminal court's aim in sentencing should now be, not so much to prevent future dominion-infringing crime, but to rectify that past infringement of dominion perpetrated by the offender's crime: which is to be done if possible by bringing the offender to *recognize* the wrongness of her crime, to *recompense* the victim, and to provide some *reassurance* against future offending. Now this picture certainly does not require the kind of consequentialist framework on which Braithwaite and Pettit insisted; and indeed, if we ask why courts should be thus concerned with rectification of the past rather than with preventing future crime, it is not obvious that a consequentialist answer will be plausible: for even if we accept that damaged dominion can be restored, surely the prevention of future crime will do more to maximize dominion, if only because it will prevent more than one crime. We might say more plausibly, in nonconsequentialist tones, that such a rectificatory response is what we owe to the victim and, indeed, to the criminal as an appropriate response to her crime.

I return to reprobation and rectification in the following two sections, in the context of some nonconsequentialist theories. The conclusion of this section should be that any purely consequentialist account of punishment, or even a consequentialist account of the goals of punishment that allows that our pursuit of those goals must be subject to side constraints that forbid both the punishment of the innocent and the excessive punishment of the guilty, remains open to the objections sketched above; that it will fail to respect (do justice to) the moral standing of those who are punished—and also, if punishment is justified as a deterrent, to the moral standing of those who are threatened with punishment. We must turn now to some of the positive retributivist writings of the last decade: for their central claim is that only a retributivist conception of punishment can do justice to the guilty, as well as to the innocent.

III. Retributivist Themes and Variations

A dominant slogan of the new retributivism of the 1970s was "just deserts": a central, if not the only, aim of punishment should be to ensure that "criminals get their 'just desserts' [*sic*]" (Home Office 1990, para. 1.6). But what do criminals deserve; why is it *punishment* that they deserve? As I noted earlier, the key problem for any retributivist is to explain this supposedly justificatory relationship between crime and punishment; we should now look at some recent attempts to articulate that relationship.

A. *The Removal of "Unfair Advantage"*

One account was for a time widely accepted as the most plausible version of retributivism. A system of law brings benefits (security, protected freedom) to all its citizens, by imposing burdens on them all (the burden of self-restraint involved in obeying the law). A criminal accepts the benefits that flow from the law-abiding self-restraint of others but refuses to accept the burden of obeying the law herself: she takes the goods, but refuses to pay for them, or to accept her fair share of the burdens on which they depend. She thus takes an unfair advantage for herself over all who obey the law: an advantage consisting not in any material profit from the crime, but in that very avoidance of the burden of self-restraint. What she deserves is to lose that unfair advantage, and punishment serves to remove that advantage by imposing an extra burden: punishment thus functions to restore that fair balance of benefits and burdens that a crime disturbs (see Morris 1968; Finnis 1972; Murphy 1973; von Hirsch 1976; Sadurski 1985, 1989; Sher 1987, chap. 5; Adler 1992, chaps. 5–8; Dagger 1993).

This is clearly a nonconsequentialist theory: the restoration of the "fair balance" of benefits and burdens, the removal of the criminal's "unfair advantage," is not a further contingent consequence of the punishment but is achieved in and by the punishment itself. It is a retributivist account, justifying punishment as an appropriate response to past crime; it aims to explain such familiar retributivist ideas as that of punishment as "annulling" the crime, or "paying the debt" that the offender owes to society. It is also a *positive* retributivism: punishment is not merely permissible, but demanded by justice, since law-abiding citizens suffer injustice if the criminal is allowed to get away with an unfair advantage.[16]

Though this kind of account still has defenders, it has been subjected to stringent criticism, even by some of its earlier adherents (see Mur-

---

[16] Some offered this as a complete account of the justifying purpose of punishment; others argued that punishment must also serve some consequentialist end—for instance, that it must both remove criminals' unfair advantage and deter crime (see von Hirsch 1976).

phy 1985; von Hirsch 1990, pp. 264–69; 1993, pp. 7–8). In particular, it is argued that the theory distorts the essential character of crime (the criminal wrongfulness of rape, for instance, in virtue of which it merits punishment, does not consist in taking an "unfair advantage" over all who obey the law); that it can give no plausible guidance on sentencing (on how we are to match the severity of punishment to the extent of the criminal's unfair advantage);[17] that it could anyway justify punishment only insofar as the law does create an initially fair balance of benefits and burdens, which is clearly not true of our existing legal systems;[18] and that it rests on a disputable liberal individualism that portrays a society as a contractual arrangement between isolated individuals (see Christie 1981, chaps. 6–7; Burgh 1982; Duff 1986, chap. 8; Falls 1987; Hudson 1987; Braithwaite and Pettit 1990, pp. 157–59; Dolinko 1991; Hampton 1992a, pp. 4–5).

A further point should be noted. Suppose we accepted that punishment can restore the fair balance of benefits and burdens that crime disturbs, by depriving criminals of the unfair advantages gained by their crimes. To justify a system of state punishment in such terms, however, we would also need to argue that such a restoration is the state's proper task (see Murphy 1985). But is it really a task that we can expect the state to carry out with tolerable efficiency and justice? Given the manifest "drawbacks" of a system of state punishment (its costs, its proneness to error and abuse), can we plausibly insist that it is so important to deprive criminals of their unfair advantages that we should create a system of state punishment for this purpose (see Husak 1992)?

This question, as Husak argues, faces any retributivist theory of punishment. Just as any consequentialist justification of punishment has to show not merely that it produces some good but that its benefits outweigh its costs, so too retributivists (even if they resist the consequentialist's calculus of benefits and costs) surely cannot justify a system of punishment by arguing only that it does justice, or secures

[17] Michael Davis, however, argues that the conception of crime as taking unfair advantage can found a plausible theory of sentencing, as distinct from a theory of punishment. See Davis (1983) and a string of subsequent articles: for criticisms, see Duff (1990c), Scheid (1990), and von Hirsch (1990); for a response (and citations of other articles in the series), see Davis (1993).

[18] As Murphy himself argued, in suggesting that the theory is "formally correct" but "materially incorrect (i.e., inapplicable to the actual world in which we live)" (Murphy 1973, p. 103). For the contrary argument that even in far from ideally just societies many criminals can still be said, in the relevant sense, to take an unfair advantage, see Sterba (1984, pp. 41–43); Davis (1991a, pp. 533–36).

some nonconsequential good: for we surely cannot assume, at least without further argument, that the state has an overriding duty to ensure that penal justice is done, or that that good is secured, *whatever* the cost. Given a system of criminal justice, we have to decide how many resources to devote to, and how enthusiastically to pursue, the tasks of detecting, prosecuting, and punishing crime: although such decisions might not be made on purely consequentialist grounds, they do at least involve some weighing of goods or duties against each other (the good of doing or the duty to do justice by detecting and punishing crime against such other goods or duties as the provision of health care, education, social welfare, etc.), and some weighing of goods or duties against costs, since we cannot plausibly insist that there is an absolute duty to detect and punish crime whatever the cost. If this is so, however, then surely some similar weighing of goods or duties against costs or drawbacks is required to justify the very creation of a system of retributive punishments in the first place.

But if punishment, as the infliction of "just deserts," cannot be justified as a matter of depriving criminals of their "unfair advantages," how can it be justified?

B. *Punitive Emotions*

Stephen notoriously argued that state punishment aims to satisfy, "in a regular public and legal manner," that "feeling of hatred and the desire of vengeance" that crime "excites in healthily constituted minds" (Stephen 1967, p. 152). Some theorists have recently tried again to justify punishment by relating it to the emotions that are properly aroused in us by crime, while giving a more subtle account than Stephen did of those emotions (he had talked rather cavalierly of "the feeling of hatred—call it revenge, resentment, or what you will" [ibid.]).

One such theorist, Moore, focuses on the feeling of guilt at our own wrongdoing rather than on the feeling of hatred or resentment at the wrongdoing of others. A system of strictly retributivist punishment, he argues, which makes criminal desert a sufficient condition for punishment, best explains the particular moral judgments we are naturally inclined to make about guilt and suffering (the only such judgments he discusses, however, concern especially horrific crimes: one must wonder how far the whole practice of state punishment could be justified on this basis; see Dolinko 1991, p. 556). I could imagine myself committing a horrific crime. If I were to commit it, I would (I hope) "feel guilty unto death"; one "ought to feel so guilty one wants to die." Given such feelings, I would judge that I ought to be punished, since restitutive action would not suffice to satisfy that guilt. If I am to respect an actual criminal as a human being, like myself, "with the capacity to will and reason—and thus to be and do evil," I must make the same judgment about his penal desert as I would about my own: that he must be punished (Moore 1987; the quotations are from pp. 213–15; see Moore 1993; for incisive criticism, on which I draw here, see Knowles 1993).

Moore's argument rests on his larger claim that virtuous emotions are a good heuristic guide to the truth of the moral judgments that they generate: feelings of guilt (which are surely virtuous) suggest the truth of those judgments of penal desert that they generate. But he seems to equivocate between talking of the emotions I *would* feel if . . . , and talking of the emotions I *do* feel. If we are to use our emotions as a heuristic guide, we must presumably appeal to our *actual* emotions (and Moore does talk of "our feelings of guilt" as if these were actual feelings; see 1987, p. 215). But while I might now judge that I would deserve punishment if I were to commit such a terrible crime, and while that judgment might reflect my actual feelings as I imagine committing such a crime, it cannot reflect any guilt that I actually feel: for I can feel no such guilt unless and until I actually commit the crime. What Moore has to claim is that I *would* feel such guilt, and *would* make such a judgment of my penal desert, if I committed such a crime; but while I might *hope* that I would feel and judge thus (that despite committing such a horrendous crime, I would not be morally completely dead), how can I *predict* that I would?

The more basic objection to Moore's argument, however, is that it rests ultimately on an appeal to unexplained intuition. A feeling of guilt might indeed, for many people, generate the judgment that one ought to suffer punishment: a judgment reflecting the intuition that the guilty deserve to suffer (see Davis 1972). But, first, we must surely explain, rather than just appeal to, that thought: *what*, and *why*, do the guilty deserve to suffer? Second, we must also show that a system of state punishment can inflict the kind of suffering that is deserved, and that it should be the state's job to inflict it.

Murphy (Murphy and Hampton 1988, chaps. 1, 3) offers a rather subtler argument, which tries to articulate more fully the meaning of those emotions that might motivate a desire for punishment. He focuses on resentment and "retributive hatred": resentment as a morally

appropriate response to wrongs that are done to me (appropriate because it expresses my own self-respect); retributive hatred, which involves a desire "to restore the proper moral balance" by making the
wrongdoer suffer so as to deprive her of her "undeserved or ill-gotten"
level of well-being, as the "in principle . . . natural, fitting and proper
response to certain instances of wrong-doing" (see pp. 89, 108).

Moore and Murphy are, I believe, right to bring the emotions back
into the picture: that is, to portray state punishment as related to (or
continuous with) our moral responses to wrongdoing, and to insist that
such moral responses are structured by certain appropriate emotions
(this is not to deny that they are rational—that they can be subject to
rational appraisal and guided by reasons; it is, rather, to deny that
sharp distinction between "reason" and "emotion" that has bedeviled
philosophy). I think too that Moore is right to focus on the significance
and implications of guilt, although his argument fails for the reasons
indicated above; and Murphy does at least make sense of resentment
as a morally respectable response to wrongs that are done to me (on
his stronger claim that it is a morally *necessary* response, see Hampton's
comments in Murphy and Hampton 1988, chap. 3; and Duff 1990*b*,
pp. 53–54). But does Murphy manage to show that "retributive hatred"
could provide a justifying foundation for a system of state punishment?
He doubts this himself: while it could *in principle* motivate a system of
punishment that aims to deprive criminals of their undeserved well-
being, we should in practice be very cautious about allowing this emotion to motivate us in this way (Murphy and Hampton 1988,
pp. 98–108), since we are ill-placed to make the requisite judgments
of wickedness; our awareness of our own moral failings should make
us "pause and at least think twice about" our hatreds (p. 103); and
retributive hatred is too often destructive, of both others and ourselves.
I am not sure, however, that his account provides even an "in principle" justification.

"Retributive hatred" involves a desire that a wrongdoer suffer a reduction in her "current level of well-being [which] is undeserved or
ill-gotten (perhaps at one's own expense)"; she should not, given what
she has done, be able or allowed to live a "life of freedom and contentment" (pp. 89, 91). Murphy seems to relate this desire to the desire to
deprive the criminal of her "unfair advantage" which could motivate a
system of "balance-restoring" punishment (pp. 94–95; above, Sec.
IIIA): but it is, surely, quite different. For retributive hatred involves
a desire that the wrongdoer be deprived not of the abstract advantage

that (on the balance-restoring account) was intrinsic to her crime, but of her current level of undeserved flourishing, which might not even be a product of her crime. A justification of punishment in terms of "retributive hatred" is thus quite different from a justification in terms of depriving criminals of their unfair advantages, and it is still unclear why the very fact of past wrongdoing either makes my current level of well-being undeserved, or justifies anyone in trying to deprive me of it.

But is there not *something* to the idea that one who has committed some serious wrong should not be able to live a life of "freedom and contentment"—should not be able to carry on as if she had done no wrong (whether or not, I would add, she is now notably flourishing)? She *should* suffer; which leads naturally to the thought that we may or should *make* her suffer. The problem, however, is still to explain that initial idea;[19] and moreover, to explain it in a way that could show state punishment to be at least in principle an appropriate way of making sure that she does suffer.

One possible explanation (which informs Moore's argument) is that she should suffer, deserves to suffer, *guilt:* for guilt is a proper response to one's own wrongdoing, and is (when sincere) painful—a matter of suffering. Guilt, however, is a kind of suffering that is essentially *self*-induced, flowing from my own perception that I did wrong: so how can it found a justification for punishment, which is typically imposed by others? One answer to this question is that the wrongdoer deserves to suffer the criticism or condemnation of others (which might induce a recognition and feeling of guilt); this leads us to the idea that punishment can be justified as a way of expressing that criticism or condemnation.

C. Punishment, Communication, and Censure

The idea of punishment as essentially expressive or communicative is not of course peculiar to retributivism. We could say that deterrent punishments have a communicative function; they are intended to tell actual and potential offenders that the threat of punishment is to be

[19] Mackie (1982) also explains this retributive thought by relating it to the "retributive emotions": but rather than looking to such emotions for a rational justification of punishment, or treating them as a guide to moral truth, he offers an evolutionary account of why the human species should have developed this emotional disposition; see Hampton (1988, pp. 117–19) for criticism of this. For a subtler version of this kind of argument, see Oldenquist (1988).

taken seriously. We will also see that consequentialists might find reason to favor a system of punishment that serves, at least in part, to express condemnation (see Primoratz 1989b on "extrinsic" as against "intrinsic" expressionism). But the idea that punishment (as distinct from mere "penalties"; see Feinberg 1970) has an essentially expressive function has been central to one recent strand of retributivist thought.[20]

If we suggest that punishment is expressive, the obvious question is: *what* is being expressed to *whom*, and *why* (see Skillen 1980)? The most plausible content for expressive punishment has to do with the disapproval or condemnation aroused and warranted by a crime: "Punishment is a conventional device for the expression of attitudes of resentment and indignation, and of judgments of disapproval and reprobation, on the part either of the punishing authority himself or of those 'in whose name' the punishment is inflicted" (Feinberg 1970, p. 98). This content might be expressed to the criminal who deserves punishment; to her victim, to declare the community's "authoritative disavowal" of the crime; to the public at large, or to potential criminals, to emphasize the community's commitment to the law and to the values it represents (on these and other purposes of expressive punishment, see Feinberg 1970, pp. 101–5).

I think, however, that we should distinguish between "expression" and "communication" and see punishment as communicative rather than expressive (see Duff 1992, pp. 51–52). For expression requires only an expresser: we express our indignation or condemnation, or the state expresses them on our behalf. It may also have an object, someone or something to or at whom the expression is directed: but this is not necessary to expression itself; and if it has an object, that object figures only as its passive recipient (as the criminal seems to figure in Stephen's account of punishment). Expression may be without further point or purpose—I simply feel the need to express my feelings, without any further aim than that; or it may be used instrumentally—to provide some relief, or to bring about some effect on others. Expression need not be a matter of reason, either in its motivation or in its intended mode of operation: that is, its content may be some immediate feeling that not even the agent sees as rational, and the effect (if any) that it is intended to produce in others may be a matter of unreasoned emotion

---

[20] See, generally, Feinberg (1970) and Primoratz (1989b); for critical discussion, see Benn (1958), Hart (1963, pp. 60–69), Walker (1978, 1981), Skillen (1980), and Davis (1991b). Both Lacey (1988) and Braithwaite and Pettit (1980), also portray punishment as expressive.

rather than anything involving their understanding. Communication, by contrast, is essentially a two-way rational activity. We communicate *with* another, who figures not simply as a passive recipient, but as a participant with us in this activity; our communication appeals to her understanding, not simply to her unreasoned feelings, and seeks a rational response from her. Communication, that is, addresses the other as a rational agent: expression need not address her at all, and might not address her as a rational agent.

I have argued elsewhere that the law should generally communicate with its citizens as rational agents—aiming not merely to control their conduct but to gain their assent to demands that are justified to them by appropriate kinds of moral reason—and that criminal trials should also constitute attempts to engage with a defendant in a rational process of judgment (see Duff 1986, chaps. 3–4). If we are to talk, as I think we should, of the *meaning* of punishment, not simply of its impact or effects (of the retributive suffering it inflicts, as some retributivists talk, or of its effects in modifying conduct, as some consequentialists talk), we should talk of its communicative rather than just its expressive meaning. For one thing, this focuses our attention on the offender, as the person with whom the communication is primarily or directly attempted; whereas if we talk only of expression, we may be accused of using the offender "as a means" to expressing something to others. This also portrays the offender as a rational and responsible agent who should be addressed as such and who should be a participant in, not merely the passive recipient of, his punishment.[21] The notion of communication brings with it demands of honesty and respect, and these are demands that the state should satisfy in its dealings with its citizens—including the criminals among them.[22]

We can understand how criminal conduct, if it constitutes genuine wrongdoing, deserves condemnation: its agent is "blameworthy"—that is, deserves blame or censure. Censure, like retributive punishment, is also essentially backward-looking, focusing on that past wrongdoing.

---

[21] I cannot here defend the claim that the criminal should (ideally) be a participant in her own punishment—but see Duff (1986); Adler (1992) develops the provocative argument that the "conscientious paradigm," of the criminal who seeks and undertakes her own punishment, is the central paradigm of justified punishment.

[22] Contrast Braithwaite and Pettit (1990, pp. 176–77) on the difference between "the Realpolitik of implementation" and the "symbolic politics" of "denunciation and reprobation": we should, they think, "tolerate the hypocrisy of maximum penalties being set reasonably high without being used, of sentences being imposed only to be suspended, because this may achieve the symbolic reprobative functions of the criminal law while toning down the excesses of its repression of dominion."

So we might hope to find here the basis for a retributivist account of the justifying relationship between past crime as wrongdoing that deserves censure, and present punishment as expressing that censure. But any such account must answer two questions. First, why should it be the *state's* task to administer that censure through a formal system of punishment: why not just leave it to other individuals (most obviously, the victim or her friends) to censure the wrongdoer? Second, our existing systems of punishment administer censure by "hard treatment" (Feinberg 1970): they express censure by material deprivations (such as the loss of liberty or money) which are painful or burdensome quite independently of their expressive meaning. We could administer censure without inflicting such hard treatment: it can be expressed by the defendant's formal conviction at his trial, or some other public and formal declaration; or by a purely symbolic punishment that causes pain only in virtue of its expressive meaning (see Duff 1986, pp. 148–49, 240–42). So why should we inflict hard treatment in order to express censure? We may agree that criminals ought to be censured, that the state should formally censure them, and that hard treatment punishments *can* express that censure. But to justify such punishments, we must surely show that hard treatment is a *necessary*, not merely a *possible*, method of expressing deserved censure; unless such hard treatment is necessary, it is surely unjustified.[23]

One might offer a consequentialist answer to the first question, since formal censure can be an effective means of modifying conduct: the person censured may avoid such conduct in future (realizing that it is wrong, or fearing the pain of censure), and others may be dissuaded from such conduct by being reminded of its wrongfulness or of the painful consequences of engaging in it (see Brandt 1961; Nowell-Smith 1961, pp. 301–4; Smart 1973, pp. 49–56). Walker indeed argues that any justification of punishment as censure must be consequentialist (Walker 1991, pp. 21–33, 78–82), while Braithwaite and Pettit explain punishment as "reprobative shaming" as an instrumental technique for censuring and inducing productive shame in the offender (see Braithwaite 1989; Braithwaite and Pettit 1990, pp. 87–91). A strictly consequentialist rationale for censure, however, is morally disputable, and there are good nonconsequentialist reasons for formally censuring offenders.

The moral objection to any purely consequentialist conception of

---

[23] See Christie (1977, p. 9; 1981, pp. 98–105): he believes in the importance of blame, but not in punishment as "pain-delivery."

censure is that blame or censure ought to mark an honest response to another's conduct, which treats her as a responsible moral agent. If we see censure as simply a useful technique for modifying conduct or attitudes, however, we cease to treat or respect the other person as a responsible agent; we instead see her as someone to be manipulated by whatever effective techniques we can find (see Charvet 1966; Duff 1986, pp. 42–53). The nonconsequentialist reason for formally censuring offenders is that the state which promulgates the criminal law as a system of supposedly stringent obligations protecting important interests and values, and the community whose law it supposedly is, ought to take breaches of that law seriously: this is owed to the citizens, and especially to the victims of crime. But to take crime seriously, while treating criminals as responsible moral agents, requires censure (see von Hirsch 1993, chap. 2). To mean what we say when we say that certain kinds of conduct are seriously wrong is to be ready to censure such conduct: someone who declared that rape was a serious wrong, but who was not prepared to condemn clear cases of rape, would find his sincerity doubted.

What of hard treatment, however: why should censure be given this form? One can easily find consequentialist answers to this question: most obviously, hard treatment offers prudential (deterrent) reasons to obey the law to those who may be unpersuaded by the moral appeal of the law or the moral import of the censure they receive, and that is why censure should be expressed in hard treatment rather than by some purely symbolic (and thus ineffectively deterrent) declaration or punishment (see Feinberg 1970, p. 101; von Hirsch 1985, chap. 5; on von Hirsch's more recent account, see Sec. III*E* below). This answer, however, revives the worries about deterrence discussed earlier: if we just add to the law's moral appeal a deterrent threat of hard treatment, we are surely again treating the potential criminal "as a dog."

It might seem obvious that a system of formal censure, especially one that expresses that censure by hard treatment, can be justified only if its purpose (and its actual effect) is to make a difference to behavior: to the behavior of those punished or of others. There is, I argue below, truth in this: but it is not a consequentialist's truth. We must rather look for a nonconsequentialist account of why censure should be expressed by hard treatment: an account that shows how such hard treatment can be an appropriate response to past crime that still treats the criminal as a responsible moral agent.[24]

[24] This will also answer Davis's (1991*b*) criticism that "intrinsic expressionism" cannot provide independent support for a retributivist account of punishment, since it "adds

D. Defeating Wrongdoers

Some argue that the censure that serious wrongdoing warrants can be adequately expressed or effectively communicated to the criminal (who might be disinclined to listen to a purely symbolic punishment) only by hard treatment (see Lucas 1980, pp. 132–36; Falls 1987; Primoratz 1989*b;* Kleinig 1991); but it is not clear that this suffices to justify penal hard treatment—unless the efficacy of the communication is just a matter of its *deterrent* efficacy (see Gur-Arye 1991; Duff 1986, pp. 240–45). If the claim is that hard treatment "translates the disesteem of society into the value system of the recalcitrant individual," so that if he does not come to see his crime as morally wrong we can at least make him "see that [it] was from his point of view a mistake" (Lucas 1980, pp. 133–34, 147), we must wonder whether such a "translation" can preserve the meaning of what it claims to translate; we must also ask why, if not for the sake of effective deterrence, it is so vital to drive this message home that the state should create a system of punishment to do so.

Hampton offers a different kind of account, portraying punishment as a communicative action whose purpose is to "defeat" the wrongdoer and so nullify the demeaning message that was implicit in her crime (see Hampton 1992*b,* developing Murphy and Hampton 1988, chap. 4; Hampton 1991, 1992*a:* for criticism, to some of which she responds in Hampton 1992*b,* see Duff 1990*b;* Dolinko 1991; Dare 1992; Marshall 1992; Slattery 1992; Golash 1994).[25]

Hampton offers an account of wrongdoing that aims to show why punishment is an appropriate response to certain kinds of wrongdoing. The kinds of wrong that require a retributive response are those that "morally injure" another person; a "moral injury" is "damage to the realization of a victim's value, or damage to the acknowledgement of the victim's value, accomplished through behavior whose meaning is such that the victim is diminished in value" (1992*b,* p. 221). Someone is diminished by conduct whose meaning is such that it portrays her as of lower value than she is: by his action, the perpetrator says that she is of inferior value to him, that her interests and rights count for

---

nothing interesting to [a nonexpressive] retributivism apart from a misleading formulation of its central thesis" (p. 3). What it should provide is an account of what criminals deserve—of why they deserve punishment.

[25] She does not now regard this as a complete account of the rationale of state punishment: retribution as she understands it is an essential, but not the only, aspect of a "morally respectable system" of state punishment, which should also take moral education and deterrence as its goals; see Hampton (1992*b,* p. 201).

less than his. Given Hampton's Kantian conception of human value, a victim's value cannot actually *be* degraded: but "diminishing" or "demeaning" action can damage her ability to "realize" that value by securing what it entitles her to (life, autonomy, bodily integrity, property), and it can damage the acknowledgment of her value by others by lowering her value in their eyes; it is wrongs that do such damage that require a "retributive response."[26]

I have doubts about her account of "moral injury" (see Duff 1990*b*, pp. 54–55). A moral injury (a wrong requiring a retributive response) must *both* have a "diminishing" meaning *and* threaten the realization or acknowledgment of the victim's value:[27] but very often at least one of these elements seems to be lacking. As to the meaning of the action, one could of course insist that any action that seriously wrongs another thereby "diminishes" her: by infringing her rights it denies her proper moral standing. But the diminishment and the moral injury are then *implications* of the wrongness of the action, rather than being *constitutive* of its wrongness, whereas Hampton wants the diminishing message to be what makes the action so wrong. Furthermore, can we plausibly find such a message in *every* kind of serious wrong? Might not some wrongs rather express a belief in the victim's equality (I see someone I defraud as a rival in the human jungle, from whom I expect no different treatment myself), or even a (misguided) belief in the victim's superiority, against which my wrong is an envious attack?

As to the actual effect of the action, will there not be wrongful actions that merit a retributive response, but which have no such effect: a failed attempt; a theft by a relatively poor person from a wealthy person, whose ability to realize her value, and whose value in others' eyes, may well not be damaged by it? Hampton might argue that such actions are nonetheless morally injurious, since we do not have a secure or unshakable commitment to the Kantian conception of human value. If we did *really* believe that all human beings have an equal value that cannot actually be degraded, "diminishing" actions that misrepresent a victim's value would not be so threatening. They could damage her ability to realize her value but would not damage, or threaten, the

---

[26] We will see shortly that this "retributive response" need not always take the form of punishment, let alone of state punishment.

[27] Hampton does seem to suggest (1992*b*, p. 223) that attempted murder might require a retributive response purely because of what it "conveys about the intended victim's worth"—regardless of its actual impact on either the realization or the acknowledgment of her value: but this seems inconsistent with her definition of a "moral injury."

acknowledgment of her value—her moral standing in others' eyes and in her own eyes: they might thus not require a retributive response that aims to rebut the degrading message about her worth implicit in the action, since there would be no danger of that message being believed. As things are, however, such actions do typically threaten both our grasp of our own value, and its acknowledgment by others, and the lack of a retributive response by others to the action would increase that threat, since it would imply that they accepted its demeaning message (Hampton 1992*b*, pp. 220, 225–26).[28]

But, first, there is a danger of circularity here. Hampton claims that a retributive response is needed to moral injuries that damage the realization or acknowledgment of the victim's value; by understanding the concept of a "moral injury," we are meant to understand why they require a retributive response. But she cannot then without circularity argue that what makes an action morally injurious is the fact that it would damage the acknowledgment of the victim's value if there was no retributive response to it: that would be to define moral injuries, in part, by reference to the need for a retributive response—whereas the notion of a moral injury was itself supposed to show why a retributive response is needed. Second, I am still not persuaded that all the kinds of action that we would want to count as criminal can plausibly be said to threaten the acknowledgment of a victim's value. If my car is vandalized, or the purse I dropped is stolen, this is inconvenient and annoying, but do I really suffer the kind of moral injury that Hampton is concerned with?

Hampton's account of "moral injury" is meant to identify the particular kind of wrongdoing that merits a retributive response, which might take the form of punishment. It should thus help to solve the problem of criminalization as well as that of punishment, by indicating the kinds of conduct that should be made criminal and thus in principle punishable. I think, however, that it is a mistake to look for any such unitary account of the kinds of wrongdoing that should be criminalized; and I have argued that Hampton's own account is not plausible. We must look now, however, at the "retributive response" that she argues is required to moral injuries, and its relation to state punishment.

In earlier versions of Hampton's account, retribution served to defeat

---

[28] She also appeals (p. 220) to the possible effect of the action in encouraging attacks on other victims: but this is not damage to this particular victim, which is what her account is meant to focus on.

the claim to superiority implicit in the wrongdoer's action and to reassert the moral truth that his action denied: it "reaffirm[s] a victim's equal worth in the face of a challenge to it," "annul[ling] the false evidence seemingly provided by the wrongdoing of the relative worth of the victim and the wrongdoer" (1988, pp. 126, 131). What mattered was that the moral truth should be reasserted, even if this did not persuade others to accept it or bring the criminal to repentance (see 1988, pp. 132–33). I doubt whether this account justifies hard treatment punishment: could we not reassert this moral truth by formal declarations or symbolic punishments? But her latest account posits more ambitious aims for retribution: it should "re-establish the acknowledgement of the victim's worth damaged by the wrongdoing, and . . . repair the damage done to the victim's ability to realize her value" (1992b, p. 228). A system of state punishment is not the only, nor necessarily the best, way to achieve this goal. It can sometimes be achieved by apology, and restitution or reparation, by the wrongdoer; or by informal community action; or by awarding punitive damages in tort cases. But it should sometimes be the state's task, "in its capacity as impartial moral representative of the entire community" (1992b, p. 236), to vindicate a victim's value; and such vindication sometimes requires the wrongdoer to be "defeated" or "lowered," in order effectively to rebut his claim to superiority. It is here that punishment, or penal hard treatment, figures, as a way of humbling the wrongdoer and, thus, of "destroy[ing] his claim to mastery" (1992b, p. 233).

On such a view, punishment is essentially communicative: it aims to communicate with the wrongdoer, the victim, and the community. It must humble the wrongdoer, to show that he is not (as he implicitly claimed by his crime) superior in value to his victim: but it must not deny his "dignity as a person," by degrading him (1992b, p. 232). This requires "creativity and flexibility in sentencing," to deal with the difficult task of fashioning "retributive punishments for serious felons that simultaneously respect the wrongdoer and defeat him in a way that destroys his claim to mastery" (1992b, p. 233);[29] but it is still not clear, I think, how penal hard treatment is to serve the aims of retribution.

Insofar as the aim is to "repair the damage done to the victim's ability to realize her value," this might sometimes be achievable by

[29] She also insists that the severity of the punishment must be proportionate to the seriousness of the crime (see 1992b, p. 232): in Sec. V, I discuss the problems of combining proportionality and creative flexibility.

compensation, restitution, or reparation from the wrongdoer. Now we can see compulsory compensation or restitution as punishment, though they are traditionally distinguished from punishment (see Ashworth 1992, pp. 249–52; Duff 1986, p. 284); but often nothing the offender can do or be required to do can repair the damage the victim suffered. If what matters is rather to repair the damage done to "the acknowledgement of the victim's worth" (to its acknowledgment by others, and to her own sense of her own worth and of its acknowledgment by others), then again I do not see why this should not be achieved by formal declarations or purely symbolic punishments. Of course, it cannot be achieved by "a few idle remarks" (Hampton 1992*b*, p. 228). But why should not a public and formal declaration, or the imposition of a purely symbolic punishment, make it clear to everyone that we do deny the demeaning message implicit in the crime?

Perhaps, however, part of the aim is to bring the wrongdoer himself to acknowledge the victim's value. Hampton talks approvingly of programs that try to make sex offenders "confront what they did to other human beings, and appreciate how badly their actions affected them": they defeat "the rapist's claim to mastery by putting him in a position where he must, through his imagination, *become* her and suffer as if he were her" (1992*b*, p. 232). Now I agree that programs of this kind can serve as appropriate forms of punishment. But, first, I do not see that their aim should be to communicate to the offender the very abstract moral message that Hampton is concerned with, about the relative values of offender and victim: should it not, rather, be to bring him to recognize the substantive harm he has done? Second, it is not clear how this aim is distinct from that of moral education, of bringing an offender to understand (and repent) what he has done: but Hampton insists that "retribution" as she defines it is distinct from moral education, although it can be "a useful . . . tool for moral education" (Hampton 1992*a*, p. 21; see also 1992*b*, p. 201).

Thus insofar as Hampton's is meant to be a strictly retributivist account, justifying punishment purely as a way of denying "the message implicit in the crime" (1992*a*, p. 22), with no further aim beyond that denial, it can justify nothing more than a practice of formal denunciations and perhaps some purely symbolic punishments. Insofar as she wants punishment also to repair the damage done to a victim's ability to realize her value, or to the acknowledgment of her value *by the offender*, she might be able to justify certain kinds of penal hard treatment (although we will need to ask more carefully just how hard treatment, and what kinds of hard treatment, can serve the latter end). But this is then to give punishment an aim beyond itself: which is to say that punishment is no longer strictly a matter of pure retribution. I discuss accounts of this kind, which portray punishment as looking both back to the past crime and forward to the "repair" of the damage wrought by crime and the moral reform or repentance of the offender, in Section IV.

E. Censure and Prudential Supplements

Before moving on to discuss more ambitious kinds of communicative theory, which find a communicative (and in a sense retributive) role for penal hard treatment, I should attend to the account that von Hirsch and Narayan have offered of the proper role of hard treatment within a primarily communicative, reprobative conception of punishment (see Narayan 1993; von Hirsch 1993, chap. 2). They reject the kinds of attempt to make retributive sense of hard treatment discussed earlier in this section, and those more ambitious attempts to give hard treatment a morally reformative or penitential role to be discussed in Section IV. But they also reject a *purely* consequentialist rationale for hard treatment as a deterrent, for the reasons I discussed above: simply to replace the law's moral appeal by the prudential threat of painful sanctions is to cease to treat potential offenders as responsible moral agents. Penal hard treatment does indeed, they argue, serve a deterrent purpose; but that deterrent purpose should not be separated, as a purely consequentialist account threatens to separate it, from the moral censure that it is the primary and central task of punishment to convey.

Most of us are to some degree sensitive to and capable of being moved by moral considerations, but also morally weak and fallible: all too often, if the only available motives for right action are moral motives, we will do what we know we ought not to do, or fail to do what we know we ought to do. If I am aware of my moral weakness, and yet concerned to get myself to act rightly despite such weakness, I might then offer myself further incentives: some modest reward for doing my duty, or some punishment or penance for failing to do it. Such rewards and penalties function as additional prudential incentives to right action, and are thus, to a degree, morally inappropriate: were I morally stronger, I would not need them; the need for them reveals my moral weakness and impairs the moral worth of my actions (though, I might properly think, better to do my duty in this imperfectly motivated way than not to do it at all). But my actions are not motivated *merely* by such prudential considerations. First, because such incentives *supplement*, rather than *replace*, the moral reasons that would ideally be sufficient: by themselves, they are not sufficient to motivate me, but their addition to those moral reasons that should, but do not, sufficiently motivate me persuades me to act as I know I should. Second, their character as rewards or punishments is crucial to their motivational efficacy: what makes them efficacious is not just their material nature, but their meaning—the thought that I will *deserve* them as rewards or punishments.

Similarly, the prospect of praise or blame, admiration or condemnation, from others can help to strengthen my moral, but weak, will. Ideally, I would act rightly even if it would gain me no praise or would actually bring condemnation or despite from others. But, given my moral weakness, the prospect of praise or blame from others (and especially, or perhaps properly only, from those I respect) can be a morally respectable supplement to my autonomous moral motivation. Of course, if I am motivated *solely* by the prospect of praise or blame, by the effect of my actions on my public reputation, my actions lose moral worth. But if such a motivation is supplementary, and if what makes it efficacious is the thought that I would *deserve* the praise or blame, it is still connected to those moral motives that should properly move me; and it is surely not a wholly disreputable kind of motivation for fallible beings like ourselves.

Von Hirsch and Narayan give an analogous rationale for penal hard treatment, as a prudential supplement to the moral reasons on which the law primarily depends, which is appropriate for moral but imperfect beings like us. We express the censure that offenders deserve by hard treatment, rather than by formal denunciation or purely symbolic punishments, because this will offer an additional, prudential incentive to obey the law; but this is intended as a supplement to, not a replacement for, the morally persuasive force of the censure. They thus aim to avoid the charge of treating potential offenders as "dogs" rather than as "men": for punishment and its threat treat us as moral, albeit imperfectly moral, agents. They also thus portray the threat of punishment as directed against "us" rather than "them": this is a kind of penal system we could adopt for ourselves to strengthen our morally weak wills (see Narayan 1993, p. 181). Finally, this account clearly implies a principle of *ordinal* proportionality: if penal hard treatment is to express the appropriate degree of censure, its hardness must be relatively proportionate to the seriousness of the crime. But it implies a *cardinal* principle too, which strictly limits the general severity of punishments:[30] if hard treatment is to supplement rather than replace the law's moral appeal, its severity must not be so great that it drowns the law's moral voice. Von Hirsch therefore advocates a "decremental strategy" of gradually reducing current levels of penal severity, towards a system that would, for instance, allow no prison sentence of more than three years, or five years for homicide (von Hirsch 1993, chap. 5).

This is, I think, the most plausible account of how we could use penal hard treatment as a deterrent within a primarily retributivist system of punishment. It does admittedly fall short of that ideal of rational persuasion that allows us to give each other only relevant (in this case moral) reasons for action, since it involves creating new and strictly speaking irrelevant prudential reasons for obeying the law; but, it might be argued, this reflects the fact that any system of criminal law must deal with beings (ourselves) who are less than ideal. Furthermore, the Hegelian objection to deterrent punishment could be argued to assume an oversimplified dichotomy: as if we treat people either *merely* as dogs, using *only* threats to secure their obedience, or as ideal moral agents, offering them *only* relevant moral reasons for obedience. Should we not instead treat people (including ourselves) as what they are: moral but imperfect beings who need prudential incentives to assist them?

Another merit of this account, at least for liberals who mistrust and seek to limit the coercive powers of the state, is that it sets relatively modest aims for a system of punishment. It is not vastly ambitious about preventing crime; it recognizes that the preventive efficacy of any morally tolerable penal system will be limited. Nor does it aim (as those more ambitious accounts to be discussed in the next section do) to secure any particular moral response from, or to bring about any desirable moral change in, the offender. Punishments of the kind it envisages *permit* such a moral response: since punishment is still essentially a matter of censure, and since penal hard treatment should supplement without drowning the voice of pure moral censure, offenders are given the *opportunity* to listen to that moral voice and so to repent their crimes and seek their own reform. But punishment does not *try* to elicit (or coerce) such a moral response: it delivers the moral message, but it is up to the offender what, if anything, to make of that message

[30] On the "ordinal" and "cardinal" dimensions of proportionality, see von Hirsch (1985, chaps. 4, 8; 1993, chaps. 2, 5).

and how to respond to it (see von Hirsch 1993, chap. 8; Narayan 1993, pp. 174–75). More ambitious theories of punishment seek to "plant the flag of truth within the fortress of a rebel soul" (Lewis 1940, p. 83, cited with approval by Hampton 1992a, pp. 1, 22): to which a liberal would respond that that is not a task which we should allot to the state. By contrast, punishment as it is envisaged here gives the offender the opportunity to examine his own soul, but it does not "impinge upon the inner citadels of his soul" (Lucas 1968, p. 221, contrasting deterrent punishment with supposedly therapeutic "treatment").

Apart from the question of whether the aims of punishment should be as modest as this account insists, however (a question addressed in Sec. IV), we must ask whether it is adequate in its own terms.

Goldman argued that the attempt to combine retributivist and utilitarian elements in an account that portrays the aim of punishment as being the deterrent prevention of crime, subject to retributivist side constraints that limit both the absolute and the relative severity of punishments, is doomed to failure: for effective deterrence will require punishments much more severe than such side constraints can allow (Goldman 1979). A similar problem seems to face von Hirsch and Narayan. Von Hirsch admits that a system of modest penal supplements such as he favors might well not be enough to deter "the most recalcitrant," but he argues that the aim of a penal system should not, and cannot realistically be, complete prevention of crime: it should give "ordinary persons good reasons for compliance," without aiming for "anything near one hundred percent efficiency"; it is enough if it induces "most people," but not "the most recalcitrant," to obey the law (von Hirsch 1993, p. 44). But we must ask, first, whether sentences of up to three years imprisonment (five for homicide), though admittedly much milder than current sentencing levels, can really be seen as *supplements* to the law's moral appeal; and, second, whether such modest supplemental punishments might not be so ineffective as motivators, failing to deter many more than "the most recalcitrant," that even von Hirsch would be worried.

On the first question, I am not sure that the prospect of a three- (or five-) year prison term can plausibly be seen merely as a supplement to the moral reasons that the potential offender is supposedly sensitive to, though not sufficiently moved by. If it is to provide, as on this account it can only provide, a prudential motive for obedience (rather than serving, as it could in more ambitious accounts, as part of some reformative or penitential process), I think it will replace, rather than merely supplement, the law's moral voice: that truly *supplementary* incentives would need to be much more modest in their severity than even von Hirsch's decremental strategy allows. On the second question, von Hirsch is skeptical about schemes that would allow upward departures from the limits set by criminal desert (the imposition of harsher sentences than the principles of proportionate censure would allow) in exceptional cases (1993, chap. 6). It is of course impossible to predict with confidence just what effect on crime rates his decremental strategy would have, but there is surely reason to fear that a system that set three years' imprisonment as the maximum for nonhomicide crimes would be moderately ineffective in preventing crime, and that one which, in order to ensure that its hard treatment penalties were indeed no more than prudential supplements, set even lower maximum sentences than this would be radically ineffective.

My point in raising these questions is not to argue for a system of more stringently deterrent kinds of hard treatment. Rather, it is to suggest that there is more tension than von Hirsch allows between the aim of preserving the communication of censure to rational moral agents as the central purpose of punishment, and that of using hard treatment as a crime-preventive prudential supplement: the kinds and levels of punishment that could be appropriate as merely prudential supplements will also be radically ineffective as deterrents.

Perhaps some such tension is unavoidable: perhaps we cannot *both* insist on treating actual and potential criminals as rational moral agents *and* hope to achieve any tolerable level (whatever that might be) of crime prevention. But before reaching such a pessimistic conclusion, we must look at some more ambitious accounts of punishment as communication: accounts that argue that penal hard treatment can itself be justified as part of a communicative process that aims to bring the criminal, as a responsible moral agent, to reform her future conduct.

IV. Teleological Communication

A strict consequentialist portrays punishment as an instrumental means to some independently identifiable end. (The contingency of the connection between punishment and its justifying goals provokes the objections to consequentialist accounts which I discussed above [see Sec. II]: that any moral constraints on the distribution of punishment or its modes [on who may be punished; on how severe, or intrusive or degrading their punishments may be] must either be merely contingent constraints, which are thus vulnerable to changing contingencies, or be based on nonconsequentialist demands of justice which are quite separate from the justifying goals of punishment; and that both pure and side-constrained consequentialists fail adequately to respect or do justice to the moral status of those who are punished or threatened with punishment.) By contrast, a strict retributivist justifies punishment purely as an appropriate, backward-looking response to a past crime, which has no purpose beyond itself. But, apart from the problem of explaining the supposedly justificatory relationship between past crime and present punishment (particularly when punishment takes the form of hard treatment), there remains for many people the feeling that a system of punishment (especially, again, one of hard treatment punishments) should have some forward-looking purpose. To insist in advance that any adequate justification of punishment must show that it achieves some (by implication consequential) good is of course to beg the question against the retributivist, who would say that it matters *in itself* that justice be done, or that criminals be deprived of their unfair advantages, or that the truth be told; and if we then say in less overtly consequentialist tones that a system of punishment must be justified by showing that it contributes something to the continuing life of the community, a retributivist might reply that on her account it does—it contributes justice or truth. Nonetheless, even among those persuaded by retributivist objections to consequentialism, there may remain the thought that there should be more to punishment than this: while punishment is, as retributivists insist, essentially a matter of responding appropriately to a past crime, that response should also look toward the future.

The accounts to be considered in this section can be seen as trying to meet this worry by giving punishment a purpose beyond itself: a purpose to which it is contingently connected in that it might not in fact achieve its purpose. That connection is not, however, *purely* contingent (this distinguishes these accounts from any strictly consequentialist theories), for two reasons. First, that purpose itself determines which means (what kinds of punishment) are appropriate to it: on these accounts, it requires that punishment be a mode of communication with a responsible moral agent, which respects her status as a rational agent, and is proportionate to the seriousness of her crime. To try to pursue punishment's proper purpose by other means, for instance, by deliberately punishing innocents or by the excessive or merely manipulative punishment of the guilty, would be not merely contingently inefficacious, or inconsistent with independent side constraints of justice, but incoherent. Second, though this purpose is a "justifying aim" in that punishment must pursue this purpose if it is to be justified, that justification does not depend wholly on its efficacy in achieving this purpose: sometimes what matters will be the *attempt* to achieve that purpose, even if we are sure that the attempt is doomed to fail.

A. *Repentance, Reform, and Reconciliation*

Some theorists have suggested that punishment should function as moral education (see Hampton 1984; Morris 1981). This idea might sound strange. We can "educate" someone only if there is something she does not yet know or understand, which we aim to teach her. But unless we take an implausibly strict Socratic view of the connection between moral knowledge and action, which ascribes all wrongdoing to ignorance of the good, we must surely see that many criminals know full well that they are doing wrong: not just that it is illegal or contrary to the moral beliefs current in their community, but that it is morally wrong. Few thieves, for instance, would agree that it is morally permissible for others to steal from them, or claim some special moral privilege that makes it right for them to steal, but not for others to steal from them. We may sometimes ascribe a crime to the agent's failure to think through the likely consequences or the moral implications of his action. But this is likely to be true only of some less serious crimes (and not of all of them): to suggest that an armed robber does not know that armed robbery is wrong would be to attribute to him a kind of moral ignorance that raises serious doubts about his status as a responsible moral agent (see Narayan 1993, p. 173).

But yet, if a responsible moral agent, without excuse or justification, breaks a criminal law that is itself justified (and if she is to be justly punished the law she breaks must be one that she was genuinely obligated to obey), there must be *something* amiss with her moral condition. Perhaps she was weak-willed: she gave in to momentary temptation, or concealed from herself the true moral character of her action. Perhaps she did not care enough for the values that the law embodies, or for the interests it protects, caring more for her own profit. Furthermore, without subscribing to the "character" conception of criminal liability that portrays the criminal action merely as evidence of some underlying defect of character (see Duff 1993), we must recognize that whatever moral defect her action manifested was a defect in her as a *continuing* moral agent: that is, it is a defect which remains with her.

Different moral and political theories give different accounts of the nature and implications of the "defect" that culpably criminal action manifests. Our concern here is with accounts that portray it as a defect not merely *within* the agent, but in those *relationships* that constitute her moral identity, and her own good. Some talk of a defect in her relationship to "correct values" (see Nozick 1981, pp. 374–79); others of a defect in her relationship with her community or her fellow citizens (whose rights or interests she has violated, whose values she has flouted); others, appealing to a Platonic conception of the self and its good, of a defect in her relationship to the Good, and therefore in her relationship with herself and her own good. These ways of talking are not wholly distinct from each other. Those who take seriously the communitarian conception of the individual as existing, and finding her identity and her good, only within a community of shared values and moral relationships, might say that crime marks a defect not merely in the agent's relationship with her fellow citizens, or to the values of her community, but also in her relationship to her own good, which depends on those other relationships (see Morris 1981, p. 265; Lacey 1988, pp. 171–73; Oldenquist 1988; Duff 1986, pp. 254–57); Platonists will portray defects in the person's relationship to "correct values" or to the Good as also injurious to her—as damaging her relationship to her own good.

We should notice, however, that such accounts do not portray the defect in, or damage to, such relationships either as an underlying condition, for which the particular criminal act provides evidence (which is how a character conception of criminal liability portrays the role of criminal conduct), or as something contingently caused by criminal action. The culpable wrongdoing itself *constitutes* that defect (see Duff 1993, pp. 371–80): it *necessarily* damages those relationships, separating the agent from the Good, her fellow citizens, and her own true good.

This way of understanding the moral significance and implications of crime underpins the idea that the purpose of punishment should be to repair or restore that which the crime has damaged: to repair not just any material harm caused by the crime (though punishment might consist in part in such material reparation), but that damage to the criminal's relationships which was intrinsic to her crime. The crime created a moral breach between the criminal and her fellow citizens or her community, or between the criminal and the Good (and her own good). That breach can be repaired, thus reconciling her with those from whom her crime threatened to separate her, only if she herself is prepared to heal it by repenting and forswearing her crime, which necessarily also involves a resolve and attempt so to reform herself that she avoids such wrongdoing in the future;[31] and punishment aims precisely to bring the criminal to recognize—more adequately than she may yet have recognized—the wrongness of her crime, to repent that crime, and to reform herself.

On this view, it is natural to say that punishment benefits the criminal herself, as well as others: it aims to repair relationships whose damage or destruction is injurious to her as well as to others (hence Morris's 1981 title "A Paternalistic Theory of Punishment"). Although punishment is not an unqualified blessing (it is better to avoid both wrongdoing and punishment than to do wrong and be punished), if I do wrong it is better to be punished than not (see Plato's *Gorgias*): punishment is therefore a good, rather than an unqualified evil for the criminal, although he might not himself recognize it as such. By contrast, deterrent theorists, and retributivists who justify punishment as an evil that is justly inflicted on those who do evil, must portray punishment simply as an evil for the person punished.

Though theorists who advocate this kind of view do typically talk of punishment as aiming to benefit the wrongdoer (see Morris 1981; Hampton 1984; Duff 1986: contrast Oldenquist 1988, p. 471), it might seem unnecessary to do so: why can we not rather say that punishment aims to benefit the community, by protecting its values and dissuading criminals from further crimes; that any benefit to the criminal is only a side effect, not the direct purpose, of such punishment? This would not open such theories to a charge of using the criminal "merely as a means" to that social benefit (for the aim would still be rational persuasion rather than coercion or manipulation, and we do not use a person "merely as a means" if we try to persuade him, rationally, to act as he ought to); while it might protect such theories from the liberal argument that it should not be the state's task to seek the wrongdoer's own moral good by such coercive methods. The answer is, I think, that what matters on such accounts is not just that the criminal be persuaded to refrain from future crime but that he be restored to full membership of the moral community by repenting his crime; it is hard to see why this should matter if we do not see that the loss of or damage to his membership of the moral community injures *him*.

[31] Her reconciliation to her fellow citizens also, of course, requires an appropriate response from them: this account of punishment places a heavy burden not just on the criminal, nor just on those who must directly administer her punishment, but on all members of the community to which she belongs.

It is crucial to note the difference between this kind of account of punishment as educative or reformative and those cruder kinds of purely consequentialist account of punishment as "rehabilitative" or "reformative" that were criticized as failing to respect the moral standing of those who are punished. Those consequentialist accounts saw "rehabilitation" as a matter of bringing about some desirable change in an offender's attitudes, dispositions, and conduct, to which punishment is at best a contingent means—and may not be an efficacious means at all (see Menninger 1968). The aim is to bring it about that the offender accepts and obeys the law or (more ambitiously) to bring it about that he can function "normally" and law-abidingly in his society, and the task is then to find some instrumentally effective means of achieving this. The offender thus figures as the *object* of our coercive attentions, in or on whom we must cause this change. The purpose of reformative punishment as it is portrayed here, however, is not so much to re-form the offender, as to persuade her to reform *herself*: to "correct" her as a rational and responsible moral agent. Now if that is our aim, the means that we use must themselves be appropriate to, respectful of, her status as a moral agent; indeed, if we are to count as pursuing *that* aim at all (as distinct from the crude aim of causing some desirable change in her attitudes and conduct), we must throughout treat and address her as a rational moral agent (see Morris 1981, p. 265; Hampton 1984, p. 222; Duff 1986, p. 278).[32] Analogously, the proper aim of philosophical persuasion is not simply to bring it about that my interlocutor accepts what I assert, but to persuade her as a rational thinker of its truth: to try to achieve *that* end by manipulation, intellectual bullying, or deceit is not simply ineffectual; it is incoherent.

It is also, of course, crucial to note that this kind of account of justified punishment does not purport to be true of or to justify our existing penal practices. It does not claim that in our existing societies

---

[32] The distinction between "education" and "indoctrination" is relevant here. My purpose in educating students should not be simply to bring it about that they accept certain theories (however justifiably sure I am of their truth), by whatever means I can find, but to persuade them to accept such truths because they understand them and see that and why they are true: not to cause beliefs in the students, but to bring them to accept beliefs for themselves. It follows that I have been more successful with a student who persists in philosophical error, but with understanding and intellectual autonomy, than with one who accepts philosophical truths without understanding them for himself. Analogously, a punishment that makes the offender think about the moral character of her crime, but does not persuade her to repent that crime or change her ways, has been more successful than one that coerces the offender into law-abiding conduct that does not reflect his moral understanding of why he should obey the law.

and legal systems every criminal offense damages the criminal's relationship to the Good or to a moral community of which she is truly a member—only that that is (would be) the implication of a crime in a well-ordered community with a just system of law. It does not claim that the kinds of punishment to which we currently subject criminals could plausibly be seen as exercises in such moral reform—only that that is what punishment should be if it is to be properly justified. Nonetheless, the claim that a system of state punishment should (even ideally) aim to benefit the criminal by enabling him to repair the moral damage wrought by his crime will still strike many as bizarre. In particular, it must face three challenges. First, can we really believe that even in a well-ordered society crime is harmful to the criminal himself? Second, how can punishment (especially hard treatment punishment) serve the aims that this kind of account sets for it? Third, should it anyway be the state's task to try, by such coercive means, to secure the moral good of its criminal citizens? I cannot discuss the first question further here: it marks one central difference between a roughly liberal conception of the person, according to which individuals might find their good in certain kinds of social or communal relationship, but might also find it in activities that involve doing serious harms or wrongs to others; and a communitarian conception, according to which we can find our individual goods (and our very identities as persons) only as members of a community of shared values and mutual concerns.[33] But by trying to answer the other two questions, I can bring out more clearly some of the central features of this kind of theory.

B. Punishment as Penance

How could a system of hard treatment punishment (even if the hard treatment is different from that typically inflicted by our existing penal systems) serve the goals of moral persuasion and reform which, on these accounts, punishment should serve? The criminal law itself declares certain kinds of conduct to be wrong; a criminal conviction condemns or censures the offender for having wrongfully breached the law's justified demands (see Duff 1986, chaps. 3–4). These are possible ways of trying to persuade citizens to accept and obey the law, and of trying to persuade an offender to repent her crime; and one could

---

[33] Plato was the first to explore this kind of dispute about the relation between individual good and moral good: see *Gorgias*, *Republic*.

imagine a system of more formal condemnations, or of purely symbolic punishments, which might also further that aim by making it clear to the criminal that and why we take her conduct seriously as something wrong.[34] We can also envisage procedures undertaken *during* an offender's punishment that have the same aim: while in prison she could be exposed to various kinds of preaching or discussion (and we would then need to ask whether imprisonment can be justified, in part, as providing the opportunity for such procedures). These accounts, however, claim that punishment itself, *as* punishment, can serve the aim of moral persuasion and reform, and we need to ask how this could be so (for critical discussion, see Deigh 1984; Shafer-Landau 1991).

Punishment must obviously, on such accounts, be communicative: it aims to bring the offender to understand and repent the wrong he has done. But what could hard treatment communicate that is not communicated by a formal conviction or a purely symbolic punishment?

One answer, resembling the suggestion that hard treatment is necessary to communicate censure adequately, is that it shows the criminal that there is a barrier, a limit, to her actions: by inflicting such hard treatment on her, we show her how seriously we take her action as something that she should not have done (see Morris 1981, p. 266; Hampton 1984, pp. 211–13). But why (if not for the sake of prudential deterrence) should this be the appropriate way of communicating such a message? Is there not a serious danger that the criminal will receive the message, and perceive the limit, in purely prudential terms—that its moral meaning will be drowned out by its character as hard treatment?

Perhaps, however, hard treatment punishment can do more than mark a barrier: it can help direct the offender's attention onto what he has done and bring him to a more adequate moral grasp of its wrongfulness. Consider the programs for sexual offenders that Hampton cites (Hampton 1992*b*, p. 232), or programs for domestically violent men that aim to "directly challenge men's violence" and "make men responsible for their violence" through "confrontational group work" involving both reenactment and discussion (Dobash and Dobash 1992, chap.

---

[34] Von Hirsch and Narayan argue that the aim of penal censure should be only to communicate the censure to the criminal, not to persuade her or to elicit any particular response (such as acceptance) from her. I would say, however, that an intention to elicit an appropriate response is internal to such communicative acts, even if we see reason (as they do) to set strict limits on what we may do to try to elicit that response.

7; Morran and Wilson 1994). An offender required to take part in such a program is *punished* by it. It is a burden imposed on him because of his crime, as a response to that crime. It is designedly painful, in that it is intended to challenge him, to confront him forcefully with the nature of what he has done, and thus to induce in him the painful recognition of his wrongdoing. It can also be said to constitute hard treatment, in that it is burdensome or painful even for those who close their ears to its moral message. Such punishments are communicative: they aim to communicate not merely censure, but a better understanding of what the offender has done. They also, therefore, aim to elicit an appropriate moral response from him: for an adequate understanding of what he has done must be a *repentant* understanding, involving his recognition of its wrongfulness. Furthermore, insofar as they aim to persuade him to confront, to understand, and to repent what he has done, such punishments aim at his moral (self-)reform: for to understand the wrong I have done must also be to recognize a need to reform my conduct and attitudes for the future.

Punishments of this kind are obviously and directly communicative in their focus on and insistent discussion of the offender's crime. But other kinds of punishment, including those familiar in existing penal systems (community service, fines, probation, even imprisonment), can serve the same communicative purpose, *if* administered in the right spirit and the right context: they too can force the criminal's attention onto his crime, thus aiming to induce his repentant understanding of what he has done (see Duff 1992). Such punishments can also assist, as well as stimulate, the further process of self-reform and reconciliation.

I have argued elsewhere that punishment should ideally constitute a penance which, though initially imposed by others on the criminal, he should ideally come to accept and will for himself (see Duff 1986, chap. 9; 1988a; 1992; see Adler 1992, on the "conscientious paradigm" of punishment: for criticism, see Bickenbach 1988; Harrison 1988; Lipkin 1988; Ten 1990; Baker 1992; Narayan 1993; von Hirsch 1993, chap. 8). A penance can serve both to induce and to express a wrongdoer's repentant recognition of what she has done: the outward burden or pain it involves expresses the inward pain of remorse, and her acceptance of the pain manifests the sincerity of her remorse. It can also strengthen what might otherwise be a shallow or incomplete repentance, by keeping her attention on her offense and providing a structure within which she can reinforce her understanding of that offense and her resolve to reform herself. It can also help reconcile her with those she has wronged: with her victim, with her fellow citizens, with her community. For it expresses her repentant acceptance of responsibility for her offense, her determined disavowal of that offense, and her desire to restore those relationships which her offense damaged.

Such an account does not, we should note, justify keeping on with increasingly harsh punishment until the offender repents (see Morris 1981, p. 268; Hampton 1984, pp. 222–23, 232–33; Duff 1986, p. 278). For, first, punishment must aim at rational moral persuasion, not co-erced (and hence inauthentic) acceptance: thus it must always address the offender as a rational moral agent and is necessarily fallible—it is intrinsic to any such rational process that it might fail to persuade (see above, n. 32). Second, because punishment must communicate an appropriate judgment on the criminal's offense: some principle of proportionality is thus intrinsic to this account. This account does, however, justify punishing those who are already repentant (see Morris 1981, p. 269; Hampton 1984, pp. 233–34): for some penance is still needed to reinforce that repentance and to manifest its sincerity to others. It also justifies punishing those who will, we are certain, remain unpersuaded and unrepentant (see Hampton 1984, p. 231; Duff 1986, pp. 264–66): for we owe it to them not to regard them as beyond moral salvation, however empirically unlikely we think that salvation is. Finally, it can also justify punishing the moral rebel who rejects the community's basic values, *if* we can properly say to him that he should accept those values (see Bickenbach 1988, pp. 780–83; Duff 1988*b*). It does not, however, justify punishing those to whom we cannot properly say that they have flouted the values and damaged the bonds of a community to which they genuinely belong, one within which they are themselves treated as full members (see Duff 1986, pp. 292–93; Hampton 1992*b*, pp. 240–42): which might well mean that it cannot justify the punishment of many actual criminals in our actual societies (see further in Sec. VI below).

C. Penitential Punishment and the Role of the State

Perhaps a system of sensitively designed and administered punishments could *ideally* serve the penitential and reformative ends that this account posits. But apart from the question of whether such an ideal is remotely practicable (to be discussed later), we must still ask whether the pursuit of such ends by such means is a proper task for the state.

To call punishments penances reveals the meaning that punishment could have, but also reveals how radical this account is in relation to existing penal actuality and to contemporary liberal conceptions of the proper role of the state. Surely, critics argue, we must distinguish the state from morally ambitious, close-knit, and voluntary communities such as monasteries (where penances have a proper role); the state should not be expected to function as an abbot, seeking, and trying by hard treatment punishments, to achieve the moral and spiritual well-being of its citizens (see von Hirsch 1993, chaps. 2, 8; Narayan 1993). One question is just how intrusive a system of penitential punishments would be: how wide would the criminal law's scope be, how deeply would penal officials be allowed to inquire into the offender's moral condition or to "impinge upon the inner citadels of his soul" (Lucas 1968, p. 221)? But even if the scope of the criminal law would be strictly limited, so that it penalizes only conduct that seriously infringes central values (see Duff 1986, pp. 274–75; also Lacey 1988, chap. 5); even if the investigative and penal powers of the system are also limited, so that it does not sanction wide-ranging inquiries into every aspect of criminals' moral character and permits only modes of punishment that genuinely leave them free to accept or reject the moral message of punishment; even if we also remember that what this account justifies is not a penal system like those we now have: should we really allow such a role, and such power, to the state?

There are different ways of construing the worries that underpin this question, reflecting different underlying political theories.

From the perspective of a liberal individualist, any such account of the proper aims of punishment is radically inconsistent with the proper functions of the state. A state that is to respect the moral freedom and the privacy of the citizen can have no concern with "the inner citadels of his soul"; nor can the state's coercive power "be rightfully exercised over a member of a civilized community, against his will" for the sake of his own supposed moral good (Mill 1972, chap. 1, para. 9). A state must of course take some moral stands, declaring some moral values to be important and some kinds of conduct to be wrong: while it can and should remain neutral between a range of different conceptions of the good, it cannot (should not) aspire to complete moral neutrality. But its role in purveying those essential values on which it must take a stand should be limited. It should declare them (for instance, through the criminal law); it should censure those who flout them; it might also offer, through a system of hard treatment punishments, either those modest kinds of prudential incentive that von Hirsch and Narayan favor (see above, Sec. IIIE) or the more stringent kinds of incentive favored by other deterrence theorists: but it should not inflict punishments that seek to secure the offender's moral repentance and reform. The kind of interest which, on a penitential account of punishment, the state should take in the moral condition of its citizens is appropriate in moral associations like monasteries; it may be appropriate within a group of friends: but these belong to the private, and voluntary, dimension of our lives; and it is a dangerous mistake to try to transfer such features of our private lives into the public, and nonvoluntary, domain of the state.

From a communitarian perspective, however, a penitential account of punishment could (as it could not for the liberal) offer a plausible *ideal* of state punishment: an ideal of how members of a genuine moral community should respond to their own and each others' wrongdoings, and thus an ideal of how the state, as aspect or expression of such a community, should respond to criminal wrongdoers. But the crucial question for such a communitarian is that of whether and how far we should try to actualize such an ideal. Should we begin now to try so to improve our penal institutions and practices that punishment can become the kind of communicative, penitential process that it should ideally be? Or should we rather recognize, not merely that we are a long way from achieving such an ideal, but that any attempt to work directly toward it would itself be morally disastrous: disastrous because the preconditions for such punishments (notably, the criminal's membership of a genuine moral community whose values her crime has flouted and which is ready to welcome her back into full membership) do not exist; and because the actual effect of trying to impose properly penitential punishments, in our present conditions, would be kinds of coercive oppression utterly inconsistent with the ideal purpose of punishment? If such pessimism is justified, we must then either forswear punishment altogether (if that is either practically or morally possible), or look for some alternative rationale for punishment in such imperfect societies as our own (see Duff 1986, chap. 10.3; 1991*a*, pp. 441–51).

The following two sections should cast further light on this problem. For, first, the moral practicability of any such conception of punishment will depend crucially on what it can say about sentencing (the topic of Sec. V): can it propose kinds of sentence (and limits on their severity) that might avert the fear that a system of would-be penitential punishments would be oppressive and unjust? Second, some of the values to which this view of punishment appeals also underpin abolitionists' arguments that punishment (or punishment as currently practiced) cannot be justified at all (the topic of Sec. VI): by assessing those arguments, we will see more clearly whether these values can in practice be served by any system of state punishment.

V. Sentencing Matters

Philosophers usually pay too little attention to sentencing. They discuss the question of whether and why we should accept a principle of proportionality between seriousness of crime and severity of punishment and (sometimes) that of how we should determine appropriate levels of punishment. But they too often ignore the kinds of problem that most concern sentencing practitioners: in particular, that of the appropriate *mode* of punishment—what kind of penalty should be imposed on this offender or this kind of offender?[35] This is a pity: not merely because it makes philosophers' voices less useful to (and thus even less likely to be listened to by) penal practitioners, but because we can throw some useful light on theories of punishment by asking how, as well as how much, we should punish.

One central issue in recent penal theory (thanks in no small part to von Hirsch's work) has been that of proportionality.[36] Why should proportionality matter? What precisely does it require? Can a principle of proportionality help set absolute levels of punishment, or only relative levels (the issue of "cardinal," as against "ordinal," proportionality)? How much weight should the principle carry: should it be used to set *the* sentence to be imposed, or only to set upper, or upper and lower, limits, below or between which courts should be free to attend to quite different kinds of consideration? If it conflicts with other concerns (with a principle of penal parsimony, or with consequentialist concerns for effective crime prevention), must it always override them? Is it even a *practicable* principle: can we hope to reach the accurate and determinate judgments about the seriousness of this crime, and about the severity of this punishment for this offender, which are necessary

[35] But see Braithwaite and Pettit (1990, chap. 7), Adler (1992, chap. 6), and Duff (1992). The great exception to this general remark is capital punishment, whose justifiability philosophers have often discussed. I cannot discuss that topic here (and find very depressing the fact that it still requires discussion): for good recent samples of arguments on either side, see Bedau (1991) and Primoratz (1989a, chap. 8).

[36] See esp. von Hirsch (1985, 1992, 1993). "Sanctioning rationales differ from one another largely in the emphasis they give the principle of proportionality . . . the choice among sanctioning rationales is, in important part, a choice about how much weight to give to proportionality" (1992, p. 56).

if we are to inflict truly proportionate punishments; can we simply ignore background social conditions in making such judgments, or hope to develop a practicable system of proportionate sentencing that attends to them (the problem of "just deserts in an unjust society")?

I do not want to engage too closely in these controversies at the moment.[37] But I must say a bit about the implications for sentencing of the communicative, penitential account punishment sketched in the last section, and attend to von Hirsch's objection that that account allows inadequate weight to, or renders impracticable, the principle of proportionality (see von Hirsch 1993, chap. 8).

As von Hirsch has argued, some form of the principle of proportionality flows directly from a communicative account of punishment as censure (von Hirsch 1992, pp. 69–71; 1993, pp. 15–17; Duff 1986, pp. 278–89): if punishment is to communicate to a wrongdoer the censure his crime deserves, then since the severity of the punishment expresses the strength of the censure, communicative honesty requires that the severity of the punishment must be at least relatively proportionate to the seriousness of the crime. It follows that, whatever the absolute levels of punishment,[38] proportionality is respected only when equally guilty offenders (those equally culpable of equally serious crimes) are punished with equal severity, while those guilty of more serious offenses are punished more severely than those who are less culpable.

Critics of the von Hirschean version of proportionality sometimes object that the principle of proportionality cannot provide precise or determinate guidance for sentencing, and that we should therefore give it a less predominant role than he allots it. Even a demand for relative proportionality requires us to assess the relative seriousness of particular offenses, and the relative severity of particular punishments. But can this practicably be done? In order to determine just how culpable a particular offender is as compared to others who committed offenses falling under the same legal definition, we would need to engage in a far deeper examination than courts are typically allowed or competent to embark on, into all the circumstances of the offense and this of-

---

[37] Many of the arguments are developed in Braithwaite and Pettit (1990), Morris and Tonry (1990), von Hirsch (1992, 1993), and Tonry (1994). For a more radical critique of the very idea of trying to "do justice" in this way, see Christie (1981, chaps. 5–7), Hudson (1987), and Sec. VI below.

[38] See Sec. IIIE above for von Hirsch's account of how we should determine absolute levels of punishment.

fender. And in order to determine just how severe this punishment would be for this offender, as compared to seemingly similar punishments imposed on seemingly similar offenders, we would need to examine the likely actual impact of this punishment on this offender: just as a fine of $1,000 bears far more heavily on (and is thus a much severer punishment for) an impoverished offender than on a rich offender (which leads theorists like von Hirsch to argue for a system of unit fines), a sentence of one year's imprisonment will bear more harshly on some than on others, depending both on the age and character of the offender and on the kind of prison in which the sentence is to be served.

We cannot expect courts to be able to make such fine judgments of offense seriousness and of penal severity. But it follows from this, the critics argue, that the principle of proportionality *cannot* determine precise (even relative) levels of punishment. Since the principle can generate only rough judgments of seriousness and severity, we should therefore use it only as a rough guide: either to set only upper limits on sentences (specifying what level of punishment would be disproportionately severe) or to set both upper and lower limits (which levels would be disproportionately severe or lenient). Below or within those limits, however, sentencing decisions would be made on grounds other than proportionality (for versions of this argument, see Morris 1974; Morris and Tonry 1990, chap. 4; Walker 1991, chap. 12; Tonry 1994; for von Hirsch's replies, see von Hirsch 1992, pp. 89–92; 1993, pp. 29–35, 53–56, 64–68).

There are two ways of reading this argument. On one reading, it argues that since the principle of proportionality cannot give more than very rough guidance in sentencing, it must be *supplemented* by other kinds of consideration: this implies that the approach that Morris and Tonry favor is fully consistent with that principle, as it must be understood. But this seems wrong. For, even granted the impossibility of making precise determinations of relative offense-seriousness or relative punishment-severity, once courts are allowed to sentence (even below, or within, limits determined by the demands of proportionality) on grounds other than proportionality, they are allowed to pass sentences of differing severity (or sentences that cannot be shown to be equally severe) on equally culpable offenders (or on offenders who cannot be shown to be unequally culpable). The suggestion must be, rather, that we should not take the principle of proportionality as our *only* guide in sentencing, since it conflicts with other important principles (notably, the principle of penal parsimony, but also consequentialist considerations of effective crime prevention), to which we must allow some weight (see Tonry 1994, pp. 79–82). We can conceal that conflict by talking of "limiting retributivism" or by suggesting that the principle of proportionality is best read as a negative principle, forbidding manifestly *disproportionate* sentences, rather than as a positive principle that requires manifestly proportionate sentences: but the suggestion is still, in substance, that we should allow the demands of proportionality to be qualified or overridden by other principles and considerations.

The argument that we cannot anyway hope to attain any precise or strict proportionality of punishment to crime may provide some support for that suggestion, but it is neither crucial to it nor fully persuasive by itself. It is not crucial, since the Morris-Tonry view gains more substantial support from the other principles to which it appeals. It is not fully persuasive, because the obvious response is that even if we cannot hope to do ideal justice, we should at least do the best we can, rather than allow ourselves to be distracted from the search for justice by other kinds of concern. We might try to structure a just system of direct taxation that would proportion tax liability to the individual's disposable income. We realize that any such system will be imperfect, even if it includes various kinds of allowance for expenses that people should in justice be allowed to set against tax: partly because we could not anyway hope to attain ideal justice in taxation; partly because some attempts to come closer to the ideal would require unacceptably intrusive (and expensive) kinds of official inquiry into individuals' financial affairs. But this does not mean that we should not try our best to do justice within the limits set by such considerations. Analogously, we cannot hope to achieve perfect penal justice, by proportioning punishments precisely to crimes: that ideal is unattainable, and to allow courts to make the kinds of detailed inquiry into each offender's situation and character necessary for any attempt to come closer to that ideal would be to allow them unacceptably intrusive powers (and would also be likely, given the vagaries of individual sentencers, to result in a decline rather than an increase in the relative proportionality of punishments to crimes; in less justice rather than more). But this does not show that we should not try as best we can to do penal justice within such moral and practical limits (see von Hirsch and Jareborg [1991] and von Hirsch [1993], pp. 29–35, for the suggestion that we can measure both the harmfulness of crimes—though not the culpability of the criminal—and the severity of penalties by identifying the interests that the crime or the penalty intrudes on, and by gauging the importance of those interests for typical people's "living standards").

We should also note, however, that the point is not just that "in practice, judgments of comparative culpability are enormously difficult to make" (Morris and Tonry 1990, p. 87) but that there are limits of *intelligibility* on the extent to which one could even try to make such judgments. We can hope to produce a tolerable ranking of types of crime, and a list of typically aggravating or mitigating factors, realizing that that ranking will be at best rough and ready, leaving out various factors that are (that would ideally be) relevant to a judgment of the seriousness of a particular crime. But to call such rankings "rough" should *not* be taken to mean that they fall short of some ideal ranking that we could, in ideal theory if not in actual practice, hope to articulate: for there is no such ideal. If every judge was a Dworkinian Hercules; if they were allowed to investigate as deeply as would be needed to make adequately sensitive and accurate determinations of guilt; if they all agreed on the meaning and the relative importance of the values or standards relevant to judging crimes and criminals: they might then be able to agree in their judgments of the seriousness of every offender's crime. But even in that ideal judicial world, they could not intelligibly hope to agree on a univocal ranking that would enable them to say of any pair of particular crimes that one is the more serious (let alone by how much; see von Hirsch [1993], p. 18, on "spacing"). They could compare and contrast different cases, noting relevant similarities and differences between them (see Wisdom 1953, pp. 157–58, 248–54; and 1965, p. 102, on "case by case" reasoning). But relevant differences are not always differences in *degree* of seriousness or culpability. Only someone gripped by the utterly implausible idea that all values are reducible to some single final (and measurable) good could suppose that such a unitary ranking of wrongdoings is even in principle possible.

But apart from the question of the relation between the principle of proportionality as von Hirsch interprets it, and other principles such as that of parsimony, there is the question of its relation to the communicative purpose that von Hirsch ascribes to punishment and on which he bases his version of the principle: for there seems to be some tension here. If I am trying to communicate with someone, I must try to make the form and content of my communication appropriate to its context, its subject matter, and my interlocutor: I must do my best to ensure both that my communication does justice to its subject matter and also that it is so phrased and expressed that my interlocutor (given what I know about her) will have the best chance of understanding it. If we apply this idea to the context of punishment, it suggests that sentencers should look for (or try to create) that particular sentence that will express most appositely the censure merited by this offender's crime and which will be appropriate to this particular offender. Now *this* communicative ideal includes a requirement for proportional severity: the stringency of the censure we communicate must not be disproportionately severe (or lenient) in comparison to the crime we are censuring. It also, however, involves a requirement of substantive appositeness of "match" or "fit" between the particular substantive punishment and this particular crime and this particular criminal: is this the best kind of punishment by which to communicate to this offender an appropriate judgment on her particular crime?

The aim of communicating censure thus entails a demand for *formal* proportionality: that the severity of the punishment should express the appropriate *degree* of censure. But it also suggests a demand for *substantive* appropriateness: that the substantive mode of punishment should be appropriate to the nature of the crime (which is not just a matter of its degree of seriousness), the culpability of the criminal (which is not just a matter of the degree of his guilt), and to the particular offender as the person who must receive and (we hope) understand the censure. Now this latter demand must lead to a demand for creativity and flexibility in sentencing (cf. Hampton 1992*b*, p. 233); but (and this is where the tension arises) such creativity and flexibility will militate *against* the demand for formal proportionality.

If our primary concern is with the demand for formal proportionality, we will want to make sure that the punishments available to the courts can be ranked in terms of their severity: that they are, that is, commensurable (albeit, we must admit, imperfectly so, given the inevitably variable character both of sentences of the same formal type—of a year in prison as served in different prisons—and of the impact of objectively similar penalties on different individual offenders). This requirement, however, motivates resistance not only to highly individualized sentencing (see von Hirsch 1993, chap. 8) but also to the availability of too wide a range of possible punishments, especially the so-called intermediate sanctions: those that fall between the two extremes of substantial imprisonment and modest fines or nonintensive probation, including such sentences as intensive probation, community service orders, home detention, compulsory attendance at specified centers, or participation in specified programs (on these, see Morris and Tonry 1990; Tonry 1994; von Hirsch and Ashworth 1992a, chap. 6; von Hirsch 1993, chap. 7). One can rank terms of imprisonment (admittedly imperfectly) by their length, and fines by their amount (relative to the offender's means); and we might make a stab at deciding whether and when a sufficiently harsh fine is more severe than a (fairly brief) term of imprisonment. But even when we turn to such familiar intermediate sanctions as community service or intensive probation that can at least be measured in terms of their length, we face difficulties in ensuring commensurability, given the great diversity of kinds of community service and of conditions and requirements of intensive probation; while the more we increase the range of possible intermediate sanctions, or let courts put together individualized packages of such sanctions for individual offenders, the more we make commensurability, and thus formal proportionality, impossible to attain (see Wasik and von Hirsch [1990] on the British government's white paper [Home Office 1990], which preceded the Criminal Justice Act of 1991; and von Hirsch 1993, chaps. 7–8).

If, by contrast, our primary concern is with the demand for substantively apposite communicative punishments, we will find some room for imprisonment and fines, though in fewer cases than they are currently used: such punishments can sometimes communicate appropriately what needs to be communicated about the offender's crime, and serve the properly penitential ends of punishment (see Duff 1991b, pp. 243–44; 1992, pp. 60–61). But we will also look for a wide and flexible range of intermediate sanctions: not only for such sanctions as community service and probation (see Duff 1992, pp. 55–60) but also for creative sanctions that will enable appropriate communication with the particular offender. We will thus, however, favor kinds of punishment that make it difficult, or impossible, to satisfy the demand for formal proportionality or at least to determine whether or not that demand is being satisfied.

Consider just two examples: the programs for sex offenders and for domestically violent men mentioned earlier, and the various kinds of "mediation" scheme that try to bring offenders and their victims together to discuss both what was done and what should now be done (see Duff 1992, pp. 48–51; for examples of such schemes in England, see Harding 1987b; Smith, Blagg, and Derricourt 1988; Marshall 1988a, 1988b; Marshall and Merry 1990; Dignan 1994). Now these count as punishments: burdensome processes that an offender undertakes or is required to undertake, because of his offense, that are intended to be painful in that they are intended to bring him to confront and to understand the wrong he did. They are communicative punishments: they aim not merely to communicate a certain quantum of censure, but to bring him to understand the wrongness of his crime. They are also (as I have suggested a penitential punishment ought to be), forward-looking: they aim to bring the offender to repent his crime and to see that and why he should (and how he can) reform himself; they aim to assist that process of penitential self-reform; and, in the case of mediation schemes, they aim directly to find some way in which he can make reparation to, and thus reconcile himself with, his victim. Such programs thus appear ideally suited to a richly communicative theory of punishment of the kind I sketched in the previous section. But they are also, of course, radically unsuitable if our aim is to come as close as we practicably can to the ideal of formal proportionality: for it is quite unclear how we could rank their severity as compared to other kinds of punishment (except perhaps by asking offenders which they would prefer); while mediation schemes involve the further difficulty that, if they aim to reach agreed decisions about what the offender should do by way of reparation (or penance), there will inevitably be significant disparities between different cases (even if the courts have the task of monitoring such agreements and striking out any that are manifestly too severe or too lenient).

We face here a conflict between two different concepts of "doing justice." We can try to do formal justice, administering (as far as we can) formally equal quanta of censure to equally culpable criminals. Or we can try to do substantive justice by finding punishments that are substantively apposite to the offender and her crime. The former aim demands that we seek proportionate equality between criminals across the whole penal system, the latter aim that we seek the substantively apposite punishment for the particular case: but it is impossible consistently to pursue both aims together.[39] We might try to reduce the tension between these aims: for instance, by suggesting that the formal principle of proportionality should figure only as a negative constraint on sentencing, precluding manifestly disproportionate sentences, rather than as a positive ambition requiring us to impose de-

[39] This problem is analogous, but not identical, to the problem identified by Morris and Tonry: that of the conflict between "the requirement of fairness—that there be general standards that apply to all—and the requirement of justice—that all legitimate grounds for distinguishing between individuals be taken into account when decisions about individuals are made" (Morris and Tonry 1990, pp. 82–83).

monstrably proportionate sentences; or by suggesting that whatever sentence is agreed as a result of a process of mediation or negotiation that is itself just (fair, open, honest) should be regarded as a just sentence (cf. Nozick [1974], pp. 153–55, on the distinction between asking about the justice of a particular distribution, and asking about the justice of the procedure by which that distribution was arrived at). But such suggestions cannot dissolve the real conflict between a demand for formal proportionality and a demand for substantive appositeness.

This conflict is another facet of the underlying conflict between liberal and communitarian conceptions of the state and of the proper aims and ambitions of punishment (see above, Sec. IV*C*). The demand for formal proportionality reflects both the positive aspiration to "do justice" and the negative concern to limit the coercively intrusive powers of the state: a concern that leads theorists like von Hirsch, who advocate a communicative conception of punishment, to set limits on the communicative ambitions of state punishment. Just as we must, he argues, aim only to communicate deserved censure to the offender, rather than try to elicit a particular response to that censure (see von Hirsch 1993, chap. 8; Narayan 1993, pp. 174–75), so we should aim to communicate only the formal degree of censure that is warranted, rather than try to communicate some more substantively ambitious message in a way suitable to the particular offender: for, quite apart from the enormous practical problems involved in trying to construct, administer, and monitor a system of ambitiously communicative (and so individualized) punishments, we should not allow (we cannot trust) the state and its coercive institutions to take such a deep and intrusive interest in the moral condition of its citizens. The demand for substantive appositeness of punishment to particular crimes and particular offenders, by contrast, reflects the more communitarian conception of an individual's relationship to her society and the state that leads to the more ambitiously communicative conception of punishment as penance sketched in the previous section.

My own inclinations are still to go further (though tentatively) down the communitarian path than von Hirsch thinks safe or appropriate (see Duff 1992; cf. von Hirsch 1993, chap. 8): to see whether we cannot, perhaps initially through small-scale local experimentation, devise modes of punishment that would be genuinely communicative and reparative, serving to reconcile offenders with those whom they have wronged and with their community. However, any such suggestion must face attack not only from liberal "just deserts" theorists who argue that we should limit our penal ambitions to the administration of just degrees of censure (and the provision of prudential supplements to such censure) but also from "abolitionists" who argue that we should aim to abolish, rather than to refine or enrich, the whole practice of punishment. Indeed, just insofar as I want to talk about reparation and reconciliation as proper aims of punishment, and see mediation schemes as appropriate ways of responding to crime, it may seem that I am moving down the abolitionist road. For they too often look for reconciliation, restoration, and reparation, but argue that such aims are *opposed* to that of retribution or punishment.[40] I must therefore face the argument that the values to which I appeal (those of community, communication, and reconciliation) should lead not to the attempt to construct a system of penitential punishments, but to an attempt to *replace* punishment by other modes of responding to and dealing with "crime."

(There is another problem for ambitiously communicative theories of punishment: that of setting the absolute levels of punishment. We might be able to determine what *modes* of punishment will be apposite for particular crimes; we can insist, for the reasons given earlier, on some [rough] requirement of relative proportionality; we can also insist that punishments must not be so harshly oppressive or degrading that they cannot function as methods of moral communication. But this falls very far short of showing us how we can determine appropriate absolute levels of punishment. For just one example, consider murder [assuming that we can provide a definition of "murder" as the most serious kind of homicide]. A communicative theory can justify a [relatively] lengthy prison term as the appropriate penalty for most murders: the murderer's physical separation from the community gives material form to the way in which his murder effectively denied his membership of the community.[41] But [apart from the question of what the conditions of imprisonment should be] how long is "lengthy"? Is five years adequate for the most serious murders, as von Hirsch suggests; or ten years; or twenty years; or the rest of the murderer's life? I do not, I confess, know just how to answer such questions [although I am not sure that other theories will fare much better in practice], but

---

[40] So advocates of "informal justice" may argue in favor of mediation schemes: not (as I portrayed them) as an appropriate kind of punishment, but precisely as an alternative to punishment.

[41] A communicative theory could in principle justify capital punishment—but need not (see Duff 1986, pp. 281–82).

suspect that the best approach may be the following. We must, of course, begin from where we are: with the kinds and levels of punishment imposed by our own penal systems. The principle of penal parsimony, as well as the need to make punishment a genuine mode of moral communication, should lead us not merely to investigate alternative modes of punishment, and to work for radical improvements in the conditions of punishment (of imprisonment, most obviously), but also to pursue a "decremental strategy" that seeks progressive reductions in general levels of punishment—again, most obviously, in the number and length of prison sentences. How far such a strategy can go will depend on how far we can persuade ourselves that lower levels of punishment suffice to mark our [and, we hope, offenders'] understanding of the moral implications of their crimes: but that is not something that we can predict in advance.)

VI. The End of Punishment?[42]

It is a striking fact that, although philosophy is supposed to be a supremely critical discipline, questioning assumptions that others take for granted, philosophers of punishment typically focus, not on the question of *whether* any system of state punishment can be justified, but on that of *how* it can be justified; they implicitly assume that there *must* be some adequate justification of state punishment, if only we can find it. Such an assumption may be justified: perhaps some system of state punishment is a necessary and inevitable aspect of human social life (which is not to say that what is necessary and inevitable is a penal system at all like our own). But it is not one that we should simply take for granted; and there are voices that argue that state punishment is neither necessary nor justified, that it should indeed be abolished. I believe that such "abolitionist" theorists are seriously misguided, but meeting their challenge will force us to think more critically and imaginatively about the penal institutions that we so easily take for granted.

"Abolitionists" do not of course (any more than "retributivists") speak with one voice: although those who wear that label (or have it pinned to them) typically share certain values, political sympathies, and attitudes and agree in opposing existing forms of state punishment, their theoretical starting points, their critiques of current modes of

[42] See Wood (1991). On abolitionism generally, see Mathiesen (1974, 1986, 1990), Christie (1977, 1981), Hulsman (1981, 1982, 1986, 1991), Abel (1982), Cohen (1985, 1991), Bianchi and van Swaaningen (1986), Scheerer (1986), Steinert (1986), Hudson (1987), de Haan (1990), and Sim (1994).

penality, their ideals and practical recommendations are as diverse as those of any other broad alliance. All that I can do here is sketch and comment on what I think are some of the more interesting themes and arguments in roughly abolitionist thought.

A. Initial Questions and Clarifications

There are two obvious questions to ask any "abolitionist." What is to be abolished (and why)? What should replace it?[43]

As to the first question, we must distinguish *radical* or *complete* abolitionists from *partial* abolitionists or *reductivists*. The claim that we should reduce our reliance on state punishment, or on particular modes of punishment (particularly imprisonment), is not itself notably radical: even a Conservative British government could argue that the use of imprisonment should be sharply reduced (Home Office 1988, 1990); and many penal theorists hold that punishment should be the response of last resort, that we should criminalize and punish only conduct that is seriously damaging to the central values of the community or to central rights and interests of its members. It is more radical to argue that we should not simply reduce, but abolish, certain modes of punishment; and the initial focus of some "abolitionist" arguments was on the abolition not of punishment as such but of imprisonment as a punishment (see Mathiesen 1974; Sim 1994). But the most radical form of abolitionism, on which I focus here, argues precisely for the complete abolition of punishment as such.

We should also distinguish *contingent* from *absolute* abolitionism—the claim that punishment, as currently practiced in our societies, cannot be justified, from the claim that no system of state punishment could ever be justified. Philosophers may offer ideal accounts of punishment, of what an adequately justified system of state punishment would need to be and to do, in the light of which current penal practices are not merely (and unsurprisingly) imperfect, but cannot be justified at all (see Murphy 1973, pp. 103–10; Duff 1986, chap. 10.3). They do typically, however, think that a system of state punishment (albeit a system very different from our own, set in a quite different social, political, and legal structure) could in principle be justified; but an absolute abolition-

---

[43] But see Mathiesen (1974, esp. pp. 11–36; 1986) for a principled refusal to offer very much in answer to the second question.

ist denies even this.[44] We must keep these positions distinct, and not confuse arguments for contingent abolitionism with arguments for absolute abolitionism.[45]

Finally, we must distinguish abolition as an *aspiration* from abolition as a *demand*. Abolitionists aspire, at least, to a wholly nonpenal society: not one in which no serious wrong is ever done, or no serious conflicts ever arise (they are not *that* unrealistic), but one whose institutions include no practice of punishment. The attainment of that ideal, however, would require radical changes in our political and legal institutions, our moral attitudes, our conceptions of ourselves, and our relationships to each other—changes that will not be wrought in a year or a decade. So we must ask of them (as we must ask of ideal penal theorists too; see Lacey 1988, pp. 195–258; Duff 1986, chap. 10.3) what we should do meanwhile, while waiting and working for those profound changes.[46] Must we forswear punishment altogether and at once, insisting that every prison gate be flung open and that the criminal courts and the whole apparatus of penality cease operation, *whatever* the consequences: is that a demand that any theorist could honestly make? Or is abolition (or the ideal of justified punishment) instead an aspiration toward which we should work, while accepting that we must meanwhile rely on admittedly unjust systems of punishment as practical necessities? Should the abolitionist, in other words, be arguing for immediate revolution, or for radical but gradual reform?

As to the second question (what should replace punishment), we can identify three key contrasts that structure abolitionist thought.

First, we should think of "conflicts," or "troubles," rather than

[44] Contingent and absolute abolitionism would converge if we could believe that any society within which punishment could be justified at all would also be a society in which punishment was unnecessary (see Murphy 1973, p. 110). But that belief seems to me to require a heroically implausible conception of human perfectibility.

[45] Compare Szasz (1961, 1963): he conflates often well-founded objections to the ways in which "mental illness" is often diagnosed and treated with ill-founded objections to the concept of mental illness itself. The distinction between contingent and absolute abolitionism matches that between contingent pacifism (which argues that though war could in principle be morally justified, it cannot in fact be justified in our present political and military conditions) and absolute pacifism (which argues that war could never even in principle be justified).

[46] See Murphy (1973, p. 110): "If we are morally sensitive enough to want to be sure that we have the moral right to punish before we inflict it, then we had better first make sure that we have restructured society in such a way that criminals do correspond to the only model that will render punishment permissible." But what are we to do, if we are morally sensitive, meanwhile?

"crimes"; abolitionists offer a critique not only of punishment but of the concept of crime as that which requires or merits punishment.

Second, we should look for reparation, restoration, and reconciliation, not for retribution and punishment ("pain-delivery"); instead of inflicting penal pain on wrongdoers, as retribution or for deterrence, we should seek negotiated reparations for those who have been harmed, the restoration of relationships between the parties to conflicts, their reconciliation with each other and with the community.

Third, we should favor informal, participatory methods of resolving conflicts, rather than formal, professional modes of responding to "crime": conflicts should be resolved by the parties to them, by informal, local, community-based procedures, rather than by the professionalized formal institutions of the law which "steal" conflicts from those to whom they properly belong. This is one part of a wider critique of the "hegemony" of legal modes of thought and discourse and of the separation of the legal (especially the criminal) process from the modes of discourse that characterize our extralegal social lives.

Abolitionist arguments reach well beyond the practice of punishment: they are also directed at the concept of crime itself, at the political structures and ideologies within which punishment is conceived and justified, at the basic structures of self-understanding (our understanding of ourselves in relation to our fellow citizens) within contemporary societies. We should notice, however, that some of these abolitionist themes also figure in theories of *punishment:* in particular, the idea that we should look for a communicative process that aims to reconcile the wrongdoer with her victim and with the community, and that might involve or make possible some kind of reparation or restoration, figured centrally in some of the theories of punishment discussed earlier. This is not to suggest that penal theorists who structure their accounts around such notions as these agree with abolitionists about the goals or values to be pursued, and disagree only about the means by which they should be pursued (about whether punishment can appropriately figure among those means), since they also differ quite radically in their understanding of those ends and values. I suggest, however, that while abolitionists are right to reject certain *conceptions* of punishment, they sometimes mistake their criticisms of such conceptions for criticisms of the very *concept* of punishment; and that at least some of their central concerns can and should be met not by urging the abolition of punishment, but by urging an alternative conception of punishment. Christie urges us to search for "alternatives to punishment, not only alternative punishments" (Christie 1981, p. 11): my suggestion will be that we should precisely look for alternative conceptions and modes of punishment.

One final point of initial clarification. There are theorists who argue for the "abolition" of punishment, but who would not be recognized as allies by those who locate themselves in the "abolitionist" movement. Those impressed by the techniques of psychological science might talk about "the crime of punishment" (see Menninger 1968) and urge us to replace punishment by a system of enforced treatment. But such a suggestion is at odds with the spirit of contemporary abolitionism: it preserves the concept of "crime" as something that should be dealt with, by doing something to the "criminal," by the coercive powers of the state. Some theorists have also argued in a different vein that we should replace punishment by a system of restitution in which victims would sue those who wrong them (Barnett 1977; Holmgren 1983; for criticisms, see Pilon 1978; Kleinberg 1980); but although this suggestion has some resemblance to abolitionist arguments that we should "civilize" our responses to "crime," it preserves a formal structure of legal institutions that is a long way from the abolitionists' ideals.

B. The Concept of Crime

An examination of the abolitionists' critique can begin with the very concept of crime (see particularly Christie 1977; Hulsman 1986). Punishment entails crime—it is (alleged) crimes for which (alleged) criminals are punished; and while crime does not entail punishment (we can ask whether our response to crime should be punitive),[47] there is a natural movement of thought from "crime" to "punishment." A critique of the concept of crime thus also constitutes a critique of punishment. But we should distinguish critiques of the particular *conceptions* of crime that structure particular legal systems from critiques of the *concept* of "crime" itself: I believe we can identify a core concept of crime that we should not be willing to abandon. Thus we should reject this aspect of the radical abolitionist case: but this need not undermine abolitionists' objections to punishment, since it leaves open the question of what forms our responses to crime should take.

There are, I suggest, three central and related features of the concept of crime. First, crime is socially proscribed wrongdoing: conduct that

---

[47] But contrast Fingarette (1977), who argues that punishment is a logically necessary feature of a system of law.

the community should not see just as a matter of private conscience, but should authoritatively proscribe as wrong. Some kinds of conduct are inconsistent with the values of other members of the community but are properly seen as belonging to a private sphere. To operate with a concept of "crime," however, involves at least insisting that not all conduct should be seen as thus private: that on some matters the community should take, and claim the right to take, an authoritative normative stance.

A system of criminal law claims the authority to condemn certain kinds of conduct as wrongful; and there is, obviously, room for more or less radical criticism both of the claims to authority and of the content of any particular system. It may be argued that the *content* of the system's rules (the judgments of wrongdoing that they embody) is unacceptable: that they proscribe what is not wrong, or what is properly a matter of private morality; that they reflect an inadequate or distorted set of values. It may be argued that their legitimacy is vitiated by the *procedures* through which they are formulated: for instance, that they cannot claim to represent the values of the community, since they reflect the imposition of sectional interests rather than any authentic community consensus. It may be argued that they lack *authority* over certain groups: that the law has no legitimate claim to the allegiance or obedience of those who are unjustly marginalized or disadvantaged in that society. And it may be argued, relatedly, that those who benefit from the unjust economic, political, and legal structures of a society (and the courts that speak on their behalf) lack the *moral standing* to condemn members of unjustly disadvantaged groups who break the law: that it is not for "us," the comfortable beneficiaries of an unjust system, to stand in judgment on the conduct of its victims.

Consider a theft by a poor, unemployed person from a supermarket. It might be argued that given her situation and the injustices that put her there, her action was justified on grounds of necessity, or as a protest against the system.[48] Or that, whatever the substantive merit of the existing law of theft, it is not validated by processes that can command her respect: given her position in relation to the existing structures of power, the law cannot be "her" law, but must instead be understood as an alien imposition on her. Or that even if her act was

---

[48] This is distinct from the argument that her theft should be excused, which accepts that it was wrong. Nor need the claim be that the law should recognize her action as justified: the critic might agree that the law could not do this, but would say that just shows how fundamentally flawed the law is.

wrong, the criminal justice system has no proper authority over her: given the social (and perhaps legal) injustices that she has suffered, we cannot claim that she has an obligation to obey the law, or that the law has the right to condemn and to punish her; nor do we who are complicit in or beneficiaries of those injustices have the moral standing to judge and condemn her action, or to call for her punishment.[49]

I do not assess such arguments here. The point to note is that, while they involve a critique of current *conceptions* of crime, it is not a critique of the very concept of crime: they do not imply that a properly ordered society would have no concept of crime, no system of authoritative norms forbidding certain kinds of conduct as wrong. The content of such norms might be very different, though they would surely include rules protecting the person against various kinds of attack (see Hart 1961, chap. 9 on the "minimum content of Natural Law"); the political and social structures and processes that produce them might be very different: but any society requires some set of shared values that will be expressed in norms prohibiting certain kinds of conduct.[50] Some abolitionists do seem tempted by a species of moral relativism that makes them reluctant to say firmly that any kind of conduct is wrong, or to allow anyone the right to declare another's conduct to be wrong (I have heard Nils Christie talk in this way; and see Bianchi 1986, pp. 117–18). But we should distinguish the limited claim that the rights and wrongs of what now count as crimes are often not as clearly or easily determined as the law implies, from the radical claim that we can never say firmly and unqualifiedly that any action is wrong: that more radical claim is ill-suited to found the abolitionist's essentially moral argument against punishment; and it rests on serious philosophical confusions (see Williams 1976, pp. 34–39).

But there is of course more to the concept of crime than that of wrongdoing under some system of authoritative social norms.

Second, crime entails a criminal: an agent who commits the crime and can be held responsible for it.[51] Within our existing systems of

---

[49] Such arguments, along with those about individual criminal responsibility which I will note shortly, underpin the slogan that we cannot hope to do (penal) justice in an unjust society: it is important to recognize the differences between them.

[50] Indeed, this is a logical requirement, reflecting what it is for a group to constitute a society: see Winch (1972).

[51] It does not, however, entail a distinct and separate class of criminals who can be identified as "them," as the "enemy," quite distinct from "us" (see Bianchi 1986, pp. 113–14; Hulsman 1991, pp. 681–84): there is a strong temptation to think in this way, but it is one that we can and should resist.

criminal justice, the criminal is typically an individual (although other kinds of "agent" can be criminally responsible). Now it is commonplace for radical critics of liberal theories of punishment to attack the concept of the "abstract individual" which they find lurking within such theories (see, for example, Hudson 1987, pp. 125–28, 166; Hulsman 1991, pp. 683–84; Norrie 1991, 1993). In part, this is a matter of the extent to which the criminal justice system, particularly the criminal trial with its allocations of individual guilt, fails to attend sufficiently to individual defendants' situations, fails to consider the particular social factors and contexts that gave birth to that crime and which should be crucially relevant to its meaning and to any judgment on it. It is also a matter of the extent to which individuals can properly be held answerable for their actions (at least for those actions that bring them to the attention of the criminal law). To identify someone as a criminal, and to maintain a system of criminal justice that will convict and punish individual criminals, is to imply that it is the individual criminal who is, in virtue of her criminal action, responsible for what went wrong: it is to focus attention on her as the cause or origin of the problem. But instead of thus focusing our punitive attention on the individual, we might do better and more justly to look instead at the context from which her action flowed, to focus our remedial efforts on the problems or injustices that we are likely to find there (and to which it might be more appropriate to ascribe responsibility for the crime).[52]

Once again, I do not want to discuss the force of such arguments, as criticisms of our existing systems of criminal justice. What matters is whether they suggest that there is something amiss with the very concept of crime—that a better ordered society would not thus hold individuals responsible for their wrongful actions; and they do not. All that this practice requires is a conception of individuals as agents who are (often) responsible for what they do: responsible in the sense that it is for them to answer for what they do to those who have the standing to call them to account.[53] Even if we reject, rightly, the conception of the atomic, asocial individual that characterizes some kinds of liberal thought, this is not to abandon any notion of responsible individual

---

[52] This is a central theme of some recent reaffirmations of "rehabilitation," which hope to avoid the moral deficiencies of earlier cruder rehabilitative conceptions of punishment: see, for instance, Cullen and Gilbert (1982); Carlen (1989); and Rotman (1990).

[53] Thus in talking of responsibility I am talking of answerability (see Duff 1990a, chap. 4.2): it is a further question whether (and when) holding people answerable for their actions should involve condemning or punishing them.

agency: even fervent communitarians talk of individual, socially situated, agents; and abolitionists who aim to enable members of the community to resolve their own problems or conflicts want precisely to enhance the responsibility of individual members of the community for their own lives. Hulsman sought a dialogue with the youths who burgled his house, as responsible individuals (Hulsman 1991, pp. 697–703); Christie wants the parties to a conflict to come together for reparative discussion (Christie 1977): in both cases an essential part of the task is to discuss, and come to understand, what these particular people have done as responsible agents. Abolitionists urge that we should not be so ready to respond punitively to those who do us wrong: but they do not and should not argue that this is because we should not hold individual agents to be answerable, or call them to account, for their actions.

This does not yet show what form such "calling to account" should take or what its outcomes should be: it does not show that those who are responsible for socially proscribed wrongdoing should be subject to criminal trial and punishment. Nor does it yet offer an adequate concept of crime, since not every kind of socially proscribed wrongdoing is the proper concern of the criminal law: some should rather be dealt with through the civil law; some perhaps should not concern the law, or provide grounds for legal action, at all. We move closer to identifying the concept of crime by noting a third feature: that crime merits *censure*. If we take our community's norms seriously, we must be prepared to criticize, to condemn, breaches of them. This is part of what it *is* to take our norms seriously; and we can say that we owe it both to the victim of wrongdoing, and to the wrongdoer, to take the wrongdoing seriously by censuring it.

Now abolitionists do not always deny the legitimacy or importance of censure (see Christie [1977], p. 9, on the need to give wrongdoers the "opportunity to receive a type of blame that it would be very difficult to neutralize"), but their suggestion that we should talk about "conflicts" or "troubles" rather than about "crime" might imply that our aim should be to resolve "conflicts" rather than to identify and censure wrongdoers. This is no doubt often good advice. In a dispute between neighbors, for instance, we might urge that, both pragmatically and morally, the best way forward is not to focus on trying to determine the rights and wrongs of what has been done or to allocate blame for it, but rather to work out how the problem can be resolved so that they can live together more peaceably in the future (a resolution that will involve some compromise between their conflicting demands); and we might regret the litigiousness that drives people to law to resolve neighborly disputes, or the insistence on allocating blame between neighbors whose relations have become "troubled" or "problematic" (see Hulsman 1986, pp. 72–73). There are also cases in which the rights or wrongs of a conflict are genuinely in doubt: in which there is a proper place for variations on Christie's question "How wrong was the thief, how right was the victim?" (Christie 1977, p. 8); in which, even once all the facts are in, we might not be able to say determinately that one person wronged another, or how serious that wrong was.

But this is not always so. There are also many cases in which to see a situation merely as a "conflict" in which it is open to question whether one person wronged another, and on which other members of the community should not pass judgment, would be to add insult to the victim's injury by refusing to recognize the wrong she suffered. Consider, for instance, what used to be a prevalent police attitude toward "domestic disturbances": disturbances that often involved the use of serious violence by men against their female partners (see Dobash and Dobash 1992, chap. 5). The official view was that such disturbances were usually not best dealt with by the police or the criminal justice system: the rights or wrongs of the dispute were too often hard to determine, and the couple should work out their problems for and between themselves. This is no doubt true of many domestic disputes: but such a policy also failed to protect the victims (usually female victims) of serious domestic violence. It implied that the violence was "their conflict," to which they should negotiate a solution: but this leaves out the crucial moral point that many kinds of domestic violence are not simply conflicts between equal parties each of whom can colorably claim to have right on their side; that they are too often a brutal exercise of power by one party, and a use of violence whose wrongfulness should not be seen as a topic for discussion or negotiation, but must be condemned unqualifiedly.[54] Or consider what it would be to say to the victim of a savage mugging or rape that we should institute discussion between her and her assailant about "how wrong was the assailant, how right was the victim?" Sometimes there is room for doubt, even when all the facts are in, about the application of such descriptions as "rapist" and "victim": but often there is no moral room

[54] Compare the programs for domestically violent men mentioned above, which require from the start a "non-negotiable abstinence from violence" (Dobash and Dobash 1992, p. 245).

for such doubts; and one thing that the rape victim should not be expected to see as being up for discussion is whether rape is wrong.[55]

A community must declare and uphold certain basic values, and be ready to recognize and censure breaches of those values, especially those involving serious victimizing wrongs. This does not yet show, however, that such censure must be formally administered through the criminal process of trial and punishment: it could instead be administered informally, by the victim or others; it could result from a civil rather than from a criminal procedure; and though censure itself can be seen as a punishment (see Duff 1986, pp. 60, 146–47), it need not be imposed by the kinds of hard treatment punishment to which abolitionists object. We must therefore turn to the question of what form our response to "crime" should take: this will also throw further light on the concept of crime itself.

C. "Civilizing" Our Responses to Crime?

Some abolitionist talk of "conflicts as property" or of "civilizing" our responses to "crime" (see Christie 1977; 1981, p. 92; Hulsman 1982, p. 38) suggests that our responses to socially proscribed wrongdoing should be modeled on the civil, rather than the criminal, law. Instead of the state "stealing" citizens' conflicts, by taking them over and prosecuting and punishing the wrongdoer, the parties to the conflict should retain control of it; they should participate in a process that aims to resolve the conflict and to provide whatever reparation is required.

In discussing, as we must now discuss, the distinction between a "civil" and a "criminal" model of responses to wrongdoing, we should keep two questions separate. One concerns the distinction between a "civil" and a "criminal" procedure; the other concerns the outcomes of those procedures and the distinction between civil remedies and punishment. The two distinctions fit together in our existing systems: civil procedures lead to civil remedies (although these might include "punitive" damages), criminal procedures lead to punishment (though they can also lead to compensation orders). But they are at least conceptually separable, and should be treated separately. We can begin with the procedural distinction.

A civil procedure is controlled by the complainant. The community declares the norms to which he appeals; it provides the institutions

---

[55] It is not improper to focus on such serious wrongs as these: for the question is whether it is ever appropriate to count and punish something as a crime, not whether this is appropriate for everything now defined as criminal.

through which he brings his case, the court that decides it, and the mechanisms for enforcing the verdict; it can offer resources to help him make out his case. But the complainant is in charge: the case is "*P v. D*": he decides whether to bring the case, whether to pursue it or not, whether to enforce any order made in his favor. A criminal procedure, however, is controlled by the community (or state).[56] The case appears as "*People [or State] v. D*" (or in Britain, where we are still portrayed as subjects rather than citizens, often as "*Regina v. D*"); it is no longer up to the victim to decide whether (or how) the case is pursued. A case might in fact be pursued only if the victim is willing that it should be: from official respect for his wishes, or because it could not succeed without his willing cooperation. But it could be pursued, or dropped, against his wishes. There are thus two aspects to a "criminal" procedure. It relieves the victim of the burden of bringing the case for himself; the community does it on his behalf. But it also ceases to be his case; it is no longer up to him whether or how it is pursued.

The criminal procedure is clearly necessary for wrongs that have no identifiable individual victim: if, for example, tax evasion and drunken driving are wrongs that the community should proscribe and respond to, the community must bring the case. But when there is an individual victim, why should we not favor something like the civil procedure? Why should we have a legal system which "steals" the conflict from the victim (see Christie 1977)?

As a comment on the way our existing legal procedures treat both victims and defendants, Christie's slogan makes an important point: too often victims and defendants are merely passive observers of an alien process conducted by lawyers. Victims who cannot secure satisfaction and protection from a criminal justice system that does not take their wrongs seriously might also seek satisfaction through the civil law instead (see, for example, Graycar and Morgan 1990, pp. 284–307, 347–52). But as a claim about how we should *ideally* respond to *all* those "conflicts" that currently count as crimes, I think that the abolitionist's demand for "civil" responses is misguided. Rather than talking of "stealing conflicts," we should talk of the need for the community to *share* certain kinds of wrong: to see the wrong done to the particular victim not merely as *her* conflict, which she must resolve (with our

---

[56] In talking thus of "the community or the state," I skate over crucial questions about the relation (ideal or actual) between community and state; some of these are touched on in Sec. VIE below.

help), but as a wrong done to *us* (though not to us as distinct from her), to which we should therefore respond on her and our behalf.

It is often said that crimes are *public* wrongs, against the community. This would show why a criminal rather than a civil procedure is appropriate: but the problem is to explain the notion of a public wrong in a way which does not denigrate the wrong done to the individual victim—as it is denigrated, for instance, by the suggestion that a mugger should be prosecuted and punished because he takes an "unfair advantage" over all the law-abiding or because his action increases "social volatility" (see Becker 1974). But we can, I think, do justice to the victim's position while also portraying crimes as "public" wrongs, by talking of wrongs in which the community should share. The wrong suffered by the mugging victim is "her" wrong: but insofar as we identify ourselves with her, as we should, as a fellow member of the community, it becomes "our" wrong too. We should therefore prosecute her attacker, rather than leaving her to bring a case for herself; we might also say that, just as we owe this to her, she owes it to us to recognize that we were wronged by the attack, so that it is not entirely up to her whether the case is pursued or not.

These comments about crimes as socially proscribed wrongs, which a community should recognize as public wrongs in the sense sketched here, clearly do not provide determinate criteria for deciding just which kinds of conduct should be criminalized. I cannot try to deal with that thorny problem here: but the core of the criminal law, I suggest, should include the kinds of wrong from which anyone should be able to expect, categorically, to be safe in the course of their normal life ("normal" here is clearly a strongly normative notion). Risks to which we can be said to have voluntarily exposed ourselves, or which we could be expected to accept (given compensation if they are actualized), as aspects of our normal life, may be dealt with by a civil process. But a community should also protect its members by certain (perhaps fairly minimal) *categorical* prohibitions on conduct that strikes at its most central values, or its members most important interests; such conduct should be prohibited and prosecuted by the whole community.[57]

(Consider the role of "contributory negligence" in civil as contrasted with criminal law. In a civil case, the defendant's liability is reduced

---

[57] That protection would also involve preventive or defensive intervention: with civil wrongs the injured party can generally take action only when the wrong has been committed; criminal wrongs are wrongs whose commission may be prevented, if necessary by force.

if he can show that the plaintiff contributed to the harm she suffered by her own negligence. Now crime victims may also have made it more likely that they would become victims: householders who leave their houses insecure, car owners who fail to lock their cars, women who dress or behave in certain ways. We might criticize their behavior as imprudent, but do not think that it mitigates the liability of the criminal who takes advantage of it. This illustrates the sense in which the core of the criminal law should be a set of categorical prohibitions.)

To argue that a criminal procedure is appropriate for some kinds of wrongdoing, however, is not yet to argue that its outcome should be *punishment:* why should it not instead result, as a civil process results, simply in victim-oriented compensation, and in formal censure? To meet the abolitionist critique of punishment, we must meet the argument that our response to such wrongdoing should not be punitive.

D. Reparation, Reconciliation, and Punishment

Radical critics of our existing penal practices (and particularly of the "just deserts" model of punishment) often talk of the need to seek "reparative," rather than "retributive," justice (see Weston 1978; Varah 1987; Marshall 1988a; Matthews 1988); reconciliation rather than pain-delivery; or rehabilitation rather than punishment. Reparation, reconciliation, and rehabilitation are indeed admirable aims: but we must ask just what they should involve, in the case of wrongs done to one's community and fellow citizens, and whether they are as distinct from "punishment" as their advocates often suppose.

As to reparation, just what is owed to whom? The direct victim of the wrongdoing (where there is one) is of course owed whatever compensation is possible for the material harm he suffered. But, first, he has also been *wronged*. While it is not clear what could count as compensation for that moral injury, the wrongdoer owes him something for this: most obviously apology, and a serious attempt to show that the apology is sincere. Second, insofar as crimes are wrongs against the entire community, moral reparation and apology are also owed to the community. But genuine apology and moral reparation must involve a repentant recognition of wrongdoing: to seek such reparation must involve bringing the offender to recognize and accept her guilt.

As for reconciling the offender with her victim and the community as a whole, an authentic reconciliation must surely involve a proper recognition of the wrong that was done, and that made reconciliation necessary. If I have wronged someone seriously, I cannot achieve any genuine reconciliation with them merely by making good any material damage I caused, and by trying to get them (and myself) to ignore or forget the wrong that I did: I must recognize and repent that wrong, as something that injured them and damaged or threatened our relationship; and such a recognition is properly expressed in apology and an attempt to make reparation.

So too with rehabilitation. If a process aimed at rehabilitation (or reform) is to treat the wrongdoer as a responsible moral agent, its goal must be to persuade and help him to rehabilitate and reform himself. Central to that endeavor must be the attempt to bring him to face up to, to recognize and to repent, the wrong that he did: the wrongdoing that makes rehabilitation and reform necessary. The programs mentioned earlier for sexual offenders and for domestically violent men are rehabilitative and reformative; but they begin by trying to bring the offenders to understand that, and why, rehabilitation and (self-)reform are necessary.

My suggestion is, therefore, that in the context of the kinds of wrongdoing that should be counted as criminal, the aims of reparation, reconciliation, and rehabilitation are properly pursued not by abandoning punishment in favor of some nonpunitive process, but by communicative punishments of the kind I discussed in Section IV: for their aim is precisely to bring the offender to a repentant understanding of his wrongdoing, and thus to enable and assist appropriate reparation, reconciliation, and rehabilitation.

Critics of existing penal practices and conceptions often draw a sharp contrast between "punishment," understood as the purely retributivist, backward-looking imposition of suffering, and the forward-looking goals of reparation, reconciliation, or rehabilitation that they favor. Thus Christie, for example, contrasts "punishment" with restitution: punishment is "suffering" that may be applied "*in addition to* those unintended constructive sufferings the offender would go through in his restitutive actions vis-à-vis the victim" (Christie 1977, p. 10; see 1981, pp. 113–16). Similarly, probation officers who objected to what they saw as the unduly "punitive" aims underpinning the English Criminal Justice Act of 1991, and to their assigned role in administering "punishments in the community," argued that their aim should be "positive influence," rather than "punishment": such "positive influence" involved "confront[ing] offenders with the effects of their offending," and trying "to influence constructively [their] future behaviour," by "constructive, personal and helpful engagement . . . which helps them to face up to the need for change in their attitudes and behaviour" (Beaumont 1989, pp. 99–101; Roberts 1989).[58]

Now punishment can of course all too often be, in intention or in fact, mere "pain-delivery" that is wholly destructive rather than to any degree constructive; it can separate offenders yet further from the community to which they supposedly belong, rather than enabling them to restore themselves to or reconcile themselves with that community. Similarly, blame or censure (which I have argued is central to punishment) can, too often, be merely exclusionary or dismissive: we condemn the wrongdoer (and the fervor of our condemnation often reflects our lurking awareness of how easily we could have done the same ourselves, or our envy that she dared do it), we ostracize her, and that is the end of it (compare Braithwaite 1989, chap. 4, on "stigmatization" as opposed to "reintegrative shaming"; and Braithwaite and Pettit 1990, pp. 88–92). But neither blame nor punishment need be like this.

It is a difficult moral question whether there are kinds of moral wrongdoing so terrible that exclusion is the only possible response: that all we can be expected to do is to condemn the wrongdoer and to exclude him (or mark our recognition of his self-exclusion) from the moral community. We must similarly ask whether there are any crimes so terrible that they leave the criminal no way back into the community. But this is certainly not true of most wrongdoings and crimes: while we owe it to the victim (and to the wrongdoer, if we are to treat him as a moral agent) to condemn the wrongdoing, we owe it to the wrongdoer (and to the victim, as a fellow member of his community) to enable or help him to repair his relationships with his victim and with the community. Our condemnation or blame must therefore be such as to allow and assist this process. That is, the "Don't you see what you have done" which is the central message of blame should not be our final word, the *end* of our engagement with the wrongdoer: it should, rather, be the *beginning* of a process whose final aspiration is to reconcile him with those whom he has wronged. So too with communicative punishments. They inflict hard treatment; and they

---

[58] The governmental green and white papers which preceded the 1991 act drew a similar contrast between "punishment" and such other forward-looking aims of sentencing as reparation and bringing offenders to face up to what they had done: see Home Office (1988), paras. 1.2, 1.5, 2.3, 2.10; Home Office (1990), paras. 1.12, 2.6, 4.12, 7.8. For a useful discussion of the possibility of reconciling reparation with retribution, see Zedner (1994).

aim to induce the pain of accepted censure and recognized guilt. But the point of doing this is precisely to work toward the goals of repentance, reparation, reconciliation, and rehabilitation. Such goals are not distinct from "punishment": rather, they are the proper goals of punishment itself, and goals that, I have argued, can be properly achieved only through a punitive, communicative, process.

I am not suggesting that the punishments typically imposed in our existing penal systems are well-suited to these ends; it is obvious that they are not. But such punishments could be conceptualized, and could ideally be actualized, as serving these ends (see Duff 1992): community service orders, for example, enable offenders to make some "reparation to the community" (Home Office 1988, para. 1.5; see Pease and McWilliams 1980; McIvor 1994); probation can "confront offenders with the effects of their offending" and help "them to face up to the need for change in their attitudes and behaviour" (Beaumont 1989, pp. 99–101; Roberts 1989; see also Bottoms and McWilliams 1979; Raynor 1985; Harding 1987a). They achieve those aims, however, in virtue of their character as punishment: through the offender's recognition that this is something that she must undergo (should indeed accept) as a punishment for her wrongdoing. Those who reject "punishment" in favor of reparation and reconciliation rightly reject a particular conception of punishment as mere, backward-looking retribution, but wrongly take that to involve a rejection of punishment as such: once we understand what must be involved in reparation or reconciliation in relation to serious wrongs against the community, we will realize that we should search, not for "alternatives to punishment," but for "alternative [and more suitable] punishments" (Christie 1981, p. 11).

E. Formality and Informality

There is, however, another aspect of the abolitionist critique of criminal justice, which is also central to the concerns of advocates of "informal justice": a critique of the formality, the "professionalization," of the criminal justice system.[59] Instead of handing our "conflicts" over to (having them "stolen" by) this formal system, we should develop more informal, noninstitutional, participatory processes, which give offenders, victims, and their local community the central role in responding to and trying to resolve the conflict. To favor such informal

[59] See, generally, Christie (1977, 1981); Abel (1982); Cain (1985); Cohen (1985); Matthews (1988); de Haan (1990); Hulsman (1991); Marshall (1994).

modes of justice and conflict resolution is not necessarily to be opposed to punishment: punishment could be imposed by informal as well as by formal processes. But we need to attend to the argument that whatever is to be done, it is better done by such informal procedures than by the institutionalized criminal justice system.

We should accept that the criminal process, as it typically operates in our existing systems, too often gives neither offenders nor their victims an appropriate role in the proceedings. The victim has her case taken over by the police, the prosecuting authorities, and the courts; and though there is room for controversy about just what role she should be allowed or encouraged to play (see Ashworth 1986) we must surely accept that she should not be left, as she too often is left, to be simply a disregarded observer of the process. So too, the offender all too often finds himself a passive and uncomprehending witness of an alien procedure that allows him no substantive or genuinely participatory role (and while his role in his punishment is substantive enough, it is too often still only passive). Nor does the community to which offender and victim belong (if there is such a community) often have much to do with the proceedings, despite the possible roles of lay magistrates and juries. Furthermore, the scope of the inquiry conducted by a criminal court is strictly limited: it must decide, in accordance with the rules of evidence and procedure, whether the defendant's action satisfied the legal definition of an offense; and while some further factors may be relevant at the stage of sentencing, a criminal trial clearly cannot have the wide-ranging and unconstrained scope that characterizes, for instance, a discussion between friends or neighbors about their difficulties and how to resolve them. So should we not then try to replace such a formal, abstracting process by more informal processes in which the parties to the conflict could really participate, and discuss all the issues relevant to a proper understanding of, and an adequate response to, the offender's action? Indeed, surely a communicative penal process of the kind I have argued for itself requires a much more open, and participatory, discussion than our criminal courts allow, if there is to be any genuine communication about the character and implications of the offender's conduct.[60]

As even its advocates typically insist, however, serious problems face this kind of suggestion. I mention three here. First (see esp. Cohen

---

[60] Compare Hudson (1994), on what she sees as the undue dominance of narrowly "legal" reasoning in the criminal justice system.

1985, pp. 116–27; Marshall 1994), such "informal justice" processes depend, as does a communicative conception of punishment, on the existence of genuine communities to which both offender and victim belong, and with which the offender can be reconciled. Reconciliatory justice is possible and appropriate only between neighbors or friends (in a broad sense of that term): between people whose lives are structured by shared values and mutual concern. By contrast, a liberal conception of punishment, either as formal censure or as a deterrent, is appropriate for strangers: for those who might have no genuinely common life together (who form no community), but who must work out a way of living next to each other (rather than truly together) that will allow them to pursue their own separate goods (see Marshall 1989; Duff 1993, pp. 380–83). But do we now live in such genuine communities? Can we plausibly say that offenders have, typically, wronged fellow members of a genuine community to which they belong, that they have flouted the values of a community that respects and cares for them, and that thus has the moral standing to criticize them? If we cannot honestly make these claims (and I suspect that we cannot), we cannot hope to create authentically community-based processes of informal justice.

Second, if conflicts and crimes are dealt with by such local and community-based processes, the outcomes of such processes (the "punishments" imposed on offenders) will of course not exhibit the kind of consistency across the whole society that "just deserts" theorists argue to be crucial: they will be the outcomes of negotiations that reflect local values and expectations, and "[j]ustice would not be quite as equal from neighbourhood to neighbourhood as it is supposed to be today" (Christie 1981, p. 112). But there is also the danger that such processes will be *more* oppressive (and less reparative and reconciliatory) even than our criminal justice system now is. Communities can, after all, be harsh, hostile, and exclusionary; and the formal apparatus of the state and the criminal justice system can help to *protect* offenders (and others who deviate from the mores of their local communities) against their neighbors (see Christie 1981, pp. 109–16).

Third, can we suppose that, at least as we and our societies are now and for the foreseeable future constituted, such informal procedures could be adequate to every kind of crime or criminal? One problem concerns crimes that do not involve a local victim or local community: but even if we think only of crimes that could in principle be dealt with in this way, surely such procedures will need to be backed up

with the coercive power of (ultimately) the state. Thus Bianchi's abolitionist manifesto proposes not only revised roles for judges, prosecutors, and the police, but also "quarantine" for those who present immediate and serious danger to others; "civilized custody" for those who
refuse to take part in the process of negotiation that is to replace punishment (until they are willing to negotiate); and "sanctuaries" where those
who commit really serious crimes will be allowed (or required?) to stay
in safety while awaiting the negotiating process (Bianchi 1986). Such
suggestions may sound odd from someone whose avowed aim is the
abolition at least of imprisonment, even if these kinds of custody are
to be "civilized"; and liberals will ask how we can provide the kinds
of protection against unduly extended detention and coercion that the
idea of punishment as just deserts claims to provide. But my point
here is just that any realistic advocate of informal justice must recognize
that its processes will need to be both monitored and supported by
what is ultimately the coercive power of the state.

I have been arguing through this section that "abolitionists" are right
to raise strenuous moral objections to state punishment, as it is now
typically practiced, and indeed to wider and deeper features of our
criminal justice systems. They are also right to raise and to insist on
taking seriously the question of whether punishment can be justified at
all: too many penal theorists talk as if there *must*, of course, be an adequate
justification for state punishment, and their task is only to find and articulate it; but that is not something we should take for granted. I have also
argued, however, that they are wrong to urge the abolition of "punishment" as such (insofar as that is what they are urging): they should rather
be urging us to develop new conceptions of both crime and punishment,
and to work toward the kinds of social and political structure within
which those new conceptions could become practicable realities; and
they should (if my claims about the importance of recognizing and responding to wrongdoing are justified) recognize that those reconciliatory, reparative aims to which they are committed should properly be
pursued by practices that are essentially punitive.

The controversies between abolitionists and those who think that
we must retain formal state systems of criminal justice, especially those
who take "just deserts" and "proportionality" as their guiding slogans,
also reflect the tension between communitarian and liberal conceptions
of society and the individual that I have already noted. Abolitionism
is typically infused by the communitarian spirit: by a conception of
human life as properly lived, indeed as humanly lived, within (rela-

tively small) communities; communities structured by the kinds of shared value and mutual concern that are necessary if the kinds of informal, reconciliatory process that abolitionists favor are to be either possible or meaningful. In a similar way, the communicative and penitential account of punishment that I favor depends on the existence of real communities: of communities to which the offender belongs, whose shared values he has flouted, and with which he may be reconciled through punishment. One kind of liberal rejects those very communitarian ideals, even as ideals: that is not how we should understand society, or the individual's role in society; we should not even aspire to such ideals of social life. Another kind of liberal, however, recognizes the moral force of the communitarian ideal as an ideal: that is how human life should ideally be. But, she argues, it is not an ideal that we can or should try directly to actualize, given our presently (radically) imperfect condition. We should rather realize that individuals need protection against the kinds of intrusive oppression into which the communitarian urge is too readily distorted: protection that can be provided by the apparatus of liberal rights, and by a penal system that forswears any ambitious goals of repentance, reform, or reconciliation in favor of the more modest goal of "doing justice" (see Waldron 1988; Duff 1991a, pp. 445–51). Von Hirsch's strong principle of proportionality (combined with his "decremental strategy") can be read as reflecting these concerns: it aims not only to "do justice," but to protect citizens (including offenders) against the kinds of oppressive punishment that would all too probably flow from an attempt to actualize an ambitiously communicative conception of punishment in such nonideal societies as our own.

VII. Concluding Remarks

My concluding remarks can be brief, partly because I have no firm conclusions to offer. I have argued that strictly consequentialist accounts of the aims of punishment (whether or not our pursuit of such aims is to be constrained by independent requirements of justice) are open to serious and, I think, conclusive moral objections, however sophisticated an account they offer of those aims: for they still remain open to some version of the charge that they cannot do justice to or respect the moral standing of the guilty. The most fruitful way forward lies, I suggested, in the idea of punishment as communication: an idea that is retributive insofar as it holds that what is appropriate to crime is communication that insists on condemning or censuring the crime.

I then sketched an ambitiously communicative account of punishment, as a penitential process that aims to bring the offender to repent her crime and, through her repentance, to repair those relationships that it damaged. Such an account has many critics. I have focused in particular on the liberal objection that it sets dangerously intrusive and oppressive aims for a system of state punishment, and on the abolitionist argument that the values of reconciliation, reparation, and community (which I share) require not a system of criminal justice and punishment, but quite different kinds of process (and quite different kinds of understanding of "crime") that would not involve the infliction of punishment on criminals.

I am by no means confident of my answers to these arguments. I am not sure, that is, whether the ideal conception of punishment I have offered is one which is, to any degree, practicable as an aspiration for our systems of criminal justice; or whether we should recognize instead that, even if it offers a morally plausible ideal for social life (which some would deny), it is not an ideal that we should try to actualize—that we should instead, out of respect for individual freedom, seek more modestly to "do justice" by administering formal censures (and perhaps offering modest prudential incentives to obedience). Nor am I sure, however, despite my objections to "absolute" abolitionism, how far we can realistically hope to do anything much resembling "justice" through our existing criminal justice systems, or so to reform them that they can really be said to do *either* "justice" *or* that kind of "good" (which is itself a substantive kind of justice) that I have suggested should be their ideal aim (see Cohen 1985, pp. 245–54)—especially if we accept that "doing justice" must be a matter not merely of administering a warranted kind of censure, but of doing more substantive justice between offenders, victims, and the state (see Carlen 1989, p. 19).

I am sure, however, that the best way forward for normative penal theorizing about how (if at all) a system of state punishment can be justified is in this direction: in exploring the possibilities, the potential (and the dangers) of a conception of punishment as communication—which must also involve engaging, more closely than penal theorists often engage, with the underlying tension between liberal and communitarian conceptions of society and of our relationships to each other (and to the state) as members of a society. Furthermore, our understanding of what state punishment could be, of the ends and values it could ideally serve, can be enriched by a closer study of noncustodial sanctions. Since imprisonment is the most severe and, in practice, most oppressively destructive kind of punishment that is commonly inflicted, its proper role is rightly central to contemporary discussions of sentencing. But we should also look carefully at such sanctions as community service and probation; various forms of victim-offender mediation scheme; and programs like those for rapists or domestically violent men discussed earlier in this essay: here, I think, we might see most clearly how punishment could be not merely the delivery of pain, but a genuinely communicative, reformative, and reconciliatory process (which can also satisfy some of the central concerns of abolitionists).

REFERENCES

Abel, R., ed. 1982. *The Politics of Informal Justice.* 2 vols. New York: Academic Press.

Abel, R. 1991. "The Failure of Punishment as Social Control." *Israel Law Review* 25:740–52.

Adler, J. 1992. *The Urgings of Conscience.* Philadelphia: Temple University Press.

Alexander, L. 1980. "The Doomsday Machine: Proportionality, Punishment and Prevention." *Monist* 63:199–227.

———. 1983. "Retributivism and the Inadvertent Punishment of the Innocent." *Law and Philosophy* 2:233–46.

Allen, F. A. 1981. *The Decline of the Rehabilitative Ideal.* New Haven, Conn.: Yale University Press.

American Friends Service Committee. 1971. *Struggle for Justice.* New York: Hill & Wang.

Ardal, P. 1984. "Does Anyone Ever Deserve to Suffer?" *Queen's Quarterly* 91–92:241–57.

Ashworth, A. J. 1986. "Punishment and Compensation: Offender, Victim and the State." *Oxford Journal of Legal Studies* 6:86–122.

———. 1992. *Sentencing and Criminal Justice.* London: Weidenfeld & Nicolson.

Baker, B. M. 1992. "Consequentialism, Punishment, and Autonomy." In *Retributivism and Its Critics*, edited by W. Cragg. Stuttgart: Franz Steiner.

Barnett, R. E. 1977. "Restitution: A New Paradigm of Criminal Justice." *Ethics* 87:279–301.

Beaumont, W. 1989. "Professional Reactions and Comments." In *Punishment, Custody and the Community*, edited by H. Rees and E. Hall Williams. London: London School of Economics.

Becker, L. C. 1974. "Criminal Attempts and the Theory of the Law of Crimes." *Philosophy and Public Affairs* 3:262–94.

Bedau, H. 1991. "How to Argue about the Death Penalty." *Israel Law Review* 25:466–80.

Benn, S. I. 1958. "An Approach to the Problems of Punishment." *Philosophy* 33:325–41.

Bentham, J. 1970. *An Introduction to the Principles of Morals and Legislation*, edited by J. H. Burns and H. L. A. Hart. London: Athlone Press. (Originally published 1789.)

Bianchi, H. 1986. "Abolition: Assensus and Sanctuary." In *Abolitionism: Towards a Non-Repressive Approach to Crime*, edited by H. Bianchi and R. van Swaaningen. Amsterdam: Free University Press.

Bianchi, H., and R. van Swaaningen, eds. 1986. *Abolitionism: Towards a Non-Repressive Approach to Crime*. Amsterdam: Free University Press.

Bickenbach, J. 1988. "Critical Notice of Duff, *Trials and Punishments*." *Canadian Journal of Philosophy* 18:765–86.

Bottoms, A. E., and R. Brownsword. 1982. "The Dangerousness Debate after the Floud Report." *British Journal of Criminology* 22:229–54.

Bottoms, A. E., and W. McWilliams. 1979. "A Non-treatment Paradigm for Probation Practice." *British Journal of Social Work* 9:159–202.

Braithwaite, J. 1989. *Crime, Shame and Reintegration*. Cambridge: Cambridge University Press.

Braithwaite, J., and P. Pettit. 1990. *Not Just Deserts*. Oxford: Oxford University Press.

Brandt, R. B. 1961. "Determinism and the Justifiability of Moral Blame." In *Determinism and Freedom in the Age of Modern Science*, edited by S. Hook. New York: Collier-Macmillan.

Burgh, R. W. 1982. "Do the Guilty Deserve Punishment?" *Journal of Philosophy* 79:193–210.

Cain, M. 1985. "Beyond Informal Justice." *Contemporary Crises* 9:335–73.

Carlen, P. 1989. "Crime, Inequality and Sentencing." In *Paying for Crime*, edited by P. Carlen and D. Cook. Milton Keynes: Open University Press.

Charvet, J. 1966. "Criticism and Punishment." *Mind* 75:573–79.

Christie, N. 1977. "Conflicts as Property." *British Journal of Criminology* 17:1–15.

———. 1981. *Limits to Pain*. London: Martin Robertson.

Cohen, S. 1985. *Visions of Social Control*. Cambridge: Polity Press; Oxford: Blackwell.

———. 1991. "Alternatives to Punishment: The Abolitionist Case." *Israel Law Review* 25:729–39.

Cottingham, J. 1979. "Varieties of Retribution." *Philosophical Quarterly* 29:238–46.

Cullen, F. T., and K. E. Gilbert. 1982. *Reaffirming Rehabilitation*. Cincinnati: Anderson.

Dagger, R. 1993. "Playing Fair with Punishment." *Ethics* 103:473–88.

Dare, T. 1992. "Retributivism, Punishment, and Public Values." In *Retributivism and Its Critics*, edited by W. Cragg. Stuttgart: Franz Steiner.

Davis, L. 1972. "They Deserve to Suffer." *Analysis* 32:136–40.

Davis, M. 1982. "Sentencing: Must Justice Be Even-Handed?" *Law and Philosophy* 1:77–117.

———. 1983. "How to Make the Punishment Fit the Crime." *Ethics* 93:726–52.

———. 1989. "The Relative Independence of Punishment Theory." *Law and Philosophy* 7:321–50.

————. 1991*a*. "Criminal Desert, Harm and Fairness." *Israel Law Review* 25:524–48.

————. 1991*b*. "Punishment as Language: Misleading Analogy for Desert Theorists." *Law and Philosophy* 10:310–22.

————. 1993. "Criminal Desert and Unfair Advantage: What's the Connection?" *Law and Philosophy* 12:133–56.

de Haan, W. 1990. *The Politics of Redress: Crime, Punishment and Penal Abolition.* London: Unwin Hyman.

Deigh, J. 1984. "On the Right to Be Punished: Some Doubts." *Ethics* 94:191–211.

Dignan, J. 1994. "Reintegration through Reparation: A Way Forward for Restorative Justice?" In *Penal Theory and Practice*, edited by R. A. Duff, S. E. Marshall, R. E. Dobash, and R. P. Dobash. Manchester: Manchester University Press.

Dobash, R. E., and R. P. Dobash. 1992. *Women, Violence and Social Change.* London: Routledge.

Dolinko, D. 1991. "Some Thoughts about Retributivism." *Ethics* 101:537–59.

Duff, R. A. 1986. *Trials and Punishments.* Cambridge: Cambridge University Press.

————. 1988*a*. "Punishment and Penance: A Reply to Harrison." *Proceedings of the Aristotelian Society* 62 (suppl.):153–67.

————. 1988*b*. "A Reply to Bickenbach." *Canadian Journal of Philosophy* 18:787–93.

————. 1990*a*. *Intention, Agency and Criminal Liability.* Oxford: Blackwell.

————. 1990*b*. "Justice, Mercy and Forgiveness." *Criminal Justice Ethics* 9:51–63.

————. 1990*c*. "Auctions, Lotteries and the Punishment of Attempts." *Law and Philosophy* 9:1–37.

————. 1991*a*. "Retributive Punishment—Ideals and Actualities." *Israel Law Review* 25:422–51.

————. 1991*b*. "Punishment, Expression and Penance." In *Recht und Moral*, edited by H. Jung, H. Muller-Dietz, and U. Neumann. Baden-Baden: Nomos-Verlagsgesellschaft.

————. 1992. "Alternatives to Punishment—or Alternative Punishments?" In *Retributivism and Its Critics*, edited by W. Cragg. Stuttgart: Franz Steiner.

————. 1993. "Choice, Character and Criminal Liability." *Law and Philosophy* 12:345–83.

Dworkin, R. 1978. *Taking Rights Seriously.* London: Duckworth.

Falls, M. M. 1987. "Retribution, Reciprocity, and Respect for Persons." *Law and Philosophy* 6:25–51.

Farrell, D. M. 1985. "The Justification of General Deterrence." *Philosophical Review* 94:367–94.

Feinberg, J. 1970. "The Expressive Function of Punishment." In *Doing and Deserving*, by J. Feinberg. Princeton, N.J.: Princeton University Press.

Fingarette, H. 1977. "Punishment and Suffering." *Proceedings of the American Philosophical Association* 51:499–525.

Finnis, J. 1972. "The Restoration of Retribution." *Analysis* 32:131–5.

Floud, J., and W. Young. 1981. *Dangerousness and Criminal Justice.* London: Heinemann.

Galligan, D. J. 1981. "The Return to Retribution in Penal Theory." In *Crime, Proof and Punishment,* edited by C. F. H. Tapper. London: Butterworths.

Gardner, M. 1976. "The Renaissance of Retribution: An Examination of 'Doing Justice.'" *Wisconsin Law Review* 1976:781–815.

Garland, D. 1990. *Punishment and Modern Society: A Study in Social Theory.* Oxford: Oxford University Press.

Golash, D. 1994. "The Retributive Paradox." *Analysis* 54:72–78.

Goldman, A. H. 1979. "The Paradox of Punishment." *Philosophy and Public Affairs* 9:42–58.

———. 1982. "Toward a New Theory of Punishment." *Law and Philosophy* 1:57–76.

Graycar, R., and J. Morgan. 1990. *The Hidden Gender of Law.* London: Federation Press/Blackstone.

Gur-Arye, M. 1991. "The Justification of Punishment: A Comment on Retribution and Deterrence." *Israel Law Review* 25:452–59.

Hampton, J. 1984. "The Moral Education Theory of Punishment." *Philosophy and Public Affairs* 13:208–38.

———. 1988. "The Retributive Idea." In *Forgiveness and Mercy,* by J. G. Murphy and J. Hampton. Cambridge: Cambridge University Press.

———. 1991. "A New Theory of Retribution." In *Liability and Responsibility,* edited by R. G. Frey and C. W. Morris. Cambridge: Cambridge University Press.

———. 1992a. "An Expressive Theory of Retribution." In *Retributivism and Its Critics,* edited by W. Cragg. Stuttgart: Franz Steiner.

———. 1992b. "Correcting Harms versus Righting Wrongs: The Goal of Retribution." *UCLA Law Review* 39:201–44.

Harding, J., ed. 1987a. *Probation and the Community.* London: Tavistock.

———. 1987b. "Reparation: The Background, Rationale and Relevance to Criminal Justice." In *Probation and the Community,* edited by J. Harding. London: Tavistock.

Hare, R. M. 1981. *Moral Thinking: Its Levels, Methods and Point.* Oxford: Oxford University Press.

Harrison, R. 1988. "Punishment No Crime." *Proceedings of the Aristotelian Society* 62 (suppl.):139–51.

Hart, H. L. A. 1961. *The Concept of Law.* Oxford: Oxford University Press.

———. 1963. *Law, Liberty and Morality.* New York: Random House.

———. 1968. "Prolegomenon to the Principles of Punishment." In *Punishment and Responsibility,* by H. L. A. Hart. Oxford: Oxford University Press.

Hegel, G. W. F. 1942. *The Philosophy of Right,* translated by T. Knox. Oxford: Oxford University Press. (Originally published 1821.)

Holmgren, M. 1983. "Punishment as Restitution: The Rights of the Community." *Criminal Justice Ethics* 2:36–49.

Home Office. 1988. *Punishment, Custody and the Community*. London: H.M. Stationery Office.

———. 1990. *Crime, Justice and Protecting the Public*. London: H.M. Stationery Office.

Honderich, T. 1982. "On Justifying Protective Punishment." *British Journal of Criminology* 22:268–75.

———. 1984a. *Punishment: The Supposed Justifications*. Rev. ed. Harmondsworth: Penguin.

———. 1984b. "Culpability and Mystery." In *Philosophy and the Criminal Law*, edited by R. A. Duff and N. E. Simmonds. Stuttgart: Franz Steiner.

Hudson, B. 1987. *Justice through Punishment: A Critique of the "Justice" Model of Corrections*. London: Macmillan.

———. 1994. "Punishing the Poor: A Critique of the Dominance of Legal Reasoning in Penal Policy and Practice." In *Penal Theory and Practice*, edited by R. A. Duff, S. E. Marshall, R. E. Dobash, and R. P. Dobash. Manchester: Manchester University Press.

Hulsman, L. 1981. "Penal Reform in the Netherlands I." *Howard Journal* 20:150–59.

———. 1982. "Penal Reform in the Netherlands II." *Howard Journal* 21:35–47.

———. 1986. "Critical Criminology and the Concept of Crime." *Contemporary Crises* 10:63–80.

———. 1991. "The Abolitionist Case: Alternative Crime Policies." *Israel Law Review* 25:681–709.

Husak, D. 1992. "Why Punish the Deserving?" *Nous* 26:447–64.

Kant, I. 1948. *Groundwork of the Metaphysic of Morals*, translated by H. Paton as *The Moral Law*. London: Hutchinson. (Originally published 1785.)

———. 1965. *The Metaphysical Elements of Justice*, pt. 1 of *The Metaphysic of Morals*, translated by J. Ladd. Indianapolis: Bobbs-Merrill. (Originally published 1797.)

Kleinberg, S. S. 1980. "Criminal Justice and Private Enterprise." *Ethics* 90:270–82.

Kleinig, J. 1991. "Punishment and Moral Seriousness." *Israel Law Review* 25:401–21.

Knowles, D. 1993. "Unjustified Retribution." *Israel Law Review* 27:50–58.

Lacey, N. 1983. "Dangerousness and Criminal Justice: The Justification of Preventive Detention." *Current Legal Problems* 36:31–49.

———. 1988. *State Punishment*. London: Routledge.

Lewis, C. S. 1940. *The Problem of Pain*. Glasgow: Collins.

———. 1953. "The Humanitarian Theory of Punishment." *Res Judicatae* 6; reprinted in *Readings in Ethical Theory*, 2d ed., edited by W. Sellars and J. Hospers. New York: Appleton-Century-Crofts, 1970.

Lipkin, R. J. 1988. "Punishment, Penance and Respect for Autonomy." *Social Theory and Practice* 14:87–104.

Lucas, J. R. 1968. "Or Else." *Proceedings of the Aristotelian Society* 69:207–22.

———. 1980. *On Justice*. Oxford: Oxford University Press.

McCloskey, H. J. 1972. " 'Two Concepts of Rules': A Note." *Philosophical Quarterly* 22:344–48.

McIvor, G. 1994. "Community Service: Progress and Prospects." In *Penal Theory and Practice*, edited by R. A. Duff, S. E. Marshall, R. E. Dobash, and R. P. Dobash. Manchester: Manchester University Press.

Mackie, J. L. 1982. "Morality and the Retributive Emotions." *Criminal Justice Ethics* 1:3–10.

Marshall, S. E. 1989. "The Community of Friends." Stirling: University of Stirling, Department of Philosophy.

———. 1992. "Harm and Punishment in the Community." In *Retributivism and Its Critics*, edited by W. Cragg. Stuttgart: Franz Steiner.

Marshall, T. F. 1988*a*. "Out of Court: More or Less Justice?" In *Informal Justice*, edited by R. Matthews. London: Sage.

———. 1988*b*. "Informal Justice: The British Experience." In *Informal Justice*, edited by R. Matthews. London: Sage.

———. 1994. "Grassroots Initiatives towards Restorative Justice: The New Paradigm?" In *Penal Theory and Practice*, edited by R. A. Duff, S. E. Marshall, R. E. Dobash, and R. P. Dobash. Manchester: Manchester University Press.

Marshall, T. F., and S. Merry. 1990. *Crime and Accountability*. London: H.M. Stationery Office.

Mathiesen, T. 1974. *The Politics of Abolition*. London: Martin Robertson.

———. 1986. "The Politics of Abolition." *Contemporary Crises* 10:81–94.

———. 1990. *Prison on Trial*. London: Sage.

Matthews, R., ed. 1988. *Informal Justice*. London: Sage.

Menninger, K. 1968. *The Crime of Punishment*. New York: Viking Press.

Mill, J. S. 1972. *On Liberty*. London: Dent. (Originally published 1859. London.)

Moore, M. S. 1987. "The Moral Worth of Retribution." In *Responsibility, Character and the Emotions*, edited by F. Schoeman. Cambridge: Cambridge University Press.

———. 1993. "Justifying Retribution." *Israel Law Review* 27:15–49.

Morison, J. 1988. "Hart's Excuses: Problems with a Compromise Theory of Punishment." In *The Jurisprudence of Orthodoxy*, edited by P. Leith and P. Ingram. London: Routledge.

Morran, D., and M. Wilson. 1994. "Confronting Domestic Violence: An Innovative Criminal Justice Response in Scotland." In *Penal Theory and Practice*, edited by R. A. Duff, S. E. Marshall, R. E. Dobash, and R. P. Dobash. Manchester: Manchester University Press.

Morris, H. 1968. "Persons and Punishment." *Monist* 52:475–501.

———. 1981. "A Paternalistic Theory of Punishment." *American Philosophical Quarterly* 18:263–71.

Morris, N. 1974. *The Future of Imprisonment*. Chicago: University of Chicago Press.

Morris, N., and M. Tonry. 1990. *Between Prison and Probation: Intermediate Punishments in a Rational Sentencing System*. New York: Oxford University Press.

Murphy, J. G. 1973. "Marxism and Retribution." *Philosophy and Public Affairs* 2:217–43.

———. 1979. "Kant's Theory of Criminal Punishment." In *Retribution, Justice, and Therapy*, by J. G. Murphy. Dordrecht: Reidel.

———. 1985. "Retributivism, Moral Education and the Liberal State." *Criminal Justice Ethics* 4:3–11.

Murphy, J. G., and J. Hampton. 1988. *Forgiveness and Mercy*. Cambridge: Cambridge University Press.

Nagel, T. 1972. "War and Massacre." *Philosophy and Public Affairs* 1:123–127.

Narayan, U. 1993. "Appropriate Responses and Preventive Benefits: Justifying Censure and Hard Treatment in Legal Punishment." *Oxford Journal of Legal Studies* 13:166–82.

Nino, C. S. 1983. "A Consensual Theory of Punishment." *Philosophy and Public Affairs* 12:289–306.

Norrie, A. W. 1991. *Law, Ideology and Punishment*. Dordrecht: Kluwer.

———. 1993. *Crime, Reason and History*. London: Weidenfeld & Nicolson.

Nowell-Smith, P. H. 1961. *Ethics*. Harmondsworth: Penguin.

Nozick, R. 1974. *Anarchy, State, and Utopia*. Oxford: Blackwell.

———. 1981. *Philosophical Explanations*. Oxford: Oxford University Press.

Oldenquist, A. 1988. "An Explanation of Retribution." *Journal of Philosophy* 85:464–78.

Parfit, D. 1984. *Reasons and Persons*. Oxford: Oxford University Press.

Pease, K., and W. McWilliams, eds. 1980. *Community Service by Order*. Aberdeen: Scottish Academic Press.

Pettit, P., and J. Braithwaite. 1993. "Not Just Deserts, Even in Sentencing." *Current Issues in Criminal Justice* 4:225–39.

Philips, M. 1986. "The Justification of Punishment and the Justification of Political Authority." *Law and Philosophy* 5:393–416.

Pilon, R. 1978. "Criminal Remedies: Restitution, Punishment, or Both?" *Ethics* 88:348–57.

Primoratz, I. 1989a. *Justifying Legal Punishment*. Atlantic Highlands, N.J.: Humanities Press.

———. 1989b. "Punishment as Language." *Philosophy* 64:187–205.

Quinn, W. 1985. "The Right to Threaten and the Right to Punish." *Philosophy and Public Affairs* 14:327–73.

Radzinowicz, L., and R. Hood. 1981. "The American Volte-Face in Sentencing Thought and Practice." In *Crime, Proof and Punishment*, edited by C. F. H. Tapper. London: Butterworths.

Rawls, J. 1955. "Two Concepts of Rules." *Philosophical Review* 64:3–32.

———. 1972. *A Theory of Justice*. Oxford: Oxford University Press.

Raynor, P. 1985. *Social Work, Justice and Control*. Oxford: Blackwell.

Roberts, J. 1989. *Guardian* (October 13), p. 4.

Robinson, P. H. 1987. "Hybrid Principles for the Distribution of Criminal Sanctions." *Northwestern University Law Review* 82:19–42.

Rotman, E. 1990. *Beyond Punishment: A New View of the Rehabilitation of Offenders*. Westport, Conn.: Greenwood Press.

Sadurski, W. 1985. "Distributive Justice and the Theory of Punishment." *Oxford Journal of Legal Studies* 5:47–59.

———. 1989. "Theory of Punishment, Social Justice, and Liberal Neutrality." *Law and Philosophy* 7:351–73.

Schedler, G. 1980. "Can Retributivists Support Legal Punishment?" *Monist* 63:185–98.

Scheerer, S. 1986. "Towards Abolitionism." *Contemporary Crises* 10:5–20.

Scheid, D. 1990. "Davis and the Unfair-Advantage Theory of Punishment: A Critique." *Philosophical Topics* 18:143–70.

Shafer-Landau, R. 1991. "Can Punishment Morally Educate?" *Law and Philosophy* 10:189–219.

Sher, G. 1987. *Desert*. Princeton, N.J.: Princeton University Press.

Sim, J. 1994. "The Abolitionist Approach: A British Perspective." In *Penal Theory and Practice*, edited by R. A. Duff, S. E. Marshall, R. E. Dobash, and R. P. Dobash. Manchester: Manchester University Press.

Skillen, A. J. 1980. "How to Say Things with Walls." *Philosophy* 55:509–23.

Slattery, B. 1992. "The Myth of Retributive Justice." In *Retributivism and Its Critics*, edited by W. Cragg. Stuttgart: Franz Steiner.

Smart, J. J. C. 1973. "An Outline of a System of Utilitarian Ethics." In *Utilitarianism: For and Against*, by J. J. C. Smart and B. Williams. Cambridge: Cambridge University Press.

Smith, D., H. Blagg, and N. Derricourt. 1988. "Mediation in the Shadow of the Law: The South Yorkshire Experience." In *Informal Justice*, edited by R. Matthews. London: Sage.

Smith, J. C., and B. Hogan. 1992. *Criminal Law*. 7th ed. London: Butterworths.

Steinert, H. 1986. "Beyond Crime and Punishment." *Contemporary Crises* 10:21–38.

Stephen, J. F. 1967. *Liberty, Equality, Fraternity*, edited by J. White. Cambridge: Cambridge University Press. (Originally published 1873.)

Sterba, J. 1984. "Is There a Rationale for Punishment?" *American Journal of Jurisprudence* 29:29–43.

Szasz, T. 1961. *The Myth of Mental Illness*. New York: Harper & Row.

———. 1963. *Law, Liberty, and Psychiatry*. New York: Macmillan.

Ten, C. L. 1987. *Crime, Guilt and Punishment*. Oxford: Oxford University Press.

———. 1990. "Positive Retributivism." *Social Philosophy and Policy* 7:194–208.

Tonry, M. 1994. "Proportionality, Parsimony, and Interchangeability of Punishments." In *Penal Theory and Practice*, edited by R. A. Duff, S. E. Marshall, R. E. Dobash, and R. P. Dobash. Manchester: Manchester University Press.

Tonry, M., and N. Morris. 1978. "Sentencing Reform in America." In *Reshaping the Criminal Law*, edited by P. R. Glazebrook. London: Stevens.

Twentieth Century Fund (Task Force on Criminal Sentencing). 1976. *Fair and Certain Punishment*. New York: McGraw-Hill.

Varah, M. 1987. "Probation and Community Service." In *Probation and the Community*, edited by J. Harding. London: Tavistock.

von Hirsch, A. 1976. *Doing Justice: The Choice of Punishments*. New York: Hill & Wang.

———. 1985. *Past or Future Crimes*. Manchester: Manchester University Press.

———. 1990. "Proportionality in the Philosophy of Punishment: From 'Why Punish?' to 'How Much?'" *Criminal Law Forum* 1:259–90.

———. 1992. "Proportionality in the Philosophy of Punishment." In *Crime and Justice: A Review of Research*, vol. 16, edited by Michael Tonry. Chicago: University of Chicago Press.

———. 1993. *Censure and Sanctions*. Oxford: Oxford University Press.

von Hirsch, A., and A. J. Ashworth., eds. 1992a. *Principled Sentencing*. Edinburgh: Edinburgh University Press; Boston: Northeastern University Press.

———. 1992b. "Not Not Just Deserts: A Response to Braithwaite and Pettit." *Oxford Journal of Legal Studies* 12:83–98.

———. 1993. "Desert and the Three Rs." *Current Issues in Criminal Justice* 5:9–12.

von Hirsch, A., and N. Jareborg. 1991. "Gauging Criminal Harm: A Living-Standard Analysis." *Oxford Journal of Legal Studies* 11:1–38.

Waldron, J. 1988. "When Justice Replaces Affection: The Need for Rights." *Harvard Journal of Law and Public Policy* 11:625–47.

Walker, N. 1978. "Punishing, Denouncing or Reducing Crime." In *Reshaping the Criminal Law*, edited by P. R. Glazebrook. London: Stevens.

———. 1980. *Punishment, Danger and Stigma*. Oxford: Blackwell.

———. 1981. "The Ultimate Justification." In *Crime, Proof and Punishment*, edited by C. F. H. Tapper. London: Butterworths.

———. 1991. *Why Punish?* Oxford: Oxford University Press.

Walker, N., and S. McCabe. 1973. *Crime and Insanity in England*. Vol. 2. Edinburgh: Edinburgh University Press.

Wasik, M., and A. von Hirsch. 1990. "Statutory Sentencing Principles: The 1990 White Paper." *Modern Law Review* 53:508–17.

Weston, W. R. 1978. "Probation in Penal Philosophy: Evolutionary Perspectives." *Howard Journal* 17:7–22.

Williams, B. 1976. *Morality*. Cambridge: Cambridge University Press.

Winch, P. 1972. "Nature and Convention." In *Ethics and Action*, by P. Winch. London: Routledge & Kegan Paul.

Wisdom, J. 1953. *Philosophy and Psycho-Analysis*. Oxford: Blackwell.

———. 1965. *Paradox and Discovery*. Oxford: Blackwell.

Wood, C. 1991. *The End of Punishment*. Edinburgh: St. Andrew Press.

Wootton, B. 1963. *Crime and the Criminal Law*. London: Stevens.

Zedner, L. 1994. "Reparation and Retribution: Are They Reconcilable?" *Modern Law Review* 57:228–50.

Michael Tonry and Mary Lynch

Intermediate Sanctions

ABSTRACT

Most American jurisdictions have recently established new intermediate sanctions programs. Few such programs have diverted large numbers of offenders from prison, saved public monies or prison beds, or reduced recidivism rates. These findings recur in evaluations of community service, intensive supervision, house arrest, day reporting centers, and boot camps. The principal problems have been high rates of revocation and subsequent incarceration (often 40–50 percent) and assignment of less serious offenders than program developers contemplated. If intermediate sanctions are to achieve their aims, means must be found to assure that they are used for the kinds of offenders for whom they are designed.

Three major developments in the 1960s and 1970s led to the perceived need in the 1980s and 1990s to develop intermediate sanctions that fall between prison and probation in their severity and intrusiveness. First, initially on the basis of doubts about the ethical justification of rehabilitative correctional programs (Allen 1964), and later on the basis of doubts about their effectiveness (Lipton, Martinson, and Wilks 1975; Brody 1976; Sechrest, White, and Brown 1979), rehabilitation lost credibility as a basis for sentencing. With it went the primary rationale for individualized sentences.

Second, initially in academic circles (e.g., Morris 1974; von Hirsch 1976) and later in the minds of many practitioners and policy makers, "just deserts" entered the penal lexicon, filled the void left by rehabilitation, and became seen as the primary rationale for sentencing. With

Michael Tonry is Sonosky Professor of Law and Public Policy at the University of Minnesota Law School. Mary Lynch graduated in 1995 from the University of Minnesota Law School.

it came a logic of punishments scaled in their severity so as to be proportionate to the seriousness of crimes committed and a movement to narrow officials' discretion by eliminating parole release, eliminating or limiting time off for good behavior, and constraining judges' discretion by use of sentencing guidelines and mandatory penalties.

Third, beginning in the 1960s and continuing into the 1990s, crime control policy became a staple issue in election campaigns, and proponents of "law and order" persistently called for harsher penalties. With this came a widespread belief that most sentences to ordinary probation are insufficiently punitive and substantial political pressure for increases in the severity of punishments. Because, however, most states lack sanctions other than prison that are widely seen as meaningful, credible, and punitive, pressure for increased severity has been satisfied mostly by increases in the use of imprisonment.

These developments resulted in a quadrupling in the number of state and federal prisoners between 1975 (240,593) and 1993 (948,881) and in substantial overcrowding of American prisons. At year end 1993, the federal prisons were operating at 136 percent of rated capacity, and thirty-nine state systems were operating above rated capacity. An additional 51,000 state prisoners in twenty-two jurisdictions were being held in county jails because prison space was unavailable (Bureau of Justice Statistics 1994).

Whatever the political and policy goals that vastly increased numbers of prisoners may have satisfied, they have also posed substantial problems for state officials. Prisons cost a great deal to build and to operate, and these costs have not been lightly borne by hard-pressed state budgets in the recessionary years of the early 1990s. In 1994, corrections budgets were the fastest rising component of state spending (National Conference of State Legislatures 1993). However, failure to deal with overcrowding attracts the attention of the federal courts, and throughout the 1990s as many as forty states have been subject to federal court orders related to overcrowding.

Intermediate sanctions have been seen as a way both to reduce the need for prison beds and to provide a continuum of sanctions that satisfies the just deserts concern for proportionality in punishment. During the mid-1980s, intermediate sanctions such as intensive supervision, house arrest, and electronic monitoring were oversold as being able simultaneously to divert offenders from incarceration, reduce recidivism rates, and save money while providing credible punishments that could be scaled in intensity to be proportionate to the severity of the offender's crime. Like most propositions that seem too good to be true, this one was not true.

During the past decade's experimentation, we have learned that some well-run programs can achieve some of their goals, that some conventional goals are incompatible, and that the availability of new sanctions presents almost irresistible temptations to judges and corrections officials to use them for offenders other than those for whom the program was created.

The goals of diverting offenders from prison and providing tough, rigorously enforced sanctions in the community have proven largely incompatible. A major problem, and it has repeatedly been shown to characterize intensive supervision programs, is that close surveillance of offenders reveals higher levels of technical violations than are discovered in less intensive sanctions. Revocations for conduct constituting new crimes are seldom higher for offenders in evaluated programs than for comparable offenders in other programs. Nor is there reason to suppose that offenders in evaluated new programs commit technical violations at higher rates. But if they do breach a curfew or stop performing community service or get drunk or violate a no-drug-use condition, the closer monitoring to which they are subject makes the chances of discovery high; once the discovery is made, many program operators believe they must take punitive action—typically revocation and resentencing to prison—to maintain the program's credibility in the eyes of judges, the media, and the community.

A second major lesson is that elected officials and practitioners often prefer to use intermediate sanctions for types of offenders other than those for whom programs were designed. Many evaluations of intensive supervision programs and boot camps, for example, have shown that any realistic prospects of saving money or prison beds require that they be used mostly for offenders who otherwise would have served prison terms. Yet many elected officials and practitioners resist.

Elected officials resist because they are risk averse. Even in the best-run programs, offenders sometimes commit serious new crimes, and officials are understandably concerned that they will be held responsible for supporting the program. The Massachusetts furlough program for prisoners serving life sentences from which Willy Horton absconded, for example, had been in operation for fifteen years and was started under a Republican governor in 1971, but Democratic governor

Michael Dukakis was held politically accountable for Horton's 1986 rape of a Maryland woman. As a result of this and similar incidents, elected officials often support new intermediate sanctions but then take pains to limit eligibility to low-risk offenders. One illustration is the series of recent federal proposals for boot camps for nonviolent first-time youthful offenders. For reasons explained in the discussion of boot camps in Section II below, young nonviolent first-offenders are among the least appropriate imaginable participants in boot camps if the aims include cost savings and reduced savings on prison beds.

Practitioners, particularly prosecutors and judges, also often resist using intermediate sanctions for the offenders for whom they were designed. Partly this is because they too are reluctant to be seen as responsible for crimes committed by participants. This is why, as the discussion of intensive supervision in Section II documents, judges are often unwilling to cooperate in projects in which—as part of experimental evaluations—target categories of offenders are to be randomly assigned to a community penalty or incarceration.

Partly judges' "misuse" of intermediate sanctions occurs because they believe new community penalties are more appropriate for some offenders than either prison or probation. Forced by limited program options to choose between prison and probation, they will often choose probation because prison is seen as too severe or too disruptive of the offender's and his family's lives, albeit with misgivings because they believe ordinary probation too slight a sanction. Once house arrest or intensive supervision become available, those penalties may appear more appropriate than either probation or prison.

This not uncommon pattern of use of intermediate sanctions by judges for offenders other than those program planners had in mind is often pejoratively characterized as "net widening." That epithet oversimplifies the problem. From the perspectives of the desirability of proportionality in punishment and of availability of a continuum of sanctions, the judge's preference to divert offenders from probation to something more intrusive is understandable, perhaps admirable. From the perspective of the designers of a program intended to save money and prison space by diverting offenders from prison, however, the judge's actions defy the program's rationale and obstruct achievement of its goals.

Probably the most important lesson learned from fifteen years' experience with intermediate sanctions is that they are seldom likely to achieve their goals unless means can be found to set and enforce policies governing their use. Otherwise, the combination of officials' risk aversion and practitioners' preferences to be guided solely by their judgments about appropriate penalties in individual cases are likely to undermine program goals.

Means must be found to establish policies governing the choice of sanction in individual cases. Two complementary means are available. First, discretion to select sanctions can be shifted from judges and prosecutors to corrections officials. "Back-end" programs to which offenders are diverted from prison by corrections officials, or released early, have been much more successful at saving money and prison space than have "front-end" programs. Similarly, parole guidelines have been much more successful and less controversial in reducing parole-release disparities than have sentencing guidelines in reducing sentencing disparities (Arthur D. Little, Inc. 1981; Blumstein et al. 1983, chap. 3). Presumably, these findings occur because decision processes in bureaucracies can be placed in fewer peoples' hands and can be regularized more readily by use of management controls than can decisions of autonomous, politically selected judges.

Second, sentencing guidelines, which in many jurisdictions have succeeded in reducing disparities in who goes to prison and for how long (Tonry 1993), can be extended to govern choices among intermediate sanctions and between them and prison and probation. Some states have made tentative steps in this direction and many are considering doing so. Section III below summarizes some of this experience and suggests how current initiatives can be advanced.

First, though, to provide a necessary backdrop, Section I gives a brief overview of problems that make reductions in recidivism, costs, and prison use difficult to achieve. Section II summarizes experience to date with the implementation and evaluation of various intermediate sanctions, including boot camps, intensive supervision, house arrest and electronic monitoring, day reporting centers, community service, and day fines. Each of these sections provides an overview of program characteristics and discusses evidence concerning various measures of effectiveness, including implementation, net widening, and success at reducing recidivism, saving money, and diminishing demand for prison beds. The emphasis is mostly on American experience and research, but research elsewhere, especially in England and Wales, is touched on as appropriate.

I. General Impediments to Effective Intermediate Sanctions

In retrospect, it was naive (albeit from good intention) for promoters of new intermediate sanctions to assure skeptics that recidivism rates would fall, costs be reduced, and pressure on prison beds diminish if new programs were established. The considerable pressures for net widening and the formidable management problems involved in implementing new programs interact in complex ways to frustrate new programs. Although these challenges are now well understood, that knowledge has been hard won.

A. Recidivism

Consider first recidivism rates. From well-known evaluations of community service (McDonald 1986), intensive supervision (Petersilia and Turner 1993), and boot camps (McKenzie and Souryal 1994), to mention only a few, comes a robust finding that recidivism rates (for new crimes) of offenders sentenced to well-managed intermediate sanctions do not differ significantly from those of comparable offenders receiving other sentences. Recidivism and revocation rates for violation of other conditions, by contrast, are generally higher.

From different perspectives, both findings may be seen as good or bad. The finding of no effect on rates of new crime may be seen by many as good if the offenders involved have been diverted from prison and the new crimes they commit are not very serious. Sentences to prison are much more expensive to administer than sentences to house arrest, intensive supervision, or day reporting centers, and if the latter are no less effective at reducing subsequent criminality, they can potentially provide nearly comparable public safety at greatly reduced cost.

But they do not provide "comparable public safety": by definition, crimes committed in the community by people who would have been in prison would not otherwise have occurred. Thus, if diverted intermediate sanction participants commonly commit violent or sexual crimes, "no difference in recidivism rates" provides little solace. If, however, participants seldom commit violent or sexual crimes, the open-eyed choice that must be made is between avoidable minor crimes and substantial costs to hold people in prison. The suggestion that every offender be confined until he will no longer offend is impracticable. Property offenders particularly have high reoffending rates, more than 30 percent of American and English males are arrested for non-trivial crimes by age thirty, and all offenders cannot be confined forever. In effect, this trade between costs and allowing avoidable crimes to happen is made whenever community sentencing programs are established.

From the other side of the punishment continuum, the finding of no effect on new crimes raises different issues. If ordinary probation is no less effective at preventing new crimes than is a new intermediate sanction at three times the cost, the case for sentencing offenders to the new program instead of probation cannot be made on cost-effectiveness terms. That does not mean that no case can be made; Petersilia and Turner (1993), among others, have offered the just-desert argument for intermediate sanctions that they can deliver a punishment that is more intrusive and burdensome than probation and appropriately proportioned to the offender's guilt. This is a plausible argument, but it shifts the rationale from utilitarian claims about crime and cost reductions to normative claims about the quality of justice.

The equally robust finding that participants in intermediate sanctions typically have higher rates of violation of technical conditions than comparable offenders otherwise punished provokes a not-quite-parallel set of concerns. Most observers agree that the raised violation (and related raised revocation) rates result from the greater likelihood that violations will be discovered in intensive programs, and not from greater underlying rates of violation. From a "the law must keep its promises" perspective, the higher failure rates are good. Offenders *should* comply with conditions, and consequences should attach when they do not.

The contrary view is that the higher failure rates expose the unreality and injustice of conditions—like prohibitions of drinking or drug use or expectations that offenders will conform to middle-class behavioral standards they have never observed before—that many offenders will foreseeably breach and that do not involve criminality. Many offenders have great difficulty in achieving conventional, law-abiding patterns of living, and many will stumble along the way; a traditional social work approach to community corrections would expect and accept the stumbles (so long as they do not involve significant new crimes) and hope that through them, with help, the offender will learn to be law-abiding. From this perspective, it is an advantage of low-intensity programs that they uncover few violations and a disadvantage of high-intensity programs that they do.

Thus the evaluation findings on recidivism and revocation rates elicit different reactions from different people and in light of different conceptions of how the corrections system ought to work. In addition, however, they illuminate a major impediment to aspirations to reduce prison use by means of establishment of intermediate sanctions.

B. Prison Beds

If all offenders in a community program were diverted from prison, a 30 percent revocation rate for technical violations (whatever the rate for new-crime violations, but here assuming 20 percent) would not be an insurmountable problem. The net savings in prison beds would be the number of persons diverted multiplied by the average time they would otherwise spend in prison less the number of persons revoked for violations multiplied by their average term to be served. Unless the gross revocation rate approached 100 percent or the average time to be served after revocation exceeded the average time that would have been served if not diverted, bed savings are inevitable.

The combination of net widening and elevated rates of technical violations and revocations makes the calculation harder and makes prison bed savings difficult to achieve. For front-end programs, a 50 percent rate of prison diversion is commonly counted a success. Consider how the numbers work out. The 50 percent diverted from prison saves prison beds, on the calculation and assumptions described in the preceding paragraph. The 50 percent diverted from probation are a different story. They would not otherwise have occupied prison beds, and if half (on the 30 percent technical, 20 percent new crime revocation assumptions) suffer revocation and imprisonment, they represent new demand for beds, and a higher demand than would otherwise exist because many more of their technical violations will be discovered and acted on.

Whether a particular program characterized by 50 percent prison diversion will save or consume net prison beds depends on why offenders' participation is revoked, in what percentage of cases, whether they are sent to prison, and for how long. But 50 percent is a high assumed-diversion rate. If the true rate is 30 percent or 20 percent, net prison bed savings are unlikely.

C. Cost Savings

The third often-claimed goal of intermediate sanctions is to save money. Interaction of all the preceding difficulties make dollar savings unlikely except in the best of cases. If a majority of program participants are diverted from probation rather than from prison, and if tech-

nical violation and revocation rates are higher in the intermediate sanction than in the ordinary probation and parole programs to which
offenders would otherwise be assigned, the chances of net cost savings
are slight. For boot camps, for example, assuming typical levels of
participant noncompletion and typical levels of postprogram revocation, Parent has calculated that "the probability of imprisonment has
to be around 80 percent just to reach a break-even point—that is, to
have a net impact of zero on prison bed-space" (1994, p. 9).

Cost analyses must, however, look beyond diversion rates, revocation rates, and prison beds. At least three other considerations are
important. First is the issue of transactions costs. Net-widening programs that shift probationers to intensive supervision and then shift
some of those to prison cost the state more because they use up additional prison space. But in addition they create new expenses for probation offices, prosecutors, courts, and corrections agencies in administering each of those transfers. Correctional cost-benefit analyses often
ignore cost ramifications for other agencies, but the other agencies
must either pay additional costs or refuse to cooperate. An example:
community corrections officials often complain that courts sometimes
do not take violations seriously and that, when they do, police assign
such low priority to execution of arrest warrants for program violators
that they are in effect meaningless (e.g., McDonald 1986).

Second is the problem of marginal costs. Especially in the 1980s,
promoters of new programs commonly contrasted the average annual
costs per offender of administering a new program (say, $4,500) with
the average annual cost of housing one prisoner (say, $18,500) and
claimed substantial potential cost savings. This ignores the complexities presented by net widening and raised revocation rates, but it also
ignores a more important problem of scale.

For an innovative small program of fifty to one hundred offenders
(and many were and are of this size or smaller), the valid comparison is
with the marginal, not the average, costs of housing diverted offenders.
Unless a prison or a housing unit will be closed or not opened because
the system has fifty fewer inmates, the only savings will be incremental
costs for food, laundry, supplies, and other routine items. The major
costs of payroll, administration, debt service, and maintenance will be
little affected. In a prison system with 5,000, 15,000, or 50,000 inmates, the costs saved by diverting a few hundred are scarcely no-
ticeable.

Third is the issue of savings to the larger community associated with crimes avoided by incapacitating offenders. If believable values could be attached to crimes that would be averted by imprisonment but that would occur if offenders were assigned to community penalties, they would provide important data for considering policy options. Unfortunately, this is a subject that has as yet received little sustained attention. Some conservative writers (e.g., Zedlewski 1987; DiIulio 1990; Barr 1992) have claimed that increased use of imprisonment is highly cost-effective. Kleiman and Cavanagh (1990), for example, claimed "benefits of incarcerating that *one inmate* for a year at between $172,000 and $2,364,000" (emphasis in original).

Liberal scholars have responded by showing the implausibility of many of the assumptions made in such calculations. Zimring and Hawkins (1991, p. 429), for example, showed that, on the assumptions made in Zedlewski's analysis about the number of crimes prevented for each inmate confined, the 237,000 increase in the prison population that occurred between 1977 and 1986 should "have reduced crime to zero on incapacitation effects alone . . . on this account, crime disappeared some years ago."

One of the conservative contributors to this debate later recanted more extreme claims and concluded that "the truth, we find, lies . . . arguably closer to the liberal than to the conservative view" (DiIulio and Piehl 1991). These debates have, however, been more ideological than scientific and offer little guidance for thinking about intermediate sanctions. What is left is the need mentioned earlier to weigh the kinds of risks particular offenders present with the costs that will be incurred if alternate sanctioning choices are made.

No one who has worked with the criminal justice system should be surprised by the observation that the system is complex and that economic and policy ramifications ripple through it when changes are made in any one of its parts. Sometimes that truism has been overlooked to the detriment of programs on behalf of which oversimplified claims were made. Georgia, for example, operated a pioneering front-end intensive supervision program (ISP) that was at one time claimed to have achieved remarkably low recidivism rates (for new crimes) and to have saved Georgia the cost of building two prisons (Erwin 1987; Erwin and Bennett 1987). It was later realized that many or most of those sentenced to ISP were low-risk offenders convicted of minor crimes who otherwise would have received probation. From serving initially as an exemplar of successful ISP programs that save money and reduce recidivism rates, Georgia's ISP program now serves as an exemplar of netwidening programs that increase system costs and produce higher rates of revocation for violations of technical conditions (Clear and Byrne 1992, p. 321).

II. Experience with Intermediate Sanctions

Writing about experience with intermediate sanctions bears some resemblance to shooting at a moving target. Although it typically takes at least three years from the time an evaluation is conceived until results are published, the programs themselves keep changing. Thus MacKenzie (1994), describing the results of an assessment of boot camps in eight states, took pains to explain that some of them changed significantly during and after the assessment. For example, the South Carolina program, initially a front-end program with admission controlled by the judge (and thus highly vulnerable to net widening) was reorganized as a back-end program in which participants were selected by the department of corrections from among offenders sentenced to prison. Similarly, programs in some states that had focused primarily on discipline and physical labor were reorganized to include a much larger component of drug treatment and educational opportunities.

Still, an evaluation literature has continued to accumulate, and lessons learned in some states a few years ago can be useful to policy makers in other states that are designing new programs or redesigning old ones. In order, the following subsections discuss research on boot camps, ISP, house arrest and electronic monitoring, day reporting centers, community service, and day fines.

A prefatory note is required. The evaluation literature for the most part raises doubts about the effectiveness of intermediate sanctions at achieving the goals their promoters have commonly set. This does not mean that there are no effective programs. Only a handful have been carefully evaluated. Many of those have in the aftermath been altered. Many sophisticated and experienced practitioners believe that their programs are effective, and some no doubt are. The evaluation literature does not "prove" that programs cannot succeed; instead, it shows that many have not and that managers can learn from these past experiences. Sometimes that learning may be expressed as program adaptations intended to make achievement of existing goals more likely. Sometimes, it may lead to a reconceptualization of goals.

The evaluation literature concerning intermediate sanctions is slight, which at first impression may seem surprising given that new programs have proliferated in every state. To anyone knowledgeable about correctional research, the relatively small amount of research will be less surprising: private foundations are conspicuously uninterested in criminal justice research, neither of the relevant specialized national funding agencies—the National Institute of Corrections and the State Justice Institute—spends much on research, and the National Institute of Justice must spread its limited research funds among a wide range of subjects.

The available literature consists of a handful of fairly sophisticated evaluations funded by the National Institute of Justice; a larger number of smaller, typically less sophisticated studies of local projects; and a large number of uncritical descriptions of innovative programs. There have been a number of efforts to synthesize the evaluation literature on intermediate sanctions, sometimes in edited collections (McCarthy 1987; Byrne, Lurigio, and Petersilia 1992; Tonry and Hamilton 1995), sometimes in unified books (Tonry and Will 1988; Morris and Tonry 1990). Given the time consumed in writing and publishing books, the collections and syntheses are current as of a year or two before their publication dates.

In order to keep this essay to a manageable length, the discussion of each intermediate sanction is held to a few pages and emphasizes the more substantial evaluations and literature reviews. In some cases—for example, concerning ISP (Petersilia and Turner 1993) and boot camps (MacKenzie 1994; MacKenzie and Piquero 1994)—relatively recent and detailed literature reviews are available for readers who want more information. In other cases—for example, concerning fines (Hillsman 1990) and community service (Pease 1985)—the best literature reviews are more dated: there has been relatively little American research on those subjects in recent years, but those articles, despite their dates, cover most of the important research. In still other cases, notably including day reporting centers, most of the available literature is descriptive, and no literature reviews are available.

A. Boot Camps

The emerging consensus from assessments of boot camps (also sometimes called "shock incarceration") must be discouraging to their founders and supporters. Although promoted as a means to reduce recidivism rates, corrections costs, and prison crowding, most boot camps have no discernible effect on subsequent offending and increase costs and crowding (Parent 1994; MacKenzie 1994). The reasons are those sketched in Section I above. Most have been front-end programs that have drawn many of their participants from among offenders who otherwise would not have been sent to prison. In many programs, a third to half of participants fail to complete the program and are sent to prison as a result. In most programs, close surveillance of offenders after completion and release produces rates of violations of technical conditions and of revocations that are higher than for comparable offenders in less intensive programs.

The news is not all bad. Back-end programs to which imprisoned offenders are transferred by corrections officials for service of a 90- or 180-day boot camp sentence in lieu of a longer conventional sentence do apparently save money and prison space, although they too often experience high failure rates and higher than normal technical violation and revocation rates.

Boot camp prisons have spread rapidly since the first two were established in Georgia and Oklahoma in 1983. By April 1993, according to a National Institute of Justice report (MacKenzie 1993), thirty states and the U.S. Bureau of Prisons were operating boot camps. According to the results of a survey of local jurisdictions in May 1992, ten jail boot camps were then in operation, and thirteen other jurisdictions were planning to open jail boot camps in 1992 or 1993 (Austin, Jones, and Bolyard 1993). The earliest were opened in 1986 in New Orleans and in 1988 in Travis County, Texas.

Boot camps vary widely in their details (MacKenzie and Parent 1992; MacKenzie and Piquero 1994). Some last 90 days, some 180. Admission in some states is controlled by judges, in others by corrections officials. Some primarily emphasize discipline and self-control; others incorporate extensive drug and other rehabilitation elements. Some eject a third to half of participants, others less than 10 percent. Most admit only males, usually under age twenty-five, and often subject to crime of conviction and criminal history limits, though there are exceptions to each of these generalizations.

The reasons for boot camps' popularity are self-evident. Many Americans have experienced life in military boot camps and remember the experience as not necessarily pleasant but as an effective way to learn self-discipline and to learn to work as part of a team. Images of offenders participating in military drill and hard physical labor make boot camps look demanding and unpleasant, characteristics that crime-conscious officials and voters find satisfying. A series of studies by the Public Agenda Foundation in Delaware, Alabama, and Pennsylvania of citizen support for intermediate sanctions, for example, found that the public is more supportive of intermediate sanctions than is widely known but also found that they want such penalties to be burdensome and for that reason were especially in favor of boot camps (Doble and Klein 1989; Doble, Immerwahr, and Robinson 1991; Public Agenda Foundation 1993).

Most of what we know about the effects of boot camps on participants comes from a series of studies by MacKenzie and colleagues at the University of Maryland (e.g., MacKenzie and Shaw 1990, Mackenzie 1993, 1994; MacKenzie and Souryal 1994), from a U.S. General Accounting Office survey of research and experience (1993), and from an early descriptive overview of boot camps commissioned by the National Institute of Justice (Parent 1989).

The conclusions with which this subsection began are drawn from MacKenzie's work and later analyses by Parent. In addition to findings on completion rates, recidivism rates, and cost and prison bed savings, MacKenzie and her colleagues looked closely in Louisiana at effects on prisoners' self-esteem (MacKenzie and Shaw 1990). One early hypothesis concerning boot camps was that successful completion would increase participants' self-esteem, which would in turn lead to more effective participation in the free community and reduced recidivism. The first half of the hypothesis was found to be correct; using psychometric measures, MacKenzie and Shaw found that successful participants' self-esteem was enhanced compared with comparable prisoners in conventional prisons. Unfortunately, later assessments of successful participants after release found that their enhanced self-esteem soon disappeared (a plausible explanation for why the second half of the hypothesis concerning recidivism was not confirmed).

One tentative finding concerning possible positive effects of rehabilitative programs on recidivism merits emphasis. Although MacKenzie and her colleagues concluded overall that boot camps do not by themselves result in reduced recidivism rates, they found evidence in Illinois, New York, and Louisiana of "lower rates of recidivism on some measures" that they associated with strong rehabilitative emphases in those states' boot camps (MacKenzie 1994, p. 16). An earlier article describes a "somewhat more positive" finding that graduates under intensive supervision after release "appear to be involved in more positive social activities (e.g., work, attending drug treatment) than similar offenders on parole or probation" (MacKenzie and Souryal 1993, p. 465).

Boot camps illustrate most vividly of all intermediate sanctions the

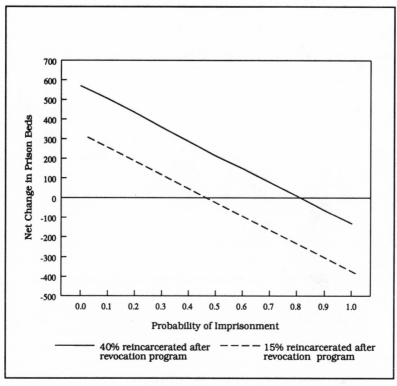

FIG. 1.—Two-hundred-bed, ninety-day boot camp (nine-month reduction). Source.—Parent (1994).

ways in which net widening, rigorous enforcement of conditions, and high revocation rates can produce the unintended side effect of increased costs and prison use from programs intended to reduce both. Both MacKenzie (MacKenzie and Piquero 1994) and Parent (1994) have used models developed by Parent for predicting the prison use implications of boot camps in light of various assumptions about net widening; within-program failure rates; and postprogram revocation rates, including estimates of time to failure, time to revocation, and length of time in the boot camp, length of time in prison if not sent to the boot camp, and length of time in prison following failure or revocation.

Figure 1, taken from Parent's work (1994), shows the effects on prison beds of a hypothetical 90-day 200-bed facility on different assumptions of prison diversion and postprogram revocation and reincarceration. Other assumptions of failure rates within the program and

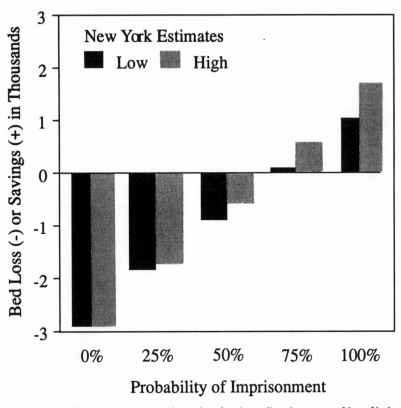

Fig. 2.—Effects on prison bed needs of prison diversion rates, New York. Source.—MacKenzie and Piquero (1994).

lengths of confinement in lieu of boot camp and after revocation, based on averages documented in MacKenzie's eight-state assessment, are built into the model. The diagonal lines show the effects of different postprogram reincarceration rates on prison bed demand. At the lower 15 percent rate, boot camps create a net demand for additional prison beds if less than half those in the program would otherwise have gone to prison. At the more realistic 40 percent rate, at least 80 percent of participants must have been diverted from prison before prison beds are saved.

MacKenzie (1994) developed similar estimates for states in her eight-state assessment. Figure 2 shows estimates based on data from New York's boot camps of bed savings given various assumptions about prison diversion. Savings occur only if at least 75 percent of participants are diverted from prison and, sizable savings occur only if nearly all are diverted.

If a primary goal of boot camps is to reduce prison use, the policy implications of research on boot camps are straightforward. Parent (1994, p. 10) sees at least three: "First, boot camps should recruit offenders who have a very high probability of imprisonment." This means that participants should be selected by corrections officials from among prisoners rather than by judges from among sentenced offenders. Second, boot camps should minimize failure rates by reducing in-program failures and post-release failures. This means that misconduct within the boot camp should be punished within the boot camp whenever possible rather than by transfer to a regular prison and that misconduct after release should be dealt with within the supervision program whenever possible rather than by revocation and reincarceration. Third, participants in boot camps should be selected from among prisoners who otherwise would serve a substantial term of imprisonment. Transfer of prisoners serving nine-month terms to a 180-day boot camp is unlikely to reduce costs and system crowding. Transfer of prisoners serving two- or three-year mandatory minimum terms is likely to reduce both.

Corrections officials are aware of these findings. Some states—for example, New York—already operate boot camps that draw their clientele from state prisons and that result in much shorter terms of confinement for those who complete the program (including many who thereby avoid mandatory minimums). Other states, like South Carolina, have shifted from judicial to correctional selection of participants. One implication is clear, however: "Boot camps for nonviolent first offenders," though often proposed, are unlikely to accomplish any of the aims for boot camps that are generally offered.

B. Intensive Supervision

Intensive supervision for probationers and parolees was initially the most popular intermediate sanction, has the longest history, and has been the most extensively and ambitiously evaluated. Intensive supervision has been the subject of the only multisite experimental evaluation involving random allocation of eligible offenders to ISP and to whatever the otherwise appropriate sentence would have been (Petersilia and Turner 1993).

Evaluation findings parallel those for boot camps. Front-end programs in which judges control placement tend to draw more heavily from offenders who would otherwise receive less restrictive sentences than from offenders who would otherwise have gone to prison or jail. The multisite ISP evaluation by the RAND Corporation, in which jurisdictions agreed in advance to cooperate with a random assignment system for allocating offenders to sanctions, was unable to evaluate front-end ISP programs when judges refused to accept the outcomes of the randomization system (Petersilia and Turner 1993). Back-end programs draw from prison populations, but even for some of these programs, suggestions have been made that their creation may lead judges to sentence more minor offenders to "a taste of prison" in the belief that they will quickly be released into ISP (Clear 1987).

Like the boot camp evaluations, the ISP evaluations have concluded that offenders sentenced to ISP do not have lower recidivism rates for new crimes than do comparable offenders receiving different sentences but, instead, typically (because of closer surveillance) experience higher rates of violation of technical conditions and higher rates of revocation. Also as with boot camps, early proponents argued that ISP, while reducing recidivism rates and rehabilitating offenders, would save money and prison resources (Petersilia, Lurigio, and Byrne 1992, pp. ix–x); evaluations suggest that the combination of net widening, high revocation rates, and related case processing costs makes the cost savings claims improbable for most programs.

There is one tantalizing positive finding from the ISP evaluation literature that parallels a boot camp finding (MacKenzie and Souryal 1993): ISP did succeed in some sites in increasing participants' involvement in counseling and other treatment programs (Petersilia and Turner 1993). The drug treatment literature demonstrates that participation, whether voluntary or coerced, can reduce both drug use and crime by drug-using offenders (Anglin and Hser 1990; President's Commission on Model State Drug Laws 1993). Because Drug Use Forecasting data (e.g., National Institute of Justice 1994) indicate that half to three-fourths of arrested felons in many cities test positive for drug abuse, ISP may hold promise as a device for getting addicted offenders into treatment and keeping them there (Gendreau, Cullen, and Bonta 1994).

Few corrections programs are new in the sense that they have not been tried before: house arrest, supervision of variable intensity, treatment conditions, community service, restitution, intermittent or partial confinement—they have all long been used on a case-by-case basis as conditions of probation. Modern ISP, however, is different in that it follows a previous generation of similar programs that was the subject of widespread programmatic adoption and evaluation.

From the 1950s through the early 1970s, probation departments experimented with caseload size in order to learn whether smaller caseloads permitting more contact between officers and probationers would enable officers to provide more and better services and thereby enhance probation's rehabilitative effectiveness. The best-known project, in California, featured caseloads ranging from "intensive" (20 offenders) to "ideal" (50), "normal" (70–130), and "minimum" (several hundred). Lower caseloads produced more technical violations but indistinguishable crime rates (Carter, Robinson, and Wilkins 1967).

A later survey of the experience of forty-six separate (mostly Law Enforcement Assistance Administration–funded) programs found that intensive supervision programs had no effect on recidivism rates or increased them, and diverted few offenders from prison but recruited instead mostly from people who otherwise would have received probation (Banks et al. 1977). Not surprisingly, ISP based on rehabilitative rationales withered away.

Contemporary programs, with caseloads ranging from two officers to twenty-five probationers to one officer to forty probationers, are typically based on surveillance, cost, and punishment rationales. More frequent contacts between officer and offender (in some programs, as many as twenty or thirty per month) lead to closer surveillance, which in turn enhances public safety by making it likelier that misconduct will be discovered and punished. Because of closer surveillance, low- to mid-risk offenders can be diverted from prison to less costly ISP without jeopardizing public safety. Because of the frequency of contacts, subjection to unannounced urinalysis tests for drugs, and rigorous enforcement of restitution, community service, and other conditions, ISP will be much more punitive than conventional probation.

Contemporary ISP programs are of three types, each with an exemplar that was the subject of a major National Institute of Justice–funded evaluation. Georgia established the most noted "prison diversion" program to which convicted offenders were sentenced by judges under criteria that directed the judge to use ISP only for offenders who otherwise would have been sent to prison. An in-house evaluation concluded that most ISP participants had been diverted from prison and, on the basis of comparisons with a matched group of offenders who were imprisoned, that the program had achieved lower recidivism rates and had reduced prison use (Erwin 1987). Subsequent analyses by others concluded that most participants had not been diverted from prison, that the comparison group was not comparable, that low rates of new crimes resulted not from the program but from the low-risk nature of the offenders, and that prison beds had not been saved (Morris and Tonry 1990, chap. 7; Clear and Byrne 1992).

The second form, "prison-release ISP," had as its evaluated exemplar a New Jersey program to which low-risk prisoners were released after a careful seven-step screening process and then placed in low caseloads with frequent contacts and urinalyses and rigorously enforced conditions. A major evaluation, based on a post hoc comparison group, concluded that the program was effectively implemented, reduced recidivism rates, and saved public moneys (Pearson 1987). Subsequent analyses by others accepted the implementation finding but challenged the recidivism findings (because the comparison group appeared to consist of higher-risk offenders and thus was not comparable) and the cost findings (nearly half of the initial participants were sent back to prison following revocation for breach of conditions, which, given the short sentences they would otherwise have served and the costs of processing the revocations, made cost-savings claims suspect) (Morris and Tonry 1990, chap. 7). Clear hypothesized that judges might sentence low-risk minor offenders to prison in the belief that they would be released to ISP and that, if under 2 percent of the eligible defendants were sentenced to prison on that basis, any possible cost savings from ISP would be lost (Clear 1987).

The third form, "case management ISP," had as its evaluated exemplar a Massachusetts program designed by the state probation department in which probationers were classified on the basis of risk of offending (using a validated risk-classification instrument). The evaluation documented significant implementation problems and concluded that offenders given intense supervision were no likelier than other comparable offenders to commit new crimes but were likelier to have their probation revoked because of technical condition violations (Byrne and Kelly 1989).

Notwithstanding the nonconfirmatory evaluation findings, ISP was adopted in most states. A General Accounting Office survey in 1989 identified programs in forty states and the District of Columbia (U.S. General Accounting Office 1990; Byrne and Pattavina 1992). Probably they exist in every state: programs can be organized by state or county correctional agencies; can be located in parole, probation, and prison departments; and as a result are easy to miss in national mail and phone surveys.

Although ad hoc intensive supervision in individual cases presumably occurs in every probation system, no other country has adopted widespread programs of intensive probation. Small-scale pilot projects were started in the Netherlands in 1993 (Tak 1994*a*, 1994*b*). In England, as in the United States, variable caseload projects to test treatment effectiveness hypotheses were conducted in the 1960s and early 1970s, with the same discouraging results (Folkard et al. 1974, 1976), and were soon abandoned. A series of pilot projects in eight sites, linked with Home Office evaluations, has been under way in England and Wales in the 1990s with as-yet inconclusive results. The programs appear to have diverted offenders from prison and to have met with approval from judges and probation officers, but in many sites they seem to have encountered substantial implementation problems (Mair 1994; Mair et al. 1994). Findings on recidivism effects will not be available until 1996 (or later).

Two exhaustive syntheses of the American ISP literature have been published (U.S. General Accounting Office 1990; Petersilia and Turner 1993) and do not differ significantly in their conclusions from those offered here. One question that naturally arises is why ISP programs have survived and continue to be created. Unlike boot camps, for which evaluation findings casting doubts on effectiveness are recent, the ISP findings have been well known and accepted since at least 1990. The answers appear to be that ISP's surveillant and punitive properties satisfy a public preference that sanctions be demanding and burdensome and that ISP is becoming seen as an appropriate mid-level punishment. Petersilia, Lurigio, and Byrne (1992, p. xiv) note, "To many observers, the goal of restoring the principle of just deserts to the criminal justice system is justification enough for the continued development of intermediate sanctions."

Here, too, the policy implications are straightforward. Because recidivism rates for new crimes are no higher for ISP participants than for comparable imprisoned offenders, ISP is a cost-effective prison alternative for offenders who do not present unacceptable risks of violence. Intensive supervision programs may offer a promising tool for facilitating treatment for drug-using offenders and can by themselves and linked with other sanctions provide credible mid-level punishments as part of a continuum of sanctions.

The challenges are to devise ways to assure that programs are used for the kinds of offenders for whom they are designed and to reduce rates of revocation for technical violations. The former problem does not exist for back-end early-release programs, and sentencing guidelines systems may hold promise for reducing the extent of net widening in front-end systems (see Section III below). The latter problem can be addressed, as Lurigio and Petersilia (1992, p. 14) note, by imposing only conditions that relate to a particular offender's circumstances rather than by imposing long lists of general standard conditions.

C. House Arrest and Electronic Monitoring

The lines that distinguish community penalties begin to blur after ISP. House arrest, often called "home confinement," has as a precursor the curfew condition traditionally attached to many probation sentences and may be ordered as a sanction in its own right or as a condition of ISP. Most affected offenders, however, do not remain in their homes but instead are authorized to work or participate in treatment, education, or training programs. Finally, house arrest is sometimes, but not necessarily, backed up by electronic monitoring; Renzema (1992), for example, reports that 10,549 people were on house arrest in Florida in August 1990, of whom 873 were on electronic monitoring.

House arrest comes in front- and back-end forms. In an early Oklahoma program (Meachum 1986), for example, prison inmates were released early subject to participation in a home confinement program. In Florida, which operates the largest and most diverse home confinement programs, most are front-end programs in which otherwise prison-bound offenders are supposed to be placed. In some states, especially in connection with electronic monitoring, house arrest is used in place of pretrial detention (Maxfield and Baumer 1990).

House arrest programs expanded rapidly beginning in the mid-1980s. The earliest programs were typically small (from thirty to fifty offenders) and often were composed mostly of driving-while-intoxicated and minor property offenders (this was also true of most of the early electronic monitoring programs) (Morris and Tonry 1990, chap. 7).

Programs have grown and proliferated. The largest program is in Florida where more than 13,000 offenders were on house arrest in 1993 (Blomberg, Bales, and Reed 1993). Programs coupled with electronic monitoring, a subset, existed nowhere in 1982, in seven states in 1986, and in all fifty states in October 1990 (Renzema 1992, p. 46).

Considered by itself, the use of electronic monitoring has grown even more from its beginnings in 1983 in the New Mexico courtroom of Judge Michael Goss and the Florida courtroom of Judge J. Allison DeFoor II (Ford and Schmidt 1985). In 1986, only ninety-five offenders were subject to monitoring (Renzema 1992, p. 41), a number that rose to 12,000 in 1990 (Baumer and Mendelsohn 1992, p. 54) and to a daily count of 30,000–50,000 in 1992 and 1993 (Lilly 1993, p. 4).

Manufacturers of electronic monitoring equipment no doubt expect eventually to sell their products worldwide. Within the English-speaking countries, the United States is at present the major market. In early 1993, the Northern Territory of Australia was the only state operating front-end house arrest programs; Western Australia, South Australia, and Queensland operated prison-release programs. Altogether, these programs contained 330-400 offenders, of whom approximately half were subject to electronic monitoring (Biles 1993).

English policy makers toyed with electronic monitoring in the late 1980s and established a pilot project in three sites in 1989–90. Judges and police were skeptical about the use of electronically monitored house arrest as a custody alternative, and rates of offender noncompliance were high (Mair and Nee 1990; Mair 1993a). The evaluators characterized their findings as inconclusive. Although the Criminal Justice Act of 1991 authorized use of electronic monitoring in conjunction with curfew orders, no monitoring equipment was in use in England and Wales late in 1994.

No American evaluations of electronic monitoring on the scale or with the sophistication of the best on boot camps or ISP have been published. One analysis of agency data for Florida's front-end house arrest program concluded that it draws more offenders from among the prison-bound than from the probation-bound (Baird and Wagner 1990). However, this conclusion is based on two dubious analyses. The first looked to see whether offenders on house arrest should, under Florida's sentencing guidelines, have been sentenced to confinement. This seemingly straightforward calculation assumes, however, that the guidelines then in effect were taken seriously by Florida judges and significantly constrain their choices; the conclusion of a legislative study committee is that they did not (Florida Legislature 1991).

The second diversion analysis was based on statistical comparison of characteristics of samples of probationers, house arrest offenders, and prisoners, and it concluded that those on house arrest more closely resembled prisoners than probationers. This is like the ISP evaluations in Georgia and New Jersey that were later challenged on the basis that seemingly comparable groups were not. Part of the problem lies in inherent limits of efforts to use statistical models to create equivalent comparison groups and part in the limited range of data about offenders that is compiled in official records.

A case study of the development, implementation, and evolution of a back-end program in Arizona cautions that house arrest programs are likely to share the prospects and problems of intermediate sanctions generally. Originally conceived as a money-saving system for early release of low-risk offenders, the program—which combined house arrest with electronic monitoring—wound up costing money. One problem was that, in addition to satisfying stringent statutory criteria (no violent or sex crimes, no prior felony convictions), inmates had to be approved for release by the parole board, which proved highly risk averse and released very few eligible inmates. When the program became operational, the rate of revocation for technical violations (34 percent of participants) was twice that for ordinary parolees. Finally, many probation officers began to justify the program, not as an early-release system for low-risk offenders, but as a mechanism for establishing tighter controls and closer surveillance for parolees than would otherwise be possible (Palumbo, Clifford, and Snyder-Joy 1992).

There are no other large-scale evaluations. House arrest coupled with electronic monitoring has been the subject of many small studies and a linked set of three studies in Indianapolis (Baumer, Maxfield, and Mendelsohn 1993). Both of two recent literature reviews (Baumer and Mendelsohn 1992; Renzema 1992) stress the scantiness of the research evidence on prison diversion, recidivism, and cost-effectiveness. On recidivism, Renzema (1992, p. 49) notes that most of the "research is uninterpretable because of shoddy or weak research designs." Baumer and Mendelsohn (1992, pp. 64–65) stress that "the incapacitative and public safety potential of this sanction has probably been considerably overstated" because the technology cannot control offenders' movement. They predict that house arrest will continue primarily to be used for low-risk offenders and will play little role as a custody alternative.

Thus, while a fair amount has been learned about the operation and management of electronic monitoring systems, about technology, and about implementation of new programs (e.g., Baumer and Mendelsohn 1992; Watts and Glaser 1992), the most comprehensive review of the research observes that "we know very little about either home confinement or electronic monitoring" (Baumer and Mendelsohn 1992,

p. 66). There seems little reason to believe that house arrest is any less vulnerable to net widening than is ISP or likely to achieve different findings on recidivism.

D. Day Reporting Centers

Day reporting centers, like the remaining two sanctions discussed, community service and day fines, differ from those discussed so far in that they were developed earlier and much more extensively outside the United States than in. The earliest American day reporting centers—places in which offenders spend their days under surveillance and participating in treatment and training programs while sleeping elsewhere—date from the mid-1980s. The English precursors, originally called day centers and now probation centers, began operation in the early 1970s. Most of our knowledge of American day reporting centers comes from descriptive writing; no published literature as yet provides credible findings on the important empirical questions.

The English programs date from creation of four "day-training centres" established under the Criminal Justice Act of 1972, charged to provide intensive training programs for persistent petty offenders whose criminality was believed rooted in general social inadequacy, and from creation of ad hoc day centers for serious offenders that were set up by a number of local probation agencies. The training centers for a number of reasons were adjudged unsuccessful and were soon canceled.

The probation-run day centers, however, thrived, becoming the "flavor of the month" after enabling legislation was enacted in 1982, numbering at least eighty by 1985, and serving thousands of offenders by the late 1980s (Mair 1993*b*, p. 6). Programs vary, with some emphasizing control and surveillance more than others, some operating as a therapeutic community, and most offering a wide range of (mostly compulsory) activities. The maximum term of involvement is sixty days, and some programs have set thirty-day or forty-five-day limits.

A major Home Office study (Mair 1988) concluded that "most centres unequivocally saw their aim as diversion from custody" (Mair 1993*b*, p. 6), that more than half of the participating offenders had previously been imprisoned, and that 47 percent had six or more prior convictions. A later reconviction study (Mair and Nee 1992) found a two-year reconviction rate of 63 percent. However, Mair writes, though "on the face of it this may look high . . . the offenders targeted by centres represent a very high-risk group in terms of probability of reconviction" (Mair 1993*b*, p. 6). In addition, the reconviction data did not distinguish between those who completed the program and those who failed. The results were seen as so promising that the Criminal Justice Act of 1991 envisioned a substantial expansion in use of day reporting centers.

A 1989 survey for the National Institute of Justice identified twenty-two day reporting centers in eight states (Parent 1990), though many others have since opened. Most American centers opened after 1985. The best-known (at least the best-documented) centers were established in Massachusetts—in Springfield (Hampton County Sheriff's Department) and in Boston (the Metropolitan Day Reporting Center)—and both were based in part on the model provided by the English day centers (Larivee 1991; McDevitt and Miliano 1992).

As with the English centers, American programs vary widely. Many are back-end programs into which offenders are released early from jail or prison. Some, however, are front-end programs to which offenders are sentenced by judges, and some are used as alternatives to pretrial detention (Parent 1990). Programs range in duration from forty days to nine months, and program content varies widely (Parent 1991). Most require development of hour-by-hour schedules of each participant's activities; some are highly intensive with ten-or-more supervision contacts per day; and a few include twenty-four-hour-per-day electronic monitoring (McDevitt and Miliano 1992). Unfortunately, no substantial evaluations have been published (a number of small in-house evaluations are cited in Larivee [1991] and McDevitt and Miliano [1992]).

E. Community Service

Community service is the most underused intermediate sanction in the United States. Used in many countries as a mid-level penalty to replace short prison terms for moderately severe crimes, community service in the United States is used primarily as a probation condition or as a penalty for trifling crimes like motor vehicle offenses. This is a pity because community service is a burdensome penalty that meets with widespread public approval (e.g., Doble, Immerwahr, and Robinson 1991), is inexpensive to administer, produces public value, and can be scaled to a degree to the seriousness of crimes.

Doing work to benefit the community as a substitute for other punishments for crime has a history that dates at least from Imperial Rome. Modern use, however, is conventionally dated from a 1960s effort by judges in Alameda County, California, to avoid having to impose fines for traffic violations on low-income women, when they knew that many would be unable to pay and would be in danger of being sent to jail as a result.

The California program attracted widespread interest and influenced the establishment of community service programs in the United States and elsewhere. The English pilot projects in the early 1970s (Young 1979), followed by Scottish pilots in the late 1970s (McIvor 1992), discussed below, both led to programs that have been fully institutionalized as a penalty that lies between probation and imprisonment in those countries' sentencing tariffs. Many millions of dollars were spent in the 1970s by the American Law Enforcement Assistance Administration, for programs for adults, and by the Office for Juvenile Justice and Delinquency Prevention, for programs for children, but with little lasting effect (McDonald 1992).

Community service did not come into widespread use as a prison alternative in the United States (Pease [1985] and McDonald [1986] provide detailed accounts with many references). Largely as a result, there has been little substantial research on the effectiveness of community service as an intermediate punishment (Pease 1985; Morris and Tonry 1990, chap. 6; McDonald 1992).

With the exception of one major American study (McDonald 1986), the most ambitious evaluation research has been carried out elsewhere. In England and Wales, Scotland, and the Netherlands, community service orders (CSOs) were statutorily authorized with the express aim that they serve as an alternative to short-term incarceration. In each of those countries, research was undertaken to discover whether CSOs were being used as replacements for short-term prison sentences (generally, yes, in about half of cases) and whether their use had any effect on recidivism rates for new crimes (generally, no). The American study, of a pilot community service program in New York City intended to substitute for jail terms up to six months, reached similar results (McDonald 1986).

Community service orders in 1993 constituted 30 percent of all sentences for serious crimes in England and Wales (Home Office 1994). In law and in practice, CSOs are regarded as more intrusive and punitive than probation and are considered an appropriate substitute for imprisonment (Lloyd 1991). Community service orders can involve between 40 and 240 hours of work supervised by a community service officer; failure to participate or cooperate can result in revocation. It is generally estimated that half of those sentenced to community service would otherwise be sentenced to prison and half to less severe penalties (Pease 1985). Reoffending rates are believed and generally found to be neither higher nor lower than those of comparable offenders sent to prison (Pease 1985).

The Scottish experience trails several years behind the English but closely resembles it. An experimental program was established in 1977; permanent enabling legislation was enacted in 1978; and CSOs were implemented nationwide in the early 1980s. Offenders are sentenced to 40–240 hours of work to be completed within one year. A five-year-long evaluation concluded that half of offenders sentenced to CSOs would otherwise have been confined, that both judges and offenders thought community service an appropriate penalty, and that reconviction rates after three years (63 percent) compared favorably with reconviction rates following incarceration (McIvor 1992, 1993).

The story in the Netherlands, where 10 percent of convicted offenders were sentenced to community service in 1992, and where government policy calls for successive annual 10 percent increases in the number of CSOs ordered, is similar. Pilot projects began in 1981 with the express aim of establishing a penalty that would be used in place of short terms of imprisonment. The British pattern of a maximum sentence of 240 hours to be performed within one year was followed. Evaluations reached the by-now expected conclusion that recidivism rates were no worse but that judges were using CSOs both for otherwise prison-bound and otherwise suspended sentence-bound offenders (with the balance as yet unknown) (van Kalmthout and Tak 1992; Tak 1994a, 1994b). In 1989, the Penal Code was amended to institutionalize CSOs as authorized sanctions.

The only well-documented American community service project, operated by the Vera Institute of Justice, was established in 1979 in the Bronx, one of the boroughs of New York, and eventually spread to Manhattan, Brooklyn, and Queens. The program was designed as a credible penalty for repetitive property offenders who had previously been sentenced to probation or jail and who faced a six-month or longer jail term for the current conviction. Offenders were sentenced to seventy hours community service under the supervision of Vera foremen. Participants were told that attendance would be closely monitored and that nonattendance and noncooperation would be punished. An agreement was struck with the judiciary that immediate arrest warrants would be issued and prompt revocation hearings held for noncompliant participants. The goal was to draw half of participants from the target prison-bound group and half from offenders with less extensive records; after initial judicial reluctance was overcome (when only a third were prison diversions), the fifty-fifty balance was achieved. An extensive and sophisticated evaluation concluded that recidivism rates were unaffected by the program, that prison diversion goals were being met, and that the program saved taxpayers' money (McDonald 1986, 1992).

For offenders who do not present unacceptable risks of future violent (including sexual) crimes, a punitive sanction that costs much less than prison to implement, that promises no higher reoffending rates, and that creates negligible risks of violence by those who would otherwise be confined has much to commend it.

Both American and European research and experience show that community service can serve as a meaningful, cost-effective sanction for offenders who would otherwise have been imprisoned. Why it has not been used in that way in the United States is a matter for conjecture, to which I return in Section III below.

F. Monetary Penalties

Monetary penalties for nontrivial crimes have yet to catch on in the United States. That is not to deny that millions of fines are imposed every year. Studies conducted as part of a fifteen-year program of fines research coordinated by the Vera Institute of Justice showed that fines are nearly the sole penalty for traffic offenses and in many courts are often imposed for misdemeanors (Hillsman, Sichel, and Mahoney 1984; Cole et al. 1987). And in many courts, most fines are collected. Although ambiguous lines of authority and absence of institutional self-interest sometimes result in haphazard and ineffective collection, courts that wish to do so can be effective collectors (Cole 1992).

Nor is it to deny that convicted offenders in some jurisdictions are routinely ordered to pay restitution and in most jurisdictions are routinely ordered to pay growing lists of fees for probation supervision, for urinalyses, and for use of electronic monitoring equipment. A survey of monetary exactions from offenders carried out in the late 1980s identified more than thirty separate charges, penalties, and fees that were imposed by courts, administrative agencies, and legislatures (Mullaney 1988). These commonly included court costs, fines, restitution, and payments to victim compensation funds. They often included a variety of supervision and monitoring fees and, in some jurisdictions (including the federal system under the Sentencing Reform Act of

1984), extended to repayment to the government of the full costs of prosecution and of carrying out any sentence imposed.

The problem is neither that monetary penalties are not imposed nor that they cannot be collected, but that, as Cole and his colleagues reported when summarizing the results of a national survey of judges' attitudes about fines, "at present, judges do not regard the fine alone as a meaningful alternative to incarceration or probation" (Cole et al. 1987).

This American inability to see a fine as a serious penalty stands in marked contrast to the legal systems of other countries. In the Netherlands, the fine is legally presumed to be the preferred penalty for every crime, and Section 359(6) of the Code of Criminal Procedure requires judges to provide a statement of reasons in every case in which a fine is not imposed. In Germany in 1986, for another example, 81 percent of all sentenced adult criminals were ordered to pay a fine, including 73 percent of those convicted of crimes of violence (Hillsman and Greene 1992, p. 125). In Sweden in 1979, fines constituted 91 percent of all sentences (Casale 1981). In England in 1980, fines were imposed in 47 percent of convictions for indictable offenses (roughly equivalent to American felonies); these included 45 percent of convicted sex offenders, 24 percent of burglars, and half of those convicted of assault (Morris and Tonry 1990, chap. 4).

European monetary penalties for serious crimes take two forms. The first is the "day fine," in use in the Scandinavian countries since the turn of the century and in Germany since the 1970s, which scales fines both to the defendant's ability to pay (some measure of daily income) and to the seriousness of the crime (expressed as the number of daily income units assessed) (Grebing 1982). The second is the use of the fine as a prosecutorial diversion device; in exchange for paying the fine, often the amount that would have been imposed after conviction, the criminal charges are dismissed.

Only the day fine has attracted much American attention. Some of the efforts to establish day-fine systems are discussed below. First, though, some discussion of the remarkable success of prosecutorial diversion programs seems warranted. In Sweden, prosecutors routinely invite defendants they intend to charge to accept a fine calculated on day-fine principles in exchange for dismissal of the charges. Nearly 70 percent of fines are imposed in this way (Casale 1981; Morris and Tonry 1990, p. 144).

Under Section 153a of the German Code of Criminal Procedure, in effect since 1974, the prosecutor, if "convinced of the defendant's guilt," may propose a conditional dismissal under which the defendant agrees to pay a fine. If the charges are serious, the judge must approve the arrangement (approval is seldom withheld). The defendant need not confess guilt. Two hundred forty thousand cases were resolved by conditional dismissal in 1989, constituting a 16 percent reduction in indictments that would otherwise have been filed (Weigend 1993).

In the Netherlands, the 1983 Financial Penalties Act authorized prosecutors to resolve criminal cases by means of an arrangement comparable to the German conditional dismissal. Defendants charged with crimes bearing maximum possible six-year prison sentences are eligible. The prosecution is terminated but can be reinstated if the defendant commits a new crime within three years. The prosecutorial diversion program has been credited with keeping the number of criminal trials stable between 1980 and 1992, despite a 60 percent increase in recorded crime. Two thirds of criminal cases are settled out of court by prosecutors (Tak 1994*a*).

Despite the substantial successes of fines as part of prosecutorial diversion programs in Sweden, Germany, and the Netherlands, the day fine has received principal attention as a penal import from Europe. The results to date are at best mildly promising. The initial pilot project was conducted in Staten Island, New York, in 1988–89, again under the auspices of the Vera Institute of Justice. Judges, prosecutors, and other court personnel were included in the planning, and implementation was remarkably successful. Most judges cooperated with the new voluntary scheme, the distribution of fines imposed changed in ways that showed that judges were following the system, the average fine imposed increased by 25 percent, the total amount ordered on all defendants increased by 14 percent, and 70 percent of defendants paid their fines in full (Hillsman and Greene 1992).

The Staten Island findings, while not unpromising, are subject to two important caveats. First, the participating court had limited jurisdiction and handled only misdemeanors; the use of day fines for felonies thus remains untested. Second, applicable statutes limited total fines for any charge to $250, $500, or $1,000, depending on the misdemeanor class, and thus artificially capped fines at those levels and precluded meaningful implementation of the scheme in relation to other than the lowest-income defendants.

A second modest pilot project was conducted for twelve weeks in 1989 in Milwaukee (McDonald, Greene, and Worzella 1992), and four projects funded by the Bureau of Justice Assistance operated for various periods between 1992 and 1994 in Maricopa County (Phoenix), Arizona; Bridgeport, Connecticut; Polk County, Iowa; and Coos, Josephine, Malheur, and Marion Counties in Oregon (Turner 1992). The Milwaukee project applied only to noncriminal violations, resulted in reduced total collections, and was abandoned. The Phoenix project, known as FARE (for Financial Assessments Related to Employability), was conceived as a mid-level sanction *between unsupervised and supervised probation*. The Iowa pilot included only misdemeanants, and the Oregon projects included misdemeanants and probationable felonies (excluding Marion County, the largest, which covered only misdemeanants). Only in the Connecticut project did the pilot cover a range of felonies and misdemeanors.

A RAND Corporation evaluation of the Arizona, Connecticut, Iowa, and Oregon projects was funded by the National Institute of Justice, but no results had been released by June 1995. Given the limited reach of the projects, however, the results are unlikely to demonstrate that day fines show promise of becoming an intermediate sanction capable—as in Europe—of diverting large numbers of felony offenders from prison.

A further cautionary note comes from England and Wales, which tried, unsuccessfully, to launch a day-fine system (because calculations were based on weekly rather than daily income, it was called a "unit-fine" system). Following a pattern that previous mentions of English research on electronic monitoring and ISP will make familiar, pilot projects to test the feasibility of unit fines were established in four magistrates' courts and evaluated by the Home Office Research and Planning Unit. The findings were positive: magistrates and other court personnel were pleased with the new system, anticipated problems about learning defendants' incomes proved soluble, low-income defendants received smaller fines, and more fines were fully paid, and earlier, than previously (Moxon, Sutton, and Hedderman 1990; Moxon 1992). As a result, the Criminal Justice Act of 1991, which effected a substantial overhaul of English sentencing laws, established a national system of unit fines to take effect in October 1992.

The unit-fines system was abandoned seven months later. The reasons remain unclear. The immediate precipitant was a series of media stories of preposterous sentences that discredited the entire system. In one case, a defendant was fined £1,200 (late in 1994, = U.S.$1,920) for throwing a potato chip bag on the ground. In another much-publicized case, a defendant was fined £500 for illegal parking after his car, worth £250, broke down on a road where parking was prohibited (Moxon 1993).

Why those (and many comparable) cases were sentenced as they were, and why the government so quickly repudiated its own innovation, are unclear. The immediate problem was overly literal application of the system. The minimum unit was set at £4 and the maximum unit at £100. To deal with the problem of defendants who do not provide income information, the policy was set in some courts that the maximum authorized amount would be presumed to apply in such cases. What was not planned for was default cases in which the defendant does not appear. What could have been a £20 fine in the illegal parking case became instead £500. In the littering case, the £1,200 fine was reduced to £48 on appeal.

The specific problems that deprived the scheme of its credibility and led to its repeal were soluble. Some observers speculated that many magistrates disapproved in principle of what were in effect sentencing guidelines for fines and used overly literal enforcement to undermine it. Some blamed the developers for setting the maximum unit amount too high (£20 was the limit in the pilot projects) and for not anticipating foreseeable problems in implementation and application. Whatever the real explanation, the system is no longer, and developers of day-fine systems in the United States will ignore the English experience at their peril.

III. Is There a Future for Intermediate Sanctions?

Despite the seemingly disheartening evaluation findings that suggest that most intermediate sanctions do not reduce recidivism, corrections costs, and prison crowding while simultaneously enhancing public safety, there is a future for intermediate sanctions.

There is a need to develop credible, enforceable sanctions between prison and probation that can provide appropriate deserved penalties for offenders convicted of mid-level crimes, and numerous studies document the capacity of well-managed corrections departments to implement such programs. There is a need, for their sake and ours, to help offenders establish conventional, law-abiding patterns of living, and the evaluation literature suggests ways that can be facilitated. There is a need to develop intermediate sanctions that can serve as cost-effective substitutes for confinement, and the evaluation literature suggests how that can be done. Finally, there is a need to devise ways to assure that intermediate sanctions are used for the kinds of offenders for whom particular programs were created, and experience with parole and sentencing guidelines shows how that can be done.

Three major obstacles stand in the way. The first, the most difficult, is the modern American preoccupation with absolute severity of punishment and the related widespread view that only imprisonment counts. The average lengths of prison sentences in the United States are much greater in the United States than in other Western countries (Tonry 1995, table 7-1). The ten-, twenty-, and thirty-year minimum sentences that are in vogue for drug crimes are unimaginable in most countries. Despite a trebling in the average severity of prison sentences for violent crimes between 1976 and 1989 established by the National Academy of Sciences Panel on the Understanding and Control of Violence (Reiss and Roth 1993), and additional increases since 1989, federal crime legislation passed in 1994 conditions prison construction grants to states on substantial additional increases in sentences for violent offenders, using 1993 averages as a base (Wallace 1994).

This absolute severity frustrates efforts to devise intermediate sanctions for the psychological (not to mention political) reason that few other sanctions seem commensurable with a multiyear prison sentence. Data presented above, for example, show that half or more offenders convicted of violent crimes in Sweden, Germany, and England are sentenced to fines (abandonment of unit fines in England did not result in a reduction in use of fines, which continued to be imposed on a "tariff" fixed-amount basis).

In those countries, the prison sentences thereby avoided would have involved months or at most a few years, making a burdensome financial penalty an imaginable alternative. By contrast, most of the American day-fine pilot projects would use day fines as punishments for misdemeanors or noncriminal ordinance violations or as a mid-level punishment between supervised and unsupervised probation. Likewise, with the rare exception of New York's community service project started by the Vera Institute, CSOs are generally ordered as probation conditions and not as sentences in their own right.

Data presented above, for another example, document successful efforts to replace prison sentences of six or fewer months (moderately severe penalties in those countries) with day fines in Germany (Weigend 1992) and with community service orders in the Netherlands (Tak 1994b). In Sweden, however, less than a quarter of prison sentences are to terms of six months or longer (Jareborg 1994), and in the

Netherlands less than 15 percent are for a year or longer. Equivalent crimes in the United States would be punished by terms measured in years; in 1991, 90 percent of state inmates were sentenced to terms longer than one year, and 57 percent to terms longer than five years (Beck et al. 1993).

Because the modern emphasis on absolute severity of crime is the product of partisan and ideological politics, it will not readily be changed. It does, however, stand in the way of substantial development of a continuum of punishments in which moderately punitive and intrusive sanctions serve as penalties—in place of incarceration—for moderately severe crimes.

The second, not unrelated obstacle to fuller development of intermediate sanctions is widespread commitment to "just deserts" rationales for punishment and the collateral idea that the severity of punishment should vary directly with the seriousness of the crime. This has been translated in the federal and most state sentencing guidelines systems into policies that tie punishments to the offender's crime and criminal history and little else.

Such policies and their commitment to "proportionality in punishment" constitute a gross oversimplification of the cases that come before criminal courts. Crimes that share a label can be very different; robberies range from schoolyard takings of basketballs to gangland assaults on banks. Offenders committing the same crime can be very different; a thief may have been motivated by a sudden impulse, by the need to feed a hungry child, by a craving to buy drugs, or by a conscious choice to make a living as a thief.

Punishments likewise vary. Despite a common label, two years' imprisonment can be served in a maximum security prison of fear and violence, in a minimum security camp, at home under house arrest, or in some combination of these and other regimes. Even a single punishment may be differently experienced: three years' imprisonment may be a rite-of-passage for a young gang member, a death sentence for a frail seventy-year-old, or the ruin of the lives of an employed forty-year-old man and his dependent spouse and children.

Nonetheless, commitment to ideas of proportionality is widespread, and it circumscribes the roles that intermediate sanctions can play. Although few people would disagree with the empirical observations in the preceding paragraph, sentencing policies based on ideas of proportionality somehow reify the sentencing categories into something meaningful. If guidelines specify a twenty-four-month prison term for offense X with criminal history Y, it seems unfair to sentence one offender to community service or house arrest when another similarly situated (in the narrow terms of the guidelines) is sentenced to twenty-four months. It seems more unfair to sentence one offender subject to a twenty-four-month guidelines sentence to house arrest when an offender convicted of a less serious crime receives an eighteen-month prison sentence.

Commitment to proportionality interacts with the modern penchant for severe penalties. If crimes punished by months of incarceration in other countries are punished in years in the United States, comparisons between offenders are more stark. If in Sweden two offenses are ordinarily punished by thirty- and sixty-day prison terms, imposition of a day-fine order on the more serious offender—out of consideration for the effects of a prison term on his family and employment—produces a contrast between a thirty-day sentence and a sixty-unit day fine. Convert the example to American presumptive sentences of two and four years, and the contrast is jarring between any intermediate sanction and a two-year sentence for someone convicted of a less serious crime.

Net widening is the third obstacle to further development of intermediate sanctions. As discussed earlier, there is a natural tension between practitioners making decisions in individual cases and policy makers trying to take a systems perspective and set policy goals for bureaucratic organizations. In a jurisdiction that lacks well-developed community penalties, it is understandable that judges and prosecutors want to use newly available resources for what seem to them suitable offenders. From the perspective of system planners, however, sentencing otherwise probation-bound offenders to a program intended for prison-bound offenders frustrates the purpose of the program.

There are two solutions to the net-widening problem. The first is to shift control over program placements from judges to corrections officials wherever possible. For some programs such as boot camps and back-end forms of ISP and house arrest, this is relatively easy and would make it likelier that such programs would achieve their goals of saving money and prison space without increasing recidivism rates.

Transfers of authority to corrections officials can, however, at best be a partial solution. No one (whom we know or can imagine) wants all sentencing authority shifted into bureaucratic hands, and judges therefore will retain authority to decide who will be sent to jail or prison. A little more plausible alternative would be to limit judicial authority to the choice between prison and probation and to allow probation and prison authorities to decide what other sanctions (house arrest, ISP, treatment participation, etc.) should be applied either as probation conditions or as custodial regimes.

Few people would want to place full authority over questions of confinement in bureaucratic hands. Judges are after all concerned with questions of liberty and justice, and most people would probably rest easier having judges making threshold decisions about confinement. In addition, it is hard to imagine any role for fines and community service in a sentencing system where judges lacked authority to order such sentences.

The alternative is to structure judges' decisions about intermediate sanctions by use of sentencing guidelines. A substantial body of evaluation and other research demonstrates that well-conceived and implemented guidelines systems can change sentencing patterns in a jurisdiction and achieve high levels of judicial compliance (sometimes, as in the federal guidelines, grudging compliance) (Tonry 1993).

Most state guidelines systems, however, establish presumptions for who is sent to state prisons, and for how long, but do not set presumptions concerning nonprison sentences or choices between prison and other sanctions. Two broad approaches for setting guidelines for nonprison sentences have been tried (the literature is tiny: von Hirsch, Wasik, and Green 1989; Morris and Tonry 1990).

The first, which seems to have been a dead end, is to establish "punishment units" in which all sanctions can be expressed. Thus, a year's confinement might equal ten units, a month of house arrest three units, and a month's community service two units. A twenty-unit sentence could be satisfied by any sanction or combination of sanctions equaling twenty. This idea was taken furthest in Oregon, where sentencing guidelines, in addition to setting presumptive ranges for jail and prison sentences, specified a number of punishment units for offenders not presumed bound for state prison. Oregon, however, never set policies governing unit values, sometimes metaphorically described as "exchange rates," and neither there nor anywhere else has the idea been taken further.

The overwhelming problem lies in the idea of proportionality mentioned earlier and can be illustrated by Washington State's more modest effort at exchange rates. Partial confinement and community service were authorized as substitutes for presumptive prison terms on the basis of one day's partial confinement or three day's community service for one day of confinement. The partial confinement/confinement exchange is probably workable (for short sentences; house arrest, assuming that to count as partial confinement, is seldom imposed for more than a few months), but the community service exchange is not.

Starting with the idea that imprisonment is more unpleasant than community service, the Washington State Sentencing Guidelines Commission (1993) initially decided that the exchange must be governed by an idea of comparable intrusion in the offender's life; hence, three eight-hour days' community service per day in prison. The difficulty is that community service programs to be credible must be enforced, and experience in this country and elsewhere instructs that they must be short. That is why the New York program provided seventy hours' obligation, and the Dutch, English, and Scottish programs established an upper limit of 240 hours. Under Washington's policy, that range would permit community service in place of three to ten days' confinement.

It is easy to criticize the Oregon commission for not carrying its innovation further and the Washington commission for lack of imagination, but that would be unfair. Working out exchange rates in a system predicated on strong ideas of proportionality in punishment is very difficult, if not impossible. If punitive literalism governs, the range for substitution between prison and community penalties is tiny. A system like New York's community service program—which substitutes seventy hours' work for six months' jail—can be justified (the idea was to give repetitive property offenders some meaningful enforced penalty rather than impose a jail term that no one expected would have deterrent effects), but it requires a loosening of proportionality constraints that no sentencing commission has yet been prepared to accept. The Pennsylvania Commission on Sentencing in 1993 gave serious consideration to a punishment unit system, but abandoned it when the problem of exchange rates proved insoluble. (There are other problems with the punishment unit approach: inevitably the exchange rates are arbitrary; if conditions like treatment participation, drug testing, and electronic monitoring are given unit values, comparisons between offenders become even more implausible.)

The other approach is to establish different areas of a guidelines grid in which different presumptions about choice of sentence govern. Both North Carolina and Pennsylvania adopted such systems in 1994. One set of crime/criminal history combinations is presumed appropriate only for prison sentences; a second is presumed subject to a judicial choice between prison sentences or intensive community sanctions (including split sentences with elements of both); a third is presumed subject to a choice between intensive or nonintensive community sanctions (or some of both); and a fourth is presumed subject only to nonintensive community sanctions. A system like this was proposed by the District of Columbia Superior Court Sentencing Commission in 1987 but never took effect. The Pennsylvania and North Carolina systems took effect in the fall of 1994; how they will work in practice remains to be seen.

Readers, we hope, will draw at least six conclusions from this essay. First, for offenders who do not present unacceptable risks of violence, well-managed intermediate sanctions offer a cost-effective way to keep them in the community at less cost than imprisonment and with no worse later prospect for criminality.

Second, boot camps, house arrest, and intensive supervision are highly vulnerable to net widening when entry is controlled by judges. For boot camps, the solution is easy: have corrections officials select participants from among admitted prisoners. For house arrest and ISP, the solution is less easy: corrections officials can control entry to back-end programs, and sentencing guidelines may be able to structure judges' decisions about admission to front-end programs.

Third, community service and monetary penalties remain woefully underdeveloped in the United States, and much could be learned from Europe. Day fines remain as yet a promising idea, but it has not yet been demonstrated that they can win acceptance as penalties for nontrivial crimes. Conditional discharges, in which convictable defendants pay a substantial fine in exchange for conditional dismissal of charges, like those common in Sweden, the Netherlands, and Germany, remain unexplored as a potentially useful European penal import.

Fourth, front-end intermediate sanctions are unlikely to come into widespread use as prison alternatives unless sentencing theories and policies become more expansive and move away from oversimplified ideas about proportionality in punishment.

Fifth, intermediate sanctions may offer promise as a way to get and keep offenders in drug and other treatment programs. With drug treatment programs, at least, there is evidence that coerced treatment programs can reduce both later drug use and later crimes, and there is evidence in the ISP and boot camp literatures that these programs can increase treatment participation.

Sixth, there is no free lunch. The failure of most intermediate sanctions to achieve promised reductions in recidivism, cost, and prison use were never realistic, though for the most part they were offered in good faith. Intermediate sanctions can reduce costs and divert offenders from imprisonment, but those results are not easy to obtain.

REFERENCES

Allen, Francis A. 1964. *The Borderland of Criminal Justice*. Chicago: University of Chicago Press.
Anglin, Douglas, and Yih-Ing Hser.. 1990. "Treatment of Drug Abuse." In *Drugs and Crime*, edited by Michael Tonry and James Q. Wilson. Volume 13 of *Crime and Justice: A Review of Research*, edited by Michael Tonry and Norval Morris. Chicago: University of Chicago Press.
Arthur D. Little, Inc. 1981. "An Evaluation of Parole Guidelines in Four Jurisdictions." Report prepared for the National Institute of Corrections. Washington, D.C., and Cambridge, Mass.: Arthur D. Little, Inc.
Austin, James, Michael Jones, and Melissa Bolyard. 1993. *The Growing Use of Jail Boot Camps: The Current State of the Art*. Research in Brief. Washington, D.C.: National Institute of Justice.
Baird, S. C., and D. Wagner. 1990. "Measuring Diversion: The Florida Community Control Program." *Crime and Delinquency* 36:112–25.
Banks, J., A. L. Porter, R. L. Rardin, T. R. Silver, and V. E. Unger. 1977. *Phase I Evaluation of Intensive Special Probation Projects*. Washington, D.C.: National Institute of Law Enforcement and Criminal Justice, Law Enforcement Assistance Administration.
Barr, William. 1992. *The Case for More Incarceration*. Washington, D.C.: U.S. Department of Justice, Office of Policy Development.
Baumer, Terry L., M. G. Maxfield, and R. I. Mendelsohn. 1993. "A Comparative Analysis of Three Electronically Monitored Home Detention Programs." *Justice Quarterly* 10:121–42.
Baumer, Terry L., and Robert I. Mendelsohn. 1992. "Electronically Monitored Home Confinement: Does It Work?" In *Smart Sentencing: The Emergence of Intermediate Sanctions*, edited by James M. Byrne, Arthur J. Lurigio, and Joan Petersilia. Newbury Park, Calif.: Sage.
Beck, Allen, et al. 1993. *Survey of State Prison Inmates, 1991*. Washington, D.C.: Bureau of Justice Statistics.
Biles, David. 1993. "Noncustodial Penalties in Australia." *Overcrowded Times* 4(1):7–9.
Blomberg, Thomas G., William Bales, and Karen Reed. 1993. "Intermediate Punishment: Redistributing or Extending Social Control?" *Crime, Law, and Social Change* 19:187–201.
Blumstein, Alfred, Jacqueline Cohen, Susan E. Martin, and Michael Tonry, eds. 1983. *Research on Sentencing: The Search for Reform*, 2 vols. Washington, D.C.: National Academy Press.

Brody, S. R. 1976. *The Effectiveness of Sentencing: A Review of the Literature.* London: H.M. Stationery Office.

Bureau of Justice Statistics. 1994. *Prisoners in 1993.* Washington, D.C.: U.S. Department of Justice, Bureau of Justice Statistics.

Byrne, James M., and Linda M. Kelly. 1989. "Restructuring Probation as an Intermediate Sanction: An Evaluation of the Massachusetts Intensive Probation Supervision Program." Final report to the National Institute of Justice. Lowell, Mass.: University of Lowell, Department of Criminal Justice.

Byrne, James M., Arthur J. Lurigio, and Joan Petersilia. 1992. *Smart Sentencing: The Emergence of Intermediate Sanctions.* Newbury Park, Calif.: Sage.

Byrne, James M., and April Pattavina. 1992. "The Effectiveness Issue: Assessing What Works in the Adult Community Corrections System." In *Smart Sentencing: The Emergence of Intermediate Sanctions,* edited by James M. Byrne, Arthur J. Lurigio, and Joan Petersilia. Newbury Park, Calif.: Sage.

Carter, R. M., J. Robinson, and L. T. Wilkins. 1967. *The San Francisco Project: A Study of Federal Probation and Parole.* Berkeley: University of California Press.

Casale, Silvia G. 1981. "Fines in Europe." Fines in Sentencing Working Paper no. 10. New York: Vera Institute of Justice.

Clear, Todd. 1987. "The New Intensive Supervision Movement." Paper presented at the annual meeting of the American Society of Criminology, Montreal, November.

Clear, Todd R., and James M. Byrne. 1992. "The Future of Intermediate Sanctions: Questions to Consider." In *Smart Sentencing: The Emergence of Intermediate Sanctions,* edited by James M. Byrne, Arthur J. Lurigio, and Joan Petersilia. Newbury Park, Calif.: Sage.

Cole, George F. 1992. "Monetary Sanctions: The Problem of Compliance." In *Smart Sentencing: The Emergence of Intermediate Sanctions,* edited by James M. Byrne, Arthur J. Lurigio, and Joan Petersilia. Newbury Park, Calif.: Sage.

Cole, George F., Barry Mahoney, Marlene Thornton, and Roger A. Hanson. 1987. *The Practices and Attitudes of Trial Court Judges Regarding Fines as a Criminal Sanction.* Washington, D.C.: National Institute of Justice.

DiIulio, John J. 1990. "Crime and Punishment in Wisconsin." *Wisconsin Policy Research Institute Report* 3(7):1–56.

DiIulio, John J., and Anne M. Piehl. 1991. "Does Prison Pay?" Unpublished manuscript. Princeton, N.J.: Princeton University, Center of Domestic and Comparative Policy Studies.

District of Columbia Superior Court, Sentencing Guidelines Commission. 1987. *Initial Report of the Superior Court Sentencing Guidelines Commission—the Development of Felony Sentencing Guidelines.* Washington, D.C.: D.C. Superior Court, Sentencing Guidelines Commission.

Doble, John, Stephen Immerwahr, and Amy Robinson. 1991. *Punishing Criminals: The People of Delaware Consider the Options.* New York: Edna McConnell Clark Foundation.

Doble, John, and Josh Klein. 1989. *Punishing Criminals: The Public's View. An Alabama Survey.* New York: Edna McConnell Clark Foundation.

Erwin, Billie. 1987. *Evaluation of Intensive Probation Supervision in Georgia.* Atlanta: Georgia Department of Corrections.

Erwin, Billie, and Lawrence Bennett. 1987. *New Dimensions in Probation: Georgia's experience with Intensive Probation Supervision.* Research in Brief. Washington, D.C.: National Institute of Justice

Florida Legislature. 1991. *An Alternative to Florida's Current Sentencing Guidelines—a Report to the Legislature and the Sentencing Guidelines Commission.* Tallahassee: Florida Legislature, Economic and Demographic Research Division, Joint Legislative Management Committee.

Folkard, M. S., et al. 1974. *IMPACT, Vol. 1: The Design of the Probation Experiment and an Interim Evaluation.* London: H.M. Stationery Office.

———. 1976. *IMPACT, Vol. 2: The Results of the Experiment.* London: H.M. Stationery Office.

Ford, Daniel, and Annesley K. Schmidt. 1985. *Electronically Monitored Home Confinement.* Research in Action. Washington, D.C.: National Institute of Justice.

Gendreau, Paul, Francis T. Cullen, and James Bonta. 1994. "Intensive Rehabilitation Supervision: The Next Generation in Community Corrections?" *Federal Probation* 58:72–78.

Grebing, Gerhardt. 1982. "The Fine in Comparative Law: A Survey of 21 Countries." Occasional Paper no. 9. Cambridge: University of Cambridge, Institute of Criminology.

Hillsman, Sally. 1990. "Fines and Day Fines." In *Crime and Justice: A Review of Research*, vol. 12, edited by Michael Tonry and Norval Morris. Chicago: University of Chicago Press.

Hillsman, Sally, and Judith A. Greene. 1992. "The Use of Fines as an Intermediate Sanction." In *Smart Sentencing: The Emergence of Intermediate Sanctions*, edited by James M. Byrne, Arthur J. Lurigio, and Joan Petersilia. Newbury Park, Calif.: Sage.

Hillsman, Sally, Joyce Sichel, and Barry Mahoney. 1984. *Fines in Sentencing: A Study of the Use of the Fine as a Criminal Sanction.* Washington, D.C.: National Institute of Justice.

Home Office. 1994. *Criminal Statistics, England and Wales.* London: H.M. Stationery Office.

Jareborg, Nils. 1994. "The Swedish Sentencing Reform." In *The Politics of Sentencing Reform*, edited by Chris Clarkson and Rod Morgan. Oxford: Oxford University Press.

Kleiman, Mark A. R., and David Cavanagh. 1990. "A Cost-Benefit Analysis of Prison Cell Construction and Alternative Sanctions." Unpublished manuscript. Cambridge, Mass.: Harvard University, Kennedy School of Government, Guggenheim Program in Criminal Justice Policy and Management.

Larivee, John J. 1991. "Day Reporting in Massachusetts: Supervision, Sanction, and Treatment." *Overcrowded Times* 2(1):7–8.

Lilly, Robert J. 1993. "Electronic Monitoring in the U.S.: An Update." *Overcrowded Times* 4(5): 4, 15.

Lipton, Douglas, Robert Martinson, and Judith Wilks. 1975. *The Effectiveness of Correctional Treatment: A Survey of Correctional Treatment Evaluations.* New York: Praeger.

Lloyd, C. 1991. *National Standards for Community Service Orders: The First Two Years of Operation.* London: Home Office Research and Planning Unit.

Lurigio, Arthur J., and Joan Petersilia. 1992. "The Emergence of Intensive Probation Supervision Programs in the United States." In *Smart Sentencing: The Emergence of Intermediate Sanctions,* edited by James M. Byrne, Arthur J. Lurigio, and Joan Petersilia. Newbury Park, Calif.: Sage.

MacKenzie, Doris Layton. 1993. "Boot Camp Prisons 1993." *National Institute of Justice Journal* 227:21–28.

———. 1994. "Boot Camps: A National Assessment." *Overcrowded Times* 5(4):1, 14–18.

MacKenzie, Doris Layton, and Dale Parent. 1992. "Boot Camp Prisons for Young Offenders." In *Smart Sentencing: The Emergence of Intermediate Sanctions,* edited by James M. Byrne, Arthur J. Lurigio, and Joan Petersilia. Newbury Park, Calif.: Sage.

MacKenzie, Doris Layton, and A. Piquero. 1994. "The Impact of Shock Incarceration Programs on Prison Crowding." *Crime and Delinquency* 40:222–49.

MacKenzie, Doris Layton, and J. W. Shaw. 1990. "Inmate Adjustment and Change during Shock Incarceration: The Impact of Correctional Boot Camp Programs." *Justice Quarterly* 7(1):125–50.

MacKenzie, Doris Layton, and C. Souryal. 1993. "The Impact of Shock Incarceration on Technical Violations and New Criminal Activities." *Justice Quarterly* 10:463–87.

———. 1994. *Multi-Site Evaluation of Shock Incarceration.* Report to the National Institute of Justice. College Park: University of Maryland, Department of Criminology and Criminal Justice.

Mair, George. 1988. *Probation Day Centres.* London: H.M. Stationery Office.

———. 1993a. "Electronic Monitoring in England and Wales." *Overcrowded Times* 4(5):5, 12.

———. 1993b. "Day Centres in England and Wales." *Overcrowded Times* 4(2):5–7.

———. 1994. "Intensive Probation in England and Wales." *Overcrowded Times* 5(4):4–6.

Mair, George, and Claire Nee. 1990. *Electronic Monitoring: The Trials and Their Results.* London: H.M. Stationery Office.

———. 1992. "Day Centre Reconviction Rates." *British Journal of Criminology* 32:329–39.

Mair, George, et al. 1994. *Intensive Probation in England and Wales: An Evaluation.* London: H.M. Stationery Office.

Maxfield, M., and T. Baumer. 1990. "Home Detention with Electronic Monitoring: Comparing Pretrial and Postconviction Programs." *Crime and Delinquency* 36:521–36.

McCarthy, Belinda, ed. 1987. *Intermediate Punishments: Intensive Supervision, Home Confinement, and Electronic Surveillance.* Monsey, N.Y.: Criminal Justice Press.

McDevitt, Jack, and Robyn Miliano. 1992. "Day Reporting Centers: An Innovative Concept in Intermediate Sanctions." In *Smart Sentencing: The Emergence of Intermediate Sanctions*, edited by James M. Byrne, Arthur J. Lurigio, and Joan Petersilia. Newbury Park, Calif.: Sage.

McDonald, Douglas. 1986. *Punishment without Walls: Community Service Sentences in New York City*. New Brunswick, N.J.: Rutgers University Press.

———. 1992. "Punishing Labor: Unpaid Community Service as a Criminal Sentence." In *Smart Sentencing: The Emergence of Intermediate Sanctions*, edited by James M. Byrne, Arthur J. Lurigio, and Joan Petersilia. Newbury Park, Calif.: Sage.

McDonald, Douglas, Judith Greene, and Charles Worzella. 1992. *Day Fines in American Courts: The Staten Island and Milwaukee Experiments*. Issues and Practices. Washington, D.C.: National Institute of Justice.

McIvor, Gill. 1992. *Sentenced to Serve: The Operation and Impact of Community Service by Offenders*. Aldershot: Avebury.

———. 1993. "CSOs Succeed in Scotland." *Overcrowded Times* 4(3):1, 6–8.

Meachum, Larry R. 1986. "House Arrest: Oklahoma Experience." *Corrections Today* 48(4):102 ff.

Morris, Norval. 1974. *The Future of Imprisonment*. Chicago: University of Chicago Press.

Morris, Norval, and Michael Tonry. 1990. *Between Prison and Probation: Intermediate Punishments in a Rational Sentencing System*. New York: Oxford University Press.

Moxon, David. 1992. "England Adopts Day Fines." *Overcrowded Times* 3(3):5, 12.

———. 1993. "England Abandons Day Fines." *Overcrowded Times* 4(4):5, 10–11.

Moxon, David, Mike Sutton, and Carol Hedderman. 1990. *Unit Fines: Experiments in Four Courts*. London: H.M. Stationery Office.

Mullaney, Fahy G. 1988. *Economic Sanctions in Community Corrections*. Washington, D.C.: National Institute of Corrections.

National Conference of State Legislatures. 1993. *State Budget Actions—1993*. Denver: National Conference of State Legislatures.

National Institute of Justice. 1994. *Drug Use Forecasting (DUF)—1993 Annual Report*. Washington, D.C.: National Institute of Justice.

North Carolina Sentencing and Policy Advisory Commission. 1993. *Report to the 1993 Session of the General Assembly of North Carolina*. Raleigh: North Carolina Sentencing and Policy Advisory Commission.

Palumbo, Dennis J., Mary Clifford, and Joann K. Snyder-Joy. 1992. "From Net-widening to Intermediate Sanctions: The Transformation of Alternatives to Incarceration from Benevolence to Malevolence." In *Smart Sentencing: The Emergence of Intermediate Sanctions*, edited by James M. Byrne, Arthur J. Lurigio, and Joan Petersilia. Newbury Park, Calif.: Sage.

Parent, Dale. 1989. *Shock Incarceration: An Overview of Existing Programs*. Washington, D.C.: National Institute of Justice.

———. 1990. *Day Reporting Centers for Criminal Offenders: A Descriptive Analysis of Existing Programs*. Washington, D.C.: National Institute of Justice.

———. 1991. "Day Reporting Centers: An Emerging Intermediate Sanction." *Overcrowded Times* 2(1):6, 8.

———. 1994. "Boot Camps Failing to Achieve Goals." *Overcrowded Times* 5(4):8–11.

Pearson, Frank. 1987. *Final Report of Research on New Jersey's Intensive Supervision Program*. New Brunswick, N.J.: Rutgers University, Department of Sociology, Institute for Criminological Research.

Pease, Ken. 1985. "Community Service Orders." In *Crime and Justice: A Review of Research*, vol. 6, edited by Michael Tonry and Norval Morris. Chicago: University of Chicago Press.

Petersilia, Joan, Arthur J. Lurigio, and James M. Byrne. 1992. "Introduction: The Emergence of Intermediate Sanctions." In *Smart Sentencing: The Emergence of Intermediate Sanctions*, edited by James M. Byrne, Arthur J. Lurigio, and Joan Petersilia. Newbury Park, Calif.: Sage.

Petersilia, Joan, and Susan Turner. 1993. "Intensive Probation and Parole." In *Crime and Justice: A Review of Research*, vol. 17, edited by Michael Tonry. Chicago: University of Chicago Press.

President's Commission on Model State Drug Laws. 1993. *Final Report*. Washington, D.C.: U.S. Government Printing Office.

Public Agenda Foundation. 1993. *Punishing Criminals: The People of Pennsylvania Speak Out*. New York: Edna McConnell Clark Foundation.

Reiss, Albert J., Jr., and Jeffrey Roth, eds. 1993. *Understanding and Controlling Violence*. Report of the National Academy of Sciences Panel on the Understanding and Control of Violence. Washington, D.C.: National Academy Press.

Renzema, Marc. 1992. "Home Confinement Programs: Development, Implementation, and Impact." In *Smart Sentencing: The Emergence of Intermediate Sanctions*, edited by James M. Byrne, Arthur J. Lurigio, and Joan Petersilia. Newbury Park, Calif.: Sage.

Sechrest, Lee B., Susan O. White, and Elizabeth D. Brown, eds. 1979. *The Rehabilitation of Criminal Offenders: Problems and Prospects*. Washington, D.C.: National Academy Press.

Tak, Peter J.P. 1994a. "Sentencing and Punishment in the Netherlands." *Overcrowded Times* 5(5):5–8.

———. 1994b. "Sentencing in the Netherlands." *Acta Criminologica* 7:7–17.

Tonry, Michael. 1993. "Sentencing Commissions and Their Guidelines." In *Crime and Justice: A Review of Research*, vol. 17, edited by Michael Tonry. Chicago: University of Chicago Press.

———. 1995. *Malign Neglect: Race, Crime, and Punishment in America*. New York: Oxford University Press.

Tonry, Michael, and Kate Hamilton. 1995. *Intermediate Sanctions in Overcrowded Times*. Boston: Northeastern University Press.

Tonry, Michael, and Richard Will. 1988. "Intermediate Sanctions." Final Report submitted by Castine Research Corporation, Castine, Maine, to the National Institute of Justice.

Turner, Susan. 1992. "Day-Fine Projects Launched in Four Jurisdictions." *Overcrowded Times* 3(6):5–6.

U.S. General Accounting Office. 1990. *Intermediate Sanctions: Their Impacts on Prison Crowding, Costs, and Recidivism are Still Unclear.* Gaithersburg, Md.: U.S. General Accounting Office.

———. 1993. *Prison Boot Camps: Short-Term Prison Costs Reduced, but Long-Term Impact Uncertain.* Washington, D.C.: U.S. General Accounting Office. ˙

van Kalmthout, Anton M., and Peter J.P. Tak. 1992. *Sanctions-Systems in the Member-States of the Council of Europe: Deprivation of Liberty, Community Service, and Other Substitutes.* Boston: Kluwer.

von Hirsch, Andrew. 1976. *Doing Justice: The Choice of Punishments.* New York: Hill & Wang.

von Hirsch, Andrew, Martin Wasik, and Judith Greene. 1989. "Punishments in the Community and the Principles of Desert." *Rutgers Law Review* 20:595–618.

Wallace, Scott. 1994. "Crime Bill Offers Funds to States for Prisons." *Overcrowded Times* 5(5):4, 12.

Washington State Sentencing Guidelines Commission. 1993. *Implementation Manual—FY 1993.* Olympia: Washington State Sentencing Guidelines Commission.

Watts, Ronald K., and Daniel Glaser. 1992. "Electronic Monitoring of Drug Offenders in California." In *Smart Sentencing: The Emergence of Intermediate Sanctions,* edited by James M. Byrne, Arthur J. Lurigio, and Joan Petersilia. Newbury Park, Calif.: Sage.

Weigend, Thomas. 1992. "Germany Reduces Use of Prison Sentences." *Overcrowded Times* 3(2):1, 11-13.

———. 1993. "In Germany, Fines Often Imposed in Lieu of Prosecution." *Overcrowded Times* 4(1):1, 15–16.

Young, Warren, 1979. *Community Service Orders.* London: Heinemann.

Zedlewski, Edwin. 1987. *Making Confinement Decisions.* Research in Brief. Washington, D.C.: National Institute of Justice.

Zimring, Franklin E., and Gordon Hawkins. 1991. *The Scale of Imprisonment.* Chicago: University of Chicago Press.

Eugene Maguin and Rolf Loeber

Academic Performance and Delinquency

ABSTRACT

A meta-analysis of naturalistic studies of the academic performance-delinquency relationship and of intervention studies aimed both at improving academic performance and reducing delinquency found that children with lower academic performance offended more frequently, committed more serious and violent offenses, and persisted in their offending. The association was stronger for males than females and for whites than for African Americans. Academic performance predicted delinquency independent of socioeconomic status. Some intervention and prevention programs, using law-related or moral education components with adolescent children and self-control, social skills, and parent training components with young school-age children, were found to effect significant improvements in academic performance and delinquency.

This essay presents the findings of a meta-analysis of quantitative relations between educational success and delinquency. It has three aims: first, to provide a quantitative summary of the magnitude of the cross-sectional and longitudinal association between academic performance

Eugene Maguin is program manager at the Research Institute on Addictions in Buffalo, N.Y. Rolf Loeber is professor of psychiatry and psychology at the University of Pittsburgh, School of Medicine, Western Psychiatric Institute and Clinic. This article was prepared under the following grants: grant 86-JN-CX-0009 from the Office of Juvenile Justice and Delinquency Prevention, U.S. Department of Justice; and grant 1R01 MH48890-01 from the National Institute of Mental Health. Points of view or opinions are those of the authors and do not necessarily represent the official position or policies of the U.S. Department of Justice or the National Institute of Mental Health.

and delinquency and to determine whether this association is different for persons of different ages, gender, or ethnicity; second, to determine which variables have common relationships with both academic performance and delinquency and which variables are related either to academic performance or delinquency but not to both; third, to determine the magnitude of improvement in academic performance and delinquency that intervention studies have shown, which program components were most likely responsible for these improvements, and whether improvements in academic performance lead to improvements in offending or vice versa.

Section I presents a brief summary of previous reviews of the academic performance and delinquency relationship and then gives an overview of several current theories of delinquency as they relate to the role of academic performance. This section then concludes with a discussion of the method of meta-analysis, which will be used to summarize relevant studies. Section II presents the results of the meta-analysis and narrative review of naturalistic studies reporting cross-sectional and longitudinal bivariate relationships or multivariate relationships. This section also includes the common causes analyses for both cross-sectional and longitudinal data. Section III presents results of the meta-analysis of prevention and intervention studies to reduce delinquency or improve academic performance. Finally, Section IV presents the conclusions and policy implications for future work.

I. Research on Education and Delinquency

Belief is widespread that educational success is an important suppressor of involvement in delinquency by children and adolescents. These beliefs have deep historical roots. What may be one of the first published "natural experiments" took place in early-nineteenth-century Ireland at a time when a large proportion of the population was illiterate. Advocates of universal education argued that with universal education crime would diminish and eventually cease. The large increase in the number of schools in Ireland at that time made it possible to examine the effects of education on the delinquency of juveniles. Publications in 1811 to 1812 claimed that out of seven thousand children educated in particular schools over a period of twenty years, only one juvenile had been "charged in any court of justice with any offence"

(Lunny 1990). The schooling consisted of training in basic academic skills and religious precepts with, presumably, strong moral overtones.

Although the results of universal education as regards crime may not have turned out as well as its advocates hoped, the two basic questions embodied in those hopes are as relevant today as they were then: is poor academic performance related to delinquency, and can intervention programs bring about reductions in delinquency and improvements in academic performance? Empirical studies on the first of these questions date from the early part of the twentieth century (e.g., Burt 1931; Bond and Fendrick 1936; Kvaraceus 1945; Glueck and Glueck 1950). These studies and later, more sophisticated studies (e.g., Rhodes and Reiss 1969; Broder et al. 1981; Hughes et al. 1991; Lynam, Moffitt, and Stouthamer-Loeber 1993) have verified that an association exists.

Yet, a key question remains unanswered. Rutter, Tizard, and Whitmore (1970) suggested three possible relationships between academic performance and delinquency: that low academic performance precedes delinquency, that delinquency precedes low academic performance, or that both academic performance and delinquency are related through a common antecedent variable. Which of these possibilities is correct will have great impact in both theoretical and applied criminology as well as in education. The resolution of this question is the overall purpose of this essay.

Four principal findings emerge from the research on educational success and delinquency. First, poor academic performance is related to the prevalence and onset of delinquency, whereas better academic performance is associated with desistance from offending. The results of the studies examined in this essay showed that the odds of delinquency for children with low academic performance is 2.07–2.11 times higher than for children with high academic performance. Both males and females with a higher frequency of offenses, more serious offenses, or violent rather than nonviolent offenses had lower levels of academic performance. Some evidence was found that low academic performance is related to an early onset of offending and its escalation in seriousness and persistence. Conversely, higher academic performance was associated with desistance from offending.

Second, intelligence and attention problems both act as a common cause of both academic performance and delinquency for males. When variation in either intelligence or attention problems is taken into account, the association between academic performance and delinquency is reduced to the extent that knowledge of academic performance adds almost nothing to predictions of the likelihood of delinquency. By contrast, neither socioeconomic status (SES) nor conduct problems appears to act as a common cause. When variation in either SES or conduct problems is taken into account, academic performance continued to add to predictions of the likelihood of delinquency.

Third, intervention studies show that improvements in academic performance co-occur with improvements in the prevalence of delinquency. Among the intervention programs that showed significant effects for either academic performance or delinquency, improvement in either or both outcome variables was equally likely. This was true of intervention studies with high-risk children and of prevention studies with community samples of children.

Fourth, effective intervention studies differed for children of broadly different ages. When the participants were adolescents, the more successful intervention programs employed law-related or moral education components. Among children of elementary school age, intervention programs that employed self-control and social skills training combined with parent training were more effective. These types of interventions tended to produce improvements in both academic performance and delinquency at termination rather than one or the other outcome measure.

A. Existing Reviews

Three major reviews of the relationship between academic performance and delinquency have been published in the past quarter century (Silberberg and Silberberg 1971; Gottfredson 1981; Hawkins and Lishner 1987). What progress have these reviews made in answering questions about academic performance and delinquency, and what criteria are available to evaluate the reviews? Data from two types of studies are needed. The first are naturalistic studies, both cross-sectional and longitudinal. These studies contribute estimates of the association between academic performance and delinquency and the data for computing the partial association between academic performance and delinquency with respect to a common variable. The second are experimental intervention studies that measure both academic performance and delinquency. These studies can establish three things: first, whether improvement on a variable having a common relationship with academic performance and delinquency leads to improvement in *both* academic performance and delinquency; second, whether academically focused interventions can improve academic performance and whether improvements in delinquency also occur either simultaneously or later; and third, whether and how delinquency-focused interventions affect academic performance and delinquency.

The review by Silberberg and Silberberg (1971) is very complete. It reviewed naturalistic studies (i.e., studies in which subjects did not receive interventions) pertaining to the bivariate academic performance and delinquency relationship. It discussed academically focused intervention studies but did not include any intervention studies focused on reducing delinquency. It included an extensive review of "correlated etiological phenomena" of physiological variables such as central nervous system disorders and genetic factors.

Gottfredson's (1981) review represented a major advance and improvement on several fronts. First of all, it explicitly recognized and addressed the relationships among social economic status, ability or intelligence, academic performance, and delinquency. It summarized in a tabular format the principal data on the quantitative bivariate relationships of academic performance, SES, and intelligence with delinquency. Thus for the first time it was possible to see at a glance the magnitudes of the relations of these variables with delinquency. It did not examine intervention studies.

Hawkins and Lishner (1987) produced a comprehensive and far-ranging review of both naturalistic and intervention studies pertaining to delinquency. They included naturalistic studies of the wide range of individual level variables that have been found to be correlated with delinquency. In addition, they reviewed studies linking school level variables such as school climate or school size to delinquency. They concluded with an extensive review of school-based delinquency intervention and prevention strategies. The range of programs reviewed included early educational (preschool) programs, behavior management and curriculum enhancements, and classroom management and instructional practices. The strength of their review is its completeness and breadth of coverage.

Knowledge concerning the relationship between academic performance and delinquency when we began work on this essay can be summarized in the following three statements. First, academic performance and delinquency are, almost without doubt, inversely related to each other. However, the past reviews did not clarify the strength of this relationship and whether the magnitude of association is the same for males and females and for younger and older children.

Second, a considerable number of other variables, but in particular SES and intelligence, are related to both academic performance and delinquency. However, only a few studies have tested whether intelligence might be a cause of both academic performance and delinquency.

Third, a wide variety of intervention programs of different theoretical orientations have been implemented to attempt to reduce delinquency. However, reviews of intervention programs have not summarized the results quantitatively in even tabular fashion. Thus it is difficult to establish what intervention programs worked because the statistical significance of the result depended on both the sample size and the magnitude of the treatment effect.

The important weaknesses of these previous reviews are methodological and conceptual. The methodological weakness stems from relying on a narrative review format to summarize the literature. The narrative review format (Hunter and Schmidt 1990) lists studies reporting significant or nonsignificant results and attempts to reconcile differing results on the basis of design characteristics (e.g., type of measures or sex of subjects) to arrive at a synthesis. The drawback of the narrative review approach is that it can not provide quantitative answers to what are, after all, quantitative questions. In addition to the central substantive question of overall relationships, these reviews have also not considered whether the quantitative relationships vary with gender or ethnicity. In addition, the literature exhibits considerable methodological variability relative to types of measures of delinquency (e.g., official records). The effects of this methodological variability have also not been considered.

Prior reviews have conceptualized delinquency as a unitary phenomenon. Past reviews have used what is essentially a trait perspective, in which some children display delinquency while others do not. Such a perspective neglects the developmental aspects of delinquency shown by the many studies of age and delinquency and life span studies of crime, which indicate that delinquency, like educational performance, is not constant over time. Furthermore, from the point of view of interventions, the more fruitful questions to ask are whether the onset of offending can be delayed, its severity minimized, or its cessation hastened. Such questions require a developmental framework.

This essay uses the quantitative methodology of meta-analysis to assess the strength of the academic performance-delinquency relationship. The source materials include both cross-sectional and longitudinal naturalistic studies and intervention studies. Where possible we examined the possibility that the relationship between academic performance and delinquency was due to common causal variables such as intelligence, attention problems, or SES. Although many of the principal analyses reported were conducted within the trait perspective, we attempted to apply a developmental perspective to both the phenomenon of delinquency and its relationship with academic performance.

B. Academic Performance and Theories of Delinquency

A considerable number of theories have been developed to explain delinquency (see Siegel [1992] for an overview). Several include academic performance directly or indirectly. In this section, we briefly examine these theories and highlight their differences and similarities. Theoretical predictions made by these theories that are testable by this meta-analysis are identified. However, before turning to theories, we first highlight recent developments in the conceptualization of delinquency.

1. *Conceptual Perspectives.*   Most often, delinquency has been conceptualized as a measure of the prevalence of violations by adolescents of laws applicable to adolescents. Although some investigators have focused on adolescents who committed particular types of crimes (e.g., Tarter et al. 1983; Busch et al. 1990), such investigators are in a minority. The principal theoretical interest has been in explaining the prevalence of delinquency or, less often, the frequency of its occurrence by resort to such concepts such as differential association, commitment, intelligence, or SES. Work based on this perspective has yielded much information on the correlates of crime using both cross-sectional and longitudinal frameworks.

An alternative conceptualization of delinquency is embodied in the perspective of developmental criminology (Loeber and Le Blanc 1990). This perspective argues that delinquent behaviors, starting with predelinquent problem behaviors, are continuous with adult offending. Delinquent individuals are thought to progress along a developmental continuum of delinquency, and types of delinquents can be distinguished accordingly. The terminology of onset, escalation, and desistance is used to study the development of delinquent offending in individuals. Thus one can investigate, for example, questions of when the onset of offending occurs and whether the correlates (such as poor academic performance) of early onset are the same as those of later onset.

2. *Delinquency Theories*. Theories of delinquency are traditionally separated into three groups in which constitutional factors, psychological factors, or social factors are seen as the principal causes of delinquency. Such theories are variously relevant to understanding the connection between poor academic performance and delinquency.

a. Psychological theories. Low intelligence was, perhaps, the first variable to be linked to offending. Although the writings of early criminologists mention the apparent low intelligence of criminals, it was not until intelligence tests were developed and employed as research tools in the early 1900s that quantitative measures became available. After a time, however, intelligence fell into disrepute as an explanation of crime, and it was not until Hirschi and Hindelang's (1977) review that low intelligence was reestablished as a cause of crime. Although the mechanism of how low intelligence leads to crime is not clearly understood, current explanations concentrate on the role of intelligence in learning, abstract thought, and problem solving.

Attention and hyperactivity problems are a much more current variable—having been implicated since 1950 (Glueck and Glueck 1950). Since that time, follow-up studies of hyperactive or attention deficit children have relatively consistently identified an excess of delinquency and academic problems in children with these problems compared with control children (e.g., Satterfield, Hoppe, and Schell 1982; McGee and Share 1988; Mannuzza et al. 1989). The mechanism of attention and activity regulation deficits also is not clearly understood; most likely, there is a disruption of processes related to learning and other cognitive/emotional processes.

Recently, Moffitt (1990) has integrated intelligence and attention problems into a model of executive functioning deficits as a causal factor for delinquency. Moffitt's work takes as its starting point the well-known differential in verbal and performance IQ scores and other neuropsychological tests, which measure the abilities to learn and evaluate. She argues that these neuropsychological tests indicate a possible deficit in the ability of the person to use verbal strategies to regulate behavioral production. The key element, she proposes, is the regulation of attention. Thus delinquency is seen as a consequence of the person's inability to modulate their behavior on the basis of past experience and present conditions. Although Moffitt has not extended her analysis to education, other studies have identified attention problems as an important correlate of poor reading (e.g., Rowe and Rowe 1992). Thus it is possible that children who display executive function deficits will also display reading problems.

b. Integrated social theories.   Integrated social theories of delinquency developed from efforts to integrate strain-based theories (e.g., Cohen 1955; Cloward and Ohlin 1960), social control theories (e.g., Hirschi 1969), and social learning theories (Burgess and Akers 1966; Akers 1977).

Strain theory contributes the idea that individuals with lower SES lack the social and intellectual resources successfully to enter the middle-class culture that is identified as a goal. Thus when low SES children enter the middle-class institution of school they fail because they lack the necessary socialization that middle-class children have had to succeed in school. Strain theory implies that these children turn to delinquency because of frustration with their failure in school.

Control theory, as articulated by Hirschi (1969), proposes that social relations (bonds) between an individual and others constrain and prevent delinquent behavior. Hirschi's formulation of the social bond consists of an affective attachment to others, a commitment to socially approved courses of action, involvement in those courses of action, and belief in the legitimacy of conventional order. Hirschi's theory emphasizes a developmental-like progression in the scope of the social bond as children move from the bond with their parents to a bond with the school and then to other, larger social institutions. Implicit is the assumption that events weakening these relationships increase the likelihood of delinquency. The role of academic performance in control theory is not clear. Although Hirschi recognized that doing poorly in school would likely weaken all aspects of the social bond, he treated academic performance as a measure of attachment. However, others (e.g., Cernkovich and Giordano 1992) have disagreed and treated academic performance as a measure of commitment.

Social learning theory (Burgess and Akers 1966; Akers 1977) is an application of Skinnerian learning theory to the development of delinquency. Akers proposed that children learn all behavior including delinquent behavior from social interaction with others. Specifically, the twin processes of reinforcement and punishment drive the acquisition and maintenance of behaviors and the supporting beliefs, attitudes, and values.

Integrations of concepts from some or all of the preceding three theories have been offered by Weis and Sederstrom (1981), Elliott,

Huizinga, and Ageton (1985), Hawkins and Weis (1985), Thornberry (1987), and Catalano and Hawkins (forthcoming). These theories are discussed briefly in terms of their conceptualization of academic performance.

Social development theory (Weis and Sederstrom 1981; Hawkins and Weis 1985; Catalano and Hawkins, forthcoming) hypothesizes that involvement and interaction with prosocial others (e.g., family, peers, teachers) interacts with the presence of sufficient skills to produce perceived rewards. Rewards from prosocial involvements lead to an attachment to these prosocial persons and, ultimately, the formation of prosocial beliefs. The presence of prosocial beliefs is believed to reduce the likelihood of delinquency. Academic performance is conceptualized as a measure of a "skills for interaction/involvement" construct. Children displaying high levels of academic performance would be hypothesized to receive substantial rewards from prosocial others in the schools and elsewhere, which would then lead to prosocial attachments and beliefs. Factors such as intelligence are hypothesized to affect delinquency only through their effects on the level of skills for interaction, perceived rewards of prosocial interactions, and opportunities for interaction.

Interactional theory (Thornberry 1987; Thornberry et al. 1991) hypothesizes that attachment to others such as parents, peers, or teachers leads to a commitment to socially endorsed modes of behavior and the development of beliefs that inhibit participation in delinquent behavior. Furthermore, interactional theory posits that attachment and commitment are also affected by current delinquent behavior. Academic performance is considered to be a component item of the "commitment to school" construct. Other items in this construct include how well students like school and how hard they work in school (Thornberry et al. 1991). Thus children with poor academic performance are conceptualized as displaying low commitment to school, which affects delinquency through beliefs. Structural factors such as SES affect the individual's level of attachment and commitment. Finally, this theory recognizes the roles of individual factors such as intelligence or attention problems.

Elliott, Ageton, and Canter (1979) and Elliott, Huizinga, and Ageton (1985) have developed an integrated social theory that emphasizes the role of bonds to both conventional persons and institutions such as schools, and to delinquent peers, as the variables directly predicting delinquency. Weak bonds to conventional persons and institutions are seen as leading to stronger bonds to delinquent peers. The presence of bonding either to conventional others or to delinquent peers is hypothesized to consist of the attachment, commitment, involvement, and belief components identified by Hirschi (1969). Both types of bonding are hypothesized to be influenced by strain theory variables that measure the dislocations between aspirations and attainment such as in educational or occupational areas. Academic performance is viewed as an indicator of the commitment aspect of the social bond. That is, low performance is a measure of low commitment and acts on delinquency through bonds to delinquent peers. Structural variables such as SES do not appear to enter directly but rather through their expressions as strains between aspiration and attainment. Individual level variables such as intelligence have not been included in the theory.

3. *Quantitative Implications.*   The theories of delinquency causation just reviewed imply two quantitative models (see fig. 1). The first is the common cause model and is implied by psychological theories. Basically, these theories propose that delinquency is caused by a factor or set of factors such as intelligence, attention problems, or executive function deficits. From reviews of the literature on learning in the field of education (e.g., Wang, Haertel, and Walberg 1993), we know that intelligence is an important correlate of academic performance. There is also considerable evidence that attention problems and hyperactivity are also important correlates of academic performance (e.g., Hinshaw 1992). Thus to the extent that academic performance and delinquency share common causes, it is possible that their association is solely spurious.

The key implication of each of the integrated theories of delinquency is that structural variables such as SES have their only effects on the strength of the social bond (Elliott, Huizinga, and Ageton 1985; Thornberry et al. 1991) or on skills for interaction, opportunities for interaction, and perceived rewards (Catalano and Hawkins, forthcoming). This is also true for psychological variables such as intelligence or attention regulation in the case of social development theory (Catalano and Hawkins, forthcoming). Since neither Elliott, Huizinga, and Ageton (1985) nor Thornberry et al. (1991) consider psychological factors, it is not clear how these variables should be modeled. Thus each of these theories implies a mediated model without direct effects. To the extent that the data are available, meta-analytic techniques can be used to summarize the data necessary for testing each of these models.

Common Cause Model

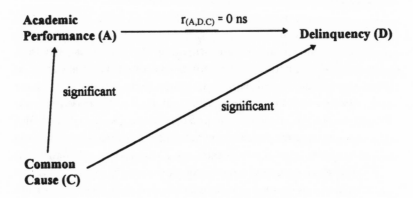

Noncommon Cause Model

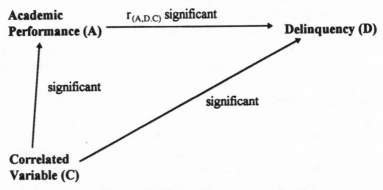

FIG. 1.—Quantitative models implied by theories of delinquency

C. Meta-analysis

Meta-analysis is a method for summarizing the relationship between two variables reported by a set of studies to arrive at a quantitative statement of the strength of that relationship. Meta-analysis uses the information from the statistical tests conducted in each study to generate a measure of the average strength of the bivariate relationships found across the studies (Hunter, Schmidt, and Jackson 1982; Hedges and Olkin 1985; Hunter and Schmidt 1990). By averaging the effect sizes together, an estimate of the magnitude of the relationship is formed. Under the hypothesis that each study in the meta-analysis has the same effect size, the mean effect size is the best estimate of the population value. Where significant variation in the mean effect size remains after removal of the variation due to sampling error, potential moderator variables (e.g., gender, ethnicity, type of measure) can be tested to determine if they can account for the variation. Thus the analyst can report an estimate of the overall relationship and then test hypotheses that may explain variations in the overall relationship.

Conducting a meta-analysis consists of four relatively straightforward steps: locate potential studies, select the studies according to some selection criteria, compute effect sizes for each bivariate relationship, and analyze the resulting effect sizes (Hunter, Schmidt, and Jackson 1982; Hunter and Schmidt 1990).

1. *Locating Potential Studies.* Several strategies were used to locate potential studies. First, previous reviews of the correlates of delinquency and of delinquency interventions (e.g., Silberberg and Silberberg 1971; Logan 1972; Lundman, McFarlane, and Scarpitti 1976; Gagne 1977; Wright and Dixon 1977; Romig 1978; Gendreau and Ross 1979; Gottfredson 1981; Hawkins and Lishner 1987) were located, and studies cited there were collected. Second, the reference lists of existing and located studies were themselves scanned, and the citations to new studies were collected. Third, database searches of Psychological Abstracts, Social Work Abstracts, Educational Resources Information Center (ERIC), Public Affairs Information Service, and Sociological Abstracts were undertaken to locate previously unknown studies. The terms used in these searches were developed from our knowledge of the area and from the descriptor terms and related synonyms used by ERIC and Psychological Abstracts. A pool of over one thousand potential studies resulted.

2. *Selecting Studies.* Each study in the pool was evaluated to determine if it met the criteria for inclusion. Each study, regardless of whether it was a naturalistic study or an intervention study, had to meet the following four criteria: one or more measures of delinquency, one or more academic performance measures, an upper age cutoff of eighteen years, and sufficient data to permit the computation of a usable effect size.

Delinquency was defined on the basis of face validity—that is, whether the measure referred to behaviors that violated the criminal code. Thus measures derived from official records such as police contacts, arrests, convictions, findings of guilt, adjudications, and correctional placement were used. Measures based on the self-reports of the subjects, their parents, or other knowledgeable adults were used if the instrument also contained criminal code violations. To maintain the clarity of the delinquency construct, measures of psychological constructs such as aggression or externalizing behavior or psychiatric diagnoses such as conduct disorder or antisocial personality disorder were not used even though they may overlap with delinquency. Studies that reported composite or "construct" measures labeled as delinquency were used only if one of the component measures met our inclusion criteria.

Academic performance was also based on a face validity definition—whether the measure referred to an evaluation of knowledge that might be gained through formal education or an outcome based on such an evaluation. Thus we used subject-specific and composite measures of performance whether made by teachers, the subjects themselves, or other knowledgeable adults or derived from standardized tests (e.g., California Achievement Tests). Measures such as grade retention or special class placement were also used since these outcomes are the outcomes of more direct performance measures. Measures of ability, such as intelligence or aptitude, were not included as academic performance measures but were considered as potential antecedent variables.

To be included, a study had to report sufficient data to compute an effect size statistic, which measures the degree to which one variable is related to another. Because meta-analysis techniques are based on either the d-statistic, which expresses effect size as the ratio of the difference between group means to the pooled group standard deviation (Glass 1977), or the algebraically equivalent correlation coefficient (Hunter and Schmidt 1990), only studies that presented these statistics directly, or their equivalents (i.e., phi coefficients or t-test values), or presented sufficient data to compute these statistics could be used. Thus studies that reported Yule's Q or the gamma coefficient could not be used.[1]

[1] Each of the statistics mentioned, including the t-test, which is algebraically equivalent to a correlation coefficient, measures the degree to which one variable is related to another on a scale of -1 to $+1$, where $+1$ indicates a perfect correspondence, -1 indicates a perfect inverse correspondence, and 0 indicates no relationship. Because the computational formulae for the correlation or phi coefficient, Yule's Q, and the gamma coefficient differ from one another, the same data would yield different numerical values of the degree of association for each of these statistics. Since meta-analysis is based on averaging the association across studies, all studies must use the same measure of association.

In addition to the aforementioned requirements, which applied to both naturalistic and intervention studies, intervention studies had to include a control or comparison group of subjects that did not receive an intervention so that other causes of any change might be ruled out. The two groups of subjects could be formed using several methods: random assignment of subjects or groups of subjects (e.g., schools or school classrooms) to groups, matching of treated and untreated subjects on plausibly relevant dimensions (e.g., academic performance or intelligence) when some evidence of the groups' equivalence at assignment also existed, or identification of a comparison group that had not received the intervention but also may not have been equivalent to the intervention subjects (i.e., a nonequivalent comparison group). An example of this last method would be a group of students from the same school who did not receive the intervention. Intervention studies had to report, at a minimum, data on both academic performance and delinquency at the conclusion of the intervention. The analyses of the resulting data had to be appropriate to the type of design used. Random assignment or matching designs could use t-tests of postintervention means, but nonequivalent comparison group designs had to use analysis of covariance or repeated measures, which take into account preexisting differences. The reason for these differing requirements is that the purpose of a nonintervention group is to rule out other causes of any observed improvement in academic performance or delinquency. Although random assignment almost perfectly rules out other explanations, more complex statistical methods can, in principle, compensate for the use of post hoc matching or nonequivalent comparison groups.

At the conclusion of the selection of the studies for the meta-analysis, a number of studies remained that were unsuitable because they did not report usable bivariate measures of association. Those studies that reported multivariate analyses involving academic performance as a predictor of delinquency were retained for presentation in sections for such analyses.

All told, a total of 106 naturalistic studies and twelve intervention studies were selected either for the meta-analysis or the sections on multivariate analysis. The data to be used in the meta-analysis and the supplementary narrative reviews come from several types of designs: cross-sectional, prospective longitudinal, and intervention. The following description of a few selected studies illustrates the range of the research projects.

Among the larger and better-known of the cross-sectional design research projects was the Richmond Youth Project (Hirschi 1969; Jensen and Eve 1976). This study consisted of a stratified probability sample of seventh- through twelfth-grade youth in the Richmond, California, schools in 1964. Participants were assessed once by means of a self-report questionnaire asking about family background and child-rearing practices, attitudes toward delinquency, school, and community institutions (e.g., police and school), and involvement in delinquency. In addition, police records were collected for boys in the sample. Significant associations were found between the educational measures and the delinquency measures.

In contrast, several research projects used prospective longitudinal designs, in which a sample is selected and then followed over time during which one or more assessments are conducted. The sample selected may be a true birth cohort such as the Dunedin Multidisciplinary Health and Development Study (e.g., Moffitt and Silva 1988; Williams and McGee 1994), whose sample consists of all children born in Queen Mary Hospital in Dunedin, New Zealand, in the one-year period beginning April 1, 1972. Children in this study were assessed at two-year intervals beginning at age three until age fifteen and then again at age eighteen. Parents and teachers completed behavior rating scales, and children were tested with standardized tests of intelligence and academic achievement. Studies found that school performance at younger ages was somewhat less strongly associated with delinquency than school performance at older ages.

The Philadelphia Collaborative Perinatal Project (Denno 1990) used a variation of this type of design. This project used a subsample of women who were enrolled in the Philadelphia branch of the Collaborative Perinatal Project, which was a national study of biological influences on pregnancy, child health, and child mortality. Children were included if they had resided in Philadelphia from age ten to seventeen and had received intelligence tests at age seven and achievement tests at ages thirteen to fourteen. Data were taken from the Perinatal Project records, school records, and police records. Here again, significant associations between school achievement tests and later delinquency were found.

Other research projects selected subjects when they were older and followed them at more closely spaced intervals. One example was the Youth in Transition project (e.g., Bachman 1970; Wiatrowski et al. 1982; Lipton and Smith 1983; Wells and Rankin 1983; Agnew 1985). This project involved a nationally representative probability sample of 2,213 tenth-grade boys (both African American and white) who were selected in 1966. Participants were assessed four times: tenth grade, fall semester; eleventh grade, spring semester; twelfth grade, spring; and thirteenth grade, summer. In addition to standardized intelligence, cognitive ability, and reading tests, and other background measures that were collected only at the first assessment, participants completed measures of delinquency and prosocial behavior, academic performance, aspirations, and expectations at each assessment. The studies have reported significant associations between academic performance and delinquency during the high school years.

Another example is the Pittsburgh Youth Study (Loeber et al. 1991; Lynam, Moffitt, and Stouthamer-Loeber 1993; Maguin, Loeber, and LeMahieu 1993). This project consists of separately selected samples of first-, fourth-, and seventh-grade boys who were attending the Pittsburgh Public Schools at the time of their selection in 1987 and 1988. On the basis of an antisocial risk score constructed from parent and teacher reports collected at the screening assessment, high-risk boys were oversampled for subsequent follow-up. Follow-up assessments were conducted at twice yearly intervals for the first five follow-ups and at yearly intervals thereafter. At each assessment, the child and his caretaker complete an extensive interview about pro- and antisocial behavior, beliefs, and attitudes and about family functioning and parent-child relationships. In addition, the child's teacher completes a behavior questionnaire, and data are collected from school, police, and court records. Studies from this project have also confirmed the association between academic performance and delinquency.

3. *Computation of Effect Sizes.* In naturalistic studies, an effect size was computed for each academic performance-delinquency measure pair. In intervention studies, an effect size was computed for each academic performance or delinquency comparison between intervention and nonintervention groups. The measure of effect size used was the correlation coefficient.[2] A positive sign for the effect size means that a high score on the first variable was associated with a high score

---

[2] Although Hedges and Olkin (1985) have proposed remedies to the bias in the sample correlation coefficient as an estimator, the correction is small (.008 for $r = .40$ and $N = 23$, the worst case in these data) in relation to other possible corrections, and it was not used. Hunter and Schmidt (1990) have argued that effect sizes should be corrected for study artifacts (e.g., error of measurement, dichotomization effects, range variation effects, construct validity deviations). However, these corrections could not be made because the necessary data (i.e., reliabilities, ranges, and validity coefficients) have generally not been reported in the literature. Thus the meta-analyses conducted here assume that variables are perfectly measured and are not attenuated by any measurement artifacts.

on the second variable. Variables measuring retardation or retention in grade (e.g., held back) were reverse coded so that a higher score indicated promotion.

Phi coefficients were computed for 2 × 2 tables. Tables with more than two levels of the delinquency measure, as would be the case if the delinquency measure were categorized by frequency or seriousness, were collapsed to form a nondelinquent-delinquent dichotomy. If a reasonable scale could be applied to the academic performance categories (e.g., A = 4, B = 3, etc.), point-biserial correlations were computed based on the assigned scale values. This was done to minimize attenuation due to the dichotomization of academic performance. This procedure was justified, we believe, by analyses to be reported that show consistent evidence of a linear relationship between academic performance and delinquency. Point-biserial correlations were also computed where t-tests were given or where the means, standard deviations, and N's were given. Finally, paired t-test values from matching designs were recomputed as independent groups t-tests. In the one case where the standard deviations were not given, values in the literature were used to estimate these values.

4. *Analysis of Effect Sizes.* The analysis of the study effect sizes (i.e., correlations) consisted of three steps. The first step is computation of the mean effect size (i.e., correlation) and its variance. The mean effect size is computed as the average of the study effect sizes after weighting by the sample size (i.e., it is N-weighted). Thus the effect size from a large study was given more weight than that from a small study. The variance of the mean effect size is the variance of the N-weighted study effect sizes. The observed variance of the mean effect size is the sum of the variance of the population effect size, which is unknown but can be calculated, and the variance due to sampling error, which is extraneous and can be removed. The second step is the removal of the variance due to sampling error, which was computed from Hunter and Schmidt (1990) from the variance of the study effect sizes. Preplanned analyses of moderator variables (e.g., gender, ethnicity) were conducted in the third step of the analysis. Both substantive (sex or ethnicity of sample) and methodological features (e.g., type of delinquency measure) were used to form homogenous subgroups for which effect sizes were compared to determine whether variation in the population effect size was related to that moderator variable.

5. *Linearity of Academic Performance with Delinquency.* Because meta-analysis is based on averaging measures of association across studies,

it is assumed that the relationship between academic performance and delinquency is linear. Using data from a number of studies to be included in the main body of the results, we were able to test the following form of this assumption: academic performance is linearly related to the likelihood of delinquency.

Data were available from six studies with seventeen sets of subjects (three sets of females and fourteen sets of males; eight sets of white subjects, seven sets of African American or nonwhite subjects, and two sets of predominant white subjects).[3] Due to the presence of multiple measures of either academic performance, delinquency, or both, a total of thirty-eight tests were possible. The academic performance data were categorized into quartiles, if possible, or were used as presented in the reports. Delinquency was dichotomized. Linear, quadratic, and, if present, cubic and quartic terms were entered simultaneously in a logistic regression of delinquency on academic performance.

The results showed that quadratic, cubic, or quartic terms were significant ($p < .05$) in only two of the thirty-eight analyses. More than this number would have been expected on the basis of chance alone. Thus we concluded that academic performance was linearly related to the likelihood of delinquency and, therefore, that measures of association such as correlations were appropriate.

II. Naturalistic Studies

There are two very important but basic questions about the academic performance-delinquency relationship. First, what is the magnitude of the association between academic performance and delinquency? Second, does the association remain after controlling for other variables? Within the first major question, we address the related questions of whether the association is the same for males and females or for persons of different ethnic backgrounds.

As noted earlier, the magnitude of the association is a measure of the strength of the relationship between two variables, such as academic performance and delinquency. The association can range from -1.0 through $+1.0$. In this essay, we have oriented the academic performance-delinquency effect data so that a negative association means that persons who have a low score on academic performance have a high

[3] The studies were Hathaway and Monachesi (1963); Hirschi (1969); Wolfgang, Figlio, and Sellin (1972); Jensen and Eve (1976); Tracy, Wolfgang, and Figlio (1990); and Maguin, Loeber, and LeMahieu (1993).

score on delinquency. An association of -1.0 means that low academic performance is perfectly associated with high delinquency. If the association were 0.0, this would indicate that no relationship exists between academic performance and delinquency. At several places, we also present some of the conclusions in terms of odds ratios, which are another measure of the association. We have oriented these data so that the odds ratio presents the likelihood of delinquency for children with low academic performance relative to children with high academic performance. An odds ratio greater than 1.0 indicates that children with low academic performance are more likely to be delinquent than those with high performance.

To begin the analysis, effect sizes were first categorized into three possible groups based on the timing of the academic performance assessment relative to the delinquency assessment. Effect sizes that were based on academic performance assessments collected at the same time as the delinquency assessment were labeled as "cross-sectional." A total of 145 raw effect sizes from forty-two studies were classified as cross-sectional. Effect sizes that were based on academic performance assessments collected prior to the delinquency assessment were labeled as "longitudinal." One hundred-seventeen effect sizes from twenty-seven studies were classified as longitudinal. Although effect sizes could also be based on academic performance assessments that were collected *after* the delinquency assessments, these were not included because only two studies reported them (Wiatrowski et al. 1982; McCarthy and Hoge 1984).

Note, however, that in many delinquency studies the period of time covered by the delinquency assessment is the lifetime of the subject in the case of self-report measures, or since the age of legal responsibility, where measures are drawn from official records such as those of police departments or juvenile courts. Thus even in studies we have labeled as "longitudinal" the period covered by academic performance assessment almost always overlapped with the period covered by the delinquency assessment.

A. Cross-sectional Bivariate Analyses

The results of the meta-analysis of association between academic performance and delinquency clearly indicate three points. First, the poorer the academic performance, the worse the delinquency. A mean effect size of $-.149$ was found, which is equivalent to an odds ratio of 2.07, and applies across males and females and across the two ethnic groups examined. The association was significantly larger for males than for females ($-.151$ vs. $-.094$). It was also larger for whites than for African Americans ($-.185$ vs. $-.134$), but this difference was not significant. Unfortunately, the subjects' ages were all in the range of mid- to late adolescence, meaning it was impossible to explore age as a substantive factor. The magnitude of the association did not depend on whether delinquency was measured by self-reports or from official records.

The 145 effect sizes identified as cross-sectional constituted the sample for this analysis. These effect sizes and the forty-two studies that reported them are presented in table 1. For each study, base population, sample selection method, and sample demographics are presented, followed by the data for specific associations reported. The sex, ethnicity, and size of the analysis sample are given. The academic performance measure used is briefly described by its type, sources (e.g., self, parent, or school record), period of coverage (e.g., past year), and age or grade of the subjects at the time of collection. Similar data are then presented for the delinquency measure. The effect size between the two measures and its statistical significance level is presented in the last column.

The forty-two studies in table 1 do not correspond to forty-two distinct, nonoverlapping groups of subjects. A particular group of subjects may be described in several studies. For example, Kelly (1971) and Polk, Frease, and Richmond (1974) both reported on subjects from the Marion County Youth Study. Likewise, Lynam, Moffitt, and Stouthamer-Loeber (1993) and Maguin, Loeber, and LeMahieu (1993) both reported on subjects from the Pittsburgh Youth Study. Several studies reported on the same group of subjects but at different times (e.g., Lynam, Moffitt, and Stouthamer-Loeber 1993; Maguin, Loeber, and LeMahieu 1993). Finally, a number of studies reported several effect sizes for a single group of subjects.

The problem that each of these arrangements poses to the meta-analysis is that of independence. Meta-analysis is based on the assumptions that each sample contributes one effect size to the meta-analysis, and samples do not have members in common. Neither of these conditions is met in this set of studies. Our approach to treating these violations of independence was to group effect sizes into sets whose subjects did not overlap as recommended by Hunter and Schmidt (1990). Each set, thus, consisted only of those effect sizes that were, in principle, based on the same group of subjects. A composite effect size for each

TABLE 1

Studies Reporting Cross-Sectional Associations between Academic Performance and Delinquency

Study	Selection and Description of Overall Sample	Analysis Sample			Academic Measure	Delinquency Measure	Association
		N	Sex	Ethnicity			
Bachman (1970)	Youth in Transition Study, national sample of tenth-grade males in public high schools (11 percent African American) at wave 1	2,213	M		SR GPA past year	SRD frequency past 3 years	−.21***
					GATB-J vocabulary		−.03
					Gates reading		−.03
Bazemore and Noblit (1978)	Marion County Youth Study, wave 2 (25 percent random sample of wave 1 sample at twelfth grade + all delinquents from wave 1)	452	M		OSR cumulative GPA at grade 12	OR lifetime prevalence at grade 12	−.25***
Broder et al. (1981)	628 adjudicated males (14.8 years old, 41.2 percent white, 41.7 percent African American) + 968 nonadjudicated males (14.1 years old, 61.1 percent white, 27.8 percent African American)	1,596	M		LD classification (reversed)	OR adjudication	−.20***
		1,542				SRD frequency	−.12***

Study	Sample	N	Sex		Academic measure	Delinquency measure	r
Cochran and Bo (1989)	Boys in ninth grade in Stavanger, Norway	92	M		OSR grade 9 GPA	SRD frequency at grade 9	−.28**
Davis, Sanger, and Morris-Friehe (1991)	One-to-one matching sample of boys in placement and nonadjudicated peers on age (range: 14–17 years) and Full-Scale IQ (range: 90–109)	48	M	W	Achievement: Reading Math Language	OR prevalence	−.46*** −.45*** −.40***
Dishion et al. (1984)	Self-selected tenth-grade boys (N = 60) and 10 boys with multiple offenses	69 67 69 67	M	W	WRAT reading achievement Parent academic rating (CBCL) WRAT reading achievement Parent academic rating (CBCL)	OR lifetime prevalence SRD delinquent life-style past year	−.29 −.33 −.30 −.37
Donovan and Jessor (1985)	Random sample of junior high students in Colorado school district; year 3 (grades 9–11) data Year 4 (grades 10–12) data	102 141 102 141	M F M F		SR GPA past semester SR GPA past semester	SRD frequency past year SRD frequency past year	−.06 −.30*** −.28** −.15*
Elliott and Voss (1974)	Ninth-grade students in two suburban California districts (73 percent white, 14 percent Hispanic, 8 percent African American)	1,338 1,279	M F		Composite of GPA, teacher rating, and achievement	SRD frequency, past 3 years	−.13*** −.08**

TABLE 1 (*Continued*)

Study	Selection and Description of Overall Sample	Analysis Sample			Academic Measure	Delinquency Measure	Association
		N	Sex	Ethnicity			
Empey and Lubeck (1971)	Unmatched groups of persistent delinquent boys (N = 233) and nondelinquent peers (N = 85) aged 15–18 years from Los Angeles area	298	M		School grades	OR conviction	– .41***
	Same selection but from Utah; 249 delinquents and 100 nondelinquents	296	M		School grades	OR conviction	– .43***
Ferguson (1952)	Males who left school legally at age 14 in Glasgow in 1947	1,349	M		OSR GPA at age 14	OR conviction age 8–14	– .10**
Glueck and Glueck (1950)	Matched sample of non–African American, nondelinquent, and delinquent boys on neighborhood, age, ethnicity, and IQ (delinquents: age: 14 years, 8 months, IQ: 92.3; nondelinquents: age: 14 years, 6 months, IQ: 94.2	999	M		Grades repeated (reversed)	OR conviction	– .24***
		1,000			Years retarded (reversed)		– .27***
		1,000			Special class placement (reversed)		– .16***
					Scholastic Aptitude Test achievement:		
		958			Reading		– .17***
		959			Math		– .37***
		999			Last year's GPA		– .37***

Study	Sample	N	Sex	Race	Ability/achievement measure	Delinquency measure	r
Gold (1963)	Matched white boys aged 12–16 years with >1 serious offenses in the past 3 years and nondelinquent boys on IQ, socioeconomic status, and school type	120	M		Fifth-grade GPA	OR adjudication	−.10
		148	M		Seventh-grade GPA	OR adjudication	−.30***
Hathaway and Monachesi (1963)	Sample of ninth-grade Minnesota students followed to twelfth grade	4,404	M		OSR class rank at grade 11 or 12	OR lifetime prevalence at grade 12	−.16***
		4,637	F				−.09***
Hindelang (1973)	Sixth–twelfth-grade students in rural New York district (98 percent white)	380	M		SR academic ability	SRD variety, past year	−.08
		395	F				−.08
Hirschi (1969)	Richmond Youth Project, random sample of seventh–twelfth grade Richmond, California, public school students	1,156	M	W	DAT scores at grade 8	SRD frequency past year	−.11**
		1,183	M	W		OR frequency police contact	−.15***
		936	M	W	OSR English grade	SRD frequency past year	−.09**
		970	M	W		OR frequency police contact	−.21***
Jensen and Eve (1976)	Richmond Youth Project, random sample of seventh–twelfth grade Richmond, California, public school students	643	M	AA	OSR GPA	SRD frequency	−.14***
		528	F	AA			−.08*
		1,052	M	W			−.14***
		444	F	W			−.16***

TABLE 1 (*Continued*)

Study	Selection and Description of Overall Sample	Analysis Sample			Academic Measure	Delinquency Measure	Association
		N	Sex	Ethnicity			
Jerse and Fakouri (1978)	Matched sample of 108 adjudicated and nondelinquents by sex, grade level, and school	216	M + F		Sixth-grade reading grade Sixth-grade math grade	OR adjudication	−.28*** −.31***
Kelly (1971)	Marion County Youth Study, wave 1; All tenth-grade male students in Oregon county (99+ percent white)	1,211	M		OSR cumulative GPA at grade 10	OR lifetime court contact, grade 10 OR lifetime frequency > 1 contact, grade 10 OR lifetime felony prevalence, grade 10	−.17*** −.20*** −.13***
Kelly and Pink (1973)	Marion County Youth Study, wave 2 (25 percent random sample of wave 1 sample at twelfth grade)	223	M		Commitment at grade 12 (GPA, college plans, homework time, and club membership)	OR lifetime court contact, grade 12 OR lifetime frequency > 1 contact, grade 12 OR lifetime felony prevalence, grade 12	−.25** −.17** −.19**
Krohn and Massey (1980)	Random sample of seventh–twelfth-grade students in six midwestern districts	3,065	M + F		SR GPA	SRD frequency, minor delinquency SRD frequency, serious delinquency	−.33*** −.27***
Lawrence (1985)	Unmatched samples of sixth–twelfth-grade students in juvenile programs or regular Texas schools	171	M + F		GPA	OR adjudication SRD theft past 3 years SRD burglary past 3 years SRD vandalism past 3 years	−.42*** −.25*** −.15* −.07

170

Study	Sample	N	Sex	Race	Predictor	Outcome	r
Le Blanc, Vallieres, and McDuff (1992)[a]	Francophone students aged 12–16 years at wave 1	454	M		SR GPA (French + math)	SRD past year at wave 1	−.06
					Years delayed (reversed)	SRD past year at wave 1	+.01
	Wave 2 sample 2 years later (aged 14–18 years)	379			SR GPA (French + math)	SRD past year at wave 2	−.10
					Years delayed (reversed)	SRD past year at wave 2	−.04
	Wave 1 sample	455	F		SR GPA (French + math)	SRD past year at wave 1	−.04
		454			Years delayed (reversed)	SRD past year at wave 1	+.04
	Wave 2 sample	379			SR GPA (French + math)	SRD past year at wave 2	−.26***
		455			Years delayed (reversed)		+.01
Lynam, Moffitt, and Stouthamer-Loeber (1993)	Pittsburgh Youth Study sample of fourth-grade males at age 12–13 (N = 508, 53.5 percent African American, remainder white)	181–218	M	W	Composite teacher rating of reading, math, writing, and spelling at age 12–13	Self-, parent-, and teacher-reported lifetime delinquency seriousness at age 12–13	−.21**
		214–67	M	AA			−.33****
Maguin, Loeber, and LeMahieu (1993)[a]	Pittsburgh Youth Study sample of first-grade males at age 6–7	199–208	M	W	Teacher rating grades 1 and 2: Reading	Self-, parent-, and teacher-reported lifetime delinquency seriousness at age 6–7	−.21**
					Math		−.11
					CAT achievement grade 1: Reading		−.20**
					Math		−.09
					Parent report *never* held back		−.25***
					In expected grade for age		−.19**

TABLE 1 (*Continued*)

Study	Selection and Description of Overall Sample	Analysis Sample			Academic Measure	Delinquency Measure	Association
		N	Sex	Ethnicity			
		264–87	M	AA	Teacher rating grades 1 and 2:	Self-, parent-, and teacher-reported lifetime delinquency seriousness at age 9–10	
					Reading		–.06
					Math		–.08
					CAT achievement grade 1:		
					Reading		–.02
					Math		–.01
					Parent report *never* held back		–.07
					In expected grade for age		–.04
Pittsburgh Youth Study sample of fourth-grade males at age 9–10		212–18	M	W	Teacher rating grades 4 and 5:		
					Reading		–.34***
					Math		–.31***
					CAT achievement grade 4:		
					Reading		–.27***
					Math		–.26***
					Parent report *never* held back		–.27***
					In expected grade for age		–.27***

				Self-, parent-, and teacher-reported life-time delinquency seriousness at age 12–13
256–72	M	AA	Teacher rating grades 4 and 5:	
			Reading	−.28***
			Math	−.33***
			CAT achievement grade 4:	
			Reading	−.13*
			Math	−.16**
			Parent report *never* held back	−.19**
			In expected grade for age	−.21***
Pittsburgh Youth Study sample of seventh-grade males at age 12–13				
174–90	M	W	Teacher rating grades 7 and 8:	
			Reading	−.21**
			Math	−.26***
			CAT achievement grade 7:	
			Reading	−.13
			Math	−.16*
			Parent report *never* held back	−.13
			In expected grade for age	−.15*
221–51	M	AA	Teacher rating grades 7 and 8:	
			Reading	−.23***
			Math	−.19**
			CAT achievement grade 7:	
			Reading	−.09
			Math	−.19**

TABLE 1 (*Continued*)

Study	Selection and Description of Overall Sample	Analysis Sample			Academic Measure	Delinquency Measure	Association
		N	Sex	Ethnicity			
Mann (1976)	National sample of boys aged 11–18: younger group age 11–14	316	M		Parent report *never* held back	SRD frequency, past 3 years age 11–14	−.26***
					In expected grade for age		−.23***
					OR current GPA age 11–14		−.12
	Older group aged 15–18	290	M		OR current GPA age 15–18	SRD frequency, past 3 years age 15–18	−.19*
McCarthy and Hoge (1984)[a]	Students in seventh, ninth, and eleventh grades of public and parochial schools in two Mid-Atlantic cities, 55 percent male, 49 percent white at time 1)	1,360	M + F		OSR grades past year at wave 1	SRD theft + vandalism frequency past year, wave 1	−.15***
		1,460			OSR grades past year at wave 2	SRD theft + vandalism frequency past year, wave 2	−.14***
		1,313			OSR grades past year at wave 3	SRD theft + vandalism frequency past year, wave 3	−.13***
Meltzer et al. (1984)	Boys aged 13–16, one group in placement (N = 53), and the other group (N = 51) from similar socioeconomic status areas	104	M	W	Achievement (current): Math	OR placement	−.52***
					Spelling		−.28**
					Reading comprehension		−.44***
					Reading accuracy		−.43***

Study	N	Sex/Race	Academic measure	Delinquency measure	r
Menard and Morse (1984)	257	M + F	OR GPA, past year DAT score	SRD frequency nonserious delinquency past 3 years	−.16* −.05
			OR GPA, past year DAT score	SRD frequency serious delinquency past 3 years	−.16* −.16*
25 percent random sample of Elliott and Voss's (1974) sample of ninth-grade students in two California school districts, time 1 data only					
Noblit (1976)	261	M	OR cumulative GPA	OR adjudication	−.22**
Marion County Youth Study, wave 2 (25 percent random sample of wave 1 sample at twelfth grade)					
Palmore and Hammond (1964)	52	M / AA	OSR GPA	OR police or court contact	−.26**
	50	F / AA			−.17
	98	M / W			−.22*
	119	F / W			−.40***
Children whose caretaker received Aid to Families with Dependent Children payments in 1950					
Patterson and Dishion (1985)	133	M	WRAT reading achievement	SRD variety	−.07
	133			OR lifetime police contact	−.11
	115		OSR GPA past 2 years	SRD variety	−.24**
	115			OR lifetime police contact	+.04
Oregon Youth Study sample of seventh- and tenth-grade boys at wave 1					
Polk (1969)	260	M	OSR GPA at grade 12	OR lifetime prevalence at grade 12	−.23***
Marion County Youth Study, wave 2 (25 percent random sample of wave 1 sample at twelfth grade)					

TABLE 1 (*Continued*)

Study	Selection and Description of Overall Sample	Analysis Sample			Academic Measure	Delinquency Measure	Association
		N	Sex	Ethnicity			
Polk (1975)	Marion County Youth Study, wave 2 (25 percent random sample of wave 1 sample at twelfth grade)	260	M		OSR cumulative GPA	OR adjudication	−.23***
Polk, Frease, and Richmond (1974)	Marion County Youth Study, wave 1, all tenth-grade students in Oregon County (99+ percent white)	1,000	M		OR cumulative GPA	OR adjudication	−.26***
Polk and Halferty (1966)	Lane County Youth Study 50 percent sample of ninth–twelfth-grade males in Oregon school	410	M		OSR cumulative GPA	OR adjudication	−.23***
Senna, Rathus, and Siegel (1974)	Suburban New York males aged 14–18 years (88 percent white)	296	M		Composite of SR modal grade, courses failed, and time spent studying	SRD frequency aggression past year SR frequency theft + vandalism past year SR frequency shake-down past year	−.15** −.21*** −.16**

Study	Sample	N	Sex	Academic measure	Antisocial measure	Correlation
Swift, Spivack, and Back (1973)	Unmatched groups of seventh–twelfth-grade girls in placement (N = 123) or attending public schools in low socioeconomic status areas (N = 201)	324	F	OSR current GPA	OR current placement	+.18**
Tygart (1988)	Seventh–twelfth-grade students in California school district	171	M + F	OSR high academic track	SRD frequency school vandalism past 6 months	−.51***
Walker et al. (1993)	Randomly selected sub-samples of low antisocial risk (N = 41) and high antisocial risk (N = 39) from Oregon Youth Study	64 / 67 / 65 / 73	M	Achievement grade 7: Total / Reading / Math / Special class placement (reversed)	OR arrest frequency to grade 7	−.28* / −.26* / −.22 / −.27*
Wells and Rankin (1983)	Youth in Transition Study, national sample of tenth-grade males in public high schools (11 percent African American) at wave 1	1,691	M	SR GPA past year	SRD frequency past 3 years: Total / Aggression / Theft + vandalism	−.22*** / −.23*** / −.10***
Wiatrowski et al. (1982)	Youth in Transition Study, national sample of tenth-grade males in public high schools (11 percent black) at wave 1	1,000	M	SR GPA past year	SRD frequency past 3 years	−.17***
	Youth in Transition data at wave 3 (twelfth grade)	1,000		SR GPA past year	SRD frequency past year	−.26***

177

TABLE 1 (*Continued*)

Study	Selection and Description of Overall Sample	Analysis Sample			Academic Measure	Delinquency Measure	Association
		N	Sex	Ethnicity			
Williams and McGee (1994)	Dunedin Multidiscipli-nary Health and Devel-opment Study, birth cohort of Dunedin, New Zealand, children (98 percent European background) at age 15	364	M		Burt reading test age 15	SRD frequency age 15	−.17***
		334	F				+.01

NOTE.—A negative sign means that delinquency involvement is associated with lower grades or special class placement. OR = officially recorded delinquency; SRD = self-reported delinquency; OSR = official school records; SR = self-reported; AA = African American; W = white; M = male; F = female; GPA = grade point average; WRAT = Wide Range Achievement Test; CAT = California Achievement Test; LD = learning disabled; GATB-J = General Aptitude Test Battery-Part J; CBCL = Child Behavior Checklist; and DAT = Differential Aptitude Test.

ᵃ This entry also reports data provided to the current investigators by the original authors.

* $p < .05$.
** $p < .01$.
*** $p < .001$.

set then was computed by taking the sample-size-weighted average of the effect sizes in that set. The sample size of the set was computed as the average of the sample size of each effect size in the set. Treating the data in this manner resulted in the formation of fifty-one nonoverlapping sets of subjects.[4] Each set of subjects represented a demographically distinct and nonoverlapping group whose data had yielded one or more effect sizes of the association between academic performance and delinquency. It is this collection of effect sizes that was used in the meta-analysis.

Thirty-five sets of subjects were drawn from sampling frames defined by a small political subdivision (e.g., city, county, or school district), and three were from statewide or multistate sampling frames. Three sets of subjects were selected from a nationally representative sampling frame. Only a few studies reported using special techniques to contact all children in the sample frame. Whereas the putative population frame may have been, for example, adolescents in a particular county, the de facto population frame for the majority of studies was adolescents *who were in school on the day of testing*. As a result, there is likely to be a nonresponse bias for studies using self-report data, which is likely to underestimate the true effect size because students who were both unsuccessful students and delinquent are disproportionately represented among those not included in the samples.

The remaining ten sets of subjects (hereafter referred to as nonrepresentatively sampled sets) were composed of approximately equal-sized groups of delinquents and nondelinquents (Broder et al. [1981], an exception, sampled at about 1.5 nondelinquents per delinquent). In all cases, the delinquent subjects were recruited from juvenile correctional facilities, and the nondelinquent subjects were recruited from local school populations. Some means of verifying a subject's official nondelinquent status was employed by all studies. In addition, in four of the data sets, delinquent and nondelinquent subjects were matched to each other on variables such as ethnicity, grade level, sex, or intelligence. Thus these sets of subjects tended to represent extreme groups.

---

[4] In the course of forming sets of subjects, we removed two studies. The first was Bazemore and Noblit (1978), who used a sample from the Marion County Youth Study that was defined differently from the sample used by Kelly and Pink (1973) as well as several other investigators who used data from this research project. Menard and Morse (1984) was removed because they pooled the sample of males and females that Elliott and Voss (1974) had analyzed separately by sex. Thus the sample from the Menard and Morse (1984) study partially overlapped both the Elliott and Voss (1974) male and female samples.

A preliminary inspection of the effect size data identified one set of subjects (Swift, Spivack, and Back 1973), which was a nonrepresentatively sampled set, as a likely outlier. Its effect size, $+.18$, was distinctly beyond the range of the remaining effect sizes (from $+.04$ to $-.51$). This study was removed, reducing the sample to fifty sets of subjects. Another likely outlier set of subjects (Tygart 1988; $r = -.51$ vs. $r = -.395$ for the next largest effect size) was identified and removed.

A preliminary analysis of the remaining forty-nine sets showed that the mean effect size for nonrepresentatively sampled sets was $-.249$, whereas that for representatively sampled sets was $-.149$. The difference was significant ($z = 2.97, p < .005$, two-tailed). Explanations of this difference are primarily statistical, although other factors may also be operative. As noted earlier, the nonrepresentatively sampled sets of subjects had approximately equal groups of nondelinquents and delinquents. The measure of association is maximized with groups of equal size. In view of the considerable differences in effect size that are confounded with a method effect, we elected to set the nine nonrepresentatively sampled sets of subjects aside and use only the forty representatively sampled sets of subjects in the remaining analyses.

The forty unweighted effect sizes ranged from $+.010$ to $-.395$ with a median of $-.169$ and a mean of $-.165$. The standard deviation of the unweighted effect sizes was .085. The total N was 28,552, with sample sizes ranging from fifty to 4,637. After weighting by the sample sizes, the mean effect size was found to be $-.149$, with a total variance of .0050. Based on the marginal distributions for academic performance and delinquency reported by Kelly (1971), this effect size is equal to an odds ratio of 2.07. An odds ratio of this magnitude indicates that children with low performance (with grades of D or F) are about twice as likely to become delinquent than children with high performance (grades of C or above). In percentage terms, these data indicate that 34.7 percent of children with low performance would be delinquent compared to 20.4 percent of children with high performance.

To estimate the true variance in the effect sizes, the variance due to sampling error (.0013) was subtracted from the total variance. The variance of the effect sizes (Var_{res}) was .0036 (SD = .060), corrected for sampling error. If sampling error were the only cause of variability in the underlying population correlation, the residual variance would be reduced to zero. That it was not indicates that sources of variability remained. The sources of this variability may be substantive effects such as gender or ethnic group differences, or method factors such as the type of delinquency measures used. We consider each of these factors in turn.

1. *Gender.* Of the forty effect sizes, twenty-seven were based on samples of males (N = 15,581), and ten were based on samples of females (N = 8,271). The remaining three effect sizes were from pooled samples of males and females and so were not used in these comparisons. The mean effect size was $-.151$ (Var$_{res}$ = .0003) for males and $-.094$ (Var$_{res}$ = .0012) for females. Comparing the mean effect sizes for males and females showed the association to be significantly larger for males than for females (z = 3.20, p < .005, two-tailed).[5]

2. *Ethnicity.* Unfortunately, only whites and African Americans could be compared because no studies reported data for either Hispanics or Asians. There were eight sets of white subjects (N = 2,385) and seven sets of African American subjects (N = 2,047). The remaining twenty-five sets of subjects included children of differing ethnic backgrounds and could not be used. The small sample size for both African Americans and whites reflects the fact that data were seldom reported for identified ethnic groups. The resulting mean effect size was $-.185$ (Var$_{res}$ = $-.0023$) for whites and $-.134$ (Var$_{res}$ = .0044) for African Americans.[6] The difference between the mean effect sizes for African Americans and whites was not significant (z = 1.53, p < .15, two-tailed).

3. *Delinquency Measures.* The two most commonly used methods of obtaining information on delinquency are self-reports and official records from police or courts. Whether both measures show equal relationships with academic performance has not been tested. In the following analysis, the raw effect sizes from each study were grouped by set within type of delinquency measure (self-report or official records). If both types of delinquency measures were collected for the same set of subjects, that set of subjects appeared in both the self-report group and the official records group. Although this violates the principle of independence, we believe the overall conclusions of the test were not

---

[5] The authors are indebted to John E. Hunter for providing the test of the moderator variables.

[6] A negative value for the residual variance simply indicates that the sample variance was smaller than would be expected, which can occur since it is an estimate (see Hunter and Schmidt 1990).

significantly affected. There were thirteen sets of subjects (N = 13,063) for whom delinquency was measured from official records and twenty-four sets of subjects (N = 15,375) for whom delinquency was measured by self-report. The mean effect size was − .140 when based on official records and − .155 when based on self-reports. This difference was not significant (z = .67, p < .60, two-tailed).

B. Cross-Sectional Multivariate Analyses

The central finding of the previous section was the association of − .149 between academic performance and delinquency across gender and ethnicity. In this section, we consider whether some variables might function as common causes of both academic performance and delinquency. If such variables were found, the association between academic performance and delinquency would be spurious.

Testing whether a variable is a common cause can be accomplished by computing the partial correlation between academic performance and delinquency while controlling for the candidate variable. All that is required, in addition to the effect size between academic performance and delinquency, are the effect sizes between the candidate variable and both academic performance and delinquency. With several candidate variables, the required effect size data might be arranged as a correlation matrix (e.g., Schmidt and Hunter 1992). However, since meta-analyses of candidate variables have not been published, we used our academic performance-delinquency literature to construct such a matrix.

Several variables were tested using cross-sectional data to determine if they fit the common cause model for academic performance and delinquency for males. First, we computed the meta-analytically-derived correlations between SES, intelligence, and attention problems as potential causes, and academic performance and delinquency as the outcomes. The results showed that both intelligence and attention problems function as common causes for males. Controlling for intelligence reduced the partial correlation between academic performance and delinquency to − .018. Controlling for attention problems reduced the partial correlation between academic performance and delinquency to − .029. However, no support was found for a similar role for SES since the partial correlation was − .139. A review of multivariate studies supported the meta-analytic findings of lower effect sizes for males than females.

Seventeen studies listed in table 1 reported measures of association between SES, intelligence, and attention problems-impulsivity and both academic performance and delinquency. These studies are listed in table 2 with the additional information included about the nature and size of the sample and the types of measures. Of the seventeen studies, thirteen included SES as the third variable, five studies included intelligence, and two included attention problems. We found that only two studies included females either as a distinct set of subjects or pooled together with males. Because of this and the significant difference between males and females in the academic performance-delinquency association, we used only males in the common causes analysis.

Using the data from table 2, we computed the effect sizes between the candidate common cause variables and both academic performance and delinquency. Since each effect size was derived from a meta-analysis, six additional meta-analyses were required in addition to the already completed meta-analysis between academic performance and delinquency. As the meta-analysis process has already been described for the academic performance and delinquency analysis, the details are not repeated except as they bear on the rejection of specific studies.

The SES-delinquency and SES-academic performance effect sizes were based on the same twelve sets of subjects. The study by Bazemore and Noblit (1978) was deleted for the reasons noted earlier. Seven of the twelve sets consisted of subjects from differing ethnic backgrounds; the remaining five were equally divided between African American subjects and white subjects. The unweighted SES-delinquency effect size distribution ranged from $+.04$ to $-.24$ with a mean of $-.10$ and revealed no outliers. The resulting weighted mean effect size was $-.079$ with the negative sign indicating that lower SES is associated with delinquency. The unweighted SES-academic performance effect size distribution ranged from .10 to .30 with a mean of .19 after removing Cochran and Bo (1989) ($r = .50$), which appeared to be an outlier. The weighted mean effect size was .178, indicating that low SES is associated with low academic performance.

The IQ-delinquency and IQ-academic performance effect sizes were based on the same five distinct sets of subjects. The ethnic composition of the six sets consisted of one set of African American subjects and two sets of white subjects. The remaining sets consisted of subjects from various ethnic backgrounds. The distribution of the unweighted IQ-delinquency effect sizes ranged from $+.02$ to $-.26$ (.02, $-.22$,

TABLE 2

Studies Reporting Cross-Sectional Associations between Both Academic Performance and Delinquency and Potential Common Cause Variables

Study	Selection and Description of Overall Sample	Analysis Sample			Potential Common Cause Measure	Academic Performance/Delinquency Measure	Association
		N	Sex	Ethnicity			
Bachman (1970)	Youth in Transition wave 1, national sample of tenth-grade males in public high schools (11 percent black)	2,213	M		Quick-Test IQ	SRD frequency past 3 years	.02
						SR GPA past year	.36
						GATB-J vocabulary	.68
						Gates reading	.66
Bazemore and Noblit (1978)	Marion County Youth Study, wave 2 (25 percent random sample of wave 1 sample at twelfth grade + all delinquents from wave 1)	452	M		SES	OR lifetime prevalence at grade 12	−.07
						OSR cumulative GPA at grade 12	.19
Cochran and Bo (1989)	Boys in ninth grade in Stavanger, Norway ($N = 97$)	92	M		SES	SRD frequency at grade 9	−.08
						OSR grade 9 GPA	.50
Dishion et al. (1984)	Self-selected tenth-grade boys ($N = 60$) and ten boys with multiple offenses	69	M	W	Ammons IQ	OR lifetime prevalence	−.24
		69				SRD delinquent lifestyle past year	−.26
		69				WRAT reading achievement	.65
		67				Parent academic rating (CBCL)	.23

Study	Sample	Sex	N	Predictor	Measure	r
Kelly and Pink (1973)	Marion County Youth Study, wave 2 (25 percent random sample of wave 1 sample at twelfth grade)	M	223	SES	OR lifetime court contact at grade 12	-.10
					OR lifetime frequency > 1 contact grade 12	
					OR prevalence grade 12	-.08
					Commitment at grade 12 (GPA, college plans, homework time, and club membership)	.28
Le Blanc, Vallieres, and McDuff (1992)*	Francophone students aged 12–16 years at wave 1	M	420–21	Parent education wave 1	SRD past year at wave 1	.00
					SR GPA (French + math) wave 1	.30
					SR years delayed wave 1 (reversed)	.07
	14–18 years at wave 2		422	Parent education wave 2	SRD past year at wave 2	.07
			353		SR GPA (French + math) wave 2	.17
			425		SR years delayed wave 2 (reversed)	.05
	Wave 1 sample	F	334	Parent education wave 1	SRD past year at wave 1	.03
					SR GPA (French + math) wave 1	.20
					SR years delayed wave 1 (reversed)	.13
			335	Parent education wave 2	SRD past year at wave 2	-.07

185

TABLE 2 (*Continued*)

Study	Selection and Description of Overall Sample	Analysis Sample			Potential Common Cause Measure	Academic Performance/Delinquency Measure	Association
		N	Sex	Ethnicity			
	Wave 2 sample	259				SR GPA (French + math) wave 2	.11
		337				SR years delayed wave 2 (reversed)	.07
Lynam, Moffitt, and Stouthamer-Loeber (1993)	Pittsburgh Youth Study sample of fourth-grade males at age 12–13 (53.5 percent African American, remainder white)	181–218	M	W	SES WAIS Full-Scale IQ Self-, parent-, and teacher-reported impulsiveness	Self-, parent-, and teacher-reported life-time delinquency seriousness	−.11 −.22 .33
					SES WAIS Full-Scale IQ Self-, parent-, and teacher-reported impulsiveness	Composite teacher rating of reading, math, writing, and spelling	.27 .65 −.40
		214–67	M	AA	SES WAIS Full-Scale IQ Self-, parent-, and teacher-reported impulsiveness	Self-, parent-, and teacher-reported life-time delinquency seriousness	−.11 −.25 .37
					SES WAIS Full-Scale IQ Self-, parent-, and teacher-reported impulsiveness	Composite teacher rating of reading, math, writing, and spelling	.05 .55 −.28

Study	Sample	N			Predictor	Outcome	r
Maguin, Loeber, and LeMahieu (1993)*	Pittsburgh Youth Study sample of first-grade males at age 6–7	205 208	M	W	Parent SES Parent- and teacher-rated attention problems	Self-, parent-, and teacher-reported life-time delinquency seriousness at age 6–7	−.08 .22
		205 208			Parent SES Parent- and teacher-rated attention problems	Teacher rating at grades 1 and 2 reading	.28 −.61
		204 207			Parent SES Parent- and teacher-rated attention problems	Teacher rating at grades 1 and 2 math	.25 −.56
		199 199			Parent SES Parent- and teacher-rated attention problems	CAT achievement at grade 1 reading	.29 −.59
		199 200			Parent SES Parent- and teacher-rated attention problems	CAT achievement at grade 1 math	.13 −.53
		205 208			Parent SES Parent- and teacher-rated attention problems	Parent report *never* held back	.30 −.42
		205 208			Parent SES Parent- and teacher-rated attention problems	In expected grade for age	.17 −.29
		285 287	M	AA	Parent SES Parent- and teacher-rated attention problems	Self-, parent-, and teacher-reported life-time delinquency seriousness at age 6–7	−.10 .17
		285 287			Parent SES Parent- and teacher-rated attention problems	Teacher rating at grades 1 and 2 reading	.19 −.57
		284			Parent SES	Teacher rating at	.14

TABLE 2 (Continued)

Study	Selection and Description of Overall Sample	Analysis Sample			Potential Common Cause Measure	Academic Performance/ Delinquency Measure	Association
		N	Sex	Ethnicity			
		286			Parent- and teacher-rated attention problems	grades 1 and 2 math	-.57
		263			Parent SES	CAT achievement at grade 1 reading	.11
		264			Parent- and teacher-rated attention problems		-.50
		264			Parent SES	CAT achievement at grade 1 math	.04
		265			Parent- and teacher-rated attention problems		-.44
		285			Parent SES	Parent report *never* held back	.19
		287			Parent- and teacher-rated attention problems		-.31
		285			Parent SES	In expected grade for age	.14
		287			Parent- and teacher-rated attention problems		-.34
Pittsburgh Youth Study sample of fourth-grade males at age 9–10		216	M	W	Parent SES	Self-, parent-, and teacher-reported life-time delinquency seriousness at age 9–10	-.19
		218			Parent- and teacher-rated attention problems		.41
		215			Parent SES	Teacher rating at grades 4 and 5 reading	.33
		217			Parent- and teacher-rated attention problems		-.69
		216			Parent SES	Teacher rating at grades 4 and 5 math	.31
		218			Parent- and teacher-rated attention problems		-.68

211		Parent SES	CAT achievement at grade 4 reading	.38
213		Parent- and teacher-rated attention problems		−.58
210		Parent SES	CAT achievement at grade 4 math	.32
219		Parent- and teacher-rated attention problems		−.59
216		Parent SES	Parent report *never* held back	.22
218		Parent- and teacher-rated attention problems		−.46
216		Parent SES	In expected grade for age	.17
218		Parent- and teacher-rated attention problems		−.40
269	M AA	Parent SES	Self-, parent-, and teacher-reported life-time delinquency seriousness at age 9–10	−.12
272		Parent- and teacher-rated attention problems		.35
266		Parent SES	Teacher rating at grades 4 and 5 reading	.11
269		Parent- and teacher-rated attention problems		−.50
266		Parent SES	Teacher rating at grades 4 and 5 math	.05
269		Parent- and teacher-rated attention problems		−.60
255		Parent SES	CAT achievement at grade 4 reading	.17
258		Parent- and teacher-rated attention problems		−.34
253		Parent SES	CAT achievement at grade 4 math	.04
256		Parent- and teacher-rated attention problems		−.47
269		Parent SES	Parent report *never* held	.18

TABLE 2 (*Continued*)

Study	Selection and Description of Overall Sample	Analysis Sample			Potential Common Cause Measure	Academic Performance/ Delinquency Measure	Association
		N	Sex	Ethnicity			
		272			Parent- and teacher-rated attention problems	back	−.37
		269			Parent SES	In expected grade for age	.18
		272			Parent- and teacher-rated attention problems		−.35
Pittsburgh Youth Study sample of seventh-grade males at age 12–13		187	M	W	Parent SES	Self-, parent-, and teacher-reported life-time delinquency seriousness at age 12–13	−.08
		190			Parent- and teacher-rated attention problems		.29
		177			Parent SES	Teacher rating at grades 7 and 8 reading	.26
		180			Parent- and teacher-rated attention problems		−.63
		171			Parent SES	Teacher rating at grades 7 and 8 math	.25
		174			Parent- and teacher-rated attention problems		−.61
		175			Parent SES	CAT achievement at grade 7 reading	.43
		178			Parent- and teacher-rated attention problems		−.50
		171			Parent SES	CAT achievement at grade 7 math	.39
		174			Parent- and teacher-rated attention problems		−.47
		187			Parent SES	Parent report *never* held back	.22
		190			Parent- and teacher-rated attention problems		−.40

N	Group	Predictor	Outcome	r
187		Parent SES	In expected grade for age	.26
190		Parent- and teacher-rated attention problems		−.31
247	M AA	Parent SES	Self-, parent-, and teacher-reported life-time delinquency seriousness at age 12–13	−.16
251		Parent- and teacher-rated attention problems		.27
235		Parent SES	Teacher rating at grades 7 and 8 reading	.22
239		Parent- and teacher-rated attention problems		−.47
230		Parent SES	Teacher rating at grades 7 and 8 math	.28
234		Parent- and teacher-rated attention problems		−.51
220		Parent SES	CAT achievement at grade 7 reading	.21
221		Parent- and teacher-rated attention problems		−.31
221		Parent SES	CAT achievement at grade 7 math	.24
222		Parent- and teacher-rated attention problems		−.55
247		Parent SES	Parent report *never* held back	.17
251		Parent- and teacher-rated attention problems		−.29
247		Parent SES	In expected grade for age	.16
251		Parent- and teacher-rated attention problems		−.18

TABLE 2 (*Continued*)

Study	Selection and Description of Overall Sample	Analysis Sample			Potential Common Cause Measure	Academic Performance/ Delinquency Measure	Association
		N	Sex	Ethnicity			
Menard and Morse (1984)	25 percent random sample of Elliot and Voss's (1974) sample of ninth-grade students in two California school districts, time 1 data only	257	M + F		OSR IQ grade 9	SRD frequency nonserious delinquency past 3 years	−.08
						SRD frequency serious delinquency past 3 years	−.16
						OSR GPA	.49
						DAT score	.78
Noblit (1976)	Marion County Youth Study, wave 2 (25 percent random sample of wave 1 sample at twelfth grade)	261	M		SES	OR adjudication	−.11
						OR cumulative GPA	.18
Patterson and Dishion (1985)	Oregon Youth Study sample of seventh- and tenth-grade boys at wave 1	133	M		Ammons IQ	SRD variety	−.28
		133				OR lifetime police contact	−.24
		133				WRAT reading achievement	.25
		115				OSR GPA past 2 years	.40
Polk (1969)	Marion County Youth Study, wave 2 (25 percent random sample of wave 1 sample at twelfth grade	260	M		SES	OR lifetime prevalence at grade 12	−.11
						OSR GPA at grade 12	.18

Study	Sample	N	Sex	Control variable	Measure	Correlation
Polk (1975)	Marion County Youth Study, wave 2 (25 percent random sample of wave 1 sample at twelfth grade)	260	M	SES	OR adjudication grade 12	−.11
					OSR cumulative GPA grade 12	.18
Polk, Frease, and Richmond (1974)	Marion County Youth Study, wave 1, all tenth-grade students in Oregon county	1,000	M	SES	OR adjudication grade 10	−.02
					OSR cumulative GPA	.22
Polk and Halferty (1966)	Lane County Youth Study, 50 percent sample of ninth-twelfth-grade males in Oregon school	410	M	Parent occupation / Parent education	OR adjudication grade 12	−.10 / −.16
				Parent occupation / Parent education	OSR cumulative GPA	.13 / .22
Wiatrowski et al. (1982)	Youth in Transition Study, national sample of tenth-grade males in public high schools (11 percent black) at wave 1	1,000	M	SES	SRD frequency past 3 years	−.02
					SR GPA past year	.19
Williams and McGee (1994)	Dunedin Multidisciplinary Health and Development Study, birth cohort of Dunedin, New Zealand, children (98 percent European background) at age 15	364	M	Family disadvantage at age 15 (reversed)	SRD frequency at age 15	−.24
					Burt reading test age 15	.10
		334	F		SRD frequency at age 15	−.11
					Burt reading test age 15	.18

NOTE.—A negative sign means that delinquency involvement is associated with lower grades or special class placement. OR = officially recorded delinquency; SRD = self-reported delinquency; OSR = official school records; SR = self-reported; AA = African American; W = white; M = male; F = female; GPA = grade point average; WRAT = Wide Range Achievement Test; CAT = California Achievement Test; WAIS = Wechsler Adult Intelligence Scale; SES = socioeconomic status; GATB-J = General Aptitude Test Battery-Part J; CBCL = Child Behavior Checklist; and DAT = Differential Aptitude Test.

* This entry also reports data provided to the current investigators by the original authors.

193

−.25, −.25, and −.26), with a mean of −.19. The distribution of the unweighted IQ-academic performance effect sizes ranged from .32 to .65 (.32, .44, .55, .57, and .65), with a mean of .51.

Since the effect sizes are weighted by sample size, an effect size from a large sample plays a critical role in determining the weighted mean effect size. The sample sizes of the six sets of subjects that made up the sample consisted of five sets that ranged in size from sixty-five to 257 and one set with a size of 2,213 (Bachman 1970). In the case of the distribution of the unweighted IQ-delinquency effect sizes, the effect size of the Bachman (1970) set was +.02. However, due to its sample size, the Bachman (1970) set almost completely determined the mean weighted effect size. With Bachman (1970) included, the mean effect size is −.034; however, with Bachman (1970) excluded, the mean effect size is −.243. In view of the singular role of this study, we elected to report both mean effect sizes. The negative sign indicates that low intelligence is associated with delinquency.

In the case of the unweighted IQ-academic performance effect sizes, the effect size from Bachman (1970) was .57, which placed it near the middle of the distribution. We examined the effects of deleting different combinations of this effect size and the .32 effect size (Patterson and Dishion 1985), which was noticeably smaller in magnitude. The mean effect size changed by less than .03 from the value obtained by using all sets. On this basis, we elected to report only the effect size based on the five sets of subjects. The resulting weighted mean effect size was .558, indicating that low intelligence is associated with low academic performance.

The attention problems-delinquency and attention problems-academic performance effect sizes were based on the same six distinct sets of subjects (three of white male children and three of African American male children), all of which were from the Pittsburgh Youth Study (Loeber et al. 1991). The distribution of the unweighted attention problems-delinquency effect sizes ranged from .17 to .37, with a mean of .28. The weighted mean effect size was .273, indicating that high attention problems are associated with delinquency. The distribution of the unweighted attention problems-academic performance effect sizes ranged from −.38 to −.55, with a mean of −.46. The weighted mean effect size was −.460, indicating that high attention problems are associated with low academic performance.

Table 3 presents the mean effect sizes for the three potential common cause variables with both academic performance and delinquency. The

TABLE 3

Cross-Sectional Correlations between Socioeconomic Status, Intelligence, Attention Problems, Academic Performance, and Delinquency for Males

	Academic Performance	Delinquency	
		Full Set	Set after Removal of Bachman (1970)
Academic performance:			
r		.151	
Subjects		15,581	
Sets		27	
Socioeconomic status:			
r	.182	−.083	
Subjects	3,937	4,002	
Sets	11	12	
Intelligence:			
r	.558	−.034	−.243
Subjects	2,800	2,810	597
Sets	5	5	4
Attention problems:			
r	−.460	.273	
Subjects	1,371	1,378	
Sets	6	6	

first line is the effect size, the second is the number of subjects, and the third is the number of groups of subjects.

The common causes hypothesis was tested by computing the partial correlation between academic performance and delinquency, controlling for the hypothesized common cause—SES, intelligence, or attention problems. Controlling for SES, the partial correlation was found to be −.138. Thus SES does not account for the academic performance-delinquency association. However, the result was different when the variable attention problems was tested as the common cause. Controlling for attention problems, the partial correlation was −.029, indicating that attention problems were a likely common cause of both academic performance and delinquency.

The results for intelligence critically depended on how the Bachman (1970) study was treated in the computation of the IQ-delinquency mean effect size. If Bachman was deleted, which yielded a mean IQ-delinquency effect size of −.243, the partial correlation was −.018. However, if Bachman was included, which yielded a mean IQ-delinquency effect size of −.034, the partial correlation was −.159.

Overall, we were inclined to consider Bachman's effect size as an outlier since the remaining effect sizes were considerably larger and generally well clustered together. We concluded that intelligence functioned as a common cause of both academic performance and delinquency. However, we acknowledge that other interpretations are possible. Only further research can clarify this issue.

Although the results of the previous section have implicated both intelligence and attention problems as common cause variables to both academic performance and delinquency, there may be other variables that function in the same manner. These variables can be suggested by examining the results of the multivariate cross-sectional analyses presented in table 4.

Seven of the nine studies included in their analyses measures of attachment to parents or school, aspirations, and involvement in school, which are constructs from social control theory. In all cases, academic performance was included by itself or as part of a composite measure, which was usually labeled as commitment. Two of the six studies (Thornton and Voigt 1984; Fiqueira-McDonough 1986) included only social control variables. Four studies used social control plus peer association or peer attachment (Johnson 1979; Krohn and Massey 1980; Gomme 1985; LaGrange and White 1985); one study (Cernkovich and Giordano 1992) used social control variables plus perceived risk of arrest, which is a variable from deterrence theory.

One way to look at these seven quite different studies is to ask how many found the multiple regression coefficient (beta) between academic performance and delinquency to be near zero after the other independent variables had been entered. Although based on only a few studies, there is little consistent evidence that peer association or perceived risk of arrest or social control variables reduce the beta coefficient to near zero. The variable that more often reduces the beta coefficient to near zero is gender. Two of the three studies that conducted within-gender analysis found weaker relationships for females than males (Johnson 1979; Gomme 1985). Only Fiqueira-McDonough (1986) found equally strong relationships for females as for males.

The first of the two remaining studies, Rankin (1980), found no association between having been ever held back and the frequency of offending, both by self-report after controlling for grade level and sex. The second study, Wolff et al. (1982), compared incarcerated boys matched on race and age to nonincarcerated boys. This study found a significant association between reading achievement and adjudication after controlling for intelligence. Although the Wolff et al. (1982) study runs counter to the results previously reported concerning the role of intelligence, we believe the matching design of the study may, in part, account for the results.

C. Longitudinal Bivariate Analyses

Our analysis of longitudinal relationships indicated several points. Earlier measured academic performance has a mean association of $-.153$ with later measured delinquency. This mean association was found to vary with each of the substantive factors examined. It was substantially stronger for males compared with females, for whites compared with African Americans, and for older children compared with younger children. It was almost independent of the interval between the measurements of academic performance and delinquency. The effect size was larger when delinquency was based on official records than on self-reports of delinquency.

One hundred and ten longitudinal effect sizes from twenty-six studies constituted the sample for this analysis (recall that "longitudinal" as used here refers to designs where the academic performance measurement preceded the delinquency measurement). These twenty-six studies are presented in table 5, with a brief description of the studys' sample demographics, selection method, types of academic performance and delinquency measures used, when the measures were administered, and the associated effect size.

As was true with the cross-sectional data, the 110 longitudinal effect sizes were not from 110 independent samples of subjects. In addition to separate effect sizes for males and females, and whites and African Americans, some studies used multiple measures of academic performance, delinquency, or both (e.g., Tremblay et al. 1992a; Williams and McGee 1994); or conducted multiple assessment waves (e.g., Wiatrowski et al. 1982; Denno 1990; Williams and McGee 1994). Finally, several studies reported results for the same set of subjects (Wiatrowski et al. 1982; Lipton and Smith 1983; Wells and Rankin 1983). We applied the same procedures as were used in the analysis of the cross-sectional data. That is, we identified distinct sets of subjects and then averaged together all effect sizes that were developed from the data for that set of subjects.[7] This resulted in thirty-one distinct sets of subjects, which spanned the remaining 105 effect sizes.

[7] Two studies, Moffitt and Silva (1988) and Walker et al. (1991), were removed because they analyzed a sample that overlapped with other studies. In the case of Moffitt and Silva (1988) the overlap was with McGee et al. (1988) and Williams and McGee (1994), and, in the case of Walker et al. (1991), the overlap was with Patterson, Capaldi, and Bank (1991).

TABLE 4
Studies Reporting Cross-Sectional Multivariate Analyses of Academic Performance as a Predictor of Delinquency with Controls for Third Variables

Study	Selection and Description of Overall Sample	Analysis Sample			Academic Measure	Delinquency Measure	Control Variables	Association
		N	Sex	Ethnicity				
Cernkovich and Giordano (1992)	Random sample of youth aged 12–19 years from Ohio city	233	M	AA	Commitment (SR grades, value of grades, and homework aspirations)	SRD frequency past year weighted by seriousness	School and teacher attachment, SES, arrest risk, age, school involvement, parent commitment, opportunities, school context	−.21*
		196	M	W				−.21*
		238	F	AA				−.18
		217	F	W				−.15
Fiqueira-McDonough (1986)	Two schools (TOPS and CENTRAL) in same community differing in school climate (that is, goals, rule making, discipline, problems, and supervision) (N = 350 tenth-grade students)	SSNR	M		SR GPA past year at TOPS	SRD frequency minor delinquency past year	Illegal opportunity, school activities, family aspirations, school attachment, career aspirations, material aspirations, public equality, private equality, self-concept	−.23[a]
		SSNR	F					−.22[a]
		SSNR	M		SR GPA past year at CENTRAL			−.26[a]
		SSNR	F					−.26[a]

198

Study	Sample	Design	N	Sex	Race	Independent measure	Dependent measure	Controls	Coefficient
Gomme (1985)	Seventh–tenth-grade students in Ontario, Canada, city (total N = 429)	SSNR		M		Failed course in past 2 years	SRD total frequency past year	SES, age, peer association, belief in law	−.16*
							SRD serious frequency past year		−.15*
							SRD theft frequency past year		−.10
							SRD status frequency past year		−.16*
		SSNR		F		Failed course in past 2 years	SRD total frequency past year	SES, age, peer association, belief in law	−.01
							SRD serious frequency past year		−.02
							SRD theft frequency past year		−.04
							SRD status frequency past year		−.02
Johnson (1979)	Tenth-grade students in 3 high schools in below-median income areas (N = 518 white, 114 Asian, 60 African American, 42 other)		207	M	W	SR composite of modal grade, work level expected, school difficulty, and success	SRD frequency past year	Social class, parental concern	.22**
			178	F	W				N.S.[b]

199

TABLE 4 (*Continued*)

Study	Selection and Description of Overall Sample	Analysis Sample			Academic Measure	Delinquency Measure	Control Variables	Association
		N	Sex	Ethnicity				
Krohn and Massey (1980)	Random sample of seventh- to twelfth-grade students in six midwestern districts (N = 3,065)	SSNR	M		SR GPA	SRD frequency minor	Maternal, paternal, and peer attachment; commitment; educational and career aspirations, beliefs in laws, parental morals, value of school	−.25[a]
						SRD frequency serious		−.19[a]
		SSNR	F			SRD frequency minor		−.17[a]
						SRD frequency serious		−.11[a]
LaGrange and White (1985)	Rutgers Health and Human Development Study sample				Composite of SR math and English grades past 3 years, SR last semester GPA	SRD frequency past 3 years	School commitment, school attachment, parent attachment, parent love, delinquent peers, SES	
	Males aged 12	122	M					−.09
	Males aged 15	138	M					−.15
	Males aged 18	81	M					−.01
Rankin (1980)	Random sample of seventh- to eleventh-grade students in 33 Michigan public school districts	385	M + F		SR ever held back	SRD frequency past year	Sex, grade level	N.S.[b]

| Thornton and Voigt (1984) | Random sample of fourth–twelfth-grade students in large city public schools | 3,500 | M + F | Commitment (SR GPA, likes school, and importance of grades) | SRD frequency: Minor theft Major theft Violence | Age, SES, gender, belief in law, involvement, attachment to school, parents, parental social control, peer delinquency, exposure to media violence, time wathcing television | −.44** −.23* −.16 |
| Wolff et al. (1982) | 56 incarcerated white boys ages 14–16 matched on age and race with 48 lower-middle- and 48 upper-middle-class boys without known or SR delinquency | 152 | M | PIAT reading achievement | OR adjudication or school and SR arrest | IPAT Culture Fair IQ | b*** |

NOTE.—A negative sign means that delinquency involvement is associated with lower grades or special class placement. OR = officially recorded delinquency; SRD = self-reported delinquency; OSR = official school records; SR = self-reported; SSNR = sample size not reported; AA = African American; W = white; M = male; F = female; GPA = grade point average; SES = socioeconomic status; PIAT = Peabody Individual Achievement Test; and IPAT = Institute for Personality and Ability Testing; N.S. = not significant.

[a] Significance level not reported.
[b] Coefficient not reported or could not be computed.

* p < .05.
** p < .01.
*** p < .001.

TABLE 5

Studies Reporting Longitudinal Associations between Academic Performance and Delinquency

Study	Selection and Description of Overall Sample	Analysis Sample			Academic Measure	Delinquency Measure	Association
		N	Sex	Ethnicity			
Denno (1990)	Philadelphia Collaborative Perinatal Project subsample of African American youth born 1959–62 and residing in Philadelphia from age 10 to 17 who attended public schools and had IQ and achievement data	487	M	AA	WRAT (age 7):	OR prevalence police contact age 10–17	
					Spelling		+ .03
					Reading		− .09*
					Arithmetic		− .03
					CAT achievement (age 14–15):		
					Total		− .10*
					Reading		− .10*
					Math		− .08*
					Spelling		− .12**
					Language		− .10*
		500	F	AA	WRAT (age 7):		
					Spelling		− .09
					Reading		− .07
					Arithmetic		− .04
					CAT achievement (age 14–15):		
					Total		− .17***
					Reading		− .16***
					Math		− .16***
					Spelling		− .15***
					Language		− .16***

Study	Sample	N	Sex	Race	GPA measure	Delinquency measure	r
Ferguson (1952)	Males who left school legally at age 14 in Glasgow in 1947	1,275	M		School GPA at age 14	OR conviction age 15–18 but not prior	−.12**
		1,349				OR conviction age 8–18	−.14***
						2 or more OR convictions age 8–18	−.13***
Kupersmidt and Coie (1990)	Fifth-grade children in semi-rural area (69 percent white, 47 percent female)	104	M + F		OSR composite GPA at grade 5	OR police contact at age 18	−.11
Le Blanc, Vallieres, and McDuff (1992)[a]	Francophone students aged 12–16 years at wave 1 and aged 14–18 years at wave 2	451	M		SR GPA (French + math) wave 1 SR years delayed (reversed)	SRD past year at wave 2	−.08 −.04
		362	F		SR GPA (French + math) wave 1 SR years delayed (reversed)	SRD past year at wave 2	−.03 +.02
Lipton and Smith (1983)	Youth in Transition sample; national sample of tenth-grade males in public high schools (11 percent African American), wave 1 (grade 10) and wave 2 (grade 11)	1,592	M	W	SR GPA past year at grade 10	SRD frequency theft + vandalism at grade 11	−.10

TABLE 5 (*Continued*)

Study	Selection and Description of Overall Sample	Analysis Sample			Academic Measure	Delinquency Measure	Association
		N	Sex	Ethnicity			
Maughan, Gray, and Rutter (1985)	10-year-old white children attending schools in an inner London borough in 1970 (N = 1,689); subsample with/without reading retardation and antisocial or mixed behavior selected for follow-up and for interview 1 year after leaving school	84	M	W	Reading retardation at age 10 (>2 years below expected grade adjusted for IQ and age)	OR caution or conviction up to age 18	−.07
McCarthy and Hoge (1984)[a]	Students in seventh, ninth, and eleventh grades of public and parochial schools in Mid-Atlantic cities (55 percent male, 49 percent white at time 1)	1,379	M + F		OSR grades past year at wave 1	SRD theft + vandalism frequency past year wave 2	−.13***
		1,485			OSR grades past year at wave 2	SRD theft + vandalism frequency past year wave 3	−.11***
		1,403			OSR grades past year at wave 1	SRD theft + vandalism frequency past year wave 3	−.10***

Study	Description	N	Sex	Reading measure	Outcome measure	r
McGee et al. (1988)	Dunedin Multidisciplinary Health and Development Study, birth cohort of Dunedin, New Zealand, children at age 13	428	M	Reading disability at ages 9 and 11	SR police contact	.01
					Parent-reported police contact	+.05
		403	F		SR police contact	–.04
					Parent-reported police contact	+.04
Moffitt and Silva (1988)	Dunedin Multidisciplinary Health and Development Study; birth cohort of Dunedin, New Zealand, children (98 percent European background) at age 13	678	M + F	Burt reading test age 11	Composite of SRD frequency, parent-reported socialized aggression, teacher-reported antisocial (age 13)	–.17***
Ouston (1984)	Children born in school-year 1959 and attending at 1 of 12 London schools	1,220	M	NFER reading test at age 14	OR caution or guilt by age 18	–.15****
		954	F			–.10**
	Subsample of children in present study who were included in another study	374	M	NFER reading test at age 10		–.14**
		483	F			–.08
Patterson, Capaldi, and Bank (1991)	Oregon Youth Study sample of fourth-grade boys from schools in high-crime areas	91	M	Teacher CBCL composite grade 4	SRD at grade 7	–.10
					OR police contact at grade 8	–.22
				OSR composite achievement grade 4	SRD at grade 7	–.09
					OR police contact at grade 8	–.07
				WRAT Reading grade 4	SRD at grade 7	–.03
					OR police contact at grade 8	–.04

TABLE 5 (*Continued*)

Study	Selection and Description of Overall Sample	Analysis Sample			Academic Measure	Delinquency Measure	Association
		N	Sex	Ethnicity			
Robins and Hill (1966)	Purposive selection of boys born 1930–34 and attending at least 6 years to yield median splits on SES, father in home, and school problems	296 256	M	AA	OSR school retardation grades 1–6 (reversed)	OR police/court contact lifetime: To age 15 To age 17 Age 16–17 only	-.20*** -.11 -.05
Schafer (1972)	Boys in 2 schools who were continuously enrolled for grades 10–12 and were not delinquent at grade 10	568	M		OSR GPA at grade 9	OR adjudication at grade 12	-.11**
Schafer, Olexa, and Polk (1972)	Boys in 2 schools who were continuously enrolled for grades 10–12 and were not delinquent at grade 10	1,157	M + F		OSR high academic track at grade 10	OR adjudication at grade 12	-.16***

Study	Sample	N	Sex	Race	Predictor measure	Outcome measure	r
Spreen (1981)	Boys who were diagnosed as LD at ages 8–12 (N = 57) and random sample of boys of average ability from high schools with no history of learning problems or brain damage (N = 52) matched at group level on sex, age, and SES	86	M		OSR LD diagnoses ages 8–12 (reversed)	SR police contact ages 16–20	−.09
						Parent report police contact ages 16–20	−.19
						SRD > 1 serious offense ages 16–20	−.07
						SRD frequency ages 16–20	−.08
Tracy, Wolfgang, and Figlio (1990)	1958 Philadelphia birth cohort of males born in 1958 and residing in Philadelphia from age 12 to 18	2,455	M	W	CAT achievement at age 12	OR police contact at ages 10–18	−.24***
		4,305	M	NW			−.17***
Tremblay and Masse (1993)	Low SES, white, Francophone boys attending kindergarten in 53 Montreal schools	587	M	W	Age 10 achievement: French	SRD frequency age 14:	
						Stealing	−.06
						Vandalism	−.07
						Aggression	−.13**
					Age 10 achievement: math	SRD frequency age 14:	
						Stealing	−.03
						Vandalism	−.03
						Aggression	−.09*

TABLE 5 (*Continued*)

Study	Selection and Description of Overall Sample	Analysis Sample			Academic Measure	Delinquency Measure	Association
		N	Sex	Ethnicity			
Tremblay et al. (1992a)	Concordia University High Risk Project sample of first-grade children from low-middle and impoverished areas of Montreal	67	M		Age 7 achievement: French	SRD frequency past year grade 7	−.33**
					Math		−.31**
					Age 7 achievement: French	SRD aggression frequency past year grade 7	−.22
					Math		−.24
					Age 10 achievement: French	SRD frequency past year grade 7	−.19
					Math		−.30**
					Age 10 achievement: French	SRD aggression frequency past year grade 7	−.20
					Math		−.32**
		80	F		Age 7 achievement: French	SRD frequency past year grade 7	+.02
					Math		+.03
					Age 7 achievement: French	SRD aggression frequency past year grade 7	−.01
					Math		−.01
					Age 10 achievement: French	SRD frequency past year grade 7	−.17
					Math		−.20
					Age 10 achievement: French	SRD aggression frequency past year grade 7	−.16
					Math		−.21

Study	N	Sex	Sample	Measure	Correlation
Walker et al. (1993)	60	M	Randomly selected subsamples of low antisocial risk (N = 41) and high antisocial risk (N = 39) fourth-grade boys from Oregon Youth Study	Achievement grade 7: Total; Reading; Math; Special class placement (reversed)	OR + SRD composite to grade 7: −.28*; −.20; −.27*; −.14
Wallander (1988)	34	M	Danish males without history of parental psychiatric hospitalization	Never held back; Special class placement (reversed)	OR arrest frequency to age 18–21: −.07; −.01
Wells and Rankin (1983)	1,691	M	Youth in Transition sample; national sample of tenth-grade males in public high schools (89 percent white); waves 1 (grade 10), 2 (grade 11), and 3 (grade 12)	SR GPA past year at grade 10; SR GPA past year at grade 10	SRD frequency at grade 12: total (−.23***); Theft + vandalism (−.12***); Aggression (−.19***); SRD frequency at wave 2: total (−.19***)
Werner and Smith (1977)	320	M	1955 birth cohort of children born on Kauai (42 percent low SES; 97 percent nonwhite)	OSR grade 4 reading achievement; OSR LD Dx at age 10 (reversed)	OR police/court contact at age 18: −.20***; −.07
	313	F		OSR grade 4 reading achievement; OSR LD Dx at age 10 (reversed)	−.18**; −.15**
West and Farrington (1973)[a]	411	M	Cambridge Study in Delinquent Development; all males in 6 lower-class London schools (90 percent white, British origin)	Secondary school allocation age 11; Junior attainment age 11	OR conviction ages 10–16: −.15**; −.18***
	409			Secondary school allocation age 11; Junior attainment age 11	SRD ages 14 and 16: −.13**; −.17***

TABLE 5 (*Continued*)

Study	Selection and Description of Overall Sample	Analysis Sample			Academic Measure	Delinquency Measure	Association
		N	Sex	Ethnicity			
Wiatrowski et al. (1982)	Youth in Transition Study; national sample of tenth-grade males in public high schools (11 percent black) at wave 1 (grade 10), wave 2 (grade 11), wave 3 (grade 12), and wave 4 (grade 13)	1,000	M		SR GPA past year at grade 10	SRD frequency past year grade 12	−.19***
						SRD frequency past year grade 13	−.13***
						SRD serious past year grade 13	−.12***
					SR GPA past year at grade 12	SRD frequency past year grade 13	−.18***
						SRD serious past year grade 13	−.13***
Williams and McGee (1994)	Dunedin Multidisciplinary Health and Development Study; birth cohort of Dunedin, New Zealand, children (N = 1,037; 98 percent European background) at age 15	364	M		Burt reading test age 7	SRD frequency age 15	−.05
					Prose reading test age 7		−.02
					Burt reading test age 9		+.02
					Dunedin spelling test age 9		−.06
		334	F		Burt reading test age 7		−.03
					Prose reading test age 7		−.01
					Burt reading test age 9		+.02
					Dunedin spelling test age 9		−.06

| Wolfgang, Figlio, and Sellin (1972) | 1945 Philadelphia birth cohort of males born in 1945 and residing in Philadelphia from age 12 to 18 ($N = 7{,}043$ whites, 2,902 non-whites) | 2,642 | M | W | Achievement test at grade 6 or below | OR police contact ages 10–18 | −.26*** |
| | | 1,207 | M | NW | | | −.12*** |

NOTE.—A negative sign means that delinquency involvement is associated with lower grades or special class placement. OR = officially recorded delinquency; SRD = self-reported delinquency; OSR = official school records; SR = self-reported; AA = African American; W = white; M = male; F = female; GPA = grade point average; WRAT = Wide Range Achievement Test; CAT = California Achievement Test; SES = socioeconomic status; LD = learning disabled; Dx = diagnosis; NFER = National Foundation for Educational Research; and CBCL = Child Behavior Checklist.

[a] This entry also reports data provided to the current investigators by the original authors.

* $p < .05$.

** $p < .01$.

*** $p < .001$.

211

Inspection of these thirty-one sets revealed that one set of subjects (Spreen 1981) was selected using a nonrepresentative sampling design. This set was removed from the data set to maintain consistency with the cross-sectional meta-analysis.

Of the remaining thirty sets of subjects, twenty-one sets were composed of males, seven sets were composed of females, and the remainder were composed of both males and females. Three of the sets of subjects were composed of African American children, three sets were composed of white children, and two sets were composed of nonwhite children. The remaining sets of subjects were from several different or unspecified ethnic backgrounds. The sample sizes of the sets of subjects ranged from a low of thirty-four (Wallander 1988) to a high of 4,305 (the nonwhite sample of Tracy, Wolfgang, and Figlio 1990).

Inspection of the 101 raw, unweighted effect sizes for the thirty sets of subjects revealed that the distribution ranged from + .045 to − .330, with a median of − .114 and a mean of − .112. The distribution of the thirty effect sizes for the thirty sets of subjects showed the range to be from − .005 to − .264, with a mean of − .118 and a standard deviation of .065. The distribution also showed the presence of a set of three effect sizes that were approximately 1.3–1.5 SD above the next largest effect size. Two of the effect sizes were from very large samples: the set of white subjects from the Tracy, Wolfgang, and Figlio 1990 study and the set of white subjects from the Wolfgang, Figlio, and Sellin (1972) study. The third was from a considerably smaller and therefore less influential sample. To represent the effects of the sets of subjects from these two studies, we computed the effect sizes with and without them. However, we emphasize the results computed with the two sets of subjects included.

The mean effect size with the two sets of subjects included was − .153, with a total variance of .0039, a sampling error variance of .0012, and an N of 24,361. However, with the two sets of subjects deleted, the mean effect size was − .127, with a total variance of .0019, a sampling error variance of .0014, and an N of 19,265. The variance of the effect sizes, corrected for sampling error, was .0028 with the two sets of subjects included and .0005 with the two sets of subjects excluded. The two sets of subjects, thus, have some impact on the mean effect size.

Based on the marginal distributions for academic performance and delinquency reported by Kelly (1971), an effect size of − .153 is equal to an odds ratio of 2.11. In percentage terms, 35.0 percent of children with low performance would be delinquent compared to 20.3 percent of children with high performance. For an effect size of $-.127$, the equivalent odds ratio is 1.87.

1. *Gender.* The comparison of the strength of the association by gender was based on twenty-one distinct sets of male subjects ($N = 19,786$) and seven distinct sets of female subjects ($N = 3,049$). The mean effect size for males was $-.166$ ($Var_{res} = .0025$) and $-.086$ ($Var_{res} = .0001$) for females. The test for differences between the effect size for males and females was significant ($z = 3.55, p < .001$, two-tailed), which indicated that the academic performance-delinquency association was larger for males than females. Removing the two previously identified effect sizes reduced the mean effect size for males to $-.137$, but the significant difference between males and females remained.

2. *Ethnicity.* Two studies (Wolfgang, Figlio, and Sellin 1972; Tracy, Wolfgang, and Figlio 1990) identified their subjects as either "whites" or "nonwhites." We interpreted their "nonwhite" label to mean primarily African American. There were five distinct sets of African Americans ($N = 6,782$), three distinct sets of whites ($N = 5,181$), and 21 sets of subjects with various ethnic heritages ($N = 12,412$). The resulting mean effect size was $-.146$ ($Var_{res} = -.0003$[6]) for African Americans, $-.246$ ($Var_{res} < .0001$) for whites, and $-.119$ ($Var_{res} = .0003$) for sets with subjects of differing heritages. The comparison for mean effect sizes revealed that the effect size for whites, which included the two large effect sizes, was significant ($z = 6.00$, $p < .001$, two-tailed). However, when the effect size for African Americans was compared to that for subjects of differing heritages, the difference ($-.146$ versus $-.119$, respectively) was just barely not significant ($z = 1.95, p < .06$, two-tailed). Although these data do not support a definitive statement, the mean effect size for African Americans and whites seem more different than alike.

3. *Age.* The third factor examined was the joint effect of age at academic performance assessment and delinquency assessment. Three groups were defined from an examination of the distributions of ages at academic performance assessment and delinquency assessment and their joint distribution. Group A (seven sets of subjects, $N = 1,863$) received academic performance assessments before age eleven and delinquency assessments before age sixteen. Group B (eight sets of subjects, $N = 2,837$) also received academic performance assessments before age eleven but received delinquency assessments at age sixteen or

after. Group C (eighteen sets of subjects, $N = 20,938$) received academic performance assessments at age eleven or after and delinquency assessments at age sixteen or after. It should be noted that some sets of subjects were allowed to contribute effect sizes to more than one group. For example, if one set of subjects had completed academic performance assessments both before and after age eleven and were assessed for delinquency after age sixteen, those subjects' data would appear in both group B and group C. Although this practice violates the principle of independence, we believe the results are sufficiently robust to mitigate any concerns.

All possible pairwise tests were examined to determine whether and where differences were to be found. The results showed no differences in mean effect size between group A and group B ($M = -.074$ vs. $-.094$, respectively). However, group C had a significantly larger mean effect size ($M = -.164$) than either group A or group B ($z = 2.91$, $p < .005$ and $z = 3.45$, $p < .001$, respectively, all two-tailed). Because both effect sizes from the large samples were in group C, we removed them and recomputed the comparisons. Although the mean effect size of this group was reduced, it remained significantly larger than that for either group A or group B. The academic performance-delinquency relationship, thus, appears to become stronger with increasing age.

4. *Delinquency Measures.*   A test for differences in the mean effect size by the type of delinquency measure (self-report or official records) was conducted by grouping the raw effect sizes from each study by subject within type of delinquency measure in the same manner as in the cross-sectional analysis. There were twenty-one sets of subjects ($N = 19,316$) for whom delinquency was measured from official records and eleven sets of subjects ($N = 5,502$) for whom delinquency was measured by self-report. The mean effect size was $-.168$ when based on official records and $-.101$ when based on self-report. This difference was significant ($z = 3.27$, $p < .005$, two-tailed). The difference remained significant when the two large effect sizes from the two large studies were removed. Thus the predictive association between poor academic performance and delinquency was stronger for official than for self-reported measures of delinquency.

D. *Longitudinal Multivariate Analyses*
The previous section reported that academic performance and delinquency were correlated even when the measurements were separated by several years. This section addresses the question of whether SES

or conduct problems might function as a common cause of both academic performance and delinquency when longitudinal data are considered. Again, these analyses are based on effect sizes developed from the already identified studies. Studies reporting other multivariate results are also examined.

Socioeconomic status and conduct problems were tested to determine if they fit a common cause model for the predictive association between academic performance and delinquency. The results showed that SES was not a common cause of both academic performance and delinquency and thus replicates the results found earlier for SES in the cross-sectional analyses. The results for conduct problems accounted for only a small part of the association between academic performance and delinquency. Therefore conduct problems did not function as a common cause of academic performance and delinquency. Multivariate analyses showed that controlling for prior delinquency reduced the contribution of prior academic performance to later delinquency. Children who have increased their offending, whether in seriousness or frequency, had poorer academic performance than those who had not.

The studies listed in table 5 were reviewed to identify potential common cause variables that could account for the association between academic performance and delinquency. Because our interest was in examining the common cause model, we judged that potential common cause variables that were measured after the academic performance measure would have very little facial validity. It could be plausibly argued that poor academic performance leads to greater attention problems or conduct problems. Although the ideal test of the common cause model in longitudinal data would be to measure both the potential common cause and academic performance at the same time, we found that this requirement imposed a severe loss of data. Thus we allowed common cause variables measured before academic performance, so long as the common cause variable was measured after the start of elementary school. Although our choice reflects an assumption of continuity in behavior and its stability over time, which has some empirical support (see, e.g., Olweus [1979], for aggression and intelligence), it should be subjected to empirical validation.

We were able to examine SES and conduct problems with academic performance and delinquency. We were not able to include intelligence and attention problems because there were few distinct sets of subjects in the studies we examined. The resulting set of studies on which the common causes analyses were based are presented in table 6.

TABLE 6

Longitudinal Follow-up Studies Reporting Associations between Both Academic Performance and Delinquency with Potential Common Cause Variables

Study	Selection and Description of Overall Sample	Analysis Sample			Potential Common Cause Measure	Academic/ Delinquency Measure	Association
		N	Sex	Ethnicity			
Le Blanc, Vallieres, and McDuff (1992)*	Francophone students aged 12–16 years at wave 1 and 14–18 years at wave 2	418	M		Parent education wave 1	SRD past year at wave 2	+.07
		421				SR GPA (French + math) wave 1	.30
		420				SR years delayed wave 1 (reversed)	.07
		332	F			SRD past year at wave 2	−.04
		334				SR GPA (French + math) wave 1	.20
		334				SR years delayed wave 1 (reversed)	.13
Lipton and Smith (1983)	Youth in Transition sample; national sample of tenth-grade males in public high schools (11 percent black), wave 1 (grade 10) and wave 2 (grade 11)	1,592	M		Parent SES grade 10	SRD frequency theft + vandalism at grade 11	+.02
						SR GPA past year at grade 10	.25

Study	N	Sex		Measure	Outcome	r
Maughan, Gray, and Rutter (1985)	84	M	W	Teacher rating antisocial behavior age 10	OR caution or conviction up to age 18	.14
					Reading retardation at age 10 (>2 years below expected grade adjusted for IQ and age)	−.10
Patterson, Capaldi, and Bank (1991)	91	M		Grade 4 ratings:		
				SR ASB	SRD at grade 7	.52
				Teacher ASB		.39
				Parent ASB		.39
				Observer ASB		.12
				SR ASB	OR police contact at grade 8	−.01
				Teacher ASB		.46
				Parent ASB		.35
				Observer ASB		.01
				SR ASB	Teacher academic composite grade 4	−.17
				Teacher ASB		−.55
				Parent ASB		−.30
				Observer ASB		−.16
				SR ASB	WRAT reading achievement grade 4	−.15
				Teacher ASB		−.25
				Parent ASB		−.08
				Observer ASB		−.16
				SR ASB	OSR composite achievement grade 4	−.16
				Teacher ASB		−.33
				Parent ASB		−.23
				Observer ASB		−.34

10-year-old white children attending schools in an inner London borough in 1970; subsample with/without reading retardation and antisocial or mixed behavior selected for follow-up and interview one year after leaving school

Oregon Youth Study sample of fourth-grade boys from schools in high-crime areas

TABLE 6 (*Continued*)

Study	Selection and Description of Overall Sample	Analysis Sample			Potential Common Cause Measure	Academic/ Delinquency Measure	Association
		N	Sex	Ethnicity			
Schafer (1969)	Boys in 2 schools who were continuously enrolled for grades 10–12 and were not delinquent at grade 10	547	M		Parent SES grade 9	OR lifetime prevalence at twelfth grade	−.16
						OSR ninth grade GPA	.22
Tremblay and Masse (1993)	Low SES, white, Francophone boys attending kindergarten in 53 Montreal schools (N = 1,161)	587	M	W	Teacher-rated oppositional behavior age 6	SRD frequency theft age 14	.13
						SRD frequency vandalism age 14	.14
						SRD frequency aggression age 14	.11
						French achievement age 10	−.12
						Math achievement age 10	−.12
					Teacher-rated oppositional behavior age 10	SRD frequency theft age 14	.16
						SRD frequency vandalism age 14	.17
						SRD frequency aggression age 14	.21
						French achievement age 10	−.26
						Math achievement age 10	−.26

218

Study	Sample	N	Sex	Disruptive behavior age 7	Method	Measure	M
Tremblay et al. (1992a)	Concordia University High Risk Project sample of first-grade children from low-middle and impoverished areas of Montreal (N = 161 boys; 163 girls)	67	M		Self-report	SRD frequency past year grade 7	.39
					Peer nominated		.46
					Self-report	SRD aggression frequency past year grade 7	.32
					Peer nominated		.41
					Self-report	French achievement age 7	−.28
					Peer nominated		−.28
					Self-report	Math achievement age 7	−.44
					Peer nominated	French achievement age 10	−.48
					Self-report		−.28
					Peer nominated	Math achievement age 10	−.39
					Self-report		−.18
					Peer nominated		−.32
		80	F		Self-report	SRD frequency past year grade 7	−.04
					Peer nominated		.11
					Self-report	SRD aggression frequency past year grade 7	−.13
					Peer nominated		.10
					Self-report	French achievement age 7	−.28
					Peer nominated		−.51
					Self-report	Math achievement age 7	−.28
					Peer nominated		−.48
					Self-report	French achievement age 10	−.11
					Peer nominated		−.48
					Self-report	Math achievement age 10	−.06
					Peer nominated		−.43

TABLE 6 (*Continued*)

Study	Selection and Description of Overall Sample	Analysis Sample			Potential Common Cause Measure	Academic/ Delinquency Measure	Association
		N	Sex	Ethnicity			
West and Farrington (1973)*	Cambridge Study in Delinquent Development; all males in 6 lower-class London schools (90 percent white, British origin)	411	M		Income age 8	OR conviction ages 10–16	−.18
		411			SES ages 8–10		−.07
		379			SES age 14		−.02
		409			Income age 8	SRD ages 14 and 16	−.12
		409			SES ages 8–10		−.13
		379			SES age 14		−.02
		411			Income age 8	Secondary school allocation age 11	.30
		411			SES ages 8–10		.09
		386			Income age 8	Junior attainment age 11	.25
		386			SES ages 8–10		.13
		411			Teacher and peer-rated troublesomeness, ages 8 and 10	OR conviction ages 10–16	.32
		409				SRD ages 14 and 16	.20
		411				Secondary school allocation age 11	−.24
		386				Junior attainment age 11	−.18
Wiatrowski et al. (1982)	Youth in Transition Study; national sample of tenth-grade males in public high schools (11 percent African American), waves 1 (grade 10), 3 (grade 12), and 4 (grade 13)	1,000–1,500	M		Parent SES grade 10	SRD frequency past year grade 12	−.06
						SRD frequency past year grade 13	+.01
						SRD serious past year grade 13	.00
						SR GPA grade 10	.19
						SR GPA grade 12	.21

Study	N	Sex		Behavior measure	Outcome measure	r
Williams and McGee (1994)	364	M	Dunedin Multidisciplinary Health and Development Study; birth cohort of Dunedin, New Zealand, children at age 15 (98 percent European background)	Family disadvantage age 7 (reversed)	SRD frequency age 15	−.17
					Burt reading test age 7	.26
					Prose reading test age 7	.26
				Oppositional behavior age 7: Teacher rating	SRD frequency age 15	.20
				Parent rating		.11
				Teacher rating	Burt reading test age 7	−.23
				Parent rating		−.19
				Teacher rating	Prose reading test age 7	−.18
				Parent rating		−.20
				Family disadvantage age 9 (reversed)	SRD frequency age 15	−.18
					Burt reading test age 9	.15
					Dunedin spelling test age 9	.17
				Oppositional behavior age 9: Teacher rating	SRD frequency age 15	.22
				Parent rating		.15
				Teacher rating	Burt reading test age 9	−.17
				Parent rating		−.14
				Teacher rating	Dunedin spelling test age 9	−.16
				Parent rating		−.16
	334	F		Family disadvantage age 7 (reversed)	SRD frequency age 15	−.10
					Burt reading test age 7	.27
					Prose reading test age 7	.22

TABLE 6 (*Continued*)

Study	Selection and Description of Overall Sample	Analysis Sample			Potential Common Cause Measure	Academic/ Delinquency Measure	Association
		N	Sex	Ethnicity			
					Oppositional behavior age 7:		
					Teacher rating	SRD frequency age 15	.00
					Parent rating		.06
					Teacher rating	Burt reading test age 7	−.21
					Parent rating		−.21
					Teacher rating	Prose reading test age 7	−.27
					Parent rating		−.17
					Family disadvantage age 9 (reversed)	SRD frequency age 15	−.07
						Burt reading test age 9	.22
						Dunedin spelling test age 9	.22
					Oppositional behavior age 9:		
					Teacher rating	SRD frequency age 15	.04
					Parent rating		.10
					Teacher rating	Burt reading test age 9	−.23
					Parent rating		−.18
					Teacher rating	Dunedin spelling test age 9	−.23
					Parent rating		−.17

NOTE.—A negative sign means that delinquency involvement is associated with lower grades or special class placement. OR = officially recorded delinquency; SRD = self-reported delinquency; OSR = official school records; SR = self-reported; W = white; M = male; F = female; GPA = grade point average; WRAT = Wide Range Achievement Test; SES = socioeconomic status; and ASB = antisocial behavior.

* This entry also reports data provided to the current investigators by the original authors.

1. *SES.* We examined SES for males only as there were five studies representing five distinct sets of subjects ($N = 2,877$) for males but only two studies for females. The five sets of subjects provided fourteen correlations between SES and delinquency. Again, we averaged all effect sizes for a set of subjects to yield an effect for each set of subjects. The set of five SES-delinquency effect sizes ranged from $+.070$ to $-.175$, with a mean of $-.074$ and a standard deviation of .104. The resulting mean effect size was $-.059$. The five sets of subjects also provided nineteen correlations between SES and academic performance. The five SES–academic performance effect sizes ranged from .184 to .221, with a mean of .205 and a standard deviation of .016. The resulting mean effect size was .209.

The common causes analysis for SES was conducted by computing the partial correlation between academic performance and delinquency while controlling for SES. Based on an academic performance–delinquency effect size of $-.166$ for males, a SES-delinquency effect size of $-.059$, and a SES–academic performance effect size of .209, the partial correlation was $-.157$. Since SES did not materially diminish the association between academic performance and delinquency, it did not qualify as a common cause. We also examined the effect of deleting the two large effect sizes from the two large samples, which yielded an academic performance–delinquency effect size of $-.137$. Although this reduced the partial association to $-.128$, the conclusion that SES is not a common cause remained firm.

2. *Conduct Problems.* Data on conduct problems as a potential common cause were provided by six studies containing seven distinct sets of subjects ($N = 3,618$). Two of the sets of subjects consisted of females, and the remaining sets consisted of males.

The seven sets of subjects provided thirty-three correlations between conduct problems and delinquency. The set of seven conduct problem–delinquency effect sizes ranged from .010 to .278, with a mean of .154 and a standard deviation of .098—a considerable spread in the distribution. The two smallest effect sizes, .010 and .050, were from sets of female subjects from different samples, whereas the remaining five effect sizes, the smallest being .143, were from sets of male subjects. To allow for the possibility of a sex difference in the association between conduct problems and delinquency, we computed the effect sizes separately for males and females. The weighted mean effect size was .203 for males and .042 for females, which indicates that high conduct problems were associated with delinquency.

There were fifty-one correlations between conduct problems and academic performance for the seven sets of subjects. The seven conduct problem–academic performance effect sizes ranged from −.096 to −.329, with a mean of .212 and a standard deviation of .070. In view of the apparent difference between males and females for association between conduct problems and delinquency, we checked the distribution of effect sizes to see if there might be similar differences for the conduct problems and academic performance association. However, we found no evidence of a clustering by gender. We, therefore, averaged the data across sex to yield a mean effect size of −.206, indicating that high conduct problems were associated with low academic performance.

The common cause model for conduct problems was tested separately for males and females. The academic performance–delinquency and the conduct problem–delinquency effect sizes for males and for females were used. However, because there appeared to be no sex differences in the conduct problems-academic performance effect size, the sets of males and the sets of females were averaged together to compute the value used.

The results for males, based on an academic performance–delinquency effect size of −.166, a conduct problem–delinquency effect size of .203, and a conduct problem–academic performance effect size of −.206, yielded a partial correlation of −.129. The results were not materially different when we deleted the values for the two large samples and recomputed the partial correlation. The results for females, based on an academic performance–delinquency effect size of −.086, a conduct problem–delinquency effect size of .042, and a conduct problem–academic performance effect size of −.206, yielded a partial correlation of −.079. Thus since conduct problems did not reduce the association between academic performance and delinquency to near zero for either males or females, it did not qualify as a common cause.

3. *Other Factors.*   We found four other multivariate studies (see table 7) (Spivack and Marcus, n.d.; White, Pandina, and LaGrange 1987; Denno 1990; and Kupersmidt and Coie 1990). Denno analyzed the data from a subsample of inner-city African American boys and girls whose families participated in the Philadelphia Collaborative Perinatal Project. The analysis included a host of variables from the pre- and postnatal period, infancy, and school-age periods. In separate structural equation models for males and females, she found partial

associations from $-.09$ to $-.12$ between achievement scores and the frequency and seriousness of official delinquency, when variables from earlier developmental periods were taken into account (e.g., parental education, IQ measures at age 4 and age 7) for both males and females. Her results indicated that academic performance retains some significance after controlling for intelligence.

Kupersmidt and Coie (1990) and Spivack and Marcus (n.d.) reported differing results from studies that controlled for aggression as well as other variables. Kupersmidt and Coie found that grades, school absences, peer rejection, gender, and ethnicity failed to remain in the logistic regression for delinquency at twelfth grade after peer-rated aggression was entered. Spivack and Marcus, by contrast, found a nonsignificant regression coefficient of .11 for males and a significant regression coefficient of .29 for females between grade retention or special class placement and official police contact after controlling for teacher ratings of negative behavior and comprehension at grade 1. The studies' differences may be substantive or due to sample selection. This highlights the difficulties of drawing conclusions from narrative statements of relationships.

The fourth study (White, Pandina, and LaGrange 1987) used a sample of male and female adolescents aged twelve ($N = 298$), fifteen ($N = 305$), or eighteen years ($N = 279$) at the initial assessment to study the relationship of academic performance to delinquent status measured three years later. An analysis of covariance design was used to control for age. The first analysis compared "heavy" (three or more index offenses in the past three years) and "nonheavy" youth, and the second analysis compared "labeled" (incarcerated, or on probation or parole in past three years) and "nonlabeled" youth. The results found that heavy delinquent youth had significantly lower grades than nonheavy youth and that labeled delinquent youth had significantly lower grades than nonlabeled youth. Thus the association between academic performance and delinquency remained after controlling for age.

4. *Prior Delinquency.* Table 8 presents the five studies that have controlled for prior delinquency as well as other variables. Two of the studies (Wiatrowski et al. 1982; Agnew 1985) used the Youth in Transition sample, and the third (Agnew 1991) used the National Youth Survey sample. Both of these are large, nationally representative samples of adolescents. Although the McCarthy and Hoge (1984) sample had substantially different participation rates from parochial and

TABLE 7
Longitudinal Follow-up Studies with Academic Performance as a Predictor of Delinquency with Controls for Third Variables

Study	Selection and Description of Overall Sample	Analysis Sample			Academic Measure	Delinquency Measure	Control Variables	Association
		N	Sex	Ethnicity				
Denno (1990)	Philadelphia Collaborative Perinatal Project subsample of African American youth born 1959–62 and residing in Philadelphia from age 10–17 who attended public schools and had IQ and achievement data	487	M	AA	CAT language achievement at age 14–15	OR frequency of police contact ages 7–17	Pregnancy and delivery, education (mother and father), income, father unemployed, hand/foot preference, physical and neurological abnormalities, anemia, lead exposure, father absence, foster placement, family size, moves, age-4 Binet IQ, age-7 WISC, school discipline, and retardation	– .10*
						OR seriousness of police contact ages 7–17		– .12**
		500	F	AA		OR frequency of police contact ages 7–17		– .10*
						OR seriousness of police contact ages 7–17		– .09*

226

Study	Sample	N	Sex	Educational measure	Delinquency measure	Controls	Effect
Kupersmidt and Coie (1990)	Fifth-grade children in semirural area (69 percent white, 47 percent female)	104	M + F	OSR composite GPA at grade 5	OR police contact at age 18	Ethnicity, gender, absences, peer rejection, aggression	N.S.
Spivack and Marcus [n.d.]	Disadvantaged, inner-city children	147 142	M F	Held back or special class placement	OR police contact at age 17	Teacher-rated negative behavior and comprehension at grade 1	−.11 −.29***
White, Pandina, and LaGrange (1987)	Rutgers Health and Human Development Study sample of males aged 15 (N = 153), 18 (N = 153), and 21 (N = 135) from New Jersey (90 percent white)	341	M	Composite of SR math and English grades past 3 years, SR last semester GPA at ages 12, 15, or 18	SRD frequency index offenses past 3 years OR incarcerated/on parole past 3 years	Age	−[a]*** −[a]****

Note.—A negative sign means that delinquency involvement is associated with lower grades or special class placement. OR = officially recorded delinquency; SRD = self-reported delinquency; OSR = official school records; SR = self-reported; AA = African American; M = male; F = female; GPA = grade point average; CAT = California Achievement Test; and WISC = Wechsler Intelligence Scale for Children; N.S. = not significant.

[a] Study provided insufficient data to compute an effect size. The significance level noted is that reported by the investigator for the analysis performed, and the sign was determined by an inspection of the group means if the analysis was significant.

* $p < .05$.
** $p < .01$.
*** $p < .001$.

TABLE 8

Longitudinal Follow-up Studies with Academic Performance as a Predictor of Delinquency, Controlling for Third Variables and Prior Delinquency

Study	Selection and Description of Overall Sample	Analysis Sample		Academic Measure	Delinquency Measure	Control Variables	Association
		N	Sex				
Agnew (1985)	Youth in Transition waves 1 (tenth grade) and 2 (eleventh grade); national sample of tenth-grade males in public high schools (11 percent African American)	1,498	M	SR GPA past year	SRD total frequency past 3 years	Parent attachment, school attachment, commitment, and involvement; peer attachment; dating index; deviant beliefs	−.06*
					SRD serious frequency past 3 years		−.04
Agnew (1991)	National Youth Survey waves 1 (ages 11–17) and 2 (ages 12–18), sample size not reported		M + F	Commitment at waves 1 and 2 (SR GPA, has high GPA, does well in hard classes)	SRD frequency minor (theft, assault, and status offenses) past year at waves 1 and 2	School attachment, parent attachment, deviant peers, deviant beliefs	−.11[a]*
Le Blanc, Vallieres, and McDuff (1992)	Francophone students aged 12–16 years at wave 1 and 14–18 years at wave 2 (55 percent male)	825	M + F	SR GPA (French + math) at wave 1	SRD past year at waves 1 and 2	Parent's education level at wave 1	−.07*

228

Study	Sample	N	Sex	School measure	Delinquency measure	Control/self-esteem variables	r
McCarthy and Hoge (1984)	Students in seventh, ninth, and eleventh grades of public and parochial schools in 2 Mid-Atlantic cities at year 1 (55 percent male, 49 percent white at year 1)	1,658 [a]	M + F	OSR grades past year at years 1 and 2	SRD theft + vandalism frequency past year at years 1 and 2	Coopersmith self-esteem at year 1	−.05
Wiatrowski et al. (1982)	Youth in Transition Study; national sample of tenth-grade males in public high schools (11 percent African American), wave 1 (grade 10), wave 2 (grade 11), wave 3 (grade 12), and wave 4 (grade 13)	1,000	M	SR GPA at tenth grade	SRD frequency past 3 years at grade 12 / SRD frequency past year at grade 13 / SRD seriousness past year at grade 13	Wave 1: SES, IQ, self-esteem, school attachment, occupational aspirations, college encouragement, college plans; wave 2: curriculum; wave 3: school attachment, self-esteem, grades	−.00 / −.01 / −.00

NOTE.—A negative sign means that delinquency involvement is associated with lower grades or special class placement. SRD = self-reported delinquency; OSR = official school records; SR = self-reported; M = male; F = female; GPA = grade point average; and SES = socioeconomic status.

[a] Correction for measurement error is included.

* $p < .05$.

public school adolescents, they believe it to be representative of the base population. Le Blanc, Vallieres, and McDuff (1992) used a sample of twelve- to sixteen-year-old Francophone students.

All studies used self-report measures of prior delinquency frequency. Wiatrowski et al. (1982) also used a self-reported seriousness measure. Academic performance was measured by grades in all studies. Self-report of grades was used in the Youth in Transition Study (Bachman 1970), the National Youth Survey (Elliott, Huizinga, and Ageton 1985), and the Le Blanc, Vallieres, and McDuff (1992) samples; and school records were used in the McCarthy and Hoge (1984) sample. The Agnew (1985, 1991) studies and Wiatrowski et al. (1982) study also used measures of attachment to parents or school, commitment, involvement, and aspirations, in addition to several other variables derived from social control theory, as control variables. McCarthy and Hoge used only self-esteem as a control variable.

Three of the five studies found at least one significant result, although all coefficients are small, ranging from 0.0 to − .07. The largest coefficient, − .11 (from Agnew 1991), was corrected for reliability and is not directly comparable to those from the other studies. These results indicated that once prior delinquency and other variables were controlled, prior academic performance only weakly predicted future delinquency.

5. *Severity and Frequency of Delinquency.* Several studies have examined academic performance as a predictor of escalation in frequency, variety, or seriousness of officially recorded delinquency among subjects who have initiated offending.

Tracy, Wolfgang, and Figlio (1990) compared achievement scores of one-time, nonchronic, and chronic offenders. The results for the 1958 cohort indicated that chronic recidivists had the lowest mean academic achievement percentiles ($M = 14.4$), whereas one-time offenders had the highest mean academic achievement percentiles ($M = 35.9$).

Blumstein, Farrington, and Moitra (1985) and Farrington (1987), using data from the Cambridge Youth Study, compared occasional offenders (who had from one to five convictions by age twenty-five) with chronic offenders (who had six or more convictions by age twenty-five). Their results showed that a significantly higher proportion of chronic offenders had low school attainment at age eleven, low intelligence scores, high troublesomeness ratings by teachers, and came from low-income families. A subsequent multivariate analysis indicated only high troublesomeness and low school attainment as predictors.

Denno (1990), using data from African American children whose mothers participated in the Philadelphia Collaborative Perinatal Project, found that both the WRAT (Wide Range Achievement Test) score at age seven and CAT (California Achievement Test) scores at age thirteen/fourteen decreased with the frequency of offending for males. However, females with two or more offenses had significantly lower CAT but not WRAT scores than did females with only one offense. Denno also found that males with index offenses (homicide, rape, robbery, aggravated assault, burglary, larceny, and auto theft) had significantly lower WRAT scores at age seven and CAT scores at age thirteen/fourteen than males with nonindex offenses. Her results for females revealed that index offenders had significantly lower CAT scores but not WRAT scores compared to nonindex offenders. She found that males with violent index offenses had significantly lower WRAT and CAT scores than did males with only property index offenses. Females with violent index offenses were found to have significantly lower CAT scores but not WRAT scores than females with only property index offenses. Unfortunately, the violent index offender group was not broken down into persons with only violent offenses and persons with both violent and property offenses.

The results of this section consistently indicate that both males and females who have escalated their offending, whether measured as increases in frequency or severity, have lower academic performance than children who have not. In several cases, that children, particularly males, had lower test scores in early elementary school argues against an explanation based solely on the effects of prior delinquency on subsequent academic performance.

E. Studies of Onset, Escalation, and Desistance

This section considers studies that have related academic performance to stages in the development of delinquency. Loeber and Le Blanc (1990) and others view delinquent offending as progressing through three broad stages: onset, escalation, and desistance. Onset marks the beginning of offending and is measured by the commission of the first delinquent act. If offending increases in seriousness or frequency or diversifies into other types of acts, that person is considered to have entered the stage of escalation. Eventually, a person's offending decreases and finally ceases. For some, the time of cessation or desistance may be in adolescence; for others, it may be in adulthood.

In contrast to the studies presented in previous sections, with their emphasis on either frequency of offending during an interval or lifetime prevalence, developmental criminology emphasizes the importance of timing—of when onset occurs as well as whether it occurs. With escalation, the interest is in the timing as well as in the magnitude of escalation. And with desistance, developmental criminology asks what factors determine whether a person continues to offend into adulthood rather than stopping at some point during adolescence.

Our review of the literature for studies of onset, escalation, or desistance identified too few studies to permit a meta-analytic review. There have been few studies of the relationship of academic performance to the stages of offending from a developmental criminology perspective. Clearly, a considerable amount of further work is needed. With only two exceptions, the studies have been restricted to univariate analyses. Multivariate studies are needed to test the effects of intelligence, attention problems, or other possible common cause variables. The samples used to date have consisted of males. These same questions need to be studied with samples of females as well. Results for onset are contradictory. Of the three onset studies, all of which employed different definitions of onset, measures of delinquency and academic performance, and method of analysis, only one found significant univariate relationships, and academic performance did not remain significant in multivariate analyses. The limited results to date indicate that academic performance is not a significant predictor of onset in a multivariate sense. Even less is known about escalation and desistance.

1. *Onset.* Farrington and Hawkins (1991) used data from the Cambridge Study in Delinquent Development to identify predictors of an early onset of delinquency (before age fourteen) based on official records. In their analysis, they compared early- to late-onset (age fourteen or later) delinquents. They found that a low school track placement at age fourteen, but not low academic attainment at the same age, was marginally associated with early onset. Subsequent multivariate analysis using low school track placement and other variables associated with early onset (low family income, low involvement with father, high troublesomeness at ages eight to ten, and low nonverbal IQ) indicated that only low involvement with father and high troublesomeness predicted early onset.

Loeber et al. (1991) examined the bivariate relationship between academic performance and onset over a one-and-a-half-year period for samples of first-, fourth-, and seventh-grade boys from the Pittsburgh Youth Study. Onset was defined as the first report of *any* delinquent act over the follow-up period, and academic performance was measured by the mean of the caretaker's and teacher's academic performance ratings of the child at the start of the study. No significant association between low academic achievement and onset was noted in any of the three samples.

Maguin and Loeber (1992) used discrete time survival analysis to study the relationship of academic performance and other variables to the onset of moderately serious delinquency over a three-year follow-up in the first-grade cohort of boys in the same study. Onset was defined as the first occurrence of a delinquent act of at least moderate seriousness (carrying weapons, joyriding, gang fighting, and theft of items over $5), and academic performance was measured by a composite of caretaker-reported reading and math performance. Univariate results showed that low academic performance and the variables of high attention problems, low family SES, grade retention (i.e., held back), and African American ethnicity were associated with a shorter time to delinquency onset. Finally, multivariate analysis was used to integrate the previous univariate analyses. This analysis found that academic performance was a predictor of delinquency onset when tested with ethnicity, family SES, and grade retention. However, when attention problems was added to the equation, academic performance was no longer a significant predictor. In summary, these three studies, using data from the same samples, do not show conclusively that academic performance is or is not associated with an earlier delinquency onset.

2. *Escalation.*   Only one study, Loeber et al. (1991), has examined the contribution of academic performance to escalation. They tested for significant bivariate associations between academic performance and escalation over a one-and-a-half-year follow-up period for boys in the first-, fourth-, and seventh- grade samples of the Pittsburgh Youth Study. Escalation was defined as an increase in delinquency seriousness during the follow-up period over that at the initial assessment. Academic performance was again the mean of the caretaker's and teacher's academic performance ratings of the child at the start of the study. Low academic performance was found to be significantly associ-

ated with escalation in the fourth-grade and seventh-grade samples but only marginally so in the first-grade sample. Inspection of the magnitudes of the associations suggested no interaction with age.

3. *Desistance.* In the same study Loeber et al. (1991) also examined the bivariate relationship between academic performance and desistance, defined as no report of a delinquent act over the follow-up period. They found that high academic performance at the initial assessment was associated with subsequent desistance for all three samples relative to boys who only deescalated their offending (committed only less serious offenses over the follow-up period).

Farrington and Hawkins (1991) examined univariate predictors of the persistence of offending into adulthood, the converse of desistance, from ages twenty-one to thirty-two, using data from the Cambridge Study in Delinquent Development. They found that *persistence* into adult offending as measured by official records was associated with low school attainment and a low school track, both measured at age eleven. However, in a multivariate analyses, they found that neither low school attainment nor low school track placement entered the equation for predicting persistence into adult offending.

Thus to date, the predictors of desistance have been examined by only two studies. Although the results of both studies indicate a role for academic performance in desistance, these data need to be replicated using both self-report and officially recorded measures of offending.

4. *Effects on Education.* Once children have experienced the onset of delinquency or escalated their offending, the consequences for their academic performance are quite important. However, we found no studies that have addressed this question. Although Le Blanc et al. (1991) compared the social functioning of boys at age ten who had an onset of serious delinquency prior to age ten to that of boys who had not experienced the onset of delinquency, the study did not include a measure of academic performance. Furthermore, data on the preonset functioning of those boys who experienced the onset of delinquency were not reported. Thus there is a great need for studies that examine the impact of the onset of delinquency on subsequent academic performance.

III. Intervention Studies

In this section, we turn to intervention and prevention studies to illuminate an important area concerning temporal and causal ordering.

Suppose that boys who received an intervention and improved their academic performance at termination then decreased their delinquency at follow-up. Such an outcome would support the ordering of academic performance as a cause of delinquency. Instead, suppose that boys who received an intervention decreased their delinquency at termination and then improved their academic performance at follow-up. Such an outcome would support the converse causal ordering. The key to distinguishing between different possible orderings is the use of several posttreatment assessments to monitor the dependent variables.

For this purpose, we sought intervention and prevention studies that employed and reported measures of both academic performance and delinquency and used methodologically appropriate designs and analyses (i.e., random assignment to an untreated control group when comparing group means at posttest or follow-up or comparison group when using pretest measures in an analysis of covariance). We found very few studies that met these criteria. Few studies employed control groups, and many studies that initially looked acceptable had to be eliminated. Furthermore, many delinquency studies did not report academic performance measures, or even such school measures as attendance, discipline contacts, or graduation/general equivalency diploma completion. Many educational studies did not report delinquency measures even though measures of negative behavior were employed. Follow-up assessments were rare. Finally, very few of the selected studies reported the necessary data for subsequent meta-analytic analyses (pre- and posttest means and standard deviations by group for continuous variables or cross-tabulations for categorical variables). A complete meta-analysis was, thus, impossible. A narrative overview is given here, supplemented where possible by effect size data.

These disparate studies shared few characteristics beyond those imposed by the selection criteria. However, one important dimension was the distinction between true primary prevention studies, where all persons, whether at risk or not, received the intervention, and high-risk intervention studies, where the intervention was offered only to children and youth at high risk for delinquency. Using this distinction, studies were categorized as either "high-risk intervention" studies or "prevention" studies. Although the studies were not explicitly selected to include only samples of children or youth who resided in their own community throughout the duration of the intervention program, the requirement that there be academic performance measures effectively excluded virtually all the studies considered by Lipsey (1992).

The results of these individual intervention studies seem promising with respect to their ability to affect delinquency and academic performance. Only four of the nine high-risk studies in table 9 failed to show at least one significant effect, and none of the prevention studies in table 10 failed to show at least one significant effect. Where effect sizes could be estimated, they were in the .15–.35 range for high-risk studies and in the .05–.10 range for prevention studies. Unfortunately, since only one study reported follow-up assessments, we have scant evidence that the effects were maintained once the intervention ended. Realistically, these studies do not provide the firm foundation needed for building an intervention knowledge base. It is too early to decide which types of interventions work and which do not and whether different interventions are more effective for one age group than another.

More methodologically well-designed studies are needed. For instance, to find the twelve studies presented here, nearly seventy were rejected because they lacked a control group or delinquency or academic performance measures. Furthermore, even among studies with control groups and measures of both academic performance and delinquency outcomes, few studies reported the data necessary to compute effect sizes. Also, in the planning of future studies, investigators need to pay more attention to ensuring adequate sample sizes to maintain power. As tables 9 and 10 show, the majority of studies do not have large enough sample sizes to ensure adequate power given the effect size they actually found. For instance, an effect size (r) of .20 requires final samples of 100 treatment and control children each. Investigators also need to specify theoretically how their interventions are expected to work. For instance, why should moral or law-related education also lead to higher grades? Could improvements in bonding to school or teachers have accounted for the results? Thus theoretical models need to incorporate a specification of mediating variables in the intervention. On this point, Hawkins and associates are on the right track, since they measured the social bond constructs that were expected to change as a result of the intervention. It also needs to be shown that treated subjects received the intervention as specified (i.e., intervention integrity was maintained). Again, the Hawkins group have incorporated these checks into their evaluation program. Finally, data on treatment integrity might be used in the evaluation model as control variables for modeling treatment effects. Thus the results to date suggest, we believe, some cause for hope. However, many improvements are

TABLE 9
Intervention Studies for At-Risk or High-Risk Children

Study	Selection and Description of Overall Sample	Intervention Description	Academic Effects				Delinquency Effects			
			Group	N	Measure	Effect Size	Group	N	Measure	Effect Size
Arbuthnot and Gordon (1986)	Children aged 13–17 (N = 48, 14.5 years, 73 percent male) rated as "behavior disordered" by teachers and randomly assigned to E or C	16–20 sessions, 1 per week, of moral reasoning education	E C	24 19	OSR GPA past term (pre/post)	+[a]*	E C	24 24	OR frequency police/court contacts past 3 months (pre/post)	+[a]*
			E C	11 9	OSR GPA past term (pre/post), past year (follow-up)	+[a]*	E C	13 9	OR frequency police court contacts past 3 months (pre/post/follow-up)	N.S.[a]
Berrueta-Clement et al. (1984)	Perry Preschool Project sample of low-IQ African American children from low-income area (N = 123); matched on IQ then randomly assigned to E or C	2-year preschool program of intellectual and social development plus weekly home visits	E C	38 39	OSR GPA in grades 9–12	+[a]*	E C	54 59	OR previous arrests lifetime age 19	.12
			E C	54 58	OSR mean number of failing marks in grades K–12	N.S.[a]	E C	58 63	OR frequency arrests lifetime age 19	N.S.[a]

TABLE 9 (*Continued*)

Study	Selection and Description of Overall Sample	Intervention Description	Academic Effects				Delinquency Effects			
			Group	N	Measure	Effect Size	Group	N	Measure	Effect Size
Emshoff and Blakely (1983)	Adjudicated youth ($N = 73$, 14.5 years, 67 percent male, 67 percent white) in community randomly assigned to E_1, E_2, or C	E_1 group received family-focused behavioral contracting and advocacy, and E_2 received multiple interventions and advocacy, each for 10 months	E_1 E_2 C	24 23 26	School performance	N.S.[a]	E_1 E_2 C	24 23 26	OR police contacts	N.S.[a]
Gottfredson (1986)	Students in 5 middle and 4 high schools in low-income inner-city and rural areas; schools assigned to E (4 high schools, and 3 middle schools) or COM; in each school (E or COM) high aca-	2-year multicomponent program of school-level change to improve climate and academic performance made with student involvement, and student career planning; 2 years of one-on-	E C E C E C E C	358 306 382 340 368 316 410 352	SR GPA OSR GPA year 2 Percent in lowest quartile of total achievement (reversed) Percent promoted year 1	.05 .02 .09 .08	E C E C	296 249 468 401	Serious SRD prevalence past year OR court contacts	.00 .00

238

demic or behavioral ioral risk students were randomly assigned to receive special services — one behavioral and academic counseling only for high-risk group

Gottfredson (1990) Self- and teacher-nominated youth in a Pasadena, California junior and senior high school; random assignment constrained by scheduling to E or C — 1-year law-related curriculum program with cooperative learning teams

Results for Program in Junior High School

E	47	SR GPA past year	.21*	E	42	Serious SRD prevalence past year	.17
C	57			C	48		
E	52	OSR GPA past year	.22**	E	56	OR court contacts	.04
C	61			C	67		

Results for Program in Senior High School

E	50	SR GPA past year	.34**	E	44	Serious SRD prevalence past year	.21*
C	36			C	32		
E	56	OSR GPA past year	.42**	E	64	OR court contacts	.09*
C	44			C	55		
E	86	OSR credits earned	.12	E	79	Serious SRD prevalence past year	-.20*
C	21			C	17		
				E	109	OR court contacts	-.06
				C	26		

Gottfredson (1990) Youth at high-delinquency risk referred from Miami public schools; E and NEC groups design — Alternative school program with token economy, individualized instruction program with tutoring, and work experience components

TABLE 9 (*Continued*)

Study	Selection and Description of Overall Sample	Intervention Description	Academic Effects				Delinquency Effects			
			Group	N	Measure	Effect Size	Group	N	Measure	Effect Size
Hawkins, Doueck, and Lishner (1988)	Seattle Social Development Project sample of grade 7 children in 5 public schools; random assignment to E or C classroom at 3 schools and whole school either E or C at 2 schools; study sample is students at third stanine or below in math achievement at grade 6	Program components: proactive classroom management, interactive teaching, cooperative learning	E	73	Achievement at grade 7: Math	N.S.[a]	E	63	SRD at grade 7: Property crime	N.S.[a]
			C	76	Reading	N.S.[a]	C	66	Violence	N.S.[a]
			E	67			E	63		
			C	72			C	65		
			E	66	Language arts	N.S.[a]	E	66	Serious crime	N.S.[a]
			C	72			C	64		
			E	77	Grade 7 grades:					
			C	81	Social studies	N.S.[a]				
			E	74	Math	N.S.[a]				
			C	52						

Study	Description of sample	Description of treatment	Group	N	Measure	Significance	Effect size
Massimo and Shore (1963)	Boys aged 15–17 with history of antisocial behavior, normal IQ, and school problems randomly assigned to group E or C (N = 20)	Individualized program of one-on-one contact with therapist on full range of issues (job, education, and so forth) lasting 10 months	E	10	Pre-/postscores achievement: Reading	+a***	
					Vocabulary	+a***	
					Math concepts	+a***	
					Math problems	+a***	
			C	10			
			E	10	OR court contact		.40
			C	10			
Tremblay et al. (1992b)	White, Francophone boys scoring >70th percentile on teacher-rated disruptive behavior at grade K and parents from schools in low SES areas; random assignment to group E and NTC	Boys: social skills and self-control training for 2 years; some boys also received fantasy play component; parents: OSLC-based parent training for up to 2 years	E	42	Grade placement for age at grade 4	a*	
			C	118			
					Grade placement for age at grade 5	N.S.a	
					Grade placement for age at grade 6	a*	
			E	42	SRD lifetime prevalence at age 12: Trespass		.19*
			C	118	Steal < $10		.23*
					Steal > $10		.16
					Steal bicycle		.17

NOTE.—E = intervention group; E₁ = intervention group for variation 1; E_1 = intervention group; E_2 = intervention group for variation 2; C = control group; NEC = nonequivalent comparison group; COM = comparison group; OR = officially recorded delinquency; SRD = self-reported delinquency; OSR = official school records; SR = self-reported; GPA = grade point average; SES = socioeconomic status; and OSLC = Oregon Social Learning Center. Positive effect sizes means that, relative to the control group, the intervention group scored higher on academic measures and lower on delinquency measures. Unless otherwise noted, effect sizes shown are computed for posttest data. N.S. = not significant.

a Study provided insufficient data to compute an effect size. The significance level noted is that reported by the investigator for the analysis performed, and the sign was determined by inspection of the group means if the analysis was significant.

* $p < .05$.

** $p < .01$.

241

TABLE 10
Prevention Studies for Children

Study	Selection and Description of Overall Sample	Intervention Description	Academic Effects			Delinquency Effects			
			Group	N	Measure	Effect Size	Group	N	Measure	Effect Size

Study	Selection and Description of Overall Sample	Intervention Description	Academic Effects Group	N	Measure	Effect Size	Delinquency Effects Group	N	Measure	Effect Size
Elias et al. (1991)	Fourth-grade children in public schools	2-year social problem-solving program implemented with higher fidelity (E_1) or lower fidelity (E_2)	E_1	39	Achievement at grade 10: total	+[a]*	E	[b]	SRD frequency for males at grades 9–11	[c]
			C	26			C	[b]		
			E_2	57	Achievement at grade 10: total	+[a]*	E	[b]	SRD frequency for females at grades 9–11	[c]
			C	26			C	[b]		
			E_1	56	Achievement at grade 11: total	N.S.[a]				
			C	20						
			E_2	60	Achievement at grade 11: total	N.S.[a]				
			C	20						
Gottfredson (1986)	Students in 5 middle schools and 4 high schools in low-income inner-city and rural areas; schools assigned to E (4 high schools and 3 middle schools) or comparison	2-year multicomponent program of organizational changes to enhance climate and academic performance, student career planning, and student involvement in school change planning	Middle Schools Receiving Intervention				Middle Schools Receiving Intervention			
					SR GPA past year at year 0 ($N = 854$) and year 2 ($N = 936$)	−.08**			Serious SRD prevalence past year at year 0 ($N = 857$) and year 2 ($N = 773$)	.04
			Middle School Receiving No Intervention (Comparisons)				Middle School Receiving No Intervention (Comparisons)			
					SR GPA past year at year 0 ($N = 299$) and year 2 ($N = 303$)	−.03			Serious SRD prevalence past year at year 0 ($N = 302$) and year 2 ($N = 270$)	−.10*
			High Schools Receiving Intervention				High Schools Receiving Intervention			
					SR GPA past year at year 0 ($N = 675$) and year 1 ($N = 1,269$)	−.04			Serious SRD prevalence past year at year 0 ($N = 649$) and year 1 ($N = 1,146$)	.06**

242

				High School Receiving No Intervention (Comparison)	
				SR GPA past year at year 0 (N = 233) and year 1 (N = 233)	.04
				Serious SRD prevalence past year at year 0 (N = 221) and year 1 (N = 254)	−.02
Hawkins et al. (1992)	Seattle Social Development Project sample of grade 1 children in 8 public schools; random assignment to E or C classroom at 6 schools and all grade 1 students either E or C at two schools; incoming students randomly assigned to E or C	Multicomponent 4-year intervention: year 1: cognitive problem solving; years 1–4: proactive classroom management, interactive teaching, cooperative learning; and voluntary parent-training classes	E 185 C 644	Composite achievement grade 5	—[a]*
			E 187 C 665	SRD prevalence at grade 5	.06*

NOTE.—E = intervention group; E$_1$ = intervention group for variation 1; E$_2$ = intervention group for variation 2; C = control group; SR = self-reported; SRD = self-reported delinquency; and GPA = grade point average. Positive effect sizes means that the intervention group scored higher on academic measures and lower on delinquency measures (a) relative to the control group for the post-only comparisons or (b) relative to pretest. Meaning is implied by context. A plus sign (+) or minus sign (−) with only a significance level indicates the direction of difference. N.S. = not significant.
[a] Study provided insufficient data to compute an effect size. The significance level noted is that reported by the investigator for the analysis performed, and the sign was determined by inspection of the group means if the analysis was significant.
[b] Sample sizes are not reported.
[c] Significance test not reported.
* $p < .05$.
** $p < .01$.

needed before we can really begin to answer the important question of what should we do for whom and when.

A. At-Risk Group Programs

This section describes studies that have targeted at-risk or high-risk youth. The at-risk status may be defined by the participant's behavioral or academic status. A total of nine studies presenting results for ten distinct samples were identified (table 9).

Two age groups of children were used by the ten samples: preschool and young school children (two samples) and adolescent children (eight samples). The intervention programs used ranged from a cognitively focused preschool program to moral education to multifocus individual counseling. Beyond the observation that law-related education programs were used for adolescents, there was no clear indication that one type of program was more commonly used for one age group than for another. However, there was a clear preference to locate more recent programs partially or completely in the schools. Also, among the more recent programs, the interventions tended to include multiple components to address both academic and behavioral problems.

Turning to the outcome measures, the ten samples reported results for a total of twenty-six academic performance measures at termination. Of these twenty-six significance tests, thirteen were significant. The thirteen significant tests were from six samples: Arbuthnot and Gordon (1986) (two of two significant), Berrueta-Clement et al. (1984) (one of three significant), Gottfredson (1990) (Pasadena junior high sample) (two of two significant), Gottfredson (1990) (Pasadena senior high sample) (two of two significant), Massimo and Shore (1963) (four of four significant), and Tremblay et al. (1992b) (two of three significant). Effect sizes that were reported or could be estimated from the significance level (most studies did not report effect sizes) ranged from .2 to .35 at termination. The positive sign indicates that the academic performance or the delinquency involvement of the intervention group improved more than that of the control or comparison group of children who did not receive the intervention. Unfortunately, only one study reported follow-up assessment data (Arbuthnot and Gordon 1986).

The delinquency measures show a similar story. Of the twenty-one delinquency measures examined from the ten samples, six were significant. The significant tests were from four samples: Arbuthnot and Gordon (1986) (one of two significant), Gottfredson (1990) (Pasadena senior high sample) (two of two significant), Gottfredson (1990) (Miami sample) (one of two significant), and Tremblay et al. (1992*b*) (two of four significant). However, the results for the Miami sample in Gottfredson (1990) favor the control group over the treatment group. Overall, the effect sizes—of those reported or of those that could be computed—tended to be somewhat smaller, though a number were in the .15–.3 range at termination. Again, only one study reported follow-up data (Arbuthnot and Gordon 1986).

Both the law-related education program used by Gottfredson (1990) (both Pasadena samples) and the moral education program used by Arbuthnot and Gordon (1986) were successful in producing improvements in academic performance and reductions in delinquency. Law-related education programs seek to educate youth about the origins and role of law in the major social systems (e.g., family, school, and criminal justice systems). Moral education is built around techniques to help participants progress to higher levels of moral reasoning as described by Kohlberg (1981). Other studies with some significant academic performance results used a comprehensive preschool program (Berrueta-Clement et al. 1984), multifocus individual counseling (Massimo and Shore 1963), and a social skills and self-control training for boys and behavioral parent training for parents (Tremblay et al. 1992*b*). Law-related or moral education components (Arbuthnot and Gordon 1986; Gottfredson 1990 [Pasadena senior high sample]) also produced significant reductions in delinquency. Other studies with significant delinquency results used an alternative schools program (Gottfredson 1990) or social skills and self-control training for boys and behavioral parent training for parents (Tremblay et al. 1992*b*). In sum, studies that produced significant results for both academic performance and delinquency used law-related or moral education (Arbuthnot and Gordon 1986; Gottfredson 1990) or a multicomponent intervention with social skills and self-control training for the boys and behavioral parent training for the parents (Tremblay et al. 1992*b*).

Although these studies' common thread may be that parent training combined with self-control and social skills is needed by young children, moral or law education is needed by younger adolescents, and counseling about jobs and other issues is needed by older adolescents, there are too few data to confirm this possibility. Instead, more replications are needed to increase the chances of finding common elements that can be compared in future analyses.

B. Prevention Programs

Three studies (table 10) presented results for prevention-focused programs. All three studies reported some significant results for either the academic performance or delinquency measures; however, the effect sizes, where available, were clearly smaller, in the .05–.10 range. However, this result would be expected if some children benefited from the intervention more than other children did. The study by Elias et al. (1991) found academic performance differences between children who had completed a two-year social problem solving program some five years earlier beginning in the fourth grade; however, no effect on delinquency was observed.

Hawkins et al. (1992) found a significant reduction in delinquency at age 10 ($r = .056$), which was one-year posttreatment. A significant result for the academic performance variable was also found but in the wrong direction (with the control group being higher). They note, however, that the reported result may have been due to accretion (new students entering the original control group) and that unreported analyses for grade 7 and grade 8 show the expected effects. This study used a multiyear, multicomponent program featuring one year of cognitive problem-solving training plus four years of classroom management and learning innovations and voluntary parent training.

Finally, Gottfredson (1986) implemented a two-year multicomponent program of organizational changes developed with student and staff involvement to enhance school climate in nonrandomly selected junior and senior high schools. She found some evidence of improvement in both academic performance and delinquency in schools receiving the program. Those schools either improved or remained constant, whereas the comparison schools remained constant or worsened. The net effect was probably significant change in both junior and senior high schools.

IV. Summary and Implications

Poor academic performance is related to the prevalence and onset of delinquency, and escalation in the frequency and seriousness of offending, while better academic performance is associated with desistance from offending.

More specifically, the results showed that the poorer the academic performance, the higher the delinquency. The odds of delinquency, given low academic performance, were about 2.1 times higher than those given high academic performance. Stated in yet another way, 35 percent of low academically performing children became delinquent compared to only about 20 percent of high performing children.

Both males and females with a higher frequency of offenses, more serious offenses, or violent rather than nonviolent offenses had lower levels of academic performance. There is some evidence that low academic performance is related to early onset of offending. Finally, low academic performance was related to escalation in delinquency seriousness and persistence in offending, and better academic performance was associated with desistance from offending. Thus data from a number of sources clearly show the relationship between academic performance and delinquency.

The mean association between poor academic performance and delinquency was significantly and consistently stronger for males than females. The mean association for white children was not significantly different from that for African American children when only cross-sectional studies were considered. However, in longitudinal studies, the mean association was significantly stronger for whites than for African American children. This difference, however, was principally due to two large samples with large effect sizes. Unfortunately, information on other ethnic groups was not available. We also found that the association between poor academic performance and delinquency became stronger with age.

Intervention studies showed that improvements in academic performance co-occurred or followed improvements in the prevalence of delinquency. Although meta-analysis was not possible, some programs for high-risk children produced small to moderate effect sizes for either academic performance or delinquency. Although only three prevention studies were found, some of these studies reported small effect sizes for both academic performance and delinquency. All intervention studies reported significant improvements for either an academic measure or a delinquency measure. However, these data are not sufficient to determine whether the improvements in academic performance and the reductions in delinquency persisted or whether academic performance improvements precede reductions in delinquency. To ascertain these relationships, follow-up data must be collected, which only one study (Arbuthnot and Gordon 1986) did.

High-risk intervention studies using law-related or moral education components showed promising results. The high-risk intervention studies that showed the most successful outcomes employed law-related or moral education components for adolescents and self-control and social skills training combined with parent training interventions for younger children. Furthermore, these types of intervention tended to produce improvements in both academic performance and delinquency at termination. The more successful prevention studies tended to use multilevel intervention strategies combining school-level interventions with individual and family interventions.

Intelligence and attention problems were found to be a likely common cause of both poor academic performance and delinquency. In contrast, SES and prior conduct problems were not common causal factors—in their presence, poor academic performance continued to predict delinquency. Four variables, intelligence, attention problems, SES, and prior conduct problems, were tested as possible common cause variables for academic performance and delinquency. When poor intelligence was controlled, the partial association of poor academic performance with delinquency decreased to nearly zero cross-sectionally. Likewise, when high attention problems were controlled, the partial association of academic performance and delinquency also decreased to nearly zero cross-sectionally. Thus both intelligence and attention problems likely function as common cause variables. Controlling for SES, the partial association of academic performance with delinquency remained essentially unchanged in both cross-sectional and longitudinal analyses. When controlling for prior conduct problems, the partial correlation of academic performance with delinquency decreased slightly for both males and females. Thus academic performance continues to make an independent contribution to delinquency after the effects of either SES or prior conduct problems are controlled.

These results suggest that interventions that improve intelligence or decrease attention problems will improve academic success and reduce delinquency. The gains obtained by these early intervention programs can be further strengthened by programs of moral education. At the same time, some children will require interventions to reduce their level of conduct problems since conduct problems affect their ability to profit from educational instruction.

A. *Implications for Research*

What are the important issues that future research efforts, both naturalistic studies and high-risk and prevention studies, should address? We offer several recommendations.

1. *Naturalistic Studies.*   The results of our analysis suggest a num-

ber of important questions for future research concerning between-individual and within-individual differences.

Priority should be given to identifying common cause variables influencing both academic performance and delinquency. These variables have immense relevance for future intervention studies since it *may* be true that interventions that alter the level of the common cause will also alter the levels of both academic performance and delinquency.

A second important question concerns the stronger association between academic performance and delinquency for older children, suggesting that interventions for academically poor performing children should take place early rather than late. However, it would be important to know whether this is due to children who have persistently poor academic records, perhaps dating from school entry. If the variation were due to a persistent group, then early intervention would seem to be recommended. However, only intervention studies can answer this question.

Gender effects are also an important question. We found the academic performance–delinquency association to be stronger for males than for females. Although the delinquency rate for females is markedly lower than that for males (e.g., Bureau of Justice Statistics 1993), and females are less likely to display reading problems (e.g., McGee et al. 1988), these findings alone are not likely to explain the lower association. However, the estimate for females is based on a relatively small number of studies, and further studies would be useful for a clearer estimate of the relationship for females. If further research corroborates our findings, considerable theoretical work will be needed to explain the source of the differences.

Ethnic differences in the academic performance–delinquency association are especially relevant for culturally appropriate interventions. To date, the association has been studied only for African American and European American children; however, it should be examined for children of other ethnic groups as well. Because the study of ethnicity in the United States is also a study of economics, it is critically important that the samples used for these studies be selected so as to disentangle these two factors. For instance, Peeples and Loeber (1994) found that African American and European American children from equivalent neighborhoods did not differ in their level of delinquency.

For future studies, the contribution of poor academic performance to other problem behaviors including truancy and early substance use is particularly important. It is crucial to know, for example, if poor academic performance leads to a deeper involvement in delinquency and if variables such as truancy, delinquent peers, or decreased commitment to school moderate this relationship. Another question concerns the role of academic performance as a promoter of deceleration and desistance from offending. Along with the level of academic performance, it may be important to consider the timing of academic failure and its persistence in relation to subsequent delinquency.

Another important question from this perspective concerns the consequences of delinquency onset and its escalation on truancy, academic performance, and substance use. Here again, it may prove important to evaluate the timing of delinquency onset or escalation and its persistence in addition to its severity or frequency. The possible consequences of delinquent involvement should also include school dropout, subsequent success or failure in obtaining legitimate employment, and involvement in illegal activities for gain.

It is important to consider the context in which individual development takes place. From the point of view of criminology, the most important context to consider may be the neighborhood. It is clear that neighborhoods differ greatly in terms of their opportunities for illegal activities. The worst neighborhoods offer a relative wealth of visible illegitimate employment opportunities and the presence of delinquent peers. In the best neighborhoods, there is a relative scarcity of these same features. Thus for children with the same individual risk factor load (i.e., lower IQ, behavior problems, poor parenting), the developmental context may lead to quite different outcomes. Clarification of these issues may allow the development of interventions that are more closely matched to needs of vulnerable children and their families living in disorganized neighborhoods.

2. *Intervention Studies.* Intervention and prevention studies need a considerable amount of work to improve their yield. A number of broad questions need to be addressed. One question concerns the effectiveness of different intervention components in improving academic performance or reducing delinquency or both. Moral or law-related education and social skills and parent-training components have been more successful than other components, but only a relatively limited number of components have been tested. Where should new components come from? Certainly, one source should be risk factors identi-

fied by naturalistic studies, especially factors that fit the common cause model.

In addition to assessing the overall effectiveness of each intervention component, several further questions should also be addressed for each. First, what is the mechanism of action? This is especially important in social interventions where several different mechanisms are plausible. For instance, consider the moral education program used by Arbuthnot and Gordon (1986). This program was found to be effective at raising academic performance and reducing delinquency at posttest and maintaining academic performance at a one-year follow-up. How did this program affect improvements in academic performance? Was it that achieving higher levels of moral development led to achieving better grades, or could successful boys have developed significant attachments to the intervenor—as social control theory might predict? From the information given, it is not possible to trace out the path of effects, yet knowing the mechanism of effect is critical to improving the intervention.

Second, it is important to identify for whom the intervention works best. This information should include age ranges but might also include gender or depth and persistence of involvement in delinquency. That adolescent children received a moral or law-related education program whereas young school-age children received self-control and parent training suggests this question may have been considered. However, would self-control or social skills training be useful for older-aged children? To the extent that attention problems are stable, the answer may be yes. Would younger-aged children benefit from moral or law-related education? These are valid questions for investigation.

Third, the duration and intensity of exposure to an intervention component necessary to produce an effect needs to be determined. The persistent nagging question with a failed intervention is whether it would have worked had it continued longer or been delivered more intensely. It would be desirable to vary the exposure to the intervention component to determine whether a dose-response relationship can be established. A related question is whether the exposure to the intervention should be intensive or structured into an initial set of sessions followed by booster sessions.

The fourth question concerns the sequence in which problems should be addressed. Our analysis showed that conduct problems overlap modestly with delinquency and academic performance; thus, it is likely that interventions for each are needed. Is the modification of conduct problems a prerequisite for effective intervention in academic performance, or can the interventions for each be implemented simultaneously?

A related question is whether it is sufficient to target only common causes or whether academic performance or delinquency must also be addressed by separate intervention components. For instance, if self-control training and medication were used to intervene with attention problems, are remedial education or moral education components also needed to assist the recovery from delinquency and disrupt the continuity of offending?

The fifth question concerns the persistence of treatment effects. We found that few previous interventions included follow-up assessments. Without these data, future users of an intervention have no way of knowing whether they will need to apply the treatment continuously, intermittently, or only once. This question is also important from an economic point of view since few school districts or local governments can afford to offer continuous, intensive intervention.

The sixth question concerns how to ensure that persons who would benefit the most actually take part in the program. As Hawkins et al. (1992) found, many parents of children at high risk choose not to take part in a voluntary parent-training program. How can these parents be "sold" on the program enough at least to give it a try? Although these issues do not appear to emerge in controlled trials, they most likely do, but they are simply called by another name—dropouts. Thus it is important to understand how parents decide whether or not to take part. Furthermore, Hawkins et al. found that African American parents were less likely to take part. What can be done to make the programs more appealing to African American parents?

B. Theoretical Implications

These results present several challenges to current and future theories of delinquency with respect to the range of variables to be included, the role of mediating processes, and gender.

The results confirm the position of SES, which is often viewed as a social structure variable in theories of delinquency. More important, the results demonstrate that the individual-level characteristics of intelligence and attention problems, hyperactivity, and impulsiveness are related to delinquency. Thus existing theories of delinquency must incorporate the effects of these variables.

These additions pose no problems for social development theory (Catalano and Hawkins, forthcoming) because these variables are subsumed under the label of constitutional factors. Since integrated theory (Thornberry et al. 1991) includes SES as an exogenous or initial causal variable, there may be little difficulty here. Placing these findings in the theory offered by Elliott, Huizinga, and Ageton (1985) poses more difficulty because of the strain-based origins of this theory. However, these variables could be incorporated by viewing them as indicators of personal resources. On the assumption that children with different levels of personal resources share similar levels of aspirations, children with low levels of such resources would be more likely to engage in delinquency.

That intelligence and attention problems are common causes of both academic performance and delinquency poses several important problems. Several existing integrated social theories of delinquency hypothesize that variables such as commitment or skills for interaction completely mediate the relationship between SES or individual-level characteristics and delinquency (e.g., Catalano and Hawkins, forthcoming). That is, intelligence affects delinquency only through its relationship to commitment and does not act directly on delinquency.

Quantitatively, for this hypothesis to be true means that the strength of the path from intelligence, for example, through the mediating variables and to delinquency must be nearly equal to the bivariate association between the individual-level characteristic (e.g., attention problems) and delinquency. The problem is that academic performance does not have a strong relationship to delinquency, and, by extension, constructs that use academic performance as an indicator variable (e.g., commitment) also are not likely to have a strong relationship to delinquency. Thus the individual-level characteristic will retain a direct relationship with delinquency. The solution to this theoretical problem may be the identification of additional processes linking the individual-level characteristic to delinquency.

The results also indicated that the association between academic performance and delinquency is stronger for males than females. Current theories treat gender differently. Social development (Catalano and Hawkins, forthcoming) and interaction theory (Thornberry et al. 1991) view gender as a structural variable whose effects are mediated through the constructs unique to that theory. Elliott's theory (Elliott, Huizinga, and Ageton 1985), by contrast, makes no explicit mention of gender, which implies that the theoretical relationships are the same for males and females.

Our results indicate that gender is a moderator variable rather than a mediator because gender determines the strength of the relationship between academic performance and delinquency. Although the relationship is small, nonetheless, it is present. Thus this difference is a point that deserves attention from future theoreticians of delinquency.

C. Policy Recommendations

A number of policy recommendations are suggested by the results of this review. These results suggest that police, schools, social workers, and parents should take the problem of truancy quite seriously. Although truancy was not addressed as an issue in this essay, children cannot be expected to do well in school if they are not there. Thus ensuring their attendance is a large step toward helping them to perform to their potential in school.

As workers in the agency that comes into daily contact with delinquent youth, members of the juvenile justice system should be especially alert to problems of academic performance. The finding that youth with serious, frequent, and varied offending also had the poorest academic performance suggests that a premium should be placed on assessing poor performance, understanding its causes, and implementing effective remedial programs. This assessment might well be part of the routine intake procedures.

Although children in detention inevitably miss some school, these results would suggest that it is important to attempt to continue to teach them. Given the importance of academic performance, judges might be advised to consider placement in specialized educational programs for some youth. Operators of juvenile residential facilities should make every effort to ensure that youth with academic problems receive diagnostic and remedial services while in their custody. Law-related education programs are a promising intervention for high risk children. Judges might consider requiring adjudicated youth to attend such a program. Finally, it would seem valuable to encourage probation officers to monitor their probationers' school attendance and coursework, perhaps through reports from the schools.

Schools should also consider offering a moral philosophy or law-related intervention program to students who display conduct problems or antisocial behavior on the school premises. It may be beneficial to develop versions of these programs for younger-aged students as well.

Schools should attempt to involve parents to a greater degree in their children's education. Although this course of action is fraught with difficulties, the gains may outweigh the disadvantages. In some cases, this may involve literacy training or other remedial programs for the parents. In other cases, it may require "selling" parents on the value of education for their children and the contribution they, as parents, can make to their children's education. When children display behavior problems in school, schools might consider extending an offer of parenting education to the parents of these children. Finally, when children have significant learning or intellectual deficits, schools might well consider offering education programs, organized around teaching techniques, to the parents of these children.

Schools offering preschool education programs such as Head Start or other early education programs should consider adding an assessment component for some children. Although both intellectual and behavioral development undergo considerable change between early childhood and high school completion, our analysis suggests that children exhibiting deficits in precursors to academic performance (e.g., language deficits, intellectual handicaps, social deprivation) or appropriate social behavior (e.g., attention or activity-level regulation, or aggression) may be a cause for concern. Where these precursor conditions are especially severe, intervention programs may be well advised. If intervention programs are undertaken, every attempt should be made to involve the child's parents in order to obtain a unified environment.

More generally, schools should consider implementing, on an experimental basis, school-level interventions that have shown promise for improving academic performance. Certainly, innovative techniques that lead to a greater sense of control and safety for both teachers and students, in conjunction with improved academic performance, are worth trying. Although the introduction of these techniques may cause controversy, a thoughtful preparation of the ground ahead of time will prevent some problems.

Parents have a unique responsibility to their children. As the persons closest to their children, they are in the best position to observe and modify their children's behavior. It is important that parents ensure that their children receive an adequate education, including access to special resources. Ensuring an education for their children should not be limited only to academic subjects but should also include appropriate social conduct toward others.

Governmental legislative bodies and agencies should consider two courses of action. One course of action is to review local, state, and federal laws and administrative regulations to determine if children in need of educational or behavioral services are prevented from receiving them. Where significant legal or administrative impediments to service access are found, legislative remedies should be used to ensure access. Their review should extend across agency boundaries to ensure that agencies whose service population includes children are not working at cross-purposes or with excessive duplication of services.

The second course of action is for legislative bodies to fund the development, evaluation, and dissemination of promising intervention and prevention programs. However, it is critical that each program funded have a methodologically rigorous evaluation component that addresses the questions set forth for interventions in the preceding section of this review. Candidate programs should not be limited to service delivery but should also include multimedia campaigns designed to build consensus for the value of education and methods of resolving social conflict.

REFERENCES

Agnew, R. 1985. "Social Control Theory and Delinquency: A Longitudinal Test." *Criminology* 23:47–61.
———. 1991. "A Longitudinal Test of Social Control Theory and Delinquency." *Journal of Research in Crime and Delinquency* 28:126–56.
Akers, R. L. 1977. *Deviant Behavior: A Social Learning Approach.* 2 ed. Belmont, Mass.: Wadsworth.
Arbuthnot, J., and D. A. Gordon. 1986. "Behavioral and Cognitive Effects of a Moral Reasoning Development Intervention for High-Risk Behavior–Disordered Adolescents." *Journal of Consulting and Clinical Psychology* 54:208–16.
Bachman, J. G. 1970. *Youth in Transition.* Vol. 2, *The Impact of Family Background and Intelligence on Tenth-Grade Boys.* Ann Arbor: University of Michigan, Institute for Social Research.
Bazemore, S. G., and G. W. Noblit. 1978. "Class Origins and Academic Achievement: An Empirical Critique of the Cultural Deprivation Perspective." *Urban Education* 13:345–60.
Berrueta-Clement, J. R., L. J. Schweinhart, W. S. Barnett, A. S. Epstein,

and D. P. Weikart. 1984. *Changed Lives: The Effects of the Perry Preschool Program on Youths through Age 19.* Monographs of the High/Scope Educational Research Foundation, no. 8. Ypsilanti, Mich.: High/Scope Educational Research Foundation.

Blumstein, A., D. P. Farrington, and S. Moitra. 1985. "Delinquency Careers: Innocents, Desisters, and Persisters." In *Crime and Justice: An Annual Review of Research*, vol. 6, edited by M. Tonry and N. Morris. Chicago: University of Chicago Press.

Bond, G., and P. Fendrick. 1936. "Delinquency and Reading." *Pedagogical Seminar and Journal of Genetic Psychology* 48:236–43.

Broder, P. K., M. Dunivant, E. C. Smith, and L. P. Sutton. 1981. "Further Observations on the Link between Learning Disabilities and Juvenile Delinquency." *Journal of Educational Psychology* 73:838–50.

Bureau of Justice Statistics. 1993. *Sourcebook of Criminal Justice Statistics.* Washington, D.C.: U.S. Government Printing Office.

Burgess, R., and R. L. Akers. 1966. "A Differential Association-Reinforcement Theory of Criminal Behavior." *Social Problems* 14:128–67.

Burt, C. 1931. *The Young Delinquent.* London: University of London Press.

Busch, K. G., R. Zagar, J. R. Huges, J. Arbit, and R. E. Russell. 1990. "Adolescents Who Kill." *Journal of Clinical Psychology* 46:472–85.

Catalano, R. F., and J. D. Hawkins. "The Social Development Model: A Theory of Antisocial Behavior." *Delinquency and Crime: Current Theories*, edited by J. D. Hawkins. New York: Cambridge University Press (forthcoming).

Cernkovich, S. A., and P. C. Giordano. 1992. "School Bonding, Race, and Delinquency." *Criminology* 30:261–91.

Cloward, R., and L. E. Ohlin. 1960. *Delinquency and Opportunity: A Theory of Delinquent Gangs.* Glencoe, Ill.: Free Press.

Cochran, M., and I. Bo. 1989. "The Social Networks, Family Involvement, and Pro- and Antisocial Behavior of Adolescent Males in Norway." *Journal of Youth and Adolescence* 18:377–98.

Cohen, A. 1955. *Delinquent Boys: Culture of the Gang.* New York: Free Press.

Davis, A. D., D. D. Sanger, and M. Morris-Friehe. 1991. "Language Skills of Delinquent and Nondelinquent Adolescent Males." *Journal of Communication Disorders* 24:251–66.

Denno, D. 1990. *Biology and Violence: From Birth to Adulthood.* New York: Cambridge University Press.

Dishion, T. J., R. Loeber, M. Stouthamer-Loeber, and G. R. Patterson. 1984. "Skill Deficit and Male Adolescent Delinquency." *Journal of Abnormal Child Psychology* 12:37–54.

Donovan, J. E., and R. Jessor. 1985. "Structure of Problem Behavior in Adolescence and Young Adulthood." *Journal of Consulting and Clinical Psychology* 53:890–904.

Elias, M. J., M. A. Gara, T. F. Schuyler, L. R. Branden-Muller, and M. A. Sayette. 1991. "The Promotion of Social Competence: Longitudinal Study of a Preventive School-Based Program." *American Journal of Orthopsychiatry* 61:409–17.

Elliott, D. S., S. S. Ageton, and R. J. Canter. 1979. "An Integrated Theoretical Perspective on Delinquent Behavior." *Journal of Research in Crime and Delinquency* 16:3–27.

Elliott, D. S., D. Huizinga, and S. S. Ageton. 1985. *Explaining Delinquency and Drug Use.* Beverly Hills, Calif.: Sage.

Elliott, D. S., and H. L. Voss. 1974. *Delinquency and Dropout.* Lexington, Mass.: Lexington Books.

Empey, L. T., and S. G. Lubeck. 1971. *Explaining Delinquency.* Lexington, Mass.: Heath.

Emshoff, J. G., and C. H. Blakely. 1983. "The Diversion of Delinquent Youth: Family Focused Intervention." *Children and Youth Services Review* 5:343–56.

Farrington, D. P. 1987. "Early Precursors of Frequent Offending." In *From Children to Citizens.* Vol. 3, *Families, Schools, and Delinquency Prevention,* edited by J. Q. Wilson and G. C. Loury. New York: Springer-Verlag.

Farrington, D. P., and J. D. Hawkins. 1991. "Predicting Participation, Early Onset, and Later Persistence in Officially Recorded Offending." *Criminal Behavior and Mental Health* 1:1–33.

Ferguson, T. 1952. *The Young Delinquent in His Social Setting: A Glasgow Study.* London: Oxford University Press.

Fiqueira-McDonough, J. 1986. "School Context, Gender, and Delinquency." *Journal of Youth and Adolescence* 15:79–98.

Gagne, E. E. 1977. "Educating Delinquents: A Review of Research." *Journal of Special Education* 11:13–27.

Gendreau, P., and B. Ross. 1979. "Effective Correctional Treatment: Bibliotherapy for Cynics." *Crime and Delinquency* 25:463–89.

Glass, G. V. 1977. "Integrating Findings: The Meta-analysis of Research." *Review of Research in Education* 5:351–79.

Glueck, S., and E. Glueck. 1950. *Unraveling Juvenile Delinquency.* New York: Commonwealth Fund.

Gold, M. 1963. *Status Forces in Delinquent Boys.* Ann Arbor: University of Michigan, Institute for Social Research.

Gomme, I. M. 1985. "Predictors of Status and Criminal Offences among Male and Female Adolescents in an Ontario Community." *Canadian Journal of Criminology* 27:147–59.

Gottfredson, D. C. 1986. "Empirical Test of School-Based Environmental and Individual Interventions to Reduce the Risk of Delinquent Behavior." *Criminology* 24:705–31.

———. 1990. "Changing School Structures to Benefit High-Risk Youth." In *Understanding Troubled and Troubling Youth,* edited by P. E. Leone. Beverly Hills, Calif.: Sage.

Gottfredson, G. D. 1981. "Schooling and Delinquency." In *New Directions in the Rehabilitation of Criminal Offenders,* edited by S. E. Martin, L. B. Sechrest, and R. Redner. Washington, D.C.: National Academy Press.

Hathaway, S. R., and E. D. Monachesi. 1963. *Adolescent Personality and Behavior.* Minneapolis: University of Minnesota Press.

Hawkins, J. D., R. F. Catalano, D. M. Morrison, J. O'Donnell, R. D. Abbott, and L. E. Day. 1992. "The Seattle Social Development Project: Effects of the First Four Years on Protective Factors and Problem Behaviors." In *The Prevention of Antisocial Behavior in Children*, edited by J. McCord and R. Tremblay. New York: Guilford.

Hawkins, J. D., H. J. Doueck, and D. M. Lishner. 1988. "Changing Teaching Practices in Mainstream Classrooms to Improve Bonding and Behavior of Low Achievers." *American Educational Research Journal* 25:31–50.

Hawkins, J. D., and D. M. Lishner. 1987. "Schooling and Delinquency." In *Handbook on Crime and Delinquency Prevention*, edited by E. H. Johnson. New York: Greenwood.

Hawkins, J. D., and J. G. Weis. 1985. "The Social Development Model: An Integrated Approach to Delinquency Prevention." *Journal of Primary Prevention* 6:73–97.

Hedges, L. V., and I. Olkin. 1985. *Statistical Methods for Meta-Analysis*. New York: Academic Press.

Hindelang, M. J. 1973. "Causes of Delinquency: A Partial Replication and Extension." *Social Problems* 20:471–87.

Hinshaw, S. P. 1992. "Externalizing Behavior Problems and Academic Underachievement in Childhood and Adolescence: Causal Relationships and Underlying Mechanisms." *Psychological Bulletin* 111:127–55.

Hirschi, T. 1969. *Causes of Delinquency*. Berkeley, Calif.: University of California Press.

Hirschi, T., and M. J. Hindelang. 1977. "Intelligence and Delinquency: A Revisionist Review." *American Sociological Review* 42:571–87.

Hughes, J. R., R. Zagar, R. B. Sylvies, J. Arbit, K. G. Busch, and N. D. Bowers. 1991. "Medical, Family, and Scholastic Conditions in Urban Delinquents." *Journal of Clinical Psychology* 47:448–64.

Hunter, J. E., and F. L. Schmidt. 1990. *Methods of Meta-analysis*. Newbury Park, Calif.: Sage.

Hunter, J. E., F. L. Schmidt, and G. B. Jackson. 1982. *Meta-analysis: Cumulating Research Findings Across Studies*. Beverly Hills, Calif.: Sage.

Jensen, G. F., and R. Eve. 1976. "Sex Differences in Delinquency: An Examination of Popular Sociological Explanations." *Criminology* 13:427–48.

Jerse, F. W., and M. E. Fakouri. 1978. "Juvenile Delinquency and Academic Deficiency." *Contemporary Education* 49:106–9.

Johnson, R. E. 1979. *Juvenile Delinquency and Its Origins*. Cambridge: Cambridge University Press.

Kelly, D. H. 1971. "School Failure, Academic Self-Evaluation, and School Avoidance and Deviant Behavior." *Youth and Society* 2:489–502.

Kelly, D. H., and W. T. Pink. 1973. "School Commitment, Youth Rebellion and Delinquency." *Criminology* 10:473–85.

Kohlberg, L. 1981. *Essays in Moral Education*. Vol. 1, *Philosophy of Moral Development*. San Francisco: Harper & Row.

Krohn, M. D., and J. L. Massey. 1980. "Social Control and Delinquency: An Examination of the Elements of the Social Bond." *Sociological Quarterly* 21:529–43.

Kupersmidt, J. B., and J. D. Coie. 1990. "Preadolescent Peer Status, Aggression, and School Adjustment as Predictors of Externalizing Problems in Adolescence." *Child Development* 61:1350–62.

Kvaraceus, W. C. 1945. *Juvenile Delinquency and the School.* Yonkers-on-Hudson, New York: World Book.

LaGrange, R. L., and H. R. White. 1985. "Age Differences in Delinquency: A Test of Theory." *Criminology* 23:19–45.

Lawrence, R. 1985. "School Performance, Containment Theory, and Delinquent Behavior." *Youth and Society* 17:69–95.

Le Blanc, Marc, Pierre McDuff, Pierre Charlebois, Claude Gagnon, Serge Larrivee, and Richard E. Tremblay. 1991. "Social and Psychological Consequences, at 10 Years Old, of an Earlier Onset of Self-Reported Delinquency." *Psychiatry* 54:133–47.

Le Blanc, M., E. Vallieres, and P. McDuff. 1992. "Adolescents' School Experience and Self-Reported Offending: An Empirical Elaboration of an Interactional and Developmental School Social Control Theory." *International Journal of Adolescence and Youth* 3:197–247.

Lipsey, M. W. 1992. "Juvenile Delinquency Treatment: A Meta-analytic Inquiry into the Variability of Effects." In *Meta-analysis for Explanation*, edited by T. D. Cook, H. Cooper, D. S. Cordray, H. Hartmann, L. V. Hedges, and R. J. Light. New York: Russell Sage Foundation.

Lipton, W. L., and M. D. Smith. 1983. "Explaining Delinquent Involvement: A Consideration of Suppressor Effects." *Journal of Research in Crime and Delinquency* 20:199–213.

Loeber, R., and M. Le Blanc. 1990. "Toward a Developmental Criminology." *Crime and Justice: A Review of Research*, vol. 12, edited by M. Tonry and N. Morris. Chicago: University of Chicago Press.

Loeber, R., M. Stouthamer-Loeber, W. B. Van Kammen, and D. P. Farrington. 1991. "Initiation, Escalation and Desistance in Juvenile Offending and Their Correlates." *Journal of Criminal Law and Criminology* 82:36–82.

Logan, C. 1972. "Evaluation Research in Crime and Delinquency: A Reappraisal." *Journal of Criminal Law, Criminology, and Police Science* 63:378–87.

Lundman, R. J., P. T. McFarlane, and F. R. Scarpitti. 1976. "Delinquency Prevention: A Description and Assessment of the Projects Reported in the Professional Literature." *Crime and Delinquency* 22:297–308.

Lunny, L. 1990. "Knowledge and Enlightenment: Attitudes to Education in Early Nineteenth Century East Ulster." In *The Origins of Popular Literacy in Ireland: Language Change and Educational Development, 1700–1920*, edited by M. Daley and D. Dickson. Dublin: Trinity College.

Lynam, D., T. E. Moffitt, and M. Stouthamer-Loeber. 1993. "Explaining the Relation between IQ and Delinquency: Class, Race, Test Motivation, School Failure, or Self-Control?" *Journal of Abnormal Psychology* 102:187–96.

Maguin, E., and R. Loeber. 1992. "Does Poor School Performance Predict the Early Onset of Delinquency?" Paper presented at the annual meeting of the American Society of Criminology, New Orleans, November.

Maguin, E., R. Loeber, and P. G. LeMahieu. 1993. "Does the Relationship between Poor Reading and Delinquency Hold for Males of Different Ages and Ethnic Groups?" *Journal of Emotional and Behavioral Disorders* 1:88–100.

Mann, D. W. 1976. "When Delinquency Is Defensive: Self Esteem in Deviant Behavior." Ph.D. dissertation, University of Michigan, Department of Psychology.

Mannuzza, S., R. Gittelmann-Klein, P. H. Konig, and T. L. Giampino. 1989. "Hyperactive Boys Almost Grown Up." *Archives of General Psychiatry* 46:1073–79.

Massimo, J., and M. Shore. 1963. "The Effectiveness of a Comprehensive, Vocationally Oriented Psychotherapeutic Program for Adolescent Delinquent Boys." *American Journal of Orthopsychiatry* 33:634–42.

Maughan, Barbara, G. Gray, and M. Rutter. 1985. "Reading Retardation and Antisocial Behavior: A Follow-Up into Employment." *Journal of Child Psychology and Psychiatry* 26:741–58.

McCarthy, J. D., and D. R. Hoge. 1984. "The Dynamics of Self-Esteem and Delinquency." *American Journal of Sociology* 90:396–410.

McGee, R., and D. Share 1988. "Attention Deficit Disorder–Hyperactivity and Academic Failure: Which Comes First and What Should Be Treated." *Journal of the American Academy of Child and Adolescent Psychiatry* 27:318–25.

McGee, R., D. Share, T. E. Moffitt, S. Williams, and P. A. Silva. 1988. "Reading Disability, Behavior Problems, and Juvenile Delinquency." In *Individual Differences in Children and Adolescents*, edited by D. Saklofske and S. Eysenck. New York: Hodder & Stoughton.

Meltzer, L. J., M. D. Levine, W. Karniski, J. S. Palfrey, and S. Clarke. 1984. "An Analysis of the Learning Styles of Adolescent Delinquents." *Journal of Learning Disabilities* 17:600–608.

Menard, S., and B. J. Morse. 1984. "A Structuralist Critique of the IQ-Delinquency Hypothesis: Theory and Evidence." *American Journal of Sociology* 89:1347–78.

Moffitt, T. E. 1990. "The Neuropsychology of Juvenile Delinquency: A Critical Review." In *Crime and Justice: A Review of Research*, vol. 12, edited by M. Tonry and N. Morris. Chicago: University of Chicago Press.

Moffitt, T. E., and P. A. Silva. 1988. "Self-Reported Delinquency, Neuropsychological Deficit, and History of Attention Deficit Disorder." *Journal of Abnormal Child Psychology* 16:553–69.

Noblit, G. W. 1976. "The Adolescent Experience and Delinquency: School versus Subcultural Effects." *Youth and Society* 8:27–44.

Olweus, Dan. 1979. "Stability of Aggressive Reaction Patterns in Males: A Review." *Psychological Bulletin* 86:852–75.

Ouston, J. 1984. "Delinquency, Family Background and Educational Attainment." *British Journal of Criminology* 24:2–26.

Palmore, E. B., and P. E. Hammond. 1964. "Interacting Factors in Juvenile Delinquency." *American Sociological Review* 29:848–54.

Patterson, G. R., D. Capaldi, and L. Bank. 1991. "An Early Starter Model for Predicting Delinquency." In *The Development and Treatment of Childhood Aggression*, edited by Debra J. Pepler and K. H. Rubin. Hillsdale, N.J.: Erlbaum.

Patterson, G. R., and T. J. Dishion. 1985. "Contributions of Families and Peers to Delinquency." *Criminology* 23:63–79.

Peeples, F., and R. Loeber. 1994. "Do Individual Factors and Neighborhood Context Explain Ethnic Differences in Juvenile Delinquency?" *Journal of Quantitative Criminology* 10:141–57.

Polk, K. 1969. "Class, Strain, and Rebellion among Adolescents." *Social Problems* 17:214–24.

———. 1975. "Schools and the Delinquency Experience." *Criminal Justice and Behavior* 2:315–38.

Polk, K., D. Frease, and F. L. Richmond. 1974. "Social Class, School Experience, and Delinquency." *Criminology* 12:84–96.

Polk, K., and D. S. Halferty. 1966. "Adolescence, Commitment, and Delinquency." *Journal of Research in Crime and Delinquency* 3:82–96.

Rankin, J. H. 1980. "School Factors and Delinquency: Interactions by Age and Sex." *Sociology and Social Research* 64:420–34.

Rhodes, A. L., and A. J. Reiss, Jr. 1969. "Apathy, Truancy, and Delinquency as Adaptations to School Failure." *Social Forces* 48:12–22.

Robins, L. N., and S. Y. Hill. 1966. "Assessing the Contribution of Family Structure, Class, and Peer Groups to Juvenile Delinquency." *Journal of Criminal Law, Criminology, and Police Science* 57:325–34.

Romig, D. 1978. "Academic Education." In *Justice for Our Children: An Examination of Juvenile Delinquency Rehabilitation Programs*, edited by D. Romig. Toronto, Calif.: Lexington.

Rowe, K. J., and K. S. Rowe. 1992. "The Relationship between Inattentiveness in the Classroom and Reading Achievement (Part B): An Explanatory Study." *Journal of the American Academy of Child and Adolescent Psychiatry* 31:357–68.

Rutter, M., J. Tizard, and K. Whitmore. 1970. *Education, Health and Behaviour.* London: Longmans.

Satterfield, J. H., C. M. Hoppe, and A. M. Schell. 1982. "A Prospective Study of Delinquency in 110 Adolescent Boys with Attention Disorder and 88 Normal Adolescent Boys." *American Journal of Psychiatry* 139:795–98.

Schafer, W. E. 1969. "Participation in Interscholastic Athletics and Delinquency: A Preliminary Study." *Social Problems* 17:40–47.

———. 1972. "Participation in Interscholastic Athletics and Delinquency." In *Schools and Delinquency*, edited by K. Polk and W. E. Schafer. Englewood Cliffs, N.J.: Prentice-Hall.

Schafer, W. E., C. Olexa, and K. Polk. 1972. "Programmed for Social Class: Tracking in High School." In *Schools and Delinquency*, edited by K. Polk and W. E. Schafer. Englewood Cliffs, N.J.: Prentice-Hall.

Schmidt, F. L., and J. E. Hunter. 1992. "Development of a Causal Model of Processes Determining Job Performance." *Science* 1:89–92.

Senna, J., S. A. Rathus, and L. Siegel. 1974. "Delinquent Behavior and Academic Investment among Suburban Youth." *Adolescence* 9:481–94.

Siegel, L. J. 1992. *Criminology.* 4th ed. St. Paul, Minn.: West.

Silberberg, N. E., and M. C. Silberberg. 1971. "School Achievement and Delinquency." *Review of Educational Research* 41:17–33.

Spivack, G., and J. Marcus. n.d. "Long-Term Effects of Retention on Grade and Special Class Placement among Inner City School Children." Unpublished manuscript. Philadelphia: Hahnemann University.

Spreen, O. 1981. "The Relationship between Learning Disability, Neurological Impairment and Delinquency." *Journal of Nervous and Mental Disease* 169:791–99.

Swift, M., G. Spivack, and L. Back. 1973. "Patterns of Disturbed Classroom Behavior of Nondelinquent and Delinquent Adolescent Girls." *Journal of Research in Crime and Delinquency* 10:59–72.

Tarter, R. E., A. M. Hegedus, A. I. Alterman, and L. Katz-Garris. 1983. "Cognitive Capacities of Juvenile Violent, Nonviolent, and Sexual Offenders." *Journal of Nervous and Mental Disease* 171:564–67.

Thornberry, T. P. 1987. "Toward an Interactional Theory of Delinquency." *Criminology* 25:863–91.

Thornberry, T. P., A. J. Lizotte, M. D. Krohn, M. Farnworth, and S. J. Jang. 1991. "Testing Interactional Theory: An Examination of Reciprocal Causal Relationships among Family, School, and Delinquency." *Journal of Criminal Law and Criminology* 82:3–35.

Thornton, W., and L. Voigt. 1984. "Television and Delinquency: A Neglected Dimension of Social Control." *Youth and Society* 15:445–68.

Tracy, P. E., M. E. Wolfgang, and R. M. Figlio. 1990. *Delinquency Careers in Two Birth Cohorts*. New York: Plenum.

Tremblay, R. E., and L. C. Masse. 1993. "Cognitive Deficits, School Adjustment, Disruptive Behavior and Juvenile Delinquency: A Longitudinal Look at Their Developmental Sequence." Paper presented at the annual meeting of the American Society of Criminology, Phoenix, October.

Tremblay, R. E., B. Masse, D. Perron, M. Le Blanc, A. E. Schwartzman, and J. E. Ledingham. 1992a. "Early Disruptive Behavior, Poor School Achievement, Delinquent Behavior, and Delinquent Personality: Longitudinal Analysis." *Journal of Consulting and Clinical Psychology* 60:64–72.

Tremblay, R. E., F. Vitaro, L. Betrand, M. Le Blanc, H. Buauchesne, H. Boileau, and L. David. 1992b. "Parent and Child Training to Prevent Early Onset of Delinquency: The Montreal Longitudinal-Experimental Study." In *Preventing Deviant Behavior from Birth to Adolescence: Experimental Approaches*, edited by J. McCord and R. E. Tremblay. New York: Guilford.

Tygart, C. E. 1988. "Public School Vandalism: Toward a Synthesis of Theories and Transition to Paradigm Analysis." *Adolescence* 23:187–200.

Walker, H. M., S. Stieber, E. Ramsey, and R. E. O'Neill. 1991. "Longitudinal Prediction of the School Achievement, Adjustment, and Delinquency of Antisocial versus At-Risk Boys." *Remedial and Special Education* 12:43–51.

———. 1993. "Fifth Grade School Adjustment and Later Arrest Rate: A Longitudinal Study of Middle School Antisocial Boys." *Journal of Child and Family Studies* 2:295–315.

Wallander, J. L. 1988. "The Relationship between Attention Problems in Childhood and Antisocial Behavior Eight Years Later." *Journal of Child Psychology and Psychiatry and Allied Disciplines* 29:53–61.

Wang, M. C., G. D. Haertel, and H. J. Walberg. 1993. "Toward a Knowledge Base for School Learning." *Review of Educational Research* 63:249–94.

Weis, J. G., and J. Sederstrom. 1981. *The Prevention of Serious Delinquency: What to Do?* Washington, D.C.: U.S. Department of Justice.

Wells, L. E., and J. H. Rankin. 1983. "Self-Concept as Mediating Factor in Delinquency." *Social Psychology Quarterly* 46:11–22.

Werner, E. E., and R. S. Smith. 1977. *Kauai's Children Come of Age.* Honolulu: University of Hawaii.

West, D. J., and D. P. Farrington. 1973. *Who Becomes Delinquent?* London: Heinemann.

White, H. R., R. J. Pandina, and R. L. LaGrange. 1987. "Longitudinal Predictors of Serious Substance Use and Delinquency." *Criminology* 25:715–40.

Wiatrowski, M. D., S. Hansell, C. R. Massey, and D. L. Wilson. 1982. "Curriculum Tracking and Delinquency." *American Sociological Review* 47:151–60.

Williams, S., and R. McGee. 1994. "Reading Attainment and Juvenile Delinquency." *Journal of Child Psychology and Psychiatry* 35:441–59.

Wolff, P. H., D. Waber, M. Bauermeister, C. Cohen, and R. Ferber. 1982. "The Neuropsychological Status of Adolescent Delinquent Boys." *Journal of Child Psychology and Psychiatry and Allied Disciplines* 23:267–79.

Wolfgang, M. E., R. M. Figlio, and T. Sellin. 1972. *Delinquency in a Birth Cohort.* Chicago: University of Chicago Press.

Wright, W., and M. Dixon. 1977. "Community Prevention and Treatment of Juvenile Delinquency: A Review and an Evaluation." *Journal of Research in Crime and Delinquency* 14:35–62.

Ellen G. Cohn and David P. Farrington

Crime and Justice and the Criminal Justice and Criminology Literature

ABSTRACT

The most-cited scholars in state-of-the-art literature reviews in general volumes of *Crime and Justice: A Review of Research* between 1986 and 1993 were significantly correlated with the most-cited scholars in three major American criminology journals, three major American criminal justice journals, and three international criminology journals between 1986 and 1990. There was also substantial overlap between the most-cited works in *Crime and Justice* and the most-cited crime and justice works in the *Social Sciences Citation Index* between 1979 and 1993. Concepts developed in criminal career research can be used to enrich citation analysis. The prevalence of citations (the number of different articles in which an author was cited) can be distinguished from the individual citation frequency (the average number of an author's works cited whenever that author was cited). Mathematical models of citation careers can be developed.

The main aim of this essay is to identify the most-cited scholars and most-cited works in the general volumes of *Crime and Justice: A Review of Research* between 1979 and 1993. However, we have widened our search to identify the most-cited works on crime and justice subjects in those years in the *Social Sciences Citation Index* (*SSCI*). In addition, we suggest methodological advances in citation analysis using concepts developed in criminal career research. We distinguish between the

Ellen G. Cohn is assistant professor of criminal justice in the School of Policy and Management, Florida International University. David P. Farrington is professor of psychological criminology in the Institute of Criminology, Cambridge University. For helpful comments and suggestions we are very grateful to Francis T. Cullen, Eugene Garfield, Loraine Gelsthorpe, Daniel Glaser, Richard Jessor, Malcolm W. Klein, Candace Kruttschnitt, Marc LeBlanc, Rolf Loeber, Joan McCord, Edwin I. Megargee, Sheldon L. Messinger, Adrian Raine, Lee N. Robins, Michael Rutter, Lawrence W. Sherman, Terence P. Thornberry, Marvin E. Wolfgang, and Richard A. Wright.

prevalence and frequency of citations, introduce the concept of coauthor citation, and discuss mathematical models of citation careers.

Crime and Justice: A Review of Research is widely regarded as the leading source of state-of-the-art reviews of key topics in crime and justice, and this is why we have chosen to study authors and works cited in it. After reviewing the first five volumes (1979–83), Trasler (1984, p. 309) concluded:

> There is no lack of new publications in the field of crime and justice, but this venture has something very special to offer. The vigorous (or should one say ruthless?) policy that has been pursued by the editorial board, of determining topics, identifying appropriate essayists, and enforcing a procedure of drafting, criticism and amendment of all contributions, no matter how eminent the writer, has undoubtedly paid off. It is difficult to identify any collection of essays in the social sciences which has achieved so high and consistent a standard of scholarship and presentation. Every school of criminology and criminal justice will need to subscribe to this series, if it maintains its present standard (and the status of its coeditors and its editorial board is a strong guarantee that it will). . . . It is in itself a small library of materials of much interest to scholars and practitioners in this field of study, put together by an outstanding team of criminologists, and a major addition to the literature of crime and justice.

Similarly, Soothill (1985, p. 82) noted that "the bibliographies compiled by all the authors are usually excellent . . . the bibliographies provided the door to an Aladdin's cave of additional sources." Much of this essay is based on these bibliographies.

Section I reviews our previous citation research, determining the most-cited scholars in three major American criminology journals, three major American criminal justice journals, and three major international criminology/criminal justice journals between 1986 and 1990. Section II analyzes the most-cited scholars and most-cited works in *Crime and Justice* between 1979 and 1985 and 1986 and 1993. The most-cited scholars in all these analyses were Marvin E. Wolfgang, Michael J. Hindelang, and Alfred Blumstein. Section III identifies the most-cited crime and justice works in the *SSCI* between 1979 and 1985 and 1986 and 1993. The most-cited items were *Asylums* (Goffman 1961) in the first time period and *Discipline and Punish* (Foucault 1977) in the second. Section IV discusses the prediction of citation careers using mathematical models. In Section V, we summarize our conclusions and argue that citation analysis is useful in identifying individual authors, works, and topics that are influential during particular time periods and, hence, that it is useful in documenting the development of knowledge of crime and justice.

I. Previous Citation Research

This essay builds on our previous research investigating the most-cited scholars in major American and international journals in criminology and criminal justice between 1986 and 1990. We determined the most-cited scholars in the major criminology journals of the major countries of the English-speaking world. Those journals are *Criminology, British Journal of Criminology, Canadian Journal of Criminology*, and *Australian and New Zealand Journal of Criminology* (Cohn and Farrington 1994*a*). Only four scholars were among the fifty most-cited authors in all four journals: Marvin E. Wolfgang, Alfred Blumstein, James Q. Wilson, and Michael J. Hindelang. Wolfgang's most-cited work was *Delinquency in a Birth Cohort* (Wolfgang, Figlio, and Sellin 1972); Blumstein's was *Criminal Careers and "Career Criminals"* (Blumstein et al. 1986); Wilson's was *Crime and Human Nature* (Wilson and Herrnstein 1985); and Hindelang's was *Measuring Delinquency* (Hindelang, Hirschi, and Weis 1981). As with "chronic offenders" in criminal career research, a small number of authors accounted for a disproportionate fraction of all citations.

We also determined the most-cited scholars in three major American criminology journals (*Criminology, Journal of Quantitative Criminology*, and *Journal of Research in Crime and Delinquency*) and three major American criminal justice journals (*Justice Quarterly, Journal of Criminal Justice*, and *Criminal Justice and Behavior*) between 1986 and 1990 (Cohn and Farrington 1994*b*). The most-cited scholars were Marvin E. Wolfgang, Michael J. Hindelang, and Alfred Blumstein. Wolfgang's most-cited works were *Delinquency in a Birth Cohort* (Wolfgang, Figlio, and Sellin 1972) in criminology journals and both *The Subculture of Violence* (Wolfgang and Ferracuti 1967) and *Patterns in Criminal Homicide* (Wolfgang 1958) in criminal justice journals. Hindelang's most-cited work was *Measuring Delinquency* (Hindelang, Hirschi, and Weis 1981) in both criminology and criminal justice journals. Blumstein's most-cited works were *Criminal Careers and "Career Criminals"* (Blumstein et al. 1986) in criminology journals and *Research on Sentencing* (Blumstein et al. 1983) in criminal justice journals.

We studied the most-cited scholars and works as one method of measuring influence in criminology and criminal justice. There are other methods, such as ratings by peers and the receipt of prizes or election to major offices in scholarly societies, but all methods tend to identify the same individuals. In our previous papers (Cohn and Farrington 1990, 1994a, 1994b), we reviewed in great detail the advantages and problems of citation analysis as a method of measuring influence. We concluded that large numbers of citations provided an imperfect but nevertheless reasonably valid measure of intellectual influence.

We also acknowledged the advantages of counting citations in a larger number of journals and in books, as Wolfgang, Figlio, and Thornberry (1978) were able to do for 1945–72, and we discussed the advantages and problems of counting citations in the SSCI. Overall, we argued that there was some merit in identifying the most-cited scholars in major journals since a larger study (e.g., based on the SSCI) had the disadvantage of giving equal weight to all journals, irrespective of their quality or eminence and irrespective of whether works published were subject to screening by peer review and, if so, of what rigor. This essay tries to get the best of both worlds by identifying the most-cited scholars and most-cited works both in Crime and Justice, which publishes only a limited number of articles but is highly eminent and subject to careful selection and rigorous screening, and in the SSCI, with a far more comprehensive but much less selective coverage.

II. Crime and Justice

Two types of volumes have been published in the Crime and Justice series: general volumes and thematic volumes on specific topics such as Communities and Crime (Reiss and Tonry 1986). In order to avoid overweighting our analysis by the topics covered in the thematic volumes, we have only analyzed the general volumes. Twelve of these were published up to the end of 1993: volumes 1 (1979), 2 (1980), 3 (1981), 4 and 5 (1983), 6 (1985), 7 (1986), 10 (1988), 12 (1990), 14 (1991), 16 (1992) and 17 (1993). All of these volumes were edited by Norval Morris and Michael Tonry except the last three, which were edited by Michael Tonry alone.

The volumes were funded by the National Institute of Justice, and the authors and topics were recommended (and the draft chapters refereed by and sometimes rejected by) a distinguished editorial board: Alfred Blumstein (1979–93), Ulla Bondeson (1986), Anthony E. Bottoms (1989–93), Shari S. Diamond (1980–90), Anthony N. Doob (1990–93), Felton Earls (1990–91), Albin Eser (1983–85), Daniel Gla-

TABLE 1

Categories of Articles in *Crime and Justice*, 1979–93

	No. of Articles	
Category	1979–85	1986–93
Explanations/theories/correlates of delinquency/crime	7	7
Measurement, methodology, crime trends and patterns, criminal careers, victimization	10	8
General criminology/criminal justice, crime control/prevention, attitudes to criminal justice	9	8
Police, enforcement, private security	4	3
Sentencing, juvenile courts, law, deterrence	7	9
Prison, community treatment, probation, parole, prediction of recidivism	10	8
Total	47	43

ser (1979–80), Ted R. Gurr (1979–81), Roger G. Hood (1989–93), Wade McCree (1979–81), Sheldon L. Messinger (1979–93), Patrick V. Murphy (1979–86), Lloyd E. Ohlin (1981–93), Albert J. Reiss, Jr. (1979–93), Patricia Wald (1980–93), Nigel D. Walker (1979–88), James Q. Wilson (1983–93), and Franklin E. Zimring (1980–93).

Since we were interested in investigating changes over time in the most-cited authors and works, we analyzed the first six volumes (1979–85) and the second six volumes (1986–93) separately. In the first six volumes, forty-seven articles were published, containing a total of 5,625 cited works (an average of 120 citations per article), excluding self-citations and institutional authors (e.g., National Institute of Justice). In the second six volumes, forty-three articles were published, containing a total of 7,971 cited works (an average of 185 citations per article), again excluding self-citations and institutional authors. The ninety articles had a total of 111 authors, of whom sixty-eight were American; twenty-five, British; eight, Canadian; and ten, from other countries (Australia, two; New Zealand, two; Denmark, two; Germany, two; and the Netherlands, two).

Table 1 shows the topics covered in *Crime and Justice* articles during the two periods using a simple classification system that we developed previously (Cohn and Farrington 1990). Any such classification system is to some extent subjective and contentious. Where an article spanned more than one category, we categorized it according to its predominant

TABLE 2

Most-Cited Authors in *Crime and Justice*, 1979–93

Rank	Author	1979–85 No. of Cites	1979–85 Score	1986–93 No. of Cites	1986–93 Score	Total Score
1	Michael J. Hindelang	28	50	32	44	94
2	Alfred Blumstein	18	45	38	48	93
3	Marvin E. Wolfgang	22	49	27	43	92
4	Donald J. West	17	44	34	45	89
5	Sheldon Glueck	20	48	23	35.5	83.5
6	Eleanor T. Glueck	19	46.5	23	35.5	82
7	Franklin E. Zimring	12	32	37	47	79
8	James Q. Wilson	15	43	22	33	76
9	Wesley G. Skogan	12	32	21	32	64
10	Albert J. Reiss, Jr.	14	40	14	14	54
11	Richard F. Sparks	11	26.5	18	25.5	52
12	David P. Farrington	8	0	54	50	50
13	Jacqueline Cohen	4	0	43	49	49
14	Thorsten Sellin	19	46.5	10	0	46.5
15	Patricia M. Mayhew	8	0	35	46	46
16	Lee N. Robins	9	12	20	30.5	42.5
17.5	Ronald V. Clarke	4	0	26	42	42
17.5	Norval Morris	10	18.5	17	23.5	42
19	J. Michael Hough	4	0	25	41	41
20	Peter W. Greenwood	11	26.5	14	14	40.5
23	Robert M. Figlio	12	32	13	8	40
23	Robert D. Hare	14	40	6	0	40
23	John Monahan	14	40	4	0	40
23	David J. Rothman	14	40	8	0	40
23	Edward P. Thompson	14	40	3	0	40
27	Lawrence E. Cohen	6	0	24	39	39
27	Andrew von Hirsch	8	0	24	39	39
27	Delbert S. Elliott	5	0	24	39	39
31.5	Karl O. Christiansen	13	35.5	3	0	35.5
31.5	LaMar T. Empey	13	35.5	8	0	35.5
31.5	Michael R. Gottfredson	8	0	23	35.5	35.5
31.5	Travis Hirschi	8	0	23	35.5	35.5
31.5	Eric H. Monkkonen	13	35.5	0	0	35.5
31.5	Leon Radzinowicz	13	35.5	7	0	35.5
35	Timothy J. Flanagan	2	0	20	30.5	30.5
37	Malcolm W. Klein	1	0	19	28	28
37	Michael Rutter	0	0	19	28	28
37	Lawrence W. Sherman	1	0	19	28	28
41.5	David F. Greenberg	11	26.5	9	0	26.5
41.5	Peter Linebaugh	11	26.5	0	0	26.5
41.5	Robert M. Martinson	11	26.5	9	0	26.5
41.5	Daniel Nagin	11	26.5	8	0	26.5
41.5	Daisy Schalling	11	26.5	0	0	26.5

TABLE 2 (*Continued*)

Rank	Author	1979–85		1986–93		Total Score
		No. of Cites	Score	No. of Cites	Score	
41.5	Clifford R. Shaw	11	26.5	7	0	26.5
45	Lloyd E. Ohlin	9	12	14	14	26
46	Gerald R. Patterson	0	0	18	25.5	25.5
47	Derek B. Cornish	4	0	17	23.5	23.5
50.5	Marcus Felson	4	0	16	20	20
50.5	Kay A. Knapp	0	0	16	20	20
50.5	Joan McCord	7	0	16	20	20
50.5	Joan Petersilia	8	0	16	20	20
50.5	James F. Short	9	12	13	8	20
50.5	Michael H. Tonry	0	0	16	20	20

NOTE.—See text for explanation of scoring.

emphasis. This analysis shows that the coverage was very wide-ranging, including articles on theory, correlates, methodology, crime trends and patterns, criminal careers, victimization, prevention, policing, sentencing, law, prison, and community treatment. There was no marked change in coverage between the two time periods.

A. Most-Cited Scholars

In order to give equal weight to citations in all journals, in our previous papers we identified the fifty most-cited scholars in each journal and gave each a score from fifty to one. The most-cited author scored fifty, the second most-cited author scored forty-nine, etc.; authors outside the top fifty scored zero. We then added up the authors' scores over several journals. We used the same method with *Crime and Justice*, except that we gave equal weight to each time period (1979–85 and 1986–93). We identified the fifty most-cited scholars in each time period, gave each a score from fifty to one, and then added up the scores over the two time periods.

Table 2 shows the fifty-three most-cited scholars in *Crime and Justice* according to this measure. For example, Michael J. Hindelang was the most-cited scholar between 1979 and 1985, with twenty-eight cites, and hence was given a score of fifty. Between 1986 and 1993, he was cited thirty-two times, but the increased number of citations in the second time period meant that he was now the seventh most-cited scholar, scoring forty-four. Hence, his total score was ninety-four.

Scholars who were among the fifty most-cited authors in the second time period but not in the first included Ronald V. Clarke, Jacqueline Cohen, Lawrence E. Cohen, Delbert S. Elliott, David P. Farrington, Michael R. Gottfredson, Travis Hirschi, J. Michael Hough, Patricia Mayhew, and Andrew von Hirsch. Scholars who were among the fifty most-cited authors in the first time period but not in the second included Karl O. Christiansen, LaMar T. Empey, Robert D. Hare, John Monahan, Eric H. Monkkonen, Leon Radzinowicz, David J. Rothman, Thorsten Sellin, and Edward P. Thompson.

As in our previous analyses of citations in criminology and criminal justice journals between 1986 and 1990, the most-cited scholars overall were Michael J. Hindelang, Alfred Blumstein, and Marvin E. Wolfgang. The scores of the fifty-three most-cited authors in *Crime and Justice* in the two time periods were compared with their scores between 1986 and 1990 in three American criminology journals (*Criminology, Journal of Quantitative Criminology, Journal of Research in Crime and Delinquency*), three American criminal justice journals (*Justice Quarterly, Journal of Criminal Justice, Criminal Justice and Behavior*), and three international criminology journals (*British Journal of Criminology, Canadian Journal of Criminology, Australian and New Zealand Journal of Criminology*).

The scores of the fifty-three most-cited authors in *Crime and Justice* between 1986 and 1993 were significantly correlated with their scores in American criminology journals ($r = .482, p < .001$), American criminal justice journals ($r = .406, p = .003$), and international criminology journals ($r = .577, p < .001$). However, the scores of these authors in *Crime and Justice* between 1979 and 1985 were negatively correlated with their scores in *Crime and Justice* between 1986 and 1993 ($r = -.316, p = .021$) and uncorrelated with their scores in the other groups of journals ($r = .024, .057, and .037$, respectively). These results perhaps indicate changes in influence between 1979 and 1985 and 1986 and 1993.

B. Coauthor Citation

Self-citations are, of course, quite legitimate because it is common for a scholar's work to build on his or her previous research. We excluded self-citations from our analysis because of our interest in assessing the influence of one scholar on other scholars. However, there is still a problem of coauthor citation. This occurs when an author of an article cites an article jointly authored by himself or herself and other persons. For example, if Jacqueline Cohen cites an article by Alfred Blumstein and Jacqueline Cohen, Alfred Blumstein will be counted as cited in our analysis, but not Jacqueline Cohen, because of the exclusion of self-citations. However, it is arguable whether and to what degree coauthor citation (the citing of Alfred Blumstein in this case) measures the influence of one scholar on another scholar since it may be in some sense a surrogate self-citation. We may be the first researchers to identify this problem of coauthor citation in citation analysis. Of the fifty-three most-cited scholars in table 2, twenty-three benefited from one or more coauthor citations.

The concepts developed to study co-offending (Reiss and Farrington 1991) might be useful in citation analysis. For example, if scholar A cites scholar B, this might be defined as a citation pair, by analogy with a co-offending pair. It would be interesting to investigate the extent to which a high proportion of a scholar's citations involve a small number of citation pairs, the persistence of citation pairs over time, and the extent to which they are reciprocal (scholar A citing scholar B, and scholar B citing scholar A). We would have preferred to use the term "cocitation" here, but cocitation has been used to refer to the citing of two or more works together in the same work (Mullens et al. 1977; Sullivan, White, and Barboni 1977). It would also be interesting to identify networks of citations, in which each scholar in a network frequently cites other scholars in the network. Research on delinquent networks might usefully guide research on citation networks.

C. Prevalence of Citations

One problem with the common use of the total number of citations as a measure of influence (Rushton et al. 1983; Rushton 1989) is that a high number of citations may be obtained either if a scholar is cited in many different articles or if a scholar is cited many times in a few articles (or, of course, from some combination of these alternatives). This is analogous to the distinction between prevalence and individual offending frequency in criminal career research (Blumstein et al. 1986). A high aggregate number of citations can reflect either a high prevalence (the proportion of different articles in which a scholar is cited) or a high individual citation frequency (the average number of citations per article in which a scholar is cited), or some combination. A high prevalence of citations may be a better measure of influence (on a large

TABLE 3

Prevalence of Author Citations, 1979–93

Rank	Author	1979–85 DA	1979–85 Percent	1986–93 DA	1986–93 Percent	Total DA	Total Percent
1	Michael J. Hindelang	14	30	14	33	28	31.1
2	Marvin E. Wolfgang	14	30	13	30	27	30.0
3	Alfred Blumstein	5	11	20	48	25	28.4
4	James Q. Wilson	11	23	14	33	25	27.8
5	Thorsten Sellin	16	34	8	19	24	26.7
6	Jacqueline Cohen	2	4	20	47	22	24.7
7.5	Michael R. Gottfredson	8	17	13	31	21	23.6
7.5	Norval Morris	9	20	12	28	21	23.6
9	David P. Farrington	7	16	13	32	20	23.5
10	Franklin E. Zimring	4	9	15	35	19	21.3
11	Robert M. Figlio	11	23	8	19	19	21.1
12.5	Joan Petersilia	7	15	10	24	17	19.3
12.5	Richard F. Sparks	9	20	8	19	17	19.3
14.5	Travis Hirschi	7	14	10	23	17	18.9
14.5	Leon Radzinowicz	12	26	5	12	17	18.9
16.5	Albert J. Reiss, Jr.	9	19	7	17	16	18.0
16.5	Wesley G. Skogan	8	17	8	19	16	18.0
18.5	Robert M. Martinson	8	17	8	19	16	17.7
18.5	Lloyd E. Ohlin	5	11	11	26	16	17.7
20	Patricia M. Mayhew	4	9	11	26	15	16.9
21.5	Jan M. Chaiken	4	9	11	26	15	16.7
21.5	J. Michael Hough	2	4	13	30	15	16.7
23	Ronald V. Clarke	3	7	11	27	14	16.3
24	Peter W. Greenwood	6	13	8	19	14	15.7
25.5	Simon Dinitz	6	13	8	19	14	15.6
25.5	Delbert S. Elliott	3	6	11	26	14	15.6
27	Andrew von Hirsch	5	11	8	19	13	14.6
29	Anthony E. Bottoms	5	11	8	19	13	14.4
29	Donald R. Cressey	8	17	5	12	13	14.4
29	Daniel Nagin	5	11	8	19	13	14.4
31	Philip J. Cook	3	7	9	22	12	14.0
32	Donald J. West	4	9	8	19	12	13.5
34.5	Lawrence E. Cohen	5	11	7	16	12	13.3
34.5	David J. Rothman	7	15	5	12	12	13.3
34.5	James F. Short	5	11	7	16	12	13.3
34.5	Nigel D. Walker	7	14	5	12	12	13.3
37	Ken Pease	3	7	8	20	11	12.5
38.5	Derek B. Cornish	3	7	8	19	11	12.4
38.5	Lawrence W. Sherman	1	2	10	24	11	12.4
41	Marcus Felson	3	6	8	19	11	12.2
41	Michel Foucault	7	14	4	9	11	12.2
41	Sheldon Glueck	6	13	5	12	11	12.2
43	Daniel Glaser	7	15	3	7	10	11.2
47	John P. Conrad	5	11	5	12	10	11.1

TABLE 3 (*Continued*)

		1979–85		1986–93		Total	
Rank	Author	DA	Percent	DA	Percent	DA	Percent
47	LaMar T. Empey	5	11	5	12	10	11.1
47	Timothy J. Flanagan	2	4	8	19	10	11.1
47	James Garofalo	4	9	6	14	10	11.1
47	Eleanor T. Glueck	5	11	5	12	10	11.1
47	Edwin Sutherland	7	14	3	7	10	11.1
47	Leslie T. Wilkins	3	6	7	16	10	11.1

NOTE.—DA = Number of different articles in which a scholar was cited. Because articles written by authors were excluded from the analyses, equal numbers of articles in which an author is cited yield slightly different percentage figures.

number of other scholars) than a high individual citation frequency (which may reflect a great influence on only a few other scholars).

Table 3 shows the scholars who had the highest prevalence of citations in *Crime and Justice* in the two time periods. For example, Michael J. Hindelang was cited in fourteen articles between 1979 and 1985, or in 30 percent of all articles published in that time period. Between 1986 and 1993, he was also cited in fourteen articles, or in 33 percent of all articles published in that time period. Overall, he was cited in twenty-eight *Crime and Justice* articles, or in 31 percent of all articles. In calculating the percentage prevalence for each scholar, *Crime and Justice* articles authored by the scholar were excluded. Because we excluded self-citations, scholars were not at risk of being counted as cited in a *Crime and Justice* article that they had authored. For example, Ken Pease, who was cited in eleven different articles, authored two articles in *Crime and Justice* (Pease 1982; Barr and Pease 1990). These articles were not considered when determining his prevalence, so that he was at risk of being cited in eighty-eight articles rather than ninety. This is why his total prevalence of 12.5 percent (eleven out of eighty-eight) is higher than that of Sheldon Glueck, for example, who was cited in eleven articles, authored none, and hence had a prevalence of 12.2 percent (eleven out of ninety).

Studying prevalence rather than the total number of citations did not affect the leading positions of Michael J. Hindelang, Alfred Blumstein, and Marvin E. Wolfgang. However, some authors in table 2 with a high individual citation frequency had lower rankings in (or disappeared from) the prevalence analysis in table 3. These included

Sheldon and Eleanor T. Glueck, Robert D. Hare, John Monahan, Lee N. Robins, Edward P. Thompson, and Donald J. West. For example, Sheldon Glueck's forty-three citations in *Crime and Justice* between 1979 and 1993 occurred in eleven different articles, giving an individual citation frequency of 3.9. In contrast, some authors in table 2 with a low individual citation frequency had higher rankings in the prevalence analysis in table 3. These included Robert M. Figlio, Michael R. Gottfredson, Travis Hirschi, Norval Morris, Joan Petersilia, Leon Radzinowicz, and Thorsten Sellin. For example, Robert M. Figlio's twenty-five citations in *Crime and Justice* between 1979 and 1993 occurred in nineteen different articles, giving an individual citation frequency of 1.3. It seems clear that, when some authors are cited, several of their works are cited, whereas, when other authors are cited, only one of their works is cited in general.

D. Most-Cited Works

Table 4 shows the most-cited single works in *Crime and Justice* in the two time periods (again excluding self-citations), and the number of articles in which they were cited. (For full details of each item, see the references.) The most-cited work between 1979 and 1985 was *Delinquency in a Birth Cohort* (Wolfgang, Figlio, and Sellin 1972), which was cited in eleven out of forty-seven articles (23 percent). The most-cited work between 1986 and 1993 was *Criminal Careers and "Career Criminals"* (Blumstein et al. 1986), which was cited in nine out of forty-one articles (22 percent).

III. *Social Sciences Citation Index*

It might be argued that, despite the excellent reputation of *Crime and Justice* and of its editorial board, the choice of authors and topics for articles may be to some extent idiosyncratic, rather than accurately reflecting the most important issues and the leading scholars in criminology and criminal justice. It might be argued that the contents of *Crime and Justice* reflect the views and interests of scholars in an elite network. While the most-cited authors in *Crime and Justice* (between 1986 and 1993) were to a considerable extent the same as the most-cited authors in the leading journals that we have searched (between 1986 and 1990), it would be desirable to search a larger number of books and journals to identify the most-cited scholars and works, as Wolfgang, Figlio, and Thornberry (1978) did for the 1945–72 time period.

The major citation index of relevance to criminology and criminal

TABLE 4

Most-Cited Works in *Crime and Justice*, 1979–93

Author(s)	No. of Cites
1979–85:	
Wolfgang, Figlio, and Sellin 1972	11
Foucault 1977	6
Morris 1974	6
Radzinowicz 1948–68	6
Becker 1963	5
Lipton, Martinson, and Wilks 1975	5
Martinson 1974	5
Rothman 1971	5
Silver 1967	5
Skolnick 1966	5
Taylor, Walton, and Young 1973	5
von Hirsch 1976	5
Wilson 1983 (1975)	5
1986–93:	
Blumstein, Cohen, Roth, and Visher 1986	9
Wolfgang, Figlio, and Sellin 1972	7
Cohen and Felson 1979	6
Wilson and Herrnstein 1985	6
Chaiken and Chaiken 1982	5
Cloward and Ohlin 1960	5
Hirschi 1969	5
Hough and Mayhew 1985	5
Martinson 1974	5
Morris 1974	5
Shane-Dubow, Brown, and Olsen 1985	5
Skogan and Maxfield 1981	5
Wilson 1983 (1975)	5

justice is the *Social Sciences Citation Index*. This lists citations in a large number of journals. It covers over three hundred psychology journals, about one hundred law journals, about seventy-five sociology journals, and about seventy-five psychiatry journals. It covers sixteen crime and justice journals, including *Criminology, British Journal of Criminology, Canadian Journal of Criminology, Australian and New Zealand Journal of Criminology, Journal of Criminal Law and Criminology, Journal of Research in Crime and Delinquency, Journal of Criminal Justice*, and *Criminal Justice and Behavior*. However, it does not (yet) include more recently established journals such as *Justice Quarterly* (begun in 1984) and *Journal of Quantitative Criminology* (begun in 1985). While the *SSCI* does not cover every possible journal that is relevant to criminology and criminal justice, it certainly includes the majority and, hence, provides excellent coverage of the field.

The use of the *SSCI* underestimates citations in the medical and physical science literature, which are included in its companion, the *Science Citation Index* (*SCI*). The *SSCI* includes citations *to* books and book chapters but excludes citations *in* books and book chapters. In principle, the *SSCI* could be searched to determine who are the most-cited scholars. However, in practice, it is not possible to carry out such a search with an acceptable degree of accuracy.

A. Problems of the SSCI

Perhaps the major problem is to determine which authors and works (both citing and cited) fall into the area of criminology and criminal justice; this is inevitably a subjective decision. A second problem is that each author is only identified in the *SSCI* by first initial and last name. For example, Jacqueline Cohen would be found under the heading "J. Cohen," and it would be extremely difficult to determine which of the citations under that heading applied to her and which were for other individuals with the same last name and first initial (such as Jacob Cohen, who has written many books and articles on statistical topics). In addition, the *SSCI* lists only the first author of a work. Without a complete vita for each scholar, it would be impossible to locate all the citations for jointly authored works, where the scholar in question was not the first author. Other problems of the *SSCI* have been discussed in detail by Cohn and Farrington (1990, 1994*a*, 1994*b*).

While it is not feasible to search the *SSCI* to determine the most-cited authors, it is more feasible to search the *SSCI* to determine the most-cited works in criminology and criminal justice, and we have done this. For comparability with our analysis of *Crime and Justice*, we have searched for the most-cited works in the *SSCI* between two time periods: 1979–85 and 1986–93. As in our previous analyses of journals, we excluded citations in book reviews, editorials, obituaries, and letters to the editor.

A major problem in searching the *SSCI* is that errors in reference lists in journals (which are quite frequent; see e.g., Sweetland 1989) are carried over in the *SSCI*. Many authors citing a work in a journal may misspell the author's name, may include the wrong initial or no initial, and may cite the wrong year. For example, Travis Hirschi was sometimes cited as "T. Hirshi," sometimes as "T. Hirsch," and also as "L. Hirschi" and "P. Hirschi." We spent a great deal of time searching around a target work in the *SSCI* to include incorrect citations. The *SSCI* searches were carried out manually using the hard copies of the *SSCI* because it was quicker and easier to search around an author/ work in the hard copies than in the computerized version of the *SSCI*. The computerized version would be preferable if all citations in the *SSCI* were correct.

It was also necessary to ensure that the same citation was not counted twice. Some citations (e.g., in legal journals) are by page number, so that the same article might separately cite page 27 and page 35 of the same book; in reality this is only one citation of one book. Another problem is that in some cases a citation in one year may appear in the following year's *SSCI*, so that, for example, a citation in an article published in 1985 may be found in the 1986 edition of the *SSCI* instead of the 1985 edition. Some of our *SSCI* searches were carried out in Miami, using yearly volumes of the *SSCI*, whereas other searches were carried out in Cambridge, which has five-year combined volumes. The problem of delayed citations is more acute with yearly volumes and causes some minor discrepancies between annual counts from yearly and five-year combined volumes.

B. Most-Cited Works

We searched for and counted the citations of major works by the scholars listed in the appendix. Since our research has been carried out with no funding and minimal resources, it was impractical to attempt to search for citations of all works in criminology and criminal justice. In deciding which works to search for, we began by searching all 174 works cited three or more times in either time period in *Crime and Justice*, regardless of whether the author of the item was among the most-cited scholars. Multiple editions of the same work (e.g., James Q. Wilson's *Thinking about Crime* [1975 and 1983]) and multivolume works (e.g., Leon Radzinowicz's *History of English Criminal Law* [1948–68]) were counted together, and citations of foreign language translations were included where possible.

We also searched works included in Thornberry's (1990) list of items that a "culturally literate" criminologist should have read, works included in Siegel and Zalman's (1991) list of items that a "culturally literate" criminal justice scholar should have read, and works identified by Wolfgang, Figlio, and Thornberry (1978) as highly cited. We supplemented these lists with items nominated by our colleagues as likely to be highly cited and items frequently cited in textbooks. Altogether,

TABLE 5

The Most-Cited Works in the *SSCI*, 1979–85

Rank	Author	*SSCI* Cites	*C&J* Cites
1	Goffman 1961	818	2
2	H. S. Becker 1963	438	5
3	Robins 1966	384	2
4	Hirschi 1969	319	2
5	Brownmiller 1975	307	0
6	Rutter et al. 1979	278	0
7	Kalven and Zeisel 1966	273	2
8.5	Cloward and Ohlin 1960	270	3
8.5	Packer 1968	270	2
10	Rothman 1971	267	5
11	Sutherland and Cressey 1974	266	3
12	G. S. Becker 1968	262	3
13	Skolnick 1966	258	5
14	Davis 1969	243	3
15	Foucault 1977	239	6
16	Hart 1968	231	1
17	Jessor and Jessor 1977	220	0
18	Wilson 1983 (1975)	198	5
19	Wolfgang, Figlio, and Sellin 1972	197	11
20.5	A. K. Cohen 1955	196	0
20.5	Whyte 1943	196	0
22	Matza 1964	189	3
23	Newman 1973	179	2
24	Platt 1969	178	3
25	Wilson 1968	176	4
26.5	Straus, Gelles, and Steinmetz 1980	175	0
26.5	Wolfgang 1958	175	4
28	Reiss 1971	174	3
29	Morris 1974	173	6
30	von Hirsch 1976	172	5
31.5	Glueck and Glueck 1950	166	3
31.5	Wolfgang and Ferracuti 1967	166	0
33	Martinson 1974	162	5
34	Amir 1971	160	1
35.5	Gelles 1972	159	0
35.5	Schur 1971	159	2
37	Lemert 1972 (1967)	157	1
38	Bowlby 1951	153	0
39	Patterson 1974	152	0
40	Suttles 1968	149	2
41	Ehrlich 1973	147	3
42	Silberman 1978	145	4
43	Chambliss and Seidman 1982 (1971)	144	2
44.5	Miller 1958	143	0
44.5	Thompson 1975	143	3

TABLE 5 (*Continued*)

Rank	Author	SSCI Cites	C&J Cites
46	Taylor, Walton, and Young 1973	142	5
47	Sykes and Matza 1957	140	0
48	Roff 1972	138	0
49	Lipton, Martinson, and Wilks 1975	137	5
50	Eysenck 1977 (1964)	129	0
51	Zimring and Hawkins 1973	127	2
52.5	Nettler 1978 (1974)	124	1
52.5	West and Farrington 1973	124	2
54	Adler 1975	123	1
55	Quinney 1970	120	2
56.5	Glaser 1964	115	3
56.5	Sykes 1958	115	2
58	Hay et al. 1975	110	4
59	Gibbs 1975	107	1
60.5	Alexander and Parsons 1973	105	1
60.5	Shaw and McKay 1969 (1942)	105	3

NOTE.—*SSCI = Social Sciences Citation Index; C&J = Crime and Justice.*

we searched the *SSCI* for citations of about 350 works that seemed likely to be highly cited. While searching for citations of these works, we also detected other highly cited works by the same authors and counted their citations. We cannot be certain that we have identified all the most-cited works in criminology and criminal justice in the *SSCI*, but we are confident that we have identified the majority. Because of the problem of the *SSCI* listing only first authors, we could not exclude self-citations from our counts.

Table 5 shows the most-cited works in the *SSCI* between 1979 and 1985, while table 6 shows the most-cited works in the *SSCI* between 1986 and 1993. The listed works are all those cited fifteen times per year or more on average (105 citations or more between 1979 and 1985, 120 citations or more between 1986 and 1993). As before, full details of all these works can be found in the references.

We had problems in deciding whether to include certain works under the headings "criminology" and "criminal justice." Our decisions about inclusion or exclusion depended on our assessment of whether the work was explicitly concerned with crime and justice. For example, we included *Asylums* (Goffman 1961) but excluded *Stigma* (Goffman 1963, which was cited 550 times between 1979 and 1985 and 584 times

TABLE 6

The Most-Cited Works in the *SSCI*, 1986–93

Rank	Author	*SSCI* Cites	*C&J* Cites
1	Foucault 1977	779	4
2	Goffman 1961	694	1
3	Jessor and Jessor 1977	619	1
4	Straus, Gelles, and Steinmetz 1980	529	2
5	Patterson 1982	495	2
6	Hirschi 1969	494	5
7	Robins 1966	405	4
8	H. S. Becker 1963	394	0
9	G. S. Becker 1968	341	1
10	Brownmiller 1975	320	0
11	Rutter et al. 1979	291	3
12	Sutherland and Cressey 1974	280	4
13	Werner and Smith 1982	269	2
14	Elliott, Huizinga, and Ageton 1985	260	3
15	Cloward and Ohlin 1960	248	5
16	Wilson and Herrnstein 1985	242	6
17	Kalven and Zeisel 1966	234	2
18	Wolfgang, Figlio, and Sellin 1972	217	7
19.5	A. K. Cohen 1955	208	4
19.5	Hart 1968	208	4
21	Hindelang, Hirschi, and Weis 1981	190	3
22	Rothman 1971	187	3
23	Packer 1968	186	0
24	Loeber and Dishion 1983	174	2
25	Rutter and Giller 1983	173	3
26	West and Farrington 1973	162	3
27	Whyte 1943	161	3
28.5	Shaw and McKay 1969 (1942)	158	1
28.5	Wilson 1983 (1975)	158	5
30	Robins 1978	157	2
31.5	Akers 1973	156	0
31.5	Wolfgang 1958	156	3
33	Glueck and Glueck 1950	155	4
34.5	Akers et al. 1979	151	0
34.5	Martinson 1974	151	5
36	Sykes and Matza 1957	150	0
37.5	L. E. Cohen and Felson 1979	149	6
37.5	Davis 1969	149	1
39	Roff 1972	148	0
40	Loeber 1982	143	1
41	Wolfgang and Ferracuti 1967	138	0
42	Matza 1964	137	1
43	von Hirsch 1976	136	3
44	S. Cohen 1985	134	3
45	Ross 1982	131	2

TABLE 6 (*Continued*)

Rank	Author	SSCI Cites	C&J Cites
46	Gelles 1972	127	0
47.5	Elliott and Voss 1974	126	3
47.5	Skogan and Maxfield 1981	126	5
49	Gelles 1985	125	0
50	Amir 1971	124	1
51	Monahan 1981	122	1
52.5	Lemert 1972 (1967)	121	0
52.5	Rothman 1980	121	3
54	Sherman and Berk 1984	120	1

NOTE.—*SSCI* = *Social Sciences Citation Index; C&J* = *Crime and Justice.*

between 1986 and 1993). Whereas *Asylums* included some discussion of penal institutions, *Stigma* had virtually no explicit discussion of delinquency or crime.

We included *Coercive Family Process* (Patterson 1982) because this explicitly focused on delinquency, but we excluded *The Moral Judgement of the Child* (Piaget 1960 [1932], which was cited 530 times between 1986 and 1993) and "Stability of Aggressive Reaction Patterns in Males: A Review" (Olweus 1979, which was cited 190 times between 1986 and 1993) because these items were less centrally concerned with delinquent behavior. We generally excluded psychiatric works such as *The Mask of Sanity* (Cleckley 1964, which was cited 120 times between 1979 and 1985 and 172 times between 1986 and 1993) and *Psychopathological Disorders of Childhood* (Quay 1972, which was cited 231 times between 1979 and 1985 and 279 times between 1986 and 1993) unless they were explicitly concerned with delinquent or criminal behavior.

Ideally, we wanted to count citations in the crime and justice literature of publications in the crime and justice literature. One problem with less clearly criminological works, such as *Social Theory and Social Structure* (Merton 1949), is that the majority of their citations were not in the crime and justice literature but in some other field (in this case, sociology). Of all the works cited three or more times in *Crime and Justice* between 1979 and 1985, the most cited in the *SSCI* in the same time period (1,515 citations) was *Experimental and Quasi-Experimental Designs for Research* (Campbell and Stanley 1966). Of all the works cited three or more times in *Crime and Justice* between 1986 and 1993, the most-cited in the *SSCI* in the same time period (1,278 citations) was

Quasi-Experimentation (Cook and Campbell 1979). These primarily methodological works were not included as works in criminology or criminal justice. Peritz (1983) noted that methodological works were more likely to become highly cited "citation classics" than other types of articles.

Table 5 shows that the most-cited crime and justice works in the *SSCI* between 1979 and 1985 were *Asylums* (Goffman 1961), *Outsiders* (Becker 1963), *Deviant Children Grown Up* (Robins 1966), *Causes of Delinquency* (Hirschi 1969), and *Against Our Will* (Brownmiller 1975). Table 6 shows that the most-cited crime and justice works between 1986 and 1993 were *Discipline and Punish* (Foucault 1977), *Asylums* (Goffman 1961), *Problem Behavior and Psychosocial Development* (Jessor and Jessor 1977), *Behind Closed Doors* (Straus, Gelles, and Steinmetz 1980), and *Coercive Family Process* (Patterson 1982).

It is striking that most of the most-cited works shown in Tables 5 and 6 were books rather than journal articles. For example, no article published in *Criminology* was cited often enough in the *SSCI* to be included in tables 5 or 6 (Garfield 1994). Generally, edited books were not among the most-cited works because their individual chapters were cited rather than the books themselves. Bott and Hargens (1991) found that, whereas the average book was cited about as often as the average article in a highly cited journal, the average chapter in an edited book was only cited about as often as the average article in an infrequently cited journal. Recent textbooks were rarely cited, as Wright and Carroll (1994) noted.

Tables 5 and 6 also show the number of citations of these works in *Crime and Justice* in each time period. Few of these works were never cited in *Crime and Justice*. The most-cited work in *Crime and Justice* in the first time period, *Delinquency in a Birth Cohort* (Wolfgang, Figlio, and Sellin 1972), had 197 citations in the *SSCI* between 1979 and 1985. The most-cited work in *Crime and Justice* in the second time period, *Criminal Careers and "Career Criminals"* (Blumstein et al. 1986) narrowly missed inclusion in table 6, being cited 103 times in the *SSCI* between 1986 and 1993. A comparison of tables 4, 5, and 6 suggests that quantitatively oriented research monographs were relatively more highly cited in *Crime and Justice*, while more qualitative, nontechnical, or theoretical works were relatively more highly cited in the *SSCI*. Works on family violence were relatively more highly cited in the *SSCI* than in the general volumes of *Crime and Justice*, but it must be remembered that *Family Violence* was the subject of a thematic volume in the series (Ohlin and Tonry 1989).

IV. Mathematical Models of Citation Careers

There have been very few longitudinal studies of citation careers (referred to as "diachronous studies" in the review by Cano and Lind [1991]). It would be interesting to develop mathematical models of citation careers, analogous to mathematical models of criminal careers (Barnett, Blumstein, and Farrington 1987), that might be used to predict the future course of the citation career at an early stage. Citation careers of scholars as well as works could be studied (e.g., Cole 1975). For example, the null hypothesis that scholars are cited in direct proportion to their numbers of publications, with an exponential decay over time in the influence of each individual publication, could be tested. However, it seems likely that the citations of prolific scholars are much greater than this null hypothesis would predict.

In this essay, we focus on citation careers of works. For example, it is clear that *A General Theory of Crime* (Gottfredson and Hirschi 1990) is destined to be a highly cited work. It was cited twice in the *SSCI* in 1990, thirteen times in 1991, twenty-six times in 1992, and thirty-nine times in 1993. The same is true of *Crime, Shame and Reintegration* (Braithwaite 1989), which was cited once in the *SSCI* in 1989, ten times in 1990, seventeen times in 1991, twenty times in 1992, and thirty times in 1993. These works did not appear in table 6 basically because they were at risk of being cited for only a portion of the 1986–93 time period.

It would be interesting to predict, on the basis of a work's citation history up to 1993, such career features as the length of its citation career in years, the total number of times that it will be cited, the average number of times that it will be cited during its career, its peak year of citation, its rate of acceleration before the peak, and its rate of deceleration after the peak. It might be interesting to establish the length of a work's career of being highly cited (e.g., a minimum of ten or fifteen citations per year), rather than the number of years in which it is cited at least once, since it may still be being cited at a low rate fifty years after its date of publication. It would also be interesting to investigate the relationship between citation career features: for example, whether a high rate of acceleration to the peak and a high magni-

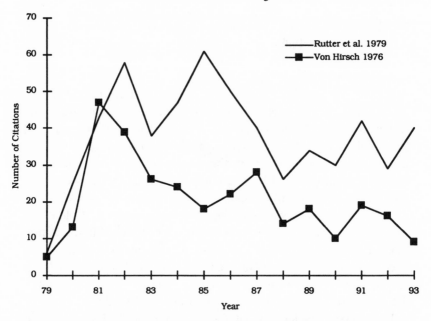

FIG. 1.—Curvilinear citation careers: Rutter et al. (1979) and von Hirsch (1976)

tude of the peak predict a slow deceleration after the peak and a long citation career, as data published by Line (1984) suggest.

At least for highly cited works, it seems plausible that the curve relating number of citations to years after publication (the "age" of the work) should rise to a single peak, remain at a high level for a few years, and then decrease. The rate of acceleration up to the peak seems likely to be greater than the rate of deceleration after the peak. However, at least for the (relatively short) 1979–93 time period, it was difficult to find clear-cut examples of such a curvilinear age-citation curve. Figure 1 shows two examples of citation careers that appear to show both an increase and a decrease over this time period. Figure 2 shows two examples of steadily increasing age-citation curves (presumably before the peak). Figure 3 shows two examples of steadily decreasing age-citation curves (presumably after the peak), while figure 4 shows two examples of relatively constant age-citation curves. Curve-smoothing techniques might be useful to display the trends in age-citation curves more clearly.

In some ways, the age-citation curve of an individual work may be similar to the aggregate age-crime curve, although the age-citation curve seems flatter. Farrington (1986) discussed possible mathematical

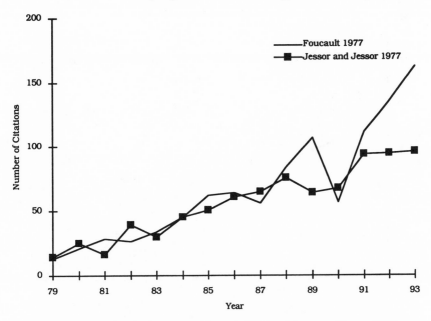

Fɪɢ. 2.—Increasing citation careers: Foucault (1977) and Jessor and Jessor (1977)

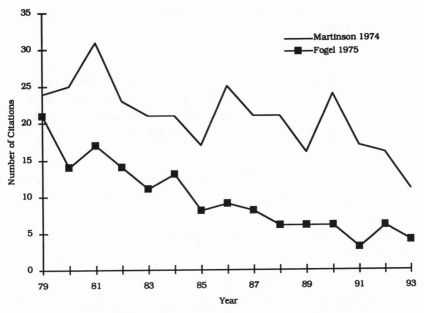

Fɪɢ. 3.—Decreasing citation careers: Martinson (1974) and Fogel (1975)

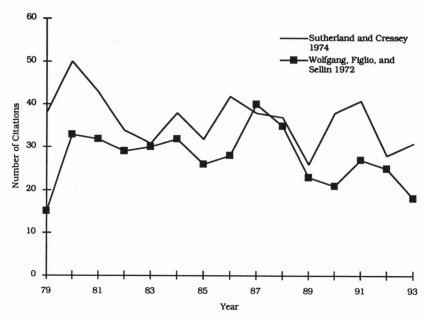

Fig. 4.—Stable citation careers: Sutherland and Cressy (1974) and Wolfgang, Figlio, and Sellin (1972).

models of the age-crime curve and suggested that this curve might be fitted by the following general model:

$$y = ax^b e^{-cx}. \tag{1}$$

In the citation context, y would be the number of citations in a year and x would be the age of a work. The parameter a essentially sets the overall height (magnitude or amplitude) of the curve, while an increase in b shifts the peak to the right and an increase in c shifts the peak to the left. It follows that

$$dy/dx = ax^{b-1} e^{-cx}(b - cx). \tag{2}$$

Since $dy/dx = 0$ at the peak, the peak occurs when $(b - cx) = 0$, or when $x = b/c$.

Previously, Avramescu (1979) suggested a different model for the age-citation curve:

$$y = c(e^{-ax} - e^{-abx}), \tag{3}$$

where c sets the overall height of the curve, a specifies the rate of decrease with age, and b is the initial increment with age. On this model, the area under the curve (the total number of citations t of a work) is specified by

$$t = c(b - 1)/ab. \tag{4}$$

It would be interesting to investigate to what degree citation careers might be fitted by these simple models. If they could, it should be possible to estimate model parameters from the number of citations in each of the first few years of a work's existence (excluding its year of publication) and, hence, to predict features of its citation career such as those listed above.

More detailed theories of citation careers might be formulated. For example, the number of citations of a work in the *SSCI* seems likely to depend on such factors as how many scholars are interested in the subject matter, how many scholars come to hear about it (influenced by the sales of a book or the circulation of a journal), how many scholars have read it, the productivity of these scholars in publishing their own works, and the number of journals in the *SSCI* covering the subject matter. Scholars may come to hear about a work by word of mouth, at conferences, or by reading other works in which the source work is cited. One possible model is that knowledge of a highly cited work spreads like a contagious disease.

An analysis of a large number of reasonably complete citation careers, extending over a long time period, would be required to develop and test mathematical models of age-citation curves and to establish which models were the most appropriate and useful. Unfortunately, like the age-crime curve, there may be complicating cohort and period effects (e.g., an increase over time in the total number of citations in the *SSCI*) that would require more complex models. For example, Cano and Lind (1991) corrected their citation data for a 7.6 percent exponential growth rate in the total number of citations in the *SCI* between 1957 and 1983. We cannot attempt to develop and test mathematical models of citation careers within the scope of this essay, but we hope that our formulation might prove useful as a basis for developing such models in the future, both for scholars and for works.

V. Conclusions

The most-cited scholars in state-of-the-art literature reviews in the general volumes of *Crime and Justice* were Michael J. Hindelang, Alfred Blumstein, and Marvin E. Wolfgang. The most-cited scholars in *Crime and Justice* between 1986 and 1993 were significantly correlated with the most-cited scholars in three major American criminology journals, three major American criminal justice journals, and three international criminology journals between 1986 and 1990. However, citations in *Crime and Justice* between 1979 and 1985 were negatively correlated with citations in *Crime and Justice* between 1986 and 1993 and uncorrelated with citations in the three groups of journals between 1986 and 1990, possibly reflecting changing influences over time.

The most-cited works in *Crime and Justice* were *Delinquency in a Birth Cohort* (Wolfgang, Figlio, and Sellin 1972) between 1979 and 1985 and *Criminal Careers and "Career Criminals"* (Blumstein et al. 1986) between 1986 and 1993. The most-cited crime and justice works in the *SSCI* were *Asylums* (Goffman 1961) between 1979 and 1985 and *Discipline and Punish* (Foucault 1977) between 1986 and 1993. Quantitatively oriented research monographs were relatively more highly cited in *Crime and Justice*, while more qualitative, nontechnical, or theoretical works were relatively more highly cited in the *SSCI*.

There are advantages in studying both *Crime and Justice* and the *SSCI*. *Crime and Justice* is highly selective and focused on the crime and justice literature, but its state-of-the-art reviews represent only a small fraction of that literature. The *SSCI* is more comprehensive but less selective, and the crime and justice literature represents only a small fraction of its coverage. Because it was impractical for us to restrict our *SSCI* study to citations in the crime and justice literature, crime and justice works with a wide appeal outside that literature tended to be the most cited.

We proposed methodological advances in citation analysis by using concepts developed in criminal career research. We distinguished the total number of citations from the prevalence of citations (the number of different articles in which an author was cited). Authors with a low individual citation frequency (defined as the average number of an author's works cited whenever that author was cited) had relatively higher rankings in a prevalence table, whereas authors with a high individual citation frequency had relatively higher rankings in a more conventional table based on the total number of citations.

We also identified the phenomenon of coauthor citation, in which a scholar's coauthor receives credit for a citation that is essentially a self-citation by the scholar. We also discussed methods of developing mathematical models of citation careers, in the interests of predicting the future course of these careers, and especially certain specified career features.

We should emphasize that we are aware of the many problems of using citation counts as a measure of influence, and we have discussed these extensively in our previous papers (Cohn and Farrington 1990, 1994*a*, 1994*b*). For example, it is possible that a work may receive mainly negative, critical citations, although we have previously found that most citations are positive or neutral. Generally, scholars ignore work that they consider to be incorrect or of poor quality, rather than bothering to criticize it. Citations may be instruments of persuasion (Gilbert 1977) and may be influenced by social factors such as likes or dislikes of individuals (Chapman 1989) or even attempts to curry favor with editors or editorial board members of a journal (Rushton 1984; Wright 1994). "Elite" scholars may be overcited to impress the reader or undercited because their contributions become part of common knowledge (Zuckerman 1987). More research on citation behavior is clearly needed, but current evidence suggests that citation counts are an imperfect but reasonably valid measure of intellectual influence. The presence of different types of error does not make it impossible to draw valid conclusions (Stigler 1987).

It might be desirable in future citation analyses to classify types of citations, not only as positive, neutral, or negative but also as essential to the argument, relevant, perfunctory, unnecessary, or irrelevant (Lalumiere 1993). Also, citations could be weighted according to the prestige of the journal citing or cited (Cole and Cole 1971), and selective citations of departmental colleagues to enhance a department's reputation could be detected. With adequate funding, it would be possible to carry out more extensive citation analyses of the crime and justice literature, covering citations in a large number of books and journals, as Wolfgang, Figlio, and Thornberry (1978) did for criminological literature in the period 1945–72.

An important question is why certain individuals and works become influential in certain periods, and whether this is related, for example, to changing priorities of funding agencies or to changing political, theoretical, empirical, or methodological concerns. A related issue is why works become highly cited and the importance of the prestige and previous citation history of the authors as opposed to features of the content of the work. For example, the recently published *Crime in the Making* (Sampson and Laub 1993) was immediately recognized as a highly significant book, and seems likely to be highly cited in the future. It would be interesting to investigate how far it is possible to predict the future citation career of a work at the time of publication and whether the fact that a book has won a prestigious prize (e.g., the Michael J. Hindelang Book Award of the American Society of Criminology) assists in this prediction. These are the kind of questions that might be addressed in future research, using citations, on influence in criminology and criminal justice.

The most-cited scholars are likely to change in different time periods. Previously, we suggested that Marvin E. Wolfgang, Michael J. Hindelang, and Alfred Blumstein were particularly influential between 1986 and 1990 because of the perceived importance at that time of criminal career research and the longitudinal method, the measurement of crime and delinquency, and the prestigious National Academy of Sciences panel reports. We believe that citation analysis is useful in identifying influential authors, works, and topics during particular time periods. Hence, it is useful in documenting the history of the development of ideas in criminology and criminal justice and the cumulative development of knowledge in crime and justice.

APPENDIX

Authors with Major Works Searched in the *SSCI*

Freda Adler, Suzanne S. Ageton, Robert S. Agnew, Ronald L. Akers, Jay S. Albanese, John F. Alexander, Francis A. Allen, Geoffrey P. Alpert, Menacham Amir, Johannes Andenaes, Dane Archer, David C. Baldus, Michael Banton, Curt R. Bartol, David H. Bayley, John M. Beattie, Gustave de Beaumont, Gary S. Becker, Howard S. Becker, Hugo A. Bedau, James A. Beha, Trevor H. Bennett, Richard A. Berk, Thomas J. Bernard, John R. Berrueta-Clement, Albert D. Biderman, Egon Bittner, Donald J. Black, Ronald Blackburn, Richard Block, Alfred Blumstein, Barbara Boland, David J. Bordua, A. Keith Bottomley, Anthony E. Bottoms, Lee H. Bowker, John Bowlby, John B. Braithwaite, Paul J. Brantingham, Patricia L. Brantingham, Stanley L. Brodsky, Stephen R. Brody, Susan Brownmiller, Lee H. Bukstel, Robert J. Bursik, Donald T. Campbell, Ruth S. Cavan, Jan M. Chaiken, Marcia R. Chaiken, William J. Chambliss, Meda Chesney-Lind, Theodore G. Chiricos, Ronald V. G. Clarke, Stevens H. Clarke, Todd R. Clear, Hervey M. Cleckley, Donald Clemmer, Marshall B. Clinard, Hugh F. Cline, Richard A. Cloward, Albert K. Cohen, Jacqueline Cohen, Lawrence E. Cohen, Stanley Cohen, John E. Conklin, John P. Conrad, Philip J. Cook, Thomas D. Cook, Derek B. Cornish, Donald R. Cressey, Frances T. Cullen, Elliott Currie, Kenneth C. Davis, Simon Dinitz, David Downes, Sheldon Eckland-Olson, Isaac Ehrlich, Delbert S. Elliott, LaMar T. Empey, Philip H. Ennis, Hans J. Eysenck,

David P. Farrington, Malcolm M. Feeley, Floyd Feeney, M. Philip Feldman, Ronald A. Feldman, Marcus Felson, Robert M. Figlio, David Fogel, Robert M. Fogelson, Michel Foucault, James A. Fox, Marvin E. Frankel, James J. Fyfe, Thomas Gabor, James Garofalo, Vincent A. C. Gattrell, Gilbert Geis, Richard J. Gelles, Paul Gendreau, Jack P. Gibbs, Daniel Glaser, Sheldon Glueck, Eleanor T. Glueck, Erving Goffman, Hermann Goldstein, Lynne Goodstein, Robert A. Gordon, Don M. Gottfredson, Michael R. Gottfredson, Stephen D. Gottfredson, Harrison G. Gough, Leroy C. Gould, David F. Greenberg, Peter W. Greenwood, John C. Gunn, Ted R. Gurr, Samuel B. Guze, Frank E. Hagan, John L. Hagan, Donna M. Hamparian, Barbara A. Hanawalt, Robert D. Hare, Herbert L. A. Hart, Douglas Hay, Kevin Heal, Michael J. Hindelang, Travis Hirschi, John Hogarth, Roger G. Hood, J. Michael Hough, L. Rowell Huesmann, David Huizinga, Michael Ignatieff, James A. Inciardi, John Irwin, George Jackson, James B. Jacobs, Gary F. Jensen, C. Ray Jeffery, Richard Jessor, Bruce D. Johnson, Carol B. Kalish, Harry Kalven, Gene Kassebaum, Alan E. Kazdin, George L. Kelling, John I. Kitsuse, Gary C. Kleck, Malcolm W. Klein, Carl B. Klockars, Kay A. Knapp, Richard C. Larson, Gloria K. Laycock, Monroe M. Lefkowitz, Edwin M. Lemert, Paul Lerman, Jack Levin, Orlando F. Lewis, W. David Lewis, Alfred R. Lindesmith, Douglas Lipton, Rolf Loeber, Colin Loftin, Cesare Lombroso, Gerald Luedtke, Michael Maguire, Peter K. Manning, Vernon H. Mark, Robert M. Martinson, Stephen D. Mastrofski, Thomas Mathieson, Ross L. Matsueda, David Matza, Michael G. Maxfield, Patricia M. Mayhew, Richard B. McCleary, Joan McCord, David McDowall, Henry D. McKay, Blake McKelvey, Sarnoff A. Mednick, Edwin I. Megargee, Karl Menninger, Robert K. Merton, Sheldon L. Messinger, Terance D. Miethe, Stuart J. Miller, Walter B. Miller, Wilbur Miller, John Monahan, Eric H. Monkkonen, Rudolf H. Moos, Norval Morris, David F. Musto, Martha A. Myers, Daniel S. Nagin, Gwynn Nettler, Oscar Newman, Arthur Niederhoffer, Michael T. Nietzel, Andre Normandeau, F. Ivan Nye, Lloyd E. Ohlin, Dan Olweus, Steven G. Osborn, Herbert L. Packer, Ted B. Palmer, Dale G. Parent, Raymond Paternoster, Gerald R. Patterson, B. K. E. Penick, Joan Petersilia, David Philips, Jean Piaget, Glenn L. Pierce, Irving M. Piliavin, Anthony M. Platt, Carl E. Pope, Herbert C. Quay, Richard Quinney, Leon Radzinowicz, Nicole H. Rafter, Walter C. Reckless, Albert J. Reiss, Jr., Thomas A. Reppetto, James F. Richardson, Lee N. Robins, Merrill F. Roff, Dennis P. Rosenbaum, H. Lawrence Ross, Robert R. Ross, Peter H. Rossi, David Rothman, Jonathan Rubinstein, George Rudé, Georg Rusche, Michael L. Rutter, Edward Sagarin, Robert J. Sampson, Harry A. Scarr, Steven L. Schlossman, Edwin M. Schur, Lawrence Schweinhart, Lee Sechrest, Thorsten J. Sellin, Hanan C. Selvin, Sandra Shane-DuBow, Clifford R. Shaw, Joseph F. Sheley, Lawrence W. Sherman, Ruel Shinnar, Milton F. Shore, James F. Short, Neil Shover, Charles E. Silberman, Allan Silver, Robert A. Silverman, Rita J. Simon, Wesley G. Skogan, Jerome H. Skolnick, Carol Smart, Douglas A. Smith, Richard F. Sparks, Cassia Spohn, Elizabeth A. Stanko, Darrell J. Steffensmeier, Susan K. Steinmetz, Murray A. Straus, David Street, David Sudnow, Edwin H. Sutherland, Gerald D. Suttles, Gresham M. Sykes, Frank Tannenbaum, Ian R. Taylor, Edward P. Thompson, Terence P. Thornberry, Charles R. Tittle, John J. Tobias, Jackson Toby, Hans Toch, Michael H. Tonry, Paul E. Tracy, Austin T. Turk, Jan J. M. van Dijk, Stephen W. van Dine, Emilio C. Viano, Christy A. Visher, George B. Vold, Andrew von Hirsch, Michael E. J. Wadsworth, Samuel Walker, J. Irvin Waller, Marguerite Q. Warren (Grant), Beatrice Webb, Sidney Webb, David P. Weikart, Joseph G. Weis, Emmy E. Werner, Donald J. West, W. Gordon West, Stanton Wheeler, William F. Whyte, Leslie T. Wilkins, James Q. Wilson, Enoch C. Wines, Marvin E. Wolfgang, Robert K. Yin, Samuel Yochelson, Franklin E. Zimring.

REFERENCES

Adler, F. 1975. *Sisters in Crime: The Rise of the New Female Criminal.* New York: McGraw-Hill.

Akers, R. L. 1973. *Deviant Behavior: A Social Learning Approach.* Belmont, Mass.: Wadsworth.

Akers, R., M. D. Krohn, L. Lanza-Kaduce, and M. Radosevich. 1979. "Social Learning and Deviant Behavior: A Specific Test of a General Theory." *American Sociological Review* 44:635–55.

Alexander, J. F., and B. V. Parsons. 1973. "Short-Term Behavioral Intervention with Delinquent Families: Impact on Family Process and Recidivism." *Journal of Abnormal Psychology* 81:219–25.

Amir, M. 1971. *Patterns in Forcible Rape.* Chicago: University of Chicago Press.

Avramescu, A. 1979. "Actuality and Obsolescence of Scientific Literature." *Journal of the American Society for Information Science* 30:296–303.

Barnett, A., A. Blumstein, and D. P. Farrington. 1987. "Probabilistic Models of Youthful Criminal Careers." *Criminology* 25:83–107.

Barr, R., and K. Pease. 1990. "Crime Placement, Displacement, and Deflection." In *Crime and Justice: A Review of Research,* vol. 12, edited by M. Tonry and N. Morris. Chicago: University of Chicago Press.

Becker, G. S. 1968. "Crime and Punishment: An Economic Approach." *Journal of Political Economy* 76:169–217.

Becker, H. S. 1963. *Outsiders: Studies in the Sociology of Deviance.* New York: Free Press.

Blumstein, A., J. Cohen, S. E. Martin, and M. Tonry, eds. 1983. *Research on Sentencing: The Search for Reform.* Washington, D.C.: National Academy Press.

Blumstein, A., J. Cohen, J. A. Roth, and C. A. Visher, eds. 1986. *Criminal Careers and "Career Criminals."* Washington, D.C.: National Academy Press.

Bott, D. M., and L. L. Hargens. 1991. "Are Sociologists' Publications Uncited? Citation Rates of Journal Articles, Chapters, and Books." *American Sociologist* 22:147–58.

Bowlby, J. 1951. *Maternal Care and Mental Health.* Geneva: World Health Organization.

Braithwaite, J. 1989. *Crime, Shame and Reintegration*. Cambridge: Cambridge University Press.

Brownmiller, S. 1975. *Against Our Will: Men, Women and Rape*. London: Secker & Warburg.

Campbell, D. T., and J. C. Stanley. 1966. *Experimental and Quasi-Experimental Designs for Research*. Chicago: Rand McNally.

Cano, V., and N. C. Lind. 1991. "Citation Life Cycles of Ten Citation Classics." *Scientometrics* 22:297–312.

Chaiken, J. M., and M. Chaiken. 1982. *Varieties of Criminal Behavior*. Santa Monica, Calif: RAND.

Chambliss, W., and R. B. Seidman. 1982. *Law, Order and Power*. Reading, Mass.: Addison-Wesley. (Originally published 1971.)

Chapman, A. J. 1989. "Assessing Research: Citation-Count Shortcomings." *Psychologist* 2:336–44.

Cleckley, H. M. 1964. *The Mask of Sanity*, 4th ed. St. Louis: Mosby.

Cloward, R. A., and L. E. Ohlin. 1960. *Delinquency and Opportunity: A Theory of Delinquent Gangs*. New York: Free Press.

Cohen, A. K. 1955. *Delinquent Boys: The Culture of the Gang*. Glencoe, Ill.: Free Press.

Cohen, L. E., and M. Felson. 1979. "Social Change and Crime Rate Trends: A Routine Activity Approach." *American Sociological Review* 44:588–607.

Cohen, S. 1985. *Visions of Social Control: Crime, Punishment, and Classification*. Oxford: Polity.

Cohn, E. G., and D. P. Farrington. 1990. "Differences between British and American Criminology: An Analysis of Citations." *British Journal of Criminology* 30:467–82.

———. 1994a. "Who Are the Most Influential Criminologists in the English-Speaking World?" *British Journal of Criminology* 34:204–25.

———. 1994b. "Who are the Most-Cited Scholars in Major American Criminology and Criminal Justice Journals?" *Journal of Criminal Justice* 22:517–34.

Cole, J., and S. Cole. 1971. "Measuring the Quality of Sociological Research: Problems in the Use of the Science Citation Index." *American Sociologist* 6:23–29.

Cole, S. 1975. "The Growth of Scientific Knowledge: Theories of Deviance as a Case Study." In *The Idea of Social Structure: Papers in Honor of Robert K. Merton*, edited by L. A. Coser. New York: Harcourt Brace Jovanovich.

Cook, T. D., and D. T. Campbell. 1979. *Quasi-Experimentation*. Chicago: Rand McNally.

Davis, K. C. 1969. *Discretionary Justice: A Preliminary Enquiry*. Baton Rouge: Louisiana State University Press.

Ehrlich, I. 1973. "Participation in Illegitimate Activities: A Theoretical and Empirical Investigation." *Journal of Political Economy* 81:521–65.

Elliott, D. S., D. Huizinga, and S. Ageton. 1985. *Explaining Delinquency and Drug Use*. Beverly Hills, Calif.: Sage.

Elliott, D. S., and H. L. Voss. 1974. *Delinquency and Dropout*. Lexington, Mass.: Heath.

Eysenck, H. J. 1977. *Crime and Personality*. London: Routledge. (Originally published 1964.)

Farrington, D. P. 1986. "Age and Crime." In *Crime and Justice: An Annual Review of Research*, vol. 7, edited by M. Tonry and N. Morris. Chicago: University of Chicago Press.

Fogel, D. 1975. ". . . *We Are the Living Proof.*" Cincinnati: Anderson.

Foucault, M. 1977. *Discipline and Punish: The Birth of the Prison.* New York: Pantheon.

Garfield, E. 1994. Personal communication with the authors. October 20.

Gelles, R. J. 1972. *The Violent Home: A Study of Physical Aggression between Husbands and Wives.* Beverly Hills, Calif.: Sage.

Gelles, R. J. 1985. *Intimate Violence in Families.* Beverly Hills, Calif.: Sage.

Gibbs, J. P. 1975. *Crime, Punishment and Deterrence.* Amsterdam: Elsevier.

Gilbert, G. N. 1977. "Referencing as Persuasion." *Social Studies of Science* 7:113–22.

Glaser, D. 1964. *The Effectiveness of a Prison and Parole System.* Indianapolis: Bobbs-Merrill.

Glueck, S., and E. T. Glueck. 1950. *Unraveling Juvenile Delinquency.* New York: Commonwealth Fund.

Goffman, E. 1961. *Asylums: Essays on the Social Situation of Mental Patients and Other Inmates.* Harmondsworth: Penguin.

———. 1963. *Stigma: Notes on the Management of Spoiled Identity.* Englewood Cliffs, N.J.: Prentice Hall.

Gottfredson, M. R., and T. Hirschi. 1990. *A General Theory of Crime.* Stanford, Calif.: Stanford University Press.

Hart, H. L. A. 1968. *Punishment and Responsibility.* New York: Oxford University Press.

Hay, D., P. Linebaugh, J. G. Rule, E. P. Thompson, and C. Winslow. 1975. *Albion's Fatal Tree: Crime and Society in Eighteenth-Century England.* New York: Pantheon.

Hindelang, M. J., T. Hirschi, and J. Weis. 1981. *Measuring Delinquency.* Beverly Hills, Calif.: Sage.

Hirschi, T. 1969. *Causes of Delinquency.* Berkeley: University of California Press.

Hough, M., and P. Mayhew. 1985. *Taking Account of Crime.* London: Her Majesty's Stationery Office.

Jessor, R., and S. L. Jessor. 1977. *Problem Behavior and Psychosocial Development: A Longitudinal Study of Youth.* New York: Academic Press.

Kalven, H., and H. Zeisel. 1966. *The American Jury.* Boston: Little, Brown.

Lalumiere, M. L. 1993. "Increasing the Precision of Citations in Scientific Writing." *American Psychologist* 48:913.

Lemert, E. M. 1972. *Human Deviance, Social Problems and Social Control.* Englewood Cliffs, N.J.: Prentice Hall. (Originally published 1967.)

Line, M. B. 1984. "Citation Decay of Scientific Papers: Variation According to Citations Received." *Journal of Information Science* 9:90–91.

Lipton, D., R. Martinson, and J. Wilks. 1975. *The Effectiveness of Correctional Treatment: A Survey of Treatment Evaluation Studies.* New York: Praeger.

Loeber, R. 1982. "The Stability of Antisocial and Delinquent Child Behavior." *Child Development* 53:1431–46.

Loeber, R., and T. Dishion. 1983. "Early Predictors of Male Delinquency: A Review." *Psychological Bulletin* 94:68–99.

Martinson, R. 1974. " 'What Works?': Questions and Answers about Prison Reform." *Public Interest* 35:22–54.

Matza, D. 1964. *Delinquency and Drift.* New York: Wiley.

Merton, R. K. 1949. *Social Theory and Social Structure.* Glencoe, Ill.: Free Press.

Miller, W. 1958. "Lower Class Culture as a Generating Milieu for Gang Delinquency." *Journal of Social Issues* 14:5–19.

Monahan, J. 1981. *Predicting Violent Behavior: An Assessment of Clinical Techniques.* Beverly Hills, Calif.: Sage.

Morris, N. 1974. *The Future of Imprisonment.* Chicago: University of Chicago Press.

Mullens, N. C., L. L. Hargens, P. K. Hecht, and E. L. Kick. 1977. "The Group Structure of Co-citation Clusters: A Comparative Study." *American Sociological Review* 42:552–62.

Nettler, G. 1978. *Explaining Crime.* New York: McGraw-Hill. (Originally published 1974.)

Newman, O. 1973. *Defensible Space.* London: Architectural Press.

Ohlin, L., and M. Tonry, eds. 1989. *Family Violence.* Vol. 11 of *Crime and Justice: A Review of Research,* edited by M. Tonry and N. Morris. Chicago: University of Chicago Press.

Olweus, D. 1979. "Stability of Aggressive Reaction Patterns in Males: A Review." *Psychological Bulletin* 86:852–75.

Packer, H. 1968. *Limits of the Criminal Sanction.* Stanford, Calif.: Stanford University Press.

Patterson, G. R. 1974. "Interventions for Boys with Conduct Problems: Multiple Settings, Treatments, and Criteria." *Journal of Consulting and Clinical Psychology* 43:471–81.

———. 1982. *Coercive Family Process.* Eugene, Oreg.: Castalia.

Pease, K. 1982. "Community Service Orders." In *Crime and Justice: An Annual Review of Research,* vol. 6, edited by M. Tonry and N. Morris. Chicago: University of Chicago Press.

Peritz, B. C. 1983. "Are Methodological Papers More Cited than Theoretical or Empirical Ones? The Case of Sociology." *Scientometrics* 5: 211–18.

Piaget, J. 1960. *The Moral Judgement of the Child.* London: Routledge & Kegan Paul. (Originally published 1932.)

Platt, A. M. 1969. *The Child Savers: The Invention of Delinquency.* Chicago: University of Chicago Press.

Quay, H. C., ed. 1972. *Psychopathological Disorders of Childhood.* New York: Wiley-Interscience.

Quinney, R. 1970. *The Social Reality of Crime.* Boston: Little, Brown.

Radzinowicz, L. 1948–68. *A History of English Criminal Law,* 4 vols. London: Stevens & Sons.

Reiss, A. J., Jr. 1971. *The Police and the Public.* New Haven, Conn.: Yale University Press.

Reiss, A. J., Jr., and D. P. Farrington. 1991. "Advancing Knowledge about Co-offending: Results from a Prospective Longitudinal Survey of London Males." *Journal of Criminal Law and Criminology* 82:360–95.

Reiss, A. J., Jr., and M. Tonry, eds. 1986. *Communities and Crime.* Vol. 8 of *Crime and Justice: A Review of Research,* edited by M. Tonry and N. Morris. Chicago: University of Chicago Press.

Robins, L. N. 1966. *Deviant Children Grown Up: A Sociological and Psychiatric Study of Sociopathic Personality.* Baltimore: Williams & Wilkins.

———. 1978. "Sturdy Childhood Predictors of Adult Outcomes: Replications from Longitudinal Studies." *Psychological Medicine* 8:611–22.

Roff, M. F. 1972. *Social Adjustment and Personality Development in Children.* Minneapolis: University of Minnesota Press.

Ross, H. L. 1982. *Deterring the Drinking Driver: Legal Policy and Social Control.* Lexington, Mass.: Lexington Books.

Rothman, D. J. 1971. *The Discovery of the Asylum: Social Order and Disorder in the New Republic.* Boston: Little, Brown.

———. 1980. *Conscience and Convenience: The Asylum and Its Alternatives in Progressive America.* Boston: Little, Brown.

Rushton, J. P. 1984. "Evaluating Research Eminence in Psychology: The Construct Validity of Citation Counts." *Bulletin of the British Psychological Society* 32:107–9.

———. 1989. "A Ten-Year Scientometric Revisit of British Psychological Departments." *Psychologist* 2:64–68.

Rushton, J. P., C. H. Littlefield, R. J. H. Russell, and S. J. Meltzer. 1983. "Research Production and Scholarly Impact in British Universities and Departments of Psychology: An Update." *Bulletin of the British Psychological Society* 36:41–44.

Rutter, M., and H. Giller, H. 1983. *Juvenile Delinquency: Trends and Perspectives.* New York: Guilford Press.

Rutter, M., B. Maughan, P. Mortimore, J. Ouston, and A. Smith. 1979. *Fifteen Thousand Hours.* Cambridge, Mass.: Harvard University Press.

Sampson, R. J., and J. H. Laub. 1993. *Crime in the Making: Pathways and Turning Points throughout Life.* Cambridge, Mass.: Harvard University Press.

Schur, E. M. 1971. *Labeling Deviant Behavior: Its Sociological Implications.* New York: Random House.

Shane-DuBow, S., A. P. Brown, and E. Olsen.1985. *Sentencing Reform in the United States: History, Content, and Effect.* Washington, D.C.: U.S. Government Printing Office.

Shaw, C. R., and H. D. McKay. 1969. *Juvenile Delinquency and Urban Areas.* Chicago: University of Chicago Press. (Originally published 1942.)

Sherman, L. W., and R. Berk. 1984. "The Specific Deterrent Effects of Arrest for Domestic Assault." *American Sociological Review* 49:261–72.

Siegel, L. J., and M. Zalman. 1991. " 'Cultural Literacy' in Criminal Justice: A Preliminary Assessment." *Journal of Criminal Justice Education* 2:15–44.

Silberman, C. E. 1978. *Criminal Violence, Criminal Justice.* New York: Random House.

Silver, A. 1967. "The Demand for Order in Civil Society: A Review of Some Themes in the History of Urban Crime, Police and Riot." In *The Police: Six Sociological Essays*, edited by D. J. Bordua. New York: Wiley.

Skogan, W. G., and M. G. Maxfield. 1981. *Coping with Crime: Individual and Neighborhood Reactions*. Beverly Hills, Calif.: Sage.

Skolnick, J. H. 1966. *Justice without Trial*. New York: Wiley.

Soothill, K. 1985. "Review of *Crime and Justice: An Annual Review of Research*, vol. 4." *British Journal of Criminology* 25:81–83.

Stigler, S. M. 1987. "Precise Measurement in the Face of Error: A Comment on MacRoberts and MacRoberts." *Social Studies of Science* 17:332–34.

Straus, M. A., R. J. Gelles, and S. Steinmetz. 1980. *Behind Closed Doors: Violence in the American Family*. New York: Doubleday.

Sullivan, D., D. H. White, and E. J. Barboni. 1977. "Co-citation Analyses of Science: An Evaluation." *Social Studies of Science* 7:223–40.

Sutherland, E. H., and D. R. Cressey. 1974. *Criminology*, 9th ed. Philadelphia: J. B. Lippincott.

Suttles, G. D. 1968. *The Social Order of the Slum: Ethnicity and Territory in the Inner City*. Chicago: University of Chicago Press.

Sweetland, J. H. 1989. "Errors in Bibliographic Citations: A Continuing Problem." *Library Quarterly* 59:291–304.

Sykes, G. M. 1958. *The Society of Captives: A Study of a Maximum Security Prison*. Princeton, N.J.: Princeton University Press.

Sykes, G. M., and D. Matza. 1957. "Techniques of Neutralization: A Theory of Delinquency." *American Sociological Review* 22:664–70.

Taylor, I., P. Walton, and J. Young. 1973. *The New Criminology*. London: Routledge & Kegan Paul.

Thompson, E. P. 1975. *Whigs and Hunters: The Origins of the Black Act*. New York: Pantheon.

Thornberry, T. P. 1990. "Cultural Literacy in Criminology." *Journal of Criminal Justice Education* 1:33–49.

Trasler, G. B. 1984. "The State of the Art." *British Journal of Criminology* 24:301–9.

von Hirsch, A. 1976. *Doing Justice: The Choice of Punishments*. New York: Hill & Wang.

Werner, E. E., and R. S. Smith. 1982. *Vulnerable but Invincible: A Longitudinal Study of Resilient Children and Youth*. New York: McGraw-Hill.

West, D. J., and D. P. Farrington. 1973. *Who Becomes Delinquent?* London: Heinemann.

Whyte, W. F. 1943. *Street Corner Society*. Chicago: University of Chicago Press.

Wilson, J. Q. 1983. *Thinking about Crime*. New York: Basic Books. (Originally published 1975.)

———. 1968. *Varieties of Police Behavior: The Management of Law and Order in Eight Communities*. Cambridge, Mass.: Harvard University Press.

Wilson, J. Q., and R. Herrnstein. 1985. *Crime and Human Nature*. New York: Simon & Schuster.

Wolfgang, M. E. 1958. *Patterns in Criminal Homicide*. Philadelphia: University of Pennsylvania Press.

Wolfgang, M. E., and F. Ferracuti. 1967. *The Subculture of Violence: Towards an Integrated Theory in Criminology*. London: Tavistock.

Wolfgang, M. E., R. M. Figlio, and T. Sellin. 1972. *Delinquency in a Birth Cohort*. Chicago: University of Chicago Press.

Wolfgang, M. E., R. M. Figlio, and T. P. Thornberry. 1978. *Evaluating Criminology*. New York: Elsevier.

Wright, R. A. 1994. "The Effect of Editorial Appointments on the Citations of Sociology Journal Editors, 1970 to 1989." *American Sociologist* 25:40–45.

Wright, R. A., and K. Carroll. 1994. "From Vanguard to Vanquished: The Declining Influence of Criminology Textbooks on Scholarship." *Journal of Criminal Justice* 22:559–67.

Zimring, F. E., and G. Hawkins. 1973. *Deterrence: The Legal Threat in Crime Control*. Chicago: University of Chicago Press.

Zuckerman, H. 1987. "Citation Analysis and the Complex Problem of Intellectual Influence." *Scientometrics* 12:329–38.

Thomas J. Bernard and Jeffrey B. Snipes

Theoretical Integration
in Criminology

ABSTRACT

Recently, there has been a vigorous debate about theoretical integration in criminology. There are many criminology theories but no agreement on which (if any) have been falsified by research. This is perceived as a problem because theory is supposed to guide interpretation of past research and chart the direction for future research. Some criminologists argue that the effort to falsify theories must continue because the theories contradict each other. Others argue that the theories are different but not contradictory, so they can be integrated with each other. Criminology theories can, however, be integrated in ways that rule out most competitive testing. This new interpretation brings criminology theory more into line with common research practices and enhances the possibility of scientific progress.

Most criminologists would agree that there are too many theories in criminology. All of the standard theories have been around for at least twenty-five years, including those by Merton (1938), Shaw and McKay (1942), Sutherland (1947), Cohen (1955), Cloward and Ohlin (1960), Wolfgang and Ferracuti (1967), Akers (Burgess and Akers 1968), and Hirschi (1969). In addition, new theories appear on the scene with astonishing frequency. A partial list of those appearing in the last ten years would include theories offered by Schwendinger and Schwendinger (1985),

Thomas J. Bernard is professor of criminal justice and sociology at Penn State University. Jeffrey B. Snipes is assistant professor of criminology and criminal justice at Florida State University.

Wilson and Herrnstein (1985), Cornish and Clarke (1986), Mawson (1987), Thornberry (1987), Cohen and Machalek (1988), Hagan (1988), Braithwaite (1989), Jeffery (1989), Katz (1989), Bernard (1990), Gottfredson and Hirschi (1990), Agnew (1992), Walters (1992), Sampson and Laub (1993), and Messner and Rosenfeld (1994).

Most criminologists would also agree that the abundance of theories does not enrich the field but impedes scientific progress (Bernard 1991). Theory is supposed to direct research and to accumulate its product into a coherent, understandable framework (Bernard and Ritti 1990). The failure to accomplish this is one reason why criminology research has tended toward a million modest little studies that produce a million tiny conflicting results (Wolfgang, Figlio, and Thornberry 1978, p. 4). This has led to considerable cynicism about criminology theories generally (see Gibbs and Erikson 1975; Geis and Meier 1978; Sagarin and Karmen 1978; Meier 1980; Williams 1984; Gibbs 1985; Meier 1985; Wilson 1983; and Weis 1987).

Criminologists may agree that it would be desirable to reduce the number of theories, but they vigorously disagree about how that can be accomplished. The traditional view is that different theories make at least some contradictory theoretical predictions. These contradictory predictions can be subjected to competitive testing in which research determines which predictions are supported by data and which are not. Theories that are falsified by this process should then be discarded, thus reducing the total number of theories.

More recently, however, some criminologists have argued that falsification has failed as a method of reducing the number of theories in criminology. They generally argue that the different theories make different, but not contradictory, predictions and can be combined through various forms of integration. Integration, then, is an alternative to falsification as a way to reduce the number of theories in criminology, and it has arisen as a result of the perceived inability of falsification to accomplish this goal.

In this essay, we examine the debate about integration of criminology theories and provide an overview of various attempts to integrate them. We argue that integration is the appropriate approach because the theories primarily make different but not contradictory predictions. Therefore, we believe that the competition among the different theories in criminology is largely empirical, over how much or how little variation can be explained by particular variables and therefore by particular theories.[1] Because of our views on integration, we favor the common research technique of simply throwing a whole bunch of variables into one gigantic regression stew. This technique has often been criticized as being theoretically sloppy, but we think it is almost always theoretically appropriate. Because of these views, we also think that competitive testing, in which two theories are tested against each other with the expectation of falsifying one or the other, is almost always inappropriate at the theoretical level.

This essay contains eight sections. First, we provide an overview of the major arguments that have formed the debate about theoretical integration in criminology. As mentioned above, this debate pits integration against falsification as the appropriate method for reducing the number of theories in criminology.

Second, we focus on integration itself and review the literature that attempts to describe the process of theoretical integration and distinguishes among its main forms. Since integration is an amorphous process, this literature is not very satisfying, but it provides a framework for discussion of the issue.

Third, we review six recent attempts at integrative theories in order to illustrate the process and forms of integration. These fit rather badly into the description of the integration process in the preceding section, and we discuss the complexities of the process in practice rather than in the abstract.

Fourth, we present our own perspective on integration and the integration debate. We largely agree with the specific arguments of those who oppose integration but argue for a variety of reasons that these arguments do not preclude integration at all. We argue, for example, that integration and falsification are not incompatible and that the purpose of integration is to enhance the falsification process. In addition, we argue that most criminology theories are not incompatible with each other. The apparent incompatibility arises, we believe, from dis-

[1] This essay uses the term "variance" or "variation" as an empirical yardstick in assessing theoretical explanatory power. This usage is for simplicity's sake and is not meant to be exhaustive. Explained variation is only relevant to a particular statistical technique (ordinary least squares regression). While this generally is adequate in discussing today's criminology theories (see Elliott 1985), integrated theories of crime in the future may involve complex dynamic or chaotic models and explained variance would not apply. While this would require some reconceptualization and rephrasing, we believe our major arguments would hold. See, for example, the discussion of Vila's (1994) general paradigm below.

tortions contained in the strain/control/cultural deviance interpretation. Ultimately, our view is that the debate about integration really is a debate about the validity of this interpretive scheme.

Fifth, since it is central in the integration debate, we examine the strain/control/cultural deviance interpretation itself. Those who oppose integration do so on the basis of this interpretation, while those who favor integration deviate from the interpretation in one way or another. We argue that this interpretation distorts two of the three types of theories and that this distortion is the basis for the argument that criminology theories are incompatible and cannot be integrated.

Sixth, we propose a new interpretation of criminology theories based on the location of independent variation and the direction of causation. Independent variation in criminology theories is located either in the individual or in the structure of society, which yields two categories of criminology theories. "Individual difference" theories describe individual-level characteristics that increase the likelihood people will engage in crime. "Structure/process" theories present arguments about the nature of "normal" biological and psychological processes and then argue that there are some social structural situations in which people with these "normal" processes are more likely to engage in crime. "Structure" and "process" theories have been categorized as two different types of theories in the past, but we argue that they must be considered part of a single coordinated theory.

Seventh, we discuss research implications of our theoretical arguments. Criminology theories can be very broadly integrated, both within the two categories and between them, and competitive testing of two or more theories is almost always inappropriate. We also point to the seemingly obvious principle that the level of data analysis must correspond to the level of theoretical argument. This principle is often violated, particularly by using individual-level data to test aggregate-level theories, and we discuss some of the complex theoretical issues that underlie this tendency.

Eighth, we conclude with some practical considerations about the extent to which integration is useful. Although full integration is theoretically possible, it may be best to attempt integration only within each category of theories, and not between them. The integration of "individual difference" and "structure/process" theories is theoretically possible but remains a long-range goal pending the development of more advanced theoretical arguments and statistical techniques.

I. The Integration Debate

Why is greater effort not directed by criminologists at theoretical integration? Tittle (1989) points out the objections of "futilitarians" toward development of general theories of crime. Crime is relative, and its definition is quick to change; its ambiguity makes it impossible to be comprehensively explained by any single theoretical framework. Behaviors captured under the label "crime" are so diverse that general theory cannot explain them all; general theory can only explain similar phenomena. Criminal behavior is so unpredictable and chaotic, a consequence of random situational events and subjective interpretations of events, that it cannot be explained. The causes of crime are too complex and diverse to fit within a single theoretical perspective, much less a single theory. Finally, efforts in the past toward a general theory of crime have failed.

While Tittle recognizes some validity in most of these objections, he argues that none of them entirely prevents the successful formulation of general theory. They are obstacles that can be surpassed by the following strategies: abstract generalization, integrative structuring of diverse causal processes, and a reciprocal relationship between theory and research. But these strategies, says Tittle, have failed because the academic community obstructs their advancement. Everyone wants to defend their own theories to their death, "as if they were the whole truth, resisting modifications" (p. 116). Additionally, academic institutions maintain such conditions by rewarding individual achievement instead of collective advancement in a particular field. Theoretical integration can only work if scholars are willing to form some consensus on an appropriate integrative framework and collaborate in the elaboration and testing of the framework.

Not only have scholars failed to form consensus on an integrative framework, but many do not believe this is a desirable goal. The formal beginning of the integration debate began in the late 1970s, when Elliott, Ageton, and Cantor (1979), Hirschi (1979), and Short (1979) each voiced their perspectives on theoretical integration in the *Journal of Research in Crime and Delinquency*. Elliott, Ageton, and Cantor offered an early version of the integrated theory discussed below, arguing that integration is the key to more powerful explanation of delinquency. Short took the pragmatist's route, seeing the advantages of integration but arguing that integration must ultimately unite three levels of analysis (individual, micro-situational, and macro), and this is a formidable task. Hirschi informed his colleagues unequivocally that he is against integration such as Elliott, Ageton, and Cantor's and that "separate and unequal is better." Hirschi argued that most theories are contradictory in that their assumptions are incompatible. Theories must be tested either on their own, for internal consistency and explanatory power, or against other theories. Theories can only be integrated if they are essentially arguing the same thing.

Several years later, Elliott, Huizinga, and Ageton (1985) provided a more in-depth defense of theoretical integration, arguing that the "oppositional tradition" has failed. The oppositional tradition refers to the primary alternative to integration-theoretical competition, which involves testing theories against each other. Some gauge is used for comparison, such as the extent to which each theory can explain a given type of behavior or the extent to which each theory is more internally consistent and logical. Theory competition has resulted in the acceptance or semiacceptance of a number of theories, each of which can only explain 10–20 percent of the variance in illegal behavior. As Elliott, Huizinga, and Ageton say, "Stated simply, the level of explained variance attributable to separate theories is embarrassingly low, and, if sociological explanations for crime and delinquency are to have any significant impact upon future planning and policy, they must be able to demonstrate greater predictive power" (p. 125).

Theoretical competition is generally pointless, according to Elliott (1985), because most of the time different theories explain independent portions of the variance in crime. Because there are multiple causes of crime, different theories that incorporate different causal factors are not necessarily incompatible. We should thus synthesize such theories, achieving a greater explanation of deviant behavior, rather than allowing them to remain in competitive isolation.

Hirschi (1989) also expanded on his argument against integration, discussing the fall of the "oppositional tradition" and the recent movement toward integration. While Hirschi recognizes that despite the prevalence of theory competition criminological theory is in need of advancement, he does not see integration as a solution. He refers to the compromises made to control theory that have been required by integrationists to make its assumptions compatible with those of other theories. Ultimately, argues Hirschi, integrationists ignore theoretical incompatibilities and plod ahead anyway. But the integrative attempt has been undermined, tainted by the decision to ignore contradictory assumptions.

Hirschi also criticizes integrationists for their slipshod approach to integration:

> Integrationists somehow conclude that variables appear in nature with opposition theory labels attached to them. This allows them to list variables by the theory that owns them. Social disorganization theory, for example, might own economic status, cultural heterogeneity, and mobility. . . . Each of the many variables is measured and, in an open and fair competition, the theories are ranked in terms of the success of their variables in explaining variation in delinquency. Because in the lists compiled by integrationists there is little or no overlap in the sets of variables claimed by various theories, it is easy to show that the data do not support one theory over another; rather, here the data support one and there support another, such that integration is in effect *required* by the evidence and surprisingly easily accomplished. [1989, p. 41]

Hirschi implies that theories do not "own" variables, and a theory of crime involves much more than variables: assumptions, relational propositions, and causal structure. Integration misrepresents individual theories.

II. Forms of Theoretical Integration

According to Liska, Krohn, and Messner (1989), there are two main types of theoretical integration: propositional and conceptual. They also suggest that a "middle range" that includes both propositional and conceptual integration might be useful.

Propositional integration involves linking separate theories by a given principle. Hirschi's (1979) typology of three such principles—"end to end," "side by side," and "up and down"—is a useful means of summarizing propositional integration.

"End-to-end" integration is developmental in that it proposes a causal order across propositions of the various theories to be integrated. The dependent variable in theory A is identified as an independent variable in theory B; thus the process described in theory A occurs prior to the process explained by theory B. For example, Edwards's (1992) integrated theory of juvenile delinquency proposes that an individual's perceived access to educational goals and perceived aspiration-opportunity (ostensibly concepts from strain theory) affects that person's exposure to definitions favorable to violating the law (differential association), and this exposure in turn contributes to de-linquent involvement. Thus, the theory that differential association varies directly with perceived strain is integrated, end to end, with the theory that juvenile delinquency varies directly with differential association.

"Side-by-side" integration involves deciding which theories best ex-plain which types of deviants (e.g., by race or gender) or which types of deviant behavior (e.g., property or violent offenses). This sort of integration should *not* be conducted merely by empirically observing which theories most successfully explain which type of deviance or deviant. Rather, side-by-side integration occurs when the assumptions and domain of each theory indicate the types of deviance that can be explained by the theory (Liska, Krohn, and Messner 1989). While these rarely allow for a complete consensus on what the theories can and cannot explain, there will be natural overlap among theories in their ability to explain different types of deviant behavior. Theory A might purport to explain violent crime, whereas theory B might explain crime committed by indigent persons. Both theories should explain violent crime committed by indigents. Each theory also has its own sphere of explanatory power. As the number of theories to be inte-grated side by side increases, this results in much confusion.

"Up-and-down" integration involves raising the level of abstraction of one theory, such that its propositions merely follow from the con-ceptually broader theory. For example, Cohen and Machalek (1988, p. 498) based their theory of expropriative crime on relatively parsimoni-ous principles from evolutionary biologists and behavioral ecologists.[2] They then "deduce most of the propositions and hypotheses featured in conventional criminological theories." To that extent, theirs is the conceptually broader theory that accomplishes an "up-and-down" inte-gration of conventional criminological theories.

Whereas propositional integration retains the premises of each the-ory—incorporating them in some fashion into a larger theory—*conceptual integration* likens a concept from one theory to a concept from another, concluding that the theories themselves are similar. Liska, Krohn, and Messner (1989) argue that this in itself is not very valuable since it is nothing but playing games with words and meanings. How-

---

[2] This theory forms the basis for Vila's general paradigm, which is more fully dis-cussed below.

ever, they suggest that conceptual integration is desirable as a means to the end of deductive ("up-and-down") integration. Conceptual clarity is necessary before one can propose that propositions of one theory are more general than and can accommodate those of another theory.

Since incorporating entire theories into an integrative framework can be an arduous task, Liska et al. suggest that a middle-range approach might be appropriate. Various concepts from different theories, but not the complete theories, may constitute a new and broader-based theory.

Finally, Thornberry took a position on "theory elaboration" that appears to be an alternative approach to integration. Theory elaboration involves the logical extension of a particular theory, in an attempt to improve its adequacy. The outcome of theoretical elaboration is described in terms that are quite similar to integration (Thornberry 1989, p. 59):

1. It is likely that propositions have been added, deleted, combined and reordered to offer a better explanation of delinquency.

2. The basic assumptions have probably been reevaluated and possibly altered to allow for the inclusion of propositions from differing perspectives.

3. The structure of the theory, including the temporal ordering of concepts and the types of relationships permitted, may well have changed.

4. It is likely that, when this process is played out over time from the point of view of a number of different focal theories, the overall result will be the blending together of originally different and competing theoretical models into a more general body of explanatory principles. In turn, this will require fundamental changes in the theories of origin as the elaborated models replace them.

Thornberry's approach, when taken to its logical extreme, would elaborate on each theory of crime until only a single theory remains. Thornberry seems to recognize this but points out that in theoretical elaboration the analyst is oriented toward maximizing the power of a single theory, whereas in integration it is toward reconciling differences across theories. Thornberry's is a diplomatic approach to the integration debate, in that it ostensibly allows a theorist to hold onto his or her theory, but his stance cannot be considered incompatible with the integrationist. Regardless of one's orientation, elaboration logically leads to integration.

III. Examples of Integrative Theories

To some extent, most theories "integrate" at least some previously existing theories in new arguments, so there is no firm and fast line between "integrated" theories and other theories. We present here six different theories that reasonably can be described as "integrated" theories, in order to facilitate further discussion of integration in general.

A. Elliott, Ageton, and Cantor's Integrated Theory

Elliott, Ageton, and Cantor (1979) opened the current round of debate on integration by publishing a paper that explicitly attempted to combine strain, control, and social learning perspectives in order to explain delinquency and drug use with greater power. They accomplish this in two steps, first by integrating strain with social control theories and then by integrating social learning.

Reviewing various interpretations of strain theory, Elliott, Huizinga, and Ageton (1985, p. 14) note a commonality across them: "that delinquency is a response to actual or anticipated failure to achieve socially induced needs or goals (status, wealth, power, social acceptance, etc.)." Control theory posits that the strength of an individual's conventional social bonds is inversely related to the probability that the individual will engage in delinquent behavior. The key difference between these two perspectives is that control theory assumes constant motivation to commit crime and variable bonding to conventional others, while strain theory assumes variable motivation but constant bonding.

Elliott, Huizinga, and Ageton circumvent these assumptions by allowing for variation in individual motivation to engage in delinquency, as well as variation in conventional bonding. Additionally, they assert that prodelinquency motivation, caused by strain, can effectuate weak social bonds. The probability of delinquency should be highest when an individual experiences strain *and* weak conventional controls. Sources of weak social controls include inadequate socialization and social disorganization, the latter also increasing the likelihood of strain.

Social learning theories suggest that delinquency is affected by a struggle between the rewards and punishments associated with both conforming and deviant patterns of socialization. Adolescents are controlled by groups such as their families, schools, and peers. While family and school generally provide a conventional context for social learning, peer groups are more likely to reinforce deviant behavior. It

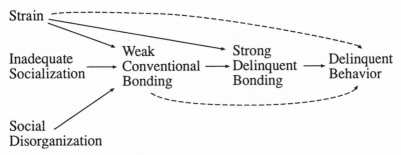

Fig. 1.—Elliott, Ageton, and Cantor's (1979) Integrated Model

is the variation in individual exposure to delinquent attitudes and behavior within this peer group that affects the probability of delinquent
behavior.

Elliott, Huizinga, and Ageton state that, whereas control theory is
interested in the strength of (conventional) socialization, learning theory is interested in its content (deviant vs. conforming socialization).
They thus find it necessary to modify control theory, taking into account the type of group to which the individual bonds. An individual
can form strong or weak bonds to conventional or deviant social
groups, resulting in a fourfold typology. Deviant behavior is most
likely in the quadrant with strong bonds to deviant groups and weak
bonds to conventional groups (high rewards and low costs), while it is
least likely in the quadrant with strong bonds to conventional groups
and weak bonds to deviant groups (low rewards and high costs).

Their final step is to integrate all three theories: strain, social control,
and social learning. Figure 1 shows their integrated model (Elliott,
Huizinga, and Ageton 1985, p. 66). Note that weak conventional bonding (low social control) is seen as causally prior to strong delinquent
bonding (social learning). Individual interactions with the family, for
example, generally occur before the individual can establish a peer
group. Also, strain, inadequate socialization, and social disorganization
are treated as the most exogenous variables in the model. These three
concepts involve social structural conditions, as well as preadolescent
developmental characteristics, and would be expected to occur before
bonding to conventional and delinquent groups occurs.

The authors identify the integrated model with the social control
rather than the social learning perspective, reasoning that control theory is more general and can explain deviance across levels of explana-

tion and that a control perspective is more sociological than social learning, as it places great importance on the role of institutional structures in controlling deviant behavior.

The dotted lines from strain and from weak conventional bonding to delinquent behavior suggest the possibility of direct effects of strain and weak social control on delinquency, but they doubt that these paths are significant. Instead, the effect of strain on delinquency should be mediated by weak conventional bonding and strong delinquent bonding, and the effect of social control on delinquency should occur indirectly, through strong delinquent bonding.

Elliott, Huizinga, and Ageton supported their model with longitudinal data from the National Youth Survey. They found *no* direct effects of strain and social control concepts on delinquent behavior. Instead, most of the explained variance in delinquent behavior was attributed to the most proximate source in the integrated model: bonding to delinquent peers.

Elliott, Huizinga, and Ageton's integration is propositional. It is a middle range form of end-to-end integration, in that independent variables are drawn from various theories—such as strain—and positioned causally prior to concepts from other theories, such as social control. It is also up and down, in that social control is subsumed under the dimensions strength and type of bonding.

B. Conceptual Integration: Pearson and Weiner

Pearson and Weiner (1985) approach integration in a very different manner from Elliott, Huizinga, and Ageton (1985). They build an integrative theory, based generally on the social learning perspective, and proceed to map concepts from almost every extant theory of criminal or delinquent behavior into their integrative framework.

The framework involves internal and external micro-level factors, social-structural factors, and feedback (or behavioral consequence) factors. Internal micro-level constructs, which occur causally prior to criminal behavior, include utility demand, behavioral skill, rules of expedience, and rules of morality. Utility demand is individual motivation for achieving a success goal. Skill relates to the learned ability to acquire the relevant utility. Rules of expedience are cognitive processes aimed at the rational optimization of utility acquisition. Rules of morality are cognitive processes orienting behavior toward principles of right and wrong.

External micro-level constructs include signs of favorable opportunities and behavioral resources. Signs of favorable opportunities are present if the individual perceives a behavior as likely to result in utility acquisition. Behavioral resources are items or people who can be used for utility acquisition.

Behavioral consequences occur after criminal behavior and affect micro-level factors in a feedback loop. These include utility reception (rewards and punishments resulting from the behavior) and information acquisition (knowledge obtained from performing the behavior that can be considered when deciding whether to repeat the behavior).

The most independent set of variables are social structural and include the social-cultural production and distribution of positive and negative utilities, opportunities, rules of expedience and morality, and beliefs about sanctioning practices. This set of factors takes into account differences across subcultures and cultures that can moderate the effect of individual factors on the likelihood of criminal behavior.

Pearson and Weiner take concepts from each of a number of criminological theories and *map* them conceptually into this theoretical framework, arguing that each concept can be likened to one or more of their twelve constructs.

In order to select the theories to be integrated, Pearson and Weiner searched five popular criminology journals from 1978 to 1985 for references to general theories. They found that thirteen theories accounted for more than 90 percent of these references: social learning, differential association, negative labeling, social control, deterrence, economic, routine activities, neutralization, relative deprivation, strain, normative (culture) conflict, Marxist-critical/group conflict, and generalized strain and normative conflict.

Strain theory can be used as an example of how an extant theory maps into Pearson and Weiner's theoretical framework since it applies to ten of the twelve constructs. Strain involves goals that are deemed desirable by one's culture, and this fits into the utility demand construct. Behavioral skill applies since the path to achieving culture goals is blocked when appropriate skills cannot be commonly obtained. Means to achieving the success goal can be perceived as moral or amoral and, independently, expedient or inefficient; thus, rules of morality and expedience apply to strain theory.

Utility reception also applies since illegitimate means *can* lead to a success-goal (utility), resulting in personal reward, which affects future considerations of illegitimate behavior. Favorable opportunities and information acquisition (as a feedback mechanism) fit strain theory as well since strain implies obstacles to legitimate means of achieving a success-goal, and the knowledge of such obstacles is reinforced when illegitimate behavior leads to the achievement of a socially accepted goal.

Three macro-level factors in the integrated framework also apply to strain theory. Central to strain theory is the idea that socially desired goals (utilities, such as high income) and favorable opportunities (means, such as professional employment) are not distributed evenly within a society, but vary across subcultures and demographical characteristics. Also, the social distribution of rules of morality and expedience applies since the value of the socially desired goals, as well as the emphasis on legitimate means to achieving them, vary across social groups.

In this fashion, Pearson and Weiner map the thirteen theories into the twelve constructs. Frequently, the connection between a concept from one of the theories and a construct from their integrated framework is tenuous. They seem to realize this, noting that their integrative effort is conceptual rather than propositional and that it is only a basis for a more systematic conceptual mapping. Pearson and Weiner do not attempt to put their general theory into testable form.

C. Thornberry's Interactional Theory

Thornberry (1987) attempts to combine control and social learning theories in order to increase their explanatory power. The most important flaw of these theories, in his view, is their use of unidirectional causal structures. In contrast, Thornberry believes that most of the concepts from control and learning theory affect each other reciprocally and that behavior reciprocally influences the concepts. In addition, Thornberry argues that control and social learning theories attempt to explain delinquency in a narrow age domain, even though the relative importance of various contributing causes to delinquency and crime are likely to change over the life course. That is, Thornberry thinks that both theories should be interpreted in a developmental context.

In order to correct these deficiencies, Thornberry proposes an "interactional" theory of delinquency, which is based predominantly on control theory. Social constraints are viewed as the primary causes of delinquency, but they are not enough to result in delinquent behavior. They merely free up behavior, and delinquency still "requires an interactive setting in which (it) is learned, performed, and reinforced" (1987, p. 865).

Interactional theory consists of six theoretical concepts, combined in a reciprocal causal structure. Three come from control theory: attachment to parents, commitment to school, and belief in conventional values; two from social learning theory: association with delinquent peers and adopting delinquent values; and the dependent variable is engagement in delinquent behavior. Because the theory is developmental he offers three models: one for early adolescence (11–13), one for middle adolescence (15–16), and one for later adolescence (18–20). These models are generally similar.

The most fundamental premise of interactional theory is that most contributors to delinquency and delinquency itself are related reciprocally. The "chicken or egg" debate in criminology most often arises in the relationship between peers and delinquency: some argue that delinquency affects whom one associates with, whereas others argue that adolescents' peer associations affect their likelihood of engaging in delinquency. Thornberry's resolution is to argue that associations with peers may affect values and behavior, but values and behavior also affect associations with peers. Thornberry's answer, then, is that it is *both* the chicken *and* the egg.

Thornberry positions the control concepts as the most fundamental contributors since delinquency has little potential when social constraints are strong. Attachment to parents and commitment to school both directly influence delinquent behavior, such that the greater the bonding, the smaller the probability of engaging in delinquency. Belief in conventional values is affected by both attachment and commitment, and affects delinquent behavior indirectly through its reciprocal influence on behavior. Delinquent behavior in turn negatively influences attachment and commitment (and belief, indirectly through attachment). As Thornberry says, "While the weakening of the bond to conventional society may be an initial cause of delinquency, delinquency eventually becomes its own indirect cause precisely because of its ability to weaken further the person's bonds to family, school, and conventional beliefs" (1987, p. 876).

In addition to social control and social learning concepts, Thornberry expects that one's position in society will influence his or her delinquent involvement. Children from lower-class families should initially be less bonded to middle-class society and more likely to form delinquent values, have delinquent friends, and behave delinquently.

This is less of a problem but still will occur somewhat for children from working-class families. Children from middle-class families should have a stronger family structure (and hence stronger bonding), greater stakes in conformity, and therefore should be less likely to engage in delinquency.

Thornberry and his colleagues have now published two tests of interactional theory (Thornberry et al. 1991, 1994). The earlier study tested the relationships among two bonding concepts (attachment to parents and commitment to school) and delinquency, whereas the later examined the relationships among associations with delinquent peers, peer reactions, delinquent beliefs, and delinquent behavior. The full theoretical model has yet to be tested. They have found general support for the reciprocal relationships between both control concepts and learning concepts with delinquent behavior.

As mentioned above, Thornberry avoids describing his theory as an "integrated" theory and prefers to call his approach "theoretical elaboration." If true theoretical integration keeps each original theory entirely intact in the merger, then Thornberry's is not an integrated theory. However, if adopting the key concepts from more than one theory and reordering the causal specifications can still constitute integrated theory, than his theory fits into this category.

D. Braithwaite's Shaming Theory

An interesting example of an integrative attempt that cannot easily be classified as propositional or conceptual is Braithwaite's (1989) theory of reintegrative shaming, which draws on labeling, subcultural, opportunity, control, differential association, and social learning theories. Propositional integration involves combining previously formed theories, and conceptual integration involves demonstrating that several concepts from different theories all relate to a more abstract concept. But Braithwaite creates a new theoretical concept—reintegrative shaming—and shows how it fits into a web of other theoretical concepts. In one sense, then, it explains a *process* by which several other theoretical concepts may be related to criminal behavior.

Shaming constitutes "all social processes of expressing disapproval which have the intention or effect of invoking remorse in the person being shamed and/or condemnation by others who become aware of the shaming" (Braithwaite 1989, p. 100). Braithwaite divides shaming into two types: stigmatization (when the shaming brings about a feeling of deviancy in the shamed) and reintegration (when the shamers ensure that they maintain bonds with the shamed). Reintegrative shaming, then, occurs when the violator is shamed into knowing what he or she did is wrong but is also allowed reentry into the conforming group. The core of the theory is that reintegrative shaming is likely to lead to lower crime rates, whereas stigmatization is likely to lead to higher crime rates.

Several other theories feed into this core theoretical relationship. Individuals with more social bonding are more likely to receive reintegrative shaming and thus less likely to commit crime. Labeling theory is drawn on to explain stigmatization, and once an individual is stigmatized, he or she is more likely to participate in a deviant subculture and, thus, more likely to commit crime. The theory also acts on a structural level. Greater urbanization and mobility (from social disorganization theory) lessen the chance that "societal communitarianism" (similar to Durkheim's social solidarity) will exist. Communitarianism, or interdependency among individuals in a culture, leads to reintegrative shaming, while the lack of it leads to stigmatization. This in turn results in blocked legitimate opportunities, formation of subcultures, presence of illegitimate opportunities, and higher crime rates. Although Braithwaite's theory applies to many different types of crimes, it is not meant to explain crimes that do not involve victimization of individuals by each other.

Because Braithwaite's theory is fairly recent, it has not yet received much discussion in the literature, nor has it been subjected to much empirical testing. Several criticisms have been offered (see Uggen 1993*a*), sparking some exploration of potential problems with the theory (Braithwaite 1993; Uggen 1993*b*). The first test of integrative theory finds support for the relationship between reintegrative shaming and criminal behavior (in this case, nursing home compliance with the law). However, this is the only link it examines, and so the relationship between shaming and concepts from other theories remains unexplored. Braithwaite's is a fresh approach to integrated criminological theory since it proposes a new theory but at the same time places it in a context of a web of established theories.

E. Hagan's Power-Control Theory

Some integrated theories set out explicitly to link explanations at one level (such as individual) with explanations at another level (such as community or society). Hagan's power-control theory of gender and delinquency is one example (Hagan, Gillis, and Simpson 1985; Hagan and Palloni 1986; Hagan 1988). Power-control theory's goal is to explain why gender has been consistently found to be related to criminality (females are less criminal than males, on the average).

The first part of the theory begins with the degree to which children in a family are controlled by their parents. Parents—especially mothers—control daughters much more than sons. This control results in less preference for risky behavior among girls than boys. Accordingly, male adolescents engage in more delinquent behavior than females.

The second part of the theory explores the possibility that this relationship will not be uniform across all families. Rather, it will be greatest in patriarchal families, in which the father has more power than the mother. This occurs when the father works outside the home, typically supervising others, and the mother works in the home, maintaining a domestic atmosphere. In egalitarian households, however, where the mother has relative power compared to the father, the daughter is not likely to be controlled more than the son. In other words, the power relations among the parents are reproduced in the form of the relative behavioral controls imposed on male and female children.

The thrust of the theory, then, is to explain the relationship between gender and delinquency with the interaction between a family's class structure and control relations within the family. Thus, two levels of explanation are integrated: the power relations between the parents relative to their position in the workplace, and the relative freedom of children in a family from parental control. The theory is designed to help reconcile the ambiguous relationship between class and delinquency by drawing on the consistent relationship between gender and delinquency.

When testing power-control theory, Hagan (1988, p. 159) focuses on "common delinquency," which includes all forms of delinquent behavior involving calculation. Behavior must be calculated to be included in the theory because the social-psychological process by which gender is posited to affect delinquency is the development of risk preferences and assessments. The first few empirical tests of power-control theory have generally supported the theory's tenets (see Hagan 1988, chaps. 7–9). Power-control theory is representative of an increasing trend toward qualifying relationships between concepts at one level of explanation by drawing on concepts at other levels of explanation.

F. Vila's General Paradigm

Criminologists are paying increased attention to efforts to understand criminality in a developmental context. Scholars are recognizing that many of the conditions they expect to affect delinquency and criminal behavior vary over time, and the weight of their effects on behavior also varies over time. As described above, Thornberry's interactional theory takes a developmental stance by revising the theory for different age groups of juveniles. A recent example of a developmental theory over the entire life course is Sampson and Laub's (1993), which examines the interaction of time, community organization, and family factors on individual behavior, exploring both stability and change in criminal careers.

Vila's (1994) general paradigm for understanding criminal behavior is perhaps the broadest of these developmental integrative approaches. This is an extension of Cohen and Machalek's (1988) theory of evolutionary ecology. Cohen and Machalek attempted to explain only expropriative crimes, such as theft and embezzlement, whereas Vila tries to explain all crime. Vila does not describe his approach as a theory; rather, he describes it as a paradigmatic model from which theory should develop.

According to Vila, if a theory is to be general enough to explain all criminal behavior, it must be ecological, integrative, and developmental, and it must include both micro-level and macro-level explanations. An ecological theory considers the interconnection of individuals and their physical environment. A developmental theory allows for changes in the causes of crime as well as in crime itself over time. Integrative theories allow for the inclusion of factors from multiple disciplines. Finally, theories that use concepts at more than one level of explanation recognize that within-person variation, variation in social structure, and variation in the person-structure interaction, all can affect individual behavior. Vila reviews a number of theories that meet at least two of these conditions but shows that no theory to date meets all of them. Therefore, he calls existing criminology theories "partial theories."

Among individual (micro-level) factors that influence behavior, Vila argues that biological contributors must be included in any theory (1994, pp. 328–30). Thus, he criticizes developmental theories such as Sampson and Laub's (1993) for ignoring the role of biological factors. Not only must individual genetic traits be considered in a general theory, but intergenerational transmission of these traits must be considered as well. For this reason, the effect of biological factors may be lagged over lengthy periods.

Vila also criticizes existing theories for not allowing macro-level correlates of crime (such as social disorganization) to vary over time. Because macro-level contributors are dynamic, an individual's position in society is in flux. Ecological contributors to crime, such as opportunities provided by one's physical environment, also have the potential to change over an individual's lifetime.

Vila stresses the *interaction* of ecological, micro, and macro causal factors. For example, macro and micro factors might interact in the effects of cultural beliefs on parental style; macro and ecological factors might interact in the effect of sociocultural heterogeneity on opportunities for crime; and micro and ecological factors might interact in an individual attempting to modify his or her local environment. When allowing for both causal directions to occur across the three types of factors, the result is six types of two-way interaction terms. Vila does not mention the possibility of a three-way interaction, but it is implied from his discussion.

A central assumption is that all crime involves the seeking of resources. Expropriative crimes (such as theft and fraud) are aimed at acquiring material resources. Expressive crimes (such as sexual assault and drug use) are aimed at obtaining hedonistic resources. Economic crimes (such as illegal gambling and narcotics trafficking) are aimed at obtaining monetary resources. Political crimes (such as terrorism) are aimed at obtaining political resources. All crimes are committed with one or more of the following strategic styles: force, stealth, and fraud. The extent to which a person develops these styles depends on the interaction between biological, sociocultural, and developmental factors. All these affect the motivation toward crime, which is determined by how many resources a person has and how much more that person desires. But only when an opportunity also exists to commit crime will the motivated individual commit a crime.

An interesting aspect of Vila's paradigm consists of its choice of an empirical method to assess theories that develop from the paradigm. Mathematical chaos theory, rather than traditional linear models, according to Vila, will best predict the development of criminality over an individual's life. Chaos theory is appropriate because initial conditions (such as early childhood experiences with parental style) set off trajectories of behavior. Thus, initial conditions are more important than most subsequent events in influencing long-term behavior. General linear models cannot appropriately model this pattern.

Vila's paradigm is frustratingly general—everything affects everything, at all levels, and these effects are continuously changing over time. However, it is intuitively appealing because criminality is so much more complex than any of the major criminological theories acknowledge. The evolutionary ecological paradigm incorporates the complexity of human behavior. The key question is whether social scientists are capable of testing theories that are as complex as this paradigm requires.

IV. Our Perspective on the Integration Debate

In our view, there are too many theories in criminology, and this impedes scientific progress (Bernard 1991). The number of theories can be reduced either through falsification (which eliminates some theories) or through integration (which combines theories without eliminating any). In the integration debate, these have had the appearance of being mutually exclusive alternatives—some believe integration is impossible and favor falsification, while others believe falsification has failed and favor integration. In fact, however, integration is not an alternative to falsification but a supplement to it. The real question is whether integration facilitates falsification or whether it simply adds more confusion to an already confused situation.

Attempts at falsification have consumed a substantial amount of criminologists' time. Regardless of what else might be said, those efforts have not reduced the number of criminology theories, and an increasing number of criminologists are trying their hand at integration as a way of addressing that problem.

We believe that integration can be beneficial to the development of criminological theory and ultimately can facilitate falsification. We do not, however, simply reject the arguments of the opponents of integration. Rather, we believe the arguments are largely correct but that their implications for integration are largely wrong.

First, we agree with Hirschi's (1979, 1989) argument that incompatible theories cannot be integrated. For example, to the extent that Elliott, Huizinga, and Ageton (1985) changed one of control theory's essential arguments, the resulting composite theory cannot be considered an "integration" that includes control theory. Integrations must accurately represent the essential arguments of their component theories. To the extent that theories are actually incompatible with each other, they cannot be integrated at all.

We differ from Hirschi in that we believe that most criminological theories do not make incompatible arguments. Hirschi's argument is based primarily on the incompatibility among "control," "strain," and "cultural deviance" theories of crime. This interpretation of criminology theories originated with Hirschi and is intimately tied to the view that the theories are incompatible and therefore cannot be integrated. In our view, the interpretation itself is the problem. It accurately represents only control theory, but it distorts the arguments of "strain" and "cultural deviance" theories. Once those distortions are corrected, the theoretical incompatibilities largely disappear.

Thus, we turn Hirschi's own argument back on him. He has argued that integrationists distort theories in order to integrate them and, therefore, that integration itself is invalid. We argue that he has distorted the theories, and those very distortions are the basis for his argument that they cannot be integrated. Once the theories are accurately represented, they can be integrated even according to Hirschi's own criteria.

Second, we agree with Hirschi's argument that variables do not "appear in nature with opposition theory labels attached to them." Theories, however, do not appear in nature at all, but variables and the relations among variables do appear in nature in the sense that they can be observed and measured. In our view, there has been too much emphasis in the integration debate on the theories themselves and not enough on the observable variables and the observable relations among them.

For example, Hirschi attributes to integrationists the view that "social disorganization theory may own economic status, cultural heterogeneity, and mobility." Our view, in contrast, is that economic status, cultural heterogeneity, and mobility are important, as are the hypothesized relationships among them and to the dependent variable. But the question of which theory "owns" those variables is not important at all. We would do better if we simply discarded that question and got on with the task of determining which variables are related to crime and in which ways.

Third, we believe that, for whatever other merits it may have, pure conceptual integration tends to result in theoretical mush (cf. Akers 1989). In the final analysis, the only meaningful integration is propositional integration. Unless theories are compatible in their actual propositions, then integration is not really meaningful.

However, an integrated theory of crime does not necessarily need to maintain intact *all* of the propositions of the component theories. Some propositions may be compatible at the theoretical level, while others may be contradictory. For example, Bernard (1989) argued that

Merton's, Cohen's, Cloward and Ohlin's, Hirschi's, and Akers's theories all contained a series of propositions that can be described as a "theory of action." One set of propositions in the "theory of action" maintains that people's actions tend to be consistent with their interests and that those interests are shaped by social structure. This results in structured regularities to individual actions. A second set of propositions argued that people tend to bring their values into line with their interests, and those values then become a separate source of independent variation explaining individual actions. Bernard argued that the same "theory of action" was at the heart of conflict theory's descriptions of the enactment and the enforcement of criminal laws. Thus all six theories could be integrated around this rather narrow and precise "theory of action," despite various contradictions in other parts of the theories.

Fourth, integration must facilitate falsification, or it is not meaningful at all. One of the problems with conceptual integration is that the resulting theory tends to be so complex, inclusive, and general that it is even more difficult to falsify than the component theories. This moves criminology theory in precisely the wrong direction. Properly done, propositional integration simplifies the complexity of multiple theories and therefore simplifies the testing of those theories. For example, Bernard (1989) argued that, if the narrow and precise "theory of action" could be falsified, then all six of the theories in which it is found would also be falsified. This would seem to simplify the falsification process considerably.

V. Interpretation as the Basis for Integration

We argued above that propositional integration is the only meaningful integration and that theories with incompatible propositions cannot be integrated. Criminology theories for the most part do not contain incompatible propositions and therefore can be integrated. To show this, we turn to the interpretation of criminology theories.

The integration debate has largely swirled around the strain/control/cultural deviance interpretation of criminology theories. Hirschi (1969) originated this interpretation and has been the strongest advocate of the position that the theories are incompatible and cannot be integrated (e.g., 1979, 1989). The interpretation was elaborated by Kornhauser (1978), who took the same position on integration. Because Hirschi's theory achieved a considerable influence, his interpretation of the other criminology theories has also proven influential. Thus, the debate about integration in criminology has largely assumed the validity of Hirschi's characterizations of other theories. Those who oppose integration defend their position largely in reference to his characterization, while those who favor integration typically deviate from it in one way or another.

In contrast, we challenge his characterizations. If they are accurate, then criminology theories cannot be integrated. However, his characterizations distort the propositions contained in what Hirschi calls "strain" and "cultural deviance" theories. That distortion, rather than the theories themselves, makes the integration of criminology theories impossible.

A. The Strain/Control/Cultural Deviance Interpretation

According to Hirschi (1969) and Kornhauser (1978), strain theories propose variable drives to crime, especially frustrations arising from limited legitimate opportunities for economic success or social status. They cite as examples of strain theories Merton (1938), Cohen (1955), and Cloward and Ohlin (1960). Control theories are said to propose variable restraints from crime, particularly attachments to legitimate people and institutions, with examples being Hirschi's (1969) and Kornhauser's (1978) own theories. Cultural deviance theories are said to propose that all individuals conform to cultures and that some cultures incorporate deviant or criminal values. They cite Miller (1958), Wolfgang and Ferracuti (1967), Sutherland and Cressey (1978), and Akers (1985) as examples.

In this interpretation, the three types of theories are comparable to each other because each makes a social psychological argument (Agnew 1992). They also are incompatible with each other because the assumptions and assertions of each theory fundamentally contradict those of the other two. Thus, if one theory is true, the others must be false (Liska 1971; Agnew 1992). Because they are social psychological theories, these theories can be tested against each other with the individual-level analysis of self-reported data. This would not be possible if any of the theories contained social structural arguments.

This interpretation virtually necessitates Hirschi's position on integration and falsification. Because the three types of theories are incompatible, they cannot be integrated. And because they are comparable, they can be tested against each other in comparative research, with the expectation that at least two out of the three will be falsified. This has not happened. The problem is that only control theory has been accurately characterized, while both "strain" and "cultural deviance" theories are distorted. Once those theories are accurately represented, a broad-ranging integration of criminology becomes possible.

B. Distortion of "Strain" Theories

Kornhauser (1978) describes "strain" theories as arguing that conforming behavior is natural and free and requires no explanation; criminal behavior must be explained by an additional variable "driving" force that determines who does and who does not engage in this behavior, as well as the extent to which they engage in it; the variable driving force is frustration; and people are aware of their frustrations and their criminality, so that these theories can be tested with the individual-level analysis of self-reported data.

Bernard (1984, 1987a, 1987b) maintains that the theories most commonly described as "strain" theories—Merton (1938), Cohen (1955), and Cloward and Ohlin (1960)—do not contain any of these arguments. In particular, these theories do not propose a "variable drive" to crime in the social psychological sense of proposing that "more frustration" is associated with "more crime." Criminals might indeed be frustrated by their structural conditions, but none of these theories assert a causal connection between frustration and criminal behavior. Rather, each theory makes a macro-level structural argument linking rates and distributions of crime to socially structured contexts.

For example, Cohen presents a theory of lower-class gang delinquency, but he does not argue that lower-class boys are "more frustrated" than middle-class boys. In fact, he clearly states the opposite: "The delinquent subculture is mostly to be found in the working class. It does not follow that working-class children are necessarily more beset with problems of adjustment than are middle-class children. It has been plausibly argued by some students of social class in America that growing up in the middle class is, on the whole, a more frustrating experience than growing up in the working class" (Cohen 1955, p. 73). Frustration plays a role in Cohen's theory, but he never argues that "more frustration" is associated with "more delinquency." Therefore frustration cannot be considered a "variable drive" to crime in Cohen's theory.

A similar argument can be made about Merton's theory. Stinchcombe (1975, p. 12) argued that anomie "structures" actions but does not drive people to crime. It does that by shaping people's self-interests and then by assuming that people, by and large, will pursue their self-interests. Hirschi (1969) makes a directly comparable argument in his discussion of commitment, except he describes the "structuring" of legal rather than criminal actions. Commitment measures the extent to which an individual's self-interests are legal. Imagine, for the sake of argument, a group of people who solely pursue their own interests. Those that are "committed" (in Hirschi's sense) will tend to act legally because their interests are largely legal, while those who are "strained" (in Merton's sense) will tend to act illegally because their interests are largely illegal. But none of them would be "restrained" or "frustrated" in a social psychological sense since they all would be pursuing their own interests. Hirschi's argument with respect to commitment and Merton's argument about the lack of opportunity are two sides of the same coin: one describes the structuring of legal behavior and the other describes the structuring of criminal behavior.

Cullen (1983, pp. 36–37) proposed a similar interpretation of strain theories. He argues that these theories propose "an indeterminate relationship between the [stress or frustration] and actual deviant outcomes, and that a variety of social circumstances structure when participation in a form of deviance will be possible." Correlating self-reported levels of stress or frustration with self-reported levels of crime therefore tends to produce weak results because nonstress variables regulate the nature of the deviant outcome. Cullen (1983, p. 40; 1988) therefore argues that nonstress variables are the central explanatory variables in these theories. These are best described as "structuring" rather than "strain" variables because they channel the motivated actor (i.e., one who is pressured or stressed or strained or frustrated) either toward or away from crime in response to that motivation.

Cullen (1983, p. 48) argues that his line of reasoning applies to all so-called strain theories of crime. But he (1983, p. 82) goes even further in his analysis of Merton's anomie theory, where he argues that criminals are not described as stressed or frustrated at all: "Merton did not maintain that an unregulated individual has to experience any special stress or pressure to become deviant. . . . In the place of (the "strained") deviant, Merton substituted a thoroughly classical view of the deviant, arguing that the deregulated or anomic actor is free to choose any course of conduct. The only guide to the person's activity is the rational calculation of the costs and benefits of the various means available. Deviant behavior occurs when illegitimate means are the 'technically most effective procedure' that can be employed to secure a desired end." This "anomie" theory operates at the societal level, linking social structural characteristics to rates and distributions of deviant behavior (Cullen 1983, pp. 80–83). Messner (1985, 1988), Rosenfeld (1989), and Messner and Rosenfeld (1994) have developed the aggregate-level "strain" theory as "the road not taken" in criminology, and it now appears to be the dominant interpretation of so-called strain theories.

Although Cullen (1983) earlier argued that Merton proposed a separate individual-level theory linking frustration to crime, he now agrees with Bernard that no such theory exists (Burton and Cullen 1992). Agnew (1992) continues to develop the individual-level frustration-based argument that Hirschi describes as a "strain" theory. Even he, however, now skirts the issue of whether this type of theory is really derived from the theories of Merton, Cohen, and Cloward and Ohlin. Rather, he focuses on developing and testing the theory itself.

Criminologists should not assume Hirschi's and Kornhauser's social psychological interpretation of so-called strain theories when discussing whether these theories can be integrated with other theories in criminology. At minimum, the structural interpretation of these theories presented here also should be considered. While the social psychological interpretation indeed makes integration impossible, the structural interpretation would form the basis for a wide-ranging integration.

C. Distortion of "Cultural Deviance" Theories

Kornhauser (1978, p. 34) summarized the "premises" of the "cultural deviance" model as "man has no nature, socialization is perfectly successful, and cultural variability is unlimited." The term "culture" refers to "those symbols by means of which a people apprehend and endow experience with ultimate human significance" (p. 6). It is independent from structure and has unlimited variability in the sense that "ultimate human significance" can be found in any type of experience, including crime (pp. 13–14). Human beings have no nature in the sense that they can be socialized into any culture, and socialization is perfect in every case, so that the individual is not free to deviate from culture.

Kornhauser then describes four theories as "cultural deviance" theories: Miller (1958), Wolfgang and Ferracuti (1967), Sutherland and Cressey (1978), and Akers (1985). But there is almost no similarity between these theories and the "cultural deviance" characterization. These theories describe the role of shared cognitions as a crucial intervening variable between social structural conditions and criminal behavior. Shared cognitions are described as an immediate cause of criminal behavior, but in each theory the source of those cognitions is said to lie in structural conditions. For example, "normative conflicts" are the "organizing principle" of differential association theory (Sutherland and Cressey 1978, p. 95). They are quite different from "cultural values" since they are defined in terms of behavioral expectations in specific situations. These originate in and are explained by "differential social organization," so they are not independent of structural conditions (pp. 99–117).

Miller (1958) used the phrase "lower-class culture" to refer to "focal concerns" that he argued were the immediate causes of delinquency and crime among lower-class people. He described these as shared thinking patterns that emerged directly from the conditions of lower-class life, having nothing to do with "ultimate human experience." Miller briefly discussed the structural origins of these shared thinking patterns in his original article and did so more extensively in an article published the following year that discussed such factors as immigration, internal migration, and vertical mobility (Miller 1959).

Wolfgang and Ferracuti (1967) used the term "values" to describe the shared ideas that they argue are immediate causes of violent crime. But they defined those values as "normative standards that are part of the repertoire of response which an individual may use as alternatives for action" (p. 114). As in Sutherland and Cressey, the focus is clearly on behavioral expectations in alternate situations, rather than on ultimate human experience. In addition, Wolfgang and Ferracuti did not argue that these values were independent from structure. Rather, they briefly discussed the possible structural conditions that might generate a subculture of violence, although they concluded that "we are not prepared to assert how a subculture arises" (1967, pp. 162–63).

The relation between "culture" and "structure" in "cultural deviance" theories is most clear in Akers's (1985) theory, which focuses on "definitions favorable to deviant behavior." Akers argues that these definitions arise in a structural context, which is then experienced in terms of differential reinforcement. Thus, Akers's theory "specifies the process by which social structure shapes individual behavior" (Akers 1985, p. 66).

More recently, Sullivan (1989) presented a cultural explanation of youth crime but explicitly rejected the "cultural deviance" characterization. Based on modern anthropological theory, Sullivan argued (pp. 242–43):

The notion that culture is a package of beliefs and customs handed down unthinkingly from one generation to the next with no modification of content or function is largely discredited. In that form, culture appears as a mysterious, exogenous force that drives human behavior inexorably and unalterably, and its contents as a mere list of traits that have accumulated accidentally. . . . The black box conception of culture . . . was at the heart of the mistaken theories of the "culture of poverty." . . . [These theories] maintained that poor people are poor because they share and transmit to their children a set of defective values, including unwillingness to defer gratification, a sense of fatalism about their conditions, and an inability to submit to authority.

Sullivan then defined culture as "the shared understandings of those in like circumstances" (p. 244) and proposed a cultural explanation of youth crime that is rooted in the structure of the situation (pp. 246–49). In this explanation, shared or "cultural" ideas are the crucial intervening variable between social structure and individual action.

As evidence against "cultural deviance" theories, Kornhauser (1978) argues that people in similar structural situations can develop similar patterns of thinking without sharing a culture. But in fact, that is essentially what Sutherland, Miller, Wolfgang and Ferracuti, and Akers also argue. These theorists go on to argue that shared patterns of thinking, once structurally generated, can operate as independent and immediate causes of crime via interpersonal transmission.

The "cultural deviance" interpretation of these theories clearly makes integration with other types of criminology theories impossible. However, we argue that, with the possible exception of Sellin's (1938) theory, no criminology theory has ever advanced the "cultural deviance" argument described by Hirschi and Kornhauser. Even Sellin's theory, which is often beaten with the "cultural deviance" club, focused on normative conflicts, not value conflicts. Thus, even it may be closer to the above "structural" interpretation than to the "cultural deviance" interpretation.

"Cultural deviance" theories have much more in common with so-called strain theories than is suggested by Hirschi's and Kornhauser's interpretation. In particular, Hirschi and Kornhauser wrongly argue that the theories of Sutherland, Miller, Wolfgang and Ferracutti, and Akers treat culture as an independent variable, whereas all of them describe structural sources for the cultural ideas in the theory. This makes them comparable to the "strain" theories of Cohen (1955) and Cloward and Ohlin (1960), both of which also describe structural sources for subcultural ideas. Hirschi's argument that these theories are fundamentally incompatible and cannot be integrated is simply wrong.

VI. A New Interpretation of Criminology Theories

The preceding analysis suggests that a crucial point in interpreting a theory is to identify the location of independent variation and the direction of causation. This is consistent with our focus, described above, on variables and the relations among them, rather than on the theories per se. Thus, both "strain" and "cultural deviance" theories locate independent variation in structural characteristics and propose a direction of causation that moves through "cultural" ideas to criminal behavior.

It is interesting to compare Hirschi's most recent theoretical contribution (Gottfredson and Hirschi 1990) with Kornhauser's (1978) with this crucial point in mind. Both of these describe themselves as "control" theories. Yet Kornhauser locates independent variation in social structure (mobility, heterogeneity, and poverty) and argues that they "cause" the individual characteristics of the people in those locations. Gottfredson and Hirschi, in contrast, locate independent variation in the individual characteristics of people (specifically, low "self-control") and argue that they "cause" the person to end up in particular social structural locations, such as those with high mobility, ethnic heterogeneity, and poverty.

Thus, these two theories use similar variables but describe different sources of independent variation and different directions of causation. Therefore, they are fundamentally different theories, despite the fact that they are both classified as "control" theories. To place them in the same category is similar to placing Hirschi's (1969) theory in the same category as Sutherland and Cressey's (1978) because they both describe a relationship between peers and delinquency; these theories use similar variables but describe different sources of independent variation and opposite directions of causation.

We hold that the most fundamental characteristic of any theory is the location of independent variation and the direction of causation. Using this as a focal point for interpreting theories clarifies the relationship theories have to each other and therefore clarifies whether they can be integrated with each other.

A. *Levels of Explanation*

Any attempt to discuss integration must include some discussion of the level of explanation. The terms "micro" and "macro" are often used to describe the level on which a theory is based. These terms can result in confusion, though, since they can mean different things to different people.

For example, Munch and Smelser (1987) point to interpretations of micro—individuals, small social units, individual interactions with limited scope, psychological propositions—and macro—populations, large social units, individual interactions with societal scope (such as value systems), and statements and laws about large-scale social processes. Short (1985) classifies criminology variables into three levels of explanation: individual, micro, and macro. Individual factors are characteristics inherently tied to the single person; the micro-level is concerned with interactional patterns among both groups and individuals; and the macro-level is concerned with properties of societies, cultures, and subcultures.

Such classification systems may be useful, but to some extent the level of explanation is more continuous than categorical. Consider the possible range of factors influencing the action of a member of a gang: his age, which members of the gang he interacts with the most, the gang's organizational structure, the gang's interactions with other gangs, residential density and mobility in the gang's neighborhood, the degree to which the gang's city is in economic transition, and the economic conditions in the country as a whole. Each of these factors can be described as being at a different level of explanation: individual, subgroup, group, intergroup, neighborhood, city, and societal.

While the "level of explanation" has a quasi-continuous nature, the level of the data used to test the theory's arguments is more clearly bifurcated. Specifically, most criminology theories use either individual-level data (such as self-report surveys) or aggregate-level data (such as official crime rates) in measuring their dependent variables. A similar bifurcation can be found in the independent variables in criminology theories where, for example, biological characteristics are individual-level data while residential density and mobility in a neighborhood are aggregate-level data.

Consistent with our focus on variables and the relations among them rather than on theories per se, we believe that levels of explanation are better interpreted in terms of the level of the data used as dependent and independent variables. Viewed this way, it is apparent that most criminology theories require the same level of data for both the independent and dependent variables, rather than proposing, for example, that aggregate-level data can be used to predict individual-level outcomes or vice versa. This means that there are two main types of criminology theories—those using aggregate-level data, and those using individual-level data. Aggregate-level theories link social structural characteristics to variations in the rates and distributions of crime and thus require aggregate-level data both in dependent and independent variables. Individual-level theories, in contrast, link individual characteristics to the probability that an individual will engage in criminal behaviors.

What follows here is a substantial reinterpretation of criminology theories. The first category of theories is similar to Akers's (1985) categorization but differs in that "structure" and "process" are described as separate arguments within the same type of theory rather than as separate types of theories. Despite the use of similar terms, there are significant differences in the interpretation of theories within this category. The second category of theories does not appear in Akers' categorization.

B. Structure/Process Theories

Theories that use aggregate-level data both as dependent and independent variables include what Hirschi calls "strain" and "cultural deviance" theories. A more accurate description of these theories is provided by Akers (1985), who describes them in terms of "structure" and "process."

Akers (1985, p. 66) argues that the so-called strain theories describe "the structure of learning environments likely to produce deviant behavior," while the "cultural deviance" theories describe "the process by which social structure produces individual behavior." Thus, Akers concludes that "social learning is complementary to, not competing with, the structural theories." He also argues that both structural and processual arguments are contained in most criminology theories, although any given theory may emphasize one and minimize the other (Akers 1985, p. 21). This is similar to the relation between "macro" and "micro" theories (e.g., Blau 1987, pp. 82–83) in that each necessarily implies the other, even if theorists often do not make that implication explicit (Alexander 1987, p. 294).

Following Akers, structure/process theories are defined as *theories that explain variations in criminal behavior by variations in social structural characteristics, as manifested in the structured environment to which the individual responds.* In these theories, structural arguments link structural conditions to the rates and distributions of criminal behavior within a society, while process arguments explain why normal individuals who experience those structural conditions are more likely to engage in that behavior.

This type of theory is based on three assertions. First, crime is said to be a response of the individuals who are freely choosing and whose choices are constrained and inspired by the immediate environment (cf. Alexander 1987). This implies a causal relationship between the immediate environment and the actions of individuals within it.

Second, the immediate environment is said to be "structured" in the sense that its most important characteristics, in terms of their effect on the individual's responses, are causally related to the broader structural features of social organization. This assertion transfers the source of independent variation in the theory from the immediate environment to social structure.

Third, criminals are said to be "normal" in that they are essentially similar to noncriminals in the *processes* by which they interact with the immediate environment and in the *motives* that direct their responses to that environment. For example, Akers (1985, p. 66) states: "The basic premise of the social learning approach is that both conforming and deviant behavior are learned in the same way." Sutherland and Cressey (1978, p. 82) state: "While criminal behavior is an expression of general needs and values, it is not explained by those general needs and values, since noncriminal behavior is an expression of the same needs and values." Merton (1938) states that his theory explains crime in terms of the "normal reaction of normal people to abnormal conditions." This assertion eliminates individual differences as a source of independent variation that can be used to explain crime in the theory.

Structure/process theories include not only "strain" and "cultural deviance" theories, but also include "structural" control theories such as Kornhauser's (1978). That theory links variations in the rates and distributions of crime to variations in poverty, heterogeneity, and mobility. Thus, this theory operates entirely at the aggregate level. In addition, it describes essentially normal individuals responding normally to abnormally structured situations. Unlike Hirschi, Kornhauser does not argue that individuals who commit crime are in some sense different from (e.g., less controlled than) individuals who conform.

Classical (e.g., Beccaria 1963) and rational choice (e.g., Cornish and Clarke 1986) theories are probably best interpreted as aggregate-level theories, although they give the appearance of being individual-level. The "structural" arguments in these theories focus on the structure of rewards and punishments implemented by the criminal justice system. As with other aggregate-level theories, the theories argue that individuals respond to the structured environment, so that behaviors take on structural regularities. The "process" arguments in these theories describe all individuals as Hobbesian actors, who are said to be free, rational, and self-interested. These are the "processes" by which normal individuals respond normally to the structured environment.

Classical and rational choice theories are sometimes linked to control theories because they have similar Hobbesian views of human nature. But when viewed in terms of the location of independent variation and the direction of causation, these theories are actually quite different. Classical and rational choice theories describe criminals as well as noncriminals in Hobbesian terms. Thus, independent variation in these theories lies in the structured environment to which the (Hobbesian) individual responds. In contrast, control theories (e.g., Hirschi 1969) describe criminals as Hobbesian but noncriminals as controlled. The source of independent variation in Hirschi's theory lies in individual differences rather than in differences in the structured situations to which the individuals respond.

The same structure/process model is found in research on structural correlates of crime. Some of this research, for example, has focused on the link between economic inequality and the rates and distributions of crime (e.g., Messner and Golden 1992). This research tends to be lightly theorized in that it does not include complex explanations on why these structural conditions may be related to crime. Nevertheless, the researchers attribute independent variation to the structural characteristics (such as economic inequality) and then typically offer at least some explanation of the "process" by which normal people responding normally to these structured situations are more likely to engage in crime (e.g., Blau and Blau 1982).

The structure/process interpretation presented here differs from the strain/control/cultural deviance interpretation in six ways. First, the theories do not argue that there are specific motivations for crime (e.g., frustration), for conformity (e.g., attachments), or for both (e.g., values), nor do they argue that variations in these motivations explain variations in crime. Rather, the theories argue that the motivations for crime are identical to the motivations for noncrime and that variations in crime result when similarly motivated individuals confront differently structured situations. Second, none of the theories describe culture as the ultimate source of independent variation. Rather, all the theories attribute ultimate independent variation to structure. Third, the theories do not describe conforming behavior as the natural behavior of free individuals. Rather, all the theories describe the processes and motivations involved in criminal behavior as being the same as those involved in noncriminal behavior. Fourth, the theories are not deterministic in their explanation of crime. Rather, the theories are better described as positing a Parsonian framework that hypothesizes a freely choosing individual in a socially structured situation (Parsons 1937). Fifth, the theories cannot be grouped into subcategories based on the motivations for crime ("drives") or conformity ("restraints"). Rather, subcategories must be based on the characteristics of the structured situations to which people respond since those exhibit variation while motivations do not. Sixth, the theories cannot be tested with individual-level data that measure the relationship between the characteristics of an individual and the extent of that individual's criminal activity. Rather, all these theories must be tested with aggregate-level data that measure the relationship between socially structured situations and the rates with which individuals in those situations engage in criminal activity.

C. Individual Difference Theories

Individual difference theories are defined as *theories that use variations in characteristics of individuals to predict the probability that an individual will commit crime.* These theories argue that the structural correlates of crime result from pooling, where "birds of a feather flock together." This type of explanation is based on three implicit assertions:

First, differences in the probability of engaging in crime are explained by differences that are uniquely attributed to the individual, such as their biological or psychological characteristics. These individuals have higher probabilities of engaging in criminal behavior regardless of the environment in which they find themselves. In that sense, crime is not a response of a normal individual to an abnormal environment, as described in the structure/process theories.

Second, the individual characteristics may be explained by interactions with other people within the environment (e.g., low self-control may be explained by parental child-rearing techniques), but the environment is not explained by social structural characteristics. Rather, the environment is explained by the characteristics of the individuals who are within it (e.g., the characteristics of the child and parent themselves). This contrasts with the structure/process theories, which explain the immediate environment in terms of broader social structural characteristics.

Third, since crime is explained by individual characteristics, criminals themselves are assumed to be different from noncriminals in some measurable ways. In addition, because criminals represent a minority of the population, criminals can be described as "abnormal" in some sense. Thus, these theories describe "abnormal processes" that contrast with the descriptions of "normal processes" that are a part of structure/process theories.

Biological and psychological theories of crime are the clearest examples of individual difference theories (Vold and Bernard 1986, chaps. 4–7) since they assert that individuals with certain characteristics have an increased probability of committing crime regardless of the situation in which they find themselves. These must be distinguished from theories that use biological and psychological research to explain why normal individuals have an increased likelihood of committing crime in certain structured situations (Bernard 1990).

Among social theories, Hirschi's (1969) appears to attribute independent variation to characteristics of the individuals and the immediate environment. However, the variable "commitment" in Hirschi's theory may describe structural rather than individual variation, and Hirschi's theoretical arguments about belief indicate that it may have structural roots (Bernard 1987c, 1989). In addition, attachment can be interpreted to be the result of broader structural factors (e.g., Sampson 1987). Thus, Hirschi's theory may attribute independent variation to individual characteristics, to social structure, or to both.

The more recent theory by Gottfredson and Hirschi (1990) is more clearly at the individual level. Low self-control is defined as entirely an individual characteristic (pp. 90–91). The structural correlates of crime are then explained as a "consequence of low self-control—i.e., people with low self-control sort themselves and are sorted into a variety of circumstances that are *as a result* correlated with crime" (p. 119).

Thus, this theory matches the description above of an individual difference theory.

D. *The Relation between Structure/Process Theories and Individual Difference Theories*

Given the contrast drawn above between individual difference theories and structure/process theories, one might imagine that these theories are mutually exclusive in that they contradict each other's major arguments. In fact, this is not the case.

Individual difference theories could argue that no independent variation whatsoever can be explained by structural characteristics. No such theories actually do this. All biological and psychological theories acknowledge that social factors also carry independent variation (e.g., Mednick et al. 1982). Among social theories of individual difference, Hirschi (1969) includes structural elements in his variables of commitment, attachment, and belief, as described above. Gottfredson and Hirschi (1990) argue that structurally generated changes in criminal opportunities, described as "routine activities" (Cohen and Felson 1979), provide an additional source of independent variation besides low self-control.

Similarly, structural variation theories could argue that no independent variation whatsoever can be explained by individual characteristics. On first impression, many of these theories appear to do this with ideological fervor. However, this is an unreasonable position in terms of the theories themselves. Even in the most criminogenic situations, many individuals remain noncriminal. This can only be explained through some individual-level variation related to the probability of engaging in crime.

The appropriate relation between individual difference and structural/process theories is modeled by the relation between the theories of low self-control (Gottfredson and Hirschi 1990) and routine activities (Cohen and Felson 1979). Routine activities theorists control for individual differences but do not deny their existence or their relation to the likelihood of engaging in crime. Rather, they assume that there is a "constant supply of motivated offenders" and that variations in the rates and distributions of crime can be explained solely by changes in the structured situation. In contrast, self-control theorists control for variations in the structure of the situation, but they do not deny the existence of such variations or their relationship to the rates and distributions of crime. Rather, they maintain that, within any given situation, people with certain characteristics are more likely to engage in crime than people with other characteristics.

This parallels the relationship found in explanations of unemployment. The rates and distributions of unemployment (whether it is high or low, whether it is concentrated in the Northeast or the Southwest) are normally explained entirely by structural factors. At the same time, within any given structural situation, people with some individual characteristics are more likely to be unemployed—for example, those with low education and poor job skills. Economists do not normally argue that there are more people with low education and poor job skills in times and places of high unemployment. Even though those characteristics are highly related to probability of being unemployed at the individual level, they usually have not been used in aggregate-level theories explaining the unemployment rate. Similarly, criminologists can argue that rates and distributions of crime are entirely explained by social structural factors and, at the same time, argue that, within particular structural situations, people with certain characteristics are more likely to engage in crime than people with other characteristics.

VII. Research Implications

This analysis of criminology theories has two implications for research methodology. The first is straightforward: *the level of data analysis must correspond to the level of theoretical argument*. In particular, individual-level analysis of data cannot test any component of a structure/process theory without resulting in some variation of the "ecological fallacy" (Robinson 1950).

Most criminology theories, including "strain" and "cultural deviance" theories, make aggregate-level arguments. Even the process arguments in these theories attribute independent variation to the structural conditions to which individuals respond and hold individual characteristics themselves constant. But because of the strain/control/cultural deviance interpretation, criminologists often have tested these theories with individual-level analysis of self-reported data.

That criminologists have repeatedly violated this self-evident point suggests that there is a complex theoretical issue that lies behind it. This issue is revealed by examining the apparently subtle distinction between "normal process" arguments in structure/process theories and "abnormal" process arguments in individual difference theories. This distinction actually is not subtle at all. It demonstrates the relationship between the two types of theories and why they can be integrated with each other.

All individual characteristics exhibit variation. Individual difference theories treat that variation as the independent variable and use individual-level analysis of data to predict probabilities that individuals will engage in criminal behavior. In essence, this research strategy controls for but does not necessarily deny the existence of structural characteristics that also may be related to crime. As indicated above, the theories themselves generally are phrased in much the same way.

Similarly, structure/process theories are aggregate-level theories, so the assumption about "normal process" should be interpreted as referring to populations rather than as making an assertion about all individuals. These theories assume there is a *normal distribution* of individual-level characteristics within a given structural situation. The normal distribution is then treated as a constant, and the characteristics of the situation are treated as the independent variable. The normal distribution, of course, can include many "abnormal" people, and these "abnormal" people may have an increased probability of engaging in crime. Thus, structure/process theories control for individual differences by dealing at the aggregate level with a normal distribution of individual characteristics, but they do not necessarily deny the existence of those differences or their possible relation to criminality.

While the first implication appears obvious, the second is less so, but stunning: *competitive testing of criminology theories, which aims at the falsification of at least some of those theories, may only rarely be appropriate.* Given two types of theories, three types of competitive tests are possible: structure/process versus individual difference, individual difference versus individual difference, and structure/process versus structure/process.

Structure/process theories cannot be tested against individual difference theories because, as the first implication states, the level of the data analysis must correspond to the level of the theoretical argument. Thus, these theories cannot be tested with the same kind of data. The proper relation between these types of theories is modeled by the relation between self-control and routine activities theories. These are complementary theories, and competitive testing can only be accomplished by distorting one or both of the theories.

This implication is consistent with the description above of "normal" versus "abnormal" process since neither type of theory denies the assertions of the other type of theory. Rather, each type of theory uses research techniques that effectively control for the variation described by the other type of theory. Thus, these types of theories simply are not competitive and cannot be tested against each other.

Competitive testing of two or more individual difference theories also seems inappropriate. These theories always have been associated with multiple-factor causation (Vold 1958). Within this perspective, different theories are conceived as making different but not contradictory predictions, and the competition among them concerns the amount of variation explained by particular variables and therefore by particular theories. This means the various individual-level theories can be integrated with each other if research indicates such integration is useful. To some extent, this approach remains so close to the data that it can be described as atheoretical (Laub and Sampson 1991; Sampson and Laub 1993).

Competitive testing of two or more "structure/process" theories may also be inappropriate. We argued above, citing Akers (1985), that the structural arguments in these theories cannot be tested against the processual arguments in them. That means that we must consider here whether structural arguments can be competitively tested against other structural arguments and processual arguments against other processual arguments.

Boiled down to a bare minimum, the structural arguments within these theories argue that certain structural characteristics are associated with certain rates and distributions of crime. Many such characteristics have been identified by different structural theories, such as the absence of legitimate economic opportunities (Merton 1938); the presence of illegitimate economic opportunities (Cloward and Ohlin 1960); the absence of legitimate status opportunities (Cohen 1955); poverty, heterogeneity, mobility (Kornhauser 1978); economic inequality (Messner and Golden 1992); discrimination, urbanization, social isolation (Bernard 1990); and criminal opportunities due to routine activities (Cohen and Felson 1979).

These theories certainly are *different* from each other, but there is no theoretical reason why they necessarily *contradict* each other. Rather, it seems reasonable to assume that there is "multiple-factor causation" for the rates and distributions of crime, much as there is for individual criminal behavior. If that is the case, then the competition among the structural arguments within structure/process theories would be similar to that among individual difference theories. The question would concern the amount of variation in the rates and distributions explained by a particular variable and, therefore, by a particular theory. It also means that structural arguments could be integrated with each other if research indicates it is useful.

This looks dangerously close to Hirschi's criticism that integrationists believe different theories "own" different variables. Our point, however, is that the variables themselves and the relations among them should be the focus of attention, not the theory to which they "belong." Once the focus is on the variables and relationships, then there seems little reason to believe that the theories contradict each other. Rather, the competition among them is empirical rather than theoretical.

Only with processual arguments is there reason to believe that competitive testing may be useful. These arguments describe the processes by which normal individuals who experience certain structural conditions become more likely to engage in criminal behavior. Using Kornhauser's (1978) theory as an example, why are normal individuals who live in neighborhoods characterized by poverty, ethnic heterogeneity, and residential mobility more likely to engage in criminal behavior than normal individuals who live in neighborhoods characterized by wealth, ethnic homogeneity, and residential stability? Like other structure and process theories, Kornhauser explains variations in crime rates entirely by variations in structural conditions. Nevertheless, the processual arguments are an important part of a complete explanation of crime.

It is at this point that conceptualizations such as strain, control, and cultural deviance become relevant. It could be, as Kornhauser argues, that structural conditions free individuals from social controls, which then is the immediate cause of criminal behavior. Or it could be that structural conditions impose negative experiences on the individual, which then are the immediate cause of criminal behavior (e.g., Agnew 1992). Or it could be that the structural conditions generate shared ideas that then are the immediate cause of criminal behaviors (e.g., Bernard 1990). It is possible (although not entirely clear) that these conceptualizations of normal processes are incompatible and could be tested against each other with the expectation that no more than one of them will be supported. Even if this were the case, however, this seems like a relatively minor place for competitive testing in criminology theories.

VIII. Practical Considerations

Broad integration is possible both between and within the categories of criminology theories. Structural and processual arguments are two sides of the same structure/process theories—each theoretical argument requires the other to be a complete theory, so that they cannot in any way be taken as incompatible. Structure/process theories and individual difference theories could contradict each other, but none of them do. All of those theories control for the variation explained by the other type of theories rather than deny it. Structural arguments can be integrated with other structural arguments and individual difference theories with other individual difference theories since the competition among these is empirical rather than theoretical. Only processual arguments may contradict other processual arguments in the sense that competitive testing may be useful.

If our arguments are correct, it would seem possible to create a single theory of crime that incorporates the structural conditions that are associated with higher crime rates, the processes that explain why normal individuals who experience these structural conditions are more likely to engage in crime, and the individual characteristics that make it more or less likely that an individual will engage in crime regardless of structural conditions. But that is not the same thing as arguing that we *should* construct such integrations. Convoluting Kurt Lewin a bit, a theory is nothing if it is not useful. We should only integrate broadly if it is useful. We raised some of these same concerns in our discussion of Vila's (1994) paradigm above.

In general, practical limitations on integration arise from the complexity of the resulting theories. For example, such complexity may make it undesirable to propose a formal integration of Gottfredson and Hirschi's (1990) individual-level theory of low self-control and Cohen and Felson's (1979) theory of routine activities. It may be better to agree that these two theories are compatible and complementary and then continue to work on them as separate theories.

Full integration between the two categories of theories would entail an enormous range of new complexities. For example, we implied above that structural characteristics are separate from the characteristics of individuals within those structures. But it seems likely that structure is created both subjectively and objectively by individuals and in turn affects those individuals (Giddens 1979). Individual characteristics and structural characteristics are inherently related in a nonrecursive fashion. Building this relationship into an integrated theory may be utterly impractical. Our major point in this essay is that such integration is possible, not that it is desirable. That is, we have attempted to refute Hirschi's argument that criminology theories are largely incompatible and cannot be integrated.

Other practical limitations would arise from the complexity of data analysis that would be required to test the resulting theories. Just as sociologists still have not come to terms with theoretical transitions from micro to macro levels, and vice versa, they have not totally resolved the complexities involved in moving between the individual and the aggregate levels of data analysis. We know it is possible to move between these levels without falling into statistical errors, but this is complex and may best be avoided at present.

While integrating previously existing theories across levels of explanation may be undesirable, new theories that incorporate arguments at both of these levels of explanation may be both useful and feasible. For example, multilevel explanations of individual criminal behavior, using a contextual approach, seem both desirable and feasible. The effect of specific individual differences on behavior may be magnified or attenuated depending on the individual's structural position. Therefore, incorporating structure as a contextual variable may add additional variation to the individual-level explanation of individual criminal behavior.

Such theories explain individual-level variation in criminal behavior using both individual differences and the interaction between individual differences and structural position. When explaining individual differences with a combination of individual and structural explanations, it is easy to avoid committing an ecological fallacy. Additionally, the last decade has resulted in a tool kit of sophisticated multilevel statistical software designed to ensure the accuracy of models that employ concepts across levels of explanation (e.g., Bryk and Raudenbush 1992).

Finally, for practical reasons, we have ignored what Vold and Bernard (1986) call "theories of the behavior of criminal law" in this discussion of integration. We believe that these theories can and should be integrated with the "theories of criminal behavior" discussed here (see Bernard 1989). However, this essay is sufficiently complex that the inclusion of that additional material seemed unwise.

Regardless of the extent to which theories are integrated in practice, it is time to recognize that it is possible to do so in principle and to stop the widespread competitive testing of criminology theories. Such testing is a waste of time and money, just as it would be a waste of time and money to test Gottfredson and Hirschi's (1990) theory against Cohen and Felson's (1979). Between categories, criminology theories are complementary and simply do not compete with each other at all. Within categories, most of the competition among the theories is empirical rather than theoretical. By looking at theories in terms of variables and the relations among them, we can build a more powerful criminology that explains increased portions of the variance.

REFERENCES

Agnew, R. S. 1992. "Foundation for a General Strain Theory of Crime and Delinquency." *Criminology* 30:47–87.

Akers, R. L. 1985. *Deviant Behavior: A Social Learning Approach.* Belmont, Calif.: Wadsworth.

———. 1989. "A Social Behavioralist's Perspective on Integration of Theories of Crime and Deviance." In *Theoretical Integration in the Study of Deviance and Crime,* edited by S. F. Messner, M. D. Krohn, and A. E. Liska. Albany, N.Y.: SUNY Press.

Alexander, J. C. 1987. "Action and Its Environments." In *The Macro-Micro Link,* edited by J. C. Alexander, B. Giesen, R. Munch, and N. J. Smelser. Berkeley and Los Angeles: University of California Press.

Beccaria, C. 1963. *On Crimes and Punishments.* Indianapolis, Ind.: Bobbs-Merrill.

Bernard, T. J. 1984. "Control Criticisms of Strain Theories." *Journal of Research in Crime and Delinquency* 21:353–72.

———. 1987a. "Testing Structural Strain Theories." *Journal of Research in Crime and Delinquency* 24:262–80.

———. 1987b. "Reply to Agnew." *Journal of Research in Crime and Delinquency* 24:287–90.

———. 1987c. "Structure and Control." *Justice Quarterly* 4:409-24.

———. 1989. "A Theoretical Approach to Integration." In *Theoretical Integration in the Study of Deviance and Crime,* edited by S. F. Messner, M. D. Krohn, and A. E. Liska. Albany, N.Y.: SUNY Press.

———. 1990. "Angry Aggression among the 'Truly Disadvantaged.'" *Criminology* 28:73–96.

———. 1991. "Twenty Years of Testing Theories." *Journal of Research in Crime and Delinquency* 27:325–47.

Bernard, T., and R. Ritti. 1990. "The Role of Theory in Scientific Research." In *Measurement Issues in Criminology,* edited by K. Kempf. New York: Springer-Verlag.

Blau, J. R., and P. M. Blau. 1982. "The Cost of Inequality." *American Sociological Review* 47:114–29.

Blau, P. M. 1987. "Contrasting Theoretical Perspectives." In *The Macro-Micro Link,* edited by J. C. Alexander, B. Giesen, R. Munch, and N. Smelser. Berkeley and Los Angeles: University of California Press.

Braithwaite, J. 1989. *Crime, Shame, and Reintegration*. Cambridge: Cambridge University Press.

———. 1993. "Pride in Criminological Dissensus." *Law and Social Inquiry* 18:501–12.

Bryk, A. S., and S. W. Raudenbush. 1992. *Hierarchical Linear Models*. Newbury Park, Calif.: Sage.

Burgess, R. L., and R. L. Akers. 1968. "A Differential Association—Reinforcement Theory of Criminal Behavior." *Social Problems* 14:128–47.

Burton, V. S., Jr., and F. T. Cullen. 1992. "The Empirical Status of Strain Theory." *Journal of Crime and Justice* 15:1–30.

Cloward, R., and L. E. Ohlin. 1960. *Delinquency and Opportunity*. New York: Free Press.

Cohen, A. 1955. *Delinquent Boys*. New York: Free Press.

Cohen, L. E., and M. Felson. 1979. "Social Change and Crime Rate Trends: A Routine Activity Approach." *American Sociological Review* 44:588–608.

Cohen, L. E., and R. Machalek. 1988. "A General Theory of Expropriative Crime." *American Journal of Sociology* 94:465–501.

Cornish, D. B., and R. V. Clarke. 1986. *The Reasoning Criminal*. New York: Springer-Verlag.

Cullen, F. T. 1983. *Rethinking Crime and Deviance Theory*. Totowa, N.J.: Rowman & Allenheld.

———. 1988. "Were Cloward and Ohlin Strain Theorists?" *Journal of Research in Crime and Delinquency* 25:214–41.

Edwards, W. J. 1992. "Predicting Juvenile Delinquency." *Justice Quarterly* 9:553–83.

Elliott, D. 1985. "The Assumption That Theories Can Be Combined with Increased Explanatory Power." In *Theoretical Methods in Criminology*, edited by R. F. Meier. Beverly Hills, Calif.: Sage.

Elliott, D., S. Ageton, and R. Cantor. 1979. "An Integrated Theoretical Perspective on Delinquent Behavior." *Journal of Research in Crime and Delinquency* 16:3–27.

Elliott, D., D. Huizinga, and S. S. Ageton. 1985. *Explaining Delinquency and Drug Use*. Beverly Hills, Calif.: Sage.

Geis, G., and R. Meier. 1978. "Looking Backward and Forward." *Criminology* 16:273–88.

Gibbs, J. 1985. "The Methodology of Theory Construction in Criminology." In *Theoretical Methods in Criminology*, edited by R. F. Meier. Beverly Hills, Calif.: Sage.

Gibbs, J., and M. Erickson. 1975. "Major Developments in the Sociological Study of Deviance." *Annual Review of Sociology* 1:21–41.

Giddens, A. 1979. *Central Problems in Social Theory: Action, Structure, and Contradiction in Social Analysis*. London: Macmillan; Berkeley and Los Angeles: University of California Press.

Gottfredson, M. R., and T. Hirschi. 1990. *A General Theory of Crime*. Stanford, Calif.: Stanford University Press.

Hagan, J. 1988. *Structural Criminology*. New Brunswick, N.J.: Rutgers University Press.

Hagan, J., A. R. Gillis, and J. Simpson. 1985. "The Class Structure of Gender and Delinquency: Toward a Power-Control Theory of Common Delinquent Behavior." *American Journal of Sociology* 90:1151–78.

Hagan, J., and A. Palloni. 1986. "Toward a Structural Criminology." *Annual Review of Sociology* 12:431–49.

Hirschi, T. 1969. *Causes of Delinquency*. Berkeley: University of California Press.

———. 1979. "Separate but Unequal Is Better." *Journal of Research in Crime and Delinquency* 16:34–38.

———. 1989. "Exploring Alternatives to Integrated Theory." In *Theoretical Integration in the Study of Deviance and Crime*, edited by S. F. Messner, M. D. Krohn, and A. E. Liska. Albany, N.Y.: SUNY Press.

Jeffery, C. R. 1989. *Criminology*. Englewood Cliffs, N.J.: Prentice-Hall.

Katz, J. 1989. *The Seductions of Crime*. New York: Basic.

Kornhauser, R. R. 1978. *Social Sources of Delinquency*. Chicago: University of Chicago Press.

Laub, J., and R. Sampson. 1991. "The Sutherland-Glueck Debate." *American Journal of Sociology* 96:1402–40.

Liska, A. 1971. "Aspirations, Expectations, and Delinquency." *Sociological Quarterly* 12:99–107.

Liska, A. E., M. D. Krohn, and S. F. Messner. 1989. "Strategies and Requisites for Theoretical Integration in the Study of Crime and Deviance." In *Theoretical Integration in the Study of Deviance and Crime*, edited by S. F. Messner, M. D. Krohn, and A. E. Liska. Albany, N.Y.: SUNY Press.

Mawson, A. R. 1987. *Transient Criminality*. New York: Praeger.

Mednick, S., V. Pollock, J. Volavka, and W. F. Gabrielli, Jr. 1982. "Biology and Violence." In *Criminal Violence*, edited by M. E. Wolfgang and N. A. Weiner. Beverly Hills, Calif.: Sage.

Meier, R. 1980. "The Arrested Development of Criminological Theory." *Contemporary Sociology* 9:374–76.

———. 1985. "An Introduction to Theoretical Methods in Criminology." In *Theoretical Methods in Criminology*, edited by R. Meier. Beverly Hills, Calif.: Sage.

Merton, R. K. 1938. "Social Structure and Anomie." *American Sociological Review* 3:672–82.

Messner, S. F. 1985. "Sex Differences in Arrest Rates for Homicide." *Comparative Social Research* 8:187–201.

———. 1988. "Merton's 'Social Structure and Anomie': The Road Not Taken." *Deviant Behavior* 9:33–53.

Messner, S. F., and R. M. Golden. 1992. "Racial Inequality and Racially Disaggregated Homicide Rates." *Criminology* 30:421–47.

Messner, S. F., and R. Rosenfeld. 1994. *Crime and the American Dream*. Belmont, Calif.: Wadsworth.

Miller, W. B. 1958. "Lower Class Culture as a Generating Milieu of Gang Delinquency." *Journal of Social Issues* 14(3):5–19.

———. 1959. "Implications of Urban Lower Class Culture for Social Work." *Social Service Review* 33:219–36.

Munch, R., and N. J. Smelser. 1987. "Conclusion." In *The Micro-Macro Link*, edited by J. C. Alexander, B. Giesen, R. Munch, and N. J. Smelser. Berkeley and Los Angeles: University of California Press.

Parsons, T. 1937. *Structure of Social Action*. New York: Free Press.

Pearson, F., and N. Weiner. 1985. "Toward an Integration of Criminological Theories." *Journal of Criminal Law and Criminology* 76:116–50.

Robinson, W. S. 1950. "Ecological Correlations and the Behavior of Individuals." *American Sociological Review* 15:351–57.

Rosenfeld, R. 1989. "Robert Merton's Contributions to the Sociology of Deviance." *Sociological Inquiry* 59:453–66.

Sagarin, E., and A. Karmen. 1978. "Criminology and the Reaffirmation of Humanist Ideals." *Criminology* 16:239–54.

Sampson, R. J. 1987. "Urban Black Violence." *American Journal of Sociology* 93:348–82.

Sampson, R., and J. Laub. 1993. *Crime in the Making*. Cambridge, Mass.: Harvard University Press.

Schwendinger, H., and J. S. Schwendinger. 1985. *Adolescent Subcultures and Delinquency*. New York: Praeger.

Sellin, T. 1938. *Culture Conflict and Crime*. New York: Social Science Research Council.

Shaw, C., and H. D. McKay. 1942. *Juvenile Delinquency and Urban Areas*. Chicago: University of Chicago Press.

Short, J. F. 1979. "On the Etiology of Delinquent Behavior." *Journal of Research in Crime and Delinquency* 16:28–33.

———. 1985. "The Level of Explanation Problem in Criminology." In *Theoretical Methods in Criminology*, edited by R. F. Meier. Beverly Hills, Calif.: Sage.

Stinchcombe, A. L. 1975. "Merton's Theory of Social Structure." In *The Idea of Social Structure*, edited by L. Coser. New York: Harcourt Brace Jovanovich.

Sullivan, M. L. 1989. *Getting Paid*. Ithaca, N.Y.: Cornell University Press.

Sutherland, E. H. 1947. *Criminology*. 4th ed. Philadelphia: Lippincott.

Sutherland, E. H., and D. R. Cressey. 1978. *Criminology*. Philadelphia: Lippincott.

Thornberry, T. P. 1987. "Toward an Interactional Theory of Delinquency." *Criminology* 25:863–87.

———. 1989. "Reflections on the Advantages and Disadvantages of Theoretical Integration." In *Theoretical Integration in the Study of Deviance and Crime*, edited by S. F. Messner, M. D. Krohn, and A. E. Liska. Albany, N.Y.: SUNY Press.

Thornberry, T. P., A. J. Lizotte, M. D. Krohn, M. Farnworth, and S. J. Jang. 1991. "Testing Interactional Theory: An Examination of Reciprocal Causal Relationships Among Family, School and Delinquency." *Journal of Criminal Law and Criminology* 82:3–35.

———. 1994. "Delinquent Peers, Beliefs, and Delinquent Behavior: A Longitudinal Test of Interactional Theory." *Criminology* 32:47–83.

Tittle, C. R. 1989. "Prospects for Synthetic Theory." In *Theoretical Integration in the Study of Deviance and Crime*, edited by S. F. Messner, M. D. Krohn, and A. E. Liska. Albany, N.Y.: SUNY Press.

Uggen, C. 1993*a*. "Reintegrating Braithwaite: Shame and Consensus in Criminological Theory." *Law and Social Inquiry* 18:481–500.

———.1993*b*. "Beyond Calvin and Hobbes: Rationality and Exchange in a Theory of Moralizing Shaming." *Law and Social Inquiry* 18:513–16.

Vila, B. 1994. "A General Paradigm for Understanding Criminal Behavior: Extending Evolutionary Ecological Theory." *Criminology* 32:311–60.

Vold, G. B. 1958. *Theoretical Criminology*. New York: Oxford.

Vold, G. B., and T. J. Bernard. 1986. *Theoretical Criminology*. New York: Oxford.

Walters, G. 1992. *Foundations of Criminal Science*. New York: Praeger.

Weis, J. 1987. "From the Editor: Special Issue on Theory." *Criminology* 25:783–84.

Williams, F. 1984. "The Demise of the Criminological Imagination." *Justice Quarterly* 1:91–106.

Wilson, J. Q. 1983. *Thinking about Crime*. Rev. ed. New York: Basic.

Wilson, J. Q., and R. J. Herrnstein. 1985. *Crime and Human Nature*. New York: Simon & Schuster.

Wolfgang, M. E., and F. Ferracuti. 1967. *The Subculture of Violence*. London: Tavistock.

Wolfgang, M. E., R. Figlio, and T. Thornberry. 1978. *Evaluating Criminology*. New York: Elsevier.

Thomas M. Mieczkowski

The Prevalence of Drug Use in the United States

ABSTRACT

The four major sources of data on the prevalence of use of illicit drugs—the National Household Survey on Drug Abuse, the High School Senior Survey (Monitoring the Future), the Drug Abuse Warning Network, and the Drug Use Forecasting System—tell us much that we want to know about drug abuse patterns and trends but not enough. The first two are self-report surveys of representative national samples, but they undercount (or exclude) high-risk groups like the homeless and active offenders. There is also doubt about the external validity of their findings. The last two have design characteristics that prevent generalization to the entire population. Recent changes in the surveys and use of synthetic techniques is improving capacity to make reliable national estimates of drug use prevalence, but current estimates differ by orders of magnitude.

Drug prevalence studies attempt to count how many people use illicit drugs and how often. Other important questions are who uses drugs, including racial, ethnic, gender, class, age, and other breakdowns, and how the population of drug users is changing over time. There are a number of rationales for the considerable (and expensive) contemporary efforts to measure the prevalence of illicit drug use. First, there is intellectual curiosity. Scholars in many disciplines have long been interested in drug phenomena because the use of psychoactive drugs is itself an ancient phenomenon (Weil 1986; Anglin, Caulkins, and Hser 1993). Second, if drug control policy is to be understood, drug prevalence data are useful and even necessary. Third, prevalence data,

Tom Mieczkowski is professor of criminology at the University of South Florida, St. Petersburg.

especially trend information, are necessary to evaluate the effects and outcomes of drug policy choices.

Rational policy making depends on knowledge about patterns of drug use and the effects of policy initiatives on those patterns. It has, however, been argued that drug policy is driven by factors other than epidemiological prevalence data (Kleiman 1992; Reuter 1993):

> For conscientious policy makers dealing with drug problems at the national and local level, prevalence estimation ought to be a fundamental element of sensible decision making, which is impossible without knowing the scale of the drug problem and how it is changing. In fact, prevalence estimates have so far been used primarily as gross measures to show the nation has a large drug problem. Most drug policy decisions, such as the allocation of resources among different kinds of programs, are now made without regard to what has been learned from prevalence estimation. Nor has the potential of prevalence estimation been realized as an adjunct to evaluation of policy or program choices. Estimates of consumption and expenditure have not even played a gross role, serving purely ritualistic goals. [Reuter 1993, p. 167]

What have we learned? Four prominent and influential sources of data are available to answer questions about drug use patterns—The Drug Abuse Warning Network (DAWN), The National Household Survey on Drug Abuse (NHSDA), Monitoring the Future (MTF; commonly called the High School Senior Survey), and the Drug Use Forecasting System (DUF). (Detailed descriptions of these surveys are provided in Secs. II–IV.) Over the long term—fifteen to twenty years—the two major surveys, NHSDA and MTF, showed first a rise and then a fall in the general prevalence rates for *all* illicit drugs. However, depending on how the data are organized, certain measures—like the proportions of people who have used drugs in their lifetimes, for example—continue to increase in trend graphs as the demographic "bump" of the most drug-active generational components matures. However, when current or very recent drug use is examined, it is clear that levels of drug use have decreased notably. Figure 1 shows this general trend.

Figure 1 presents data from the NHSDA and the MTF surveys of self-reported drug use. The MTF data show the percentages of high school student and young adult respondents who answered "yes" when

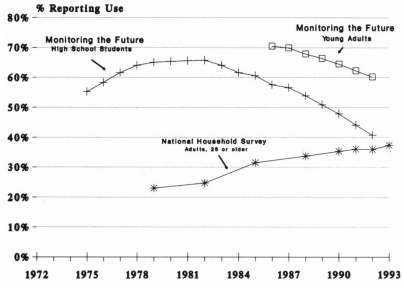

Fig. 1.—General drug trends, lifetime use, Monitoring the Future and the National Household Survey on Drug Abuse. Sources: Johnston, O'Malley, and Bachman (1992); National Institute on Drug Abuse (1993a, 1993d, 1994b). Note: Drug categories for both surveys are comparable. They are marijuana, heroin, cocaine, hallucinogens, inhalants, tranquilizers, sedatives, and stimulants. (None of the figures in this essay include alcohol or tobacco, except figure 15 from the Drug Abuse Warning Network, which includes alcohol.)

asked if they have ever used any illicit drug. The data from the NHSDA include only adults who are twenty-six years of age and older. The MTF data are either high school seniors or "young adults" (eighteen to twenty-six), as labeled on the graph. For younger Americans (persons twenty-six years of age or less), lifetime drug use prevalence has fallen consistently for the last twelve years. While the NHSDA data show consistent increases of lifetime use over that period for adults twenty-six and older, that is inherent in measures of lifetime exposure (it reflects the higher levels of use in earlier decades of people who are aging). Measures of current use (i.e., last thirty days) show declines for all age groups. Figure 2 shows the trend since 1979 for reporting current or thirty-day use for the NHSDA. When NHSDA data are stratified by age, persons from eighteen to twenty-five years old show the most marked decrease in self-reported current use of drugs, followed by youth (twelve to seventeen), and then adults twenty-six years and older.

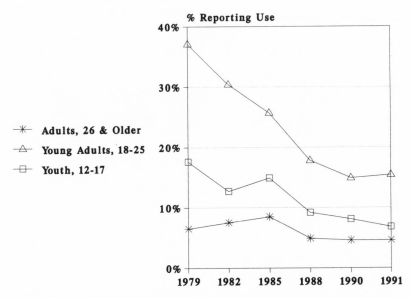

Fig. 2.—General illicit drug trends, National Household Survey on Drug Abuse: use in previous thirty days, any illicit drug. Sources: National Institute on Drug Abuse (1993*a*). Note: Drugs include marijuana, heroin, cocaine, hallucinogens, inhalants, tranquilizers, sedatives, and stimulants.

Figure 3 presents data from DAWN, which is based on hospital emergency room events, or "mentions" as recorded by an official DAWN observer, or outcome data from medical examiners' investigations into suspicious deaths. The Drug Abuse Warning Network is an incident-based medical measure both of "illness" associated with drug use (emergency room mentions) and of death associated with drug use (the medical examiners' reports). The general DAWN data trends show that morbidity and mortality, if measured as a direct consequence of drug use, are relatively stable. They also indicate that only a tiny fraction of all persons exposed to drugs experience measurable mortality or morbidity effects. When DAWN data are examined in detail, alcohol is much more strongly associated with the onset of morbidity and mortality than is any other psychoactive substance.

Drug Use Forecast trend data are shown in figure 4, which displays urinalysis outcomes of arrestees from five selected cities. These data show that drug use prevalence among criminally involved populations appears markedly higher than in the general population. While there are some slight downward trends, the general prevalence pattern measured by DUF has remained relatively stable over the last five years.

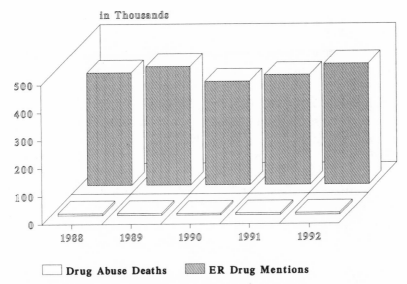

FIG. 3.—Drug Abuse Warning Network, National Trend Data from 1988 to 1992. Sources: National Institute on Drug Abuse (1994c, 1994e).

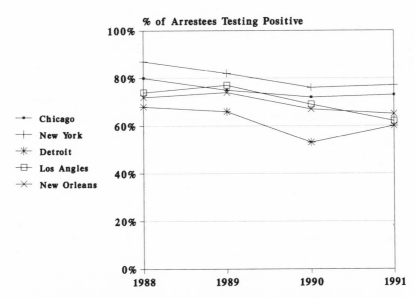

FIG. 4.—Drug use forecast trends for five select cities, 1988–91. Percentage of arrestees testing positive by urinalysis for any illicit drug. Source: National Institute of Justice (1993). Note: Drugs include cannabinoids, opiates, cocaine, amphetamines, barbiturates, tranquilizers, diazepam, methaqualone, PCP, and Darvon.

It is important to bear in mind that the DAWN and DUF data, unlike MTF and NHSDA, do not reflect self-reported drug use. The Drug Abuse Warning Network is based on clinical observations or post-mortem examinations, and DUF data report principally the age, race, gender, charge, and the urinalysis results of its subjects.

Comparing these measurement systems raises concerns, of course, because they use different methodologies. Broadly, there are two sets of issues. First, to what degree are the different systems comparable? Since they look at the phenomenon differently, how does that affect the validity of comparisons of their findings? Second, each system has a particular methodology it uses to accomplish its measurement goals. Considering each system as a stand-alone, how do the method-ological features influence the data, and how should the data from each be "weighed" (if at all) when examined for purposes of general estimation?

All the systems are professionally managed and have changed over time in response to criticisms, and they continue to make meaningful efforts at quality control and improvement. Each, however, has intrin-sic limitations, and none alone captures the "truth" of drug prevalence. Both of the self-report surveys suffer from a lack of external validation, especially the use of bioassays to gauge the accuracy of self-reported levels and frequencies of use. This is a growing problem as drug use has increasingly been stigmatized in the last ten years, which likely inhibits frank reporting. The DUF system, based on urinalyses of persons arrested for felonies, does not employ a random sample, and thus its generalizability is restricted. The DAWN system has suffered from sample degradation and lost its representative character, a condi-tion that has only recently been rectified. Thus its long-term integrity for analyzing trends has been compromised.

This essay examines each of these four systems in detail, highlights their strengths and weaknesses, and offers suggestions for improve-ments. The essay is organized into six sections. Section I briefly men-tions attempts to estimate drug prevalence in earlier generations (the appendix provides more detail) and introduces important epidemiologi-cal concepts. Section II discusses the two major self-report surveys, the NHSDA and the MTF, presents current findings, and considers criticisms of both surveys. Sections III and IV discuss the DAWN and DUF systems. Section V examines recent attempts to integrate these findings using synthetic estimation techniques. Synthetic estima-tion attempts to correct for biases in self-report surveys and offers plausible ways to compensate for errors in data sources and to integrate data drawn from different populations and gathered by distinct methodologies. Section VI contains concluding observations.

I. Drug Use Epidemiology

Drug epidemiology has a long history in the United States, going back at least to the eighteenth century. Many problems associated with current drug prevalence measures are reminiscent of early periods. Several histories (e.g., Musto 1973; Morgan 1974; Courtwright 1982; Courtwright, Joseph, and Des Jarlais 1989) have described the social climate surrounding drug consumption in earlier eras as generally anxious, moralistic, and, after 1914, fearful. Because of this, as Courtwright (1982, p. 9) observes, "reconstructing the pattern of opiate addiction in the United States is difficult, not only because addicts tend to conceal their condition, but because much of the historical evidence has been exaggerated and distorted."

Two complications—skepticism about self-reported survey data and the effect on data of a highly charged political and moral climate—occur in our own era. They affect all categories of prevalence estimation and various types of deviant and illegal behavior (Mieczkowski et al. 1992; Wish 1993). The appendix offers a brief summary of efforts in earlier periods to estimate the prevalence of drug use.

In 1938, when the first methodical studies of drug addiction got underway at the Lexington Narcotics Farm in Kentucky, Dr. Lawrence Kolb submitted a proposal for a study on the "epidemiology" of heroin use to the Public Health Service. It was sent back for revision. "Drug addiction," a Public Health Service supervisor cannily noted, "is not a contagious disease" (Latimer and Goldberg 1981, p. 4).

Despite the rebuke to Kolb that drug use was not a "contagious disease," the concepts used to describe drug prevalence are largely taken from medical epidemiology. This paradigm was developed by adapting methods developed in the study of infectious diseases and the analysis of associated contagion patterns.

While some concepts used in classical medical epidemiology are "borrowed" by drug epidemiologists, they come with some limitations. The classical epidemiological constructs that are most directly applicable to drug epidemiology are prevalence and derivative aspects of prevalence, such as changes in the population over time (generally termed "incidence" measures). Drug epidemiology measures the prevalence and incidence of drug use. While the similarities between the spread of a classic infectious disease and the occurrence and proliferation of illicit drug use suggest the use of medical epidemiological measures, there are also some distinctions that limit the degree of borrowing.

Classic epidemiology does not consider a medical infection as a willful decision (Frauenthal 1980). For the most part, willfulness of exposure is irrelevant to classical medical epidemiology. Drug-taking has notable elements of willfulness, even if one accepts a notion of physical compulsion as an element in end-stage addiction. This complicates certain medical epidemiology concepts such as "people vulnerable to the disease" since for drug use it is not clear what the definition of "vulnerable" or "at risk" means, especially in a prospective sense.

There are two basic types of mechanical epidemiological measures reported for drug use: *prevalence* (counts/frequencies) and *incidence* (proportions/rates involving change over time). Of these, the single most popular epidemiological measure of drug use has been the prevalence ratio. The drug prevalence ratio is simply the portion of persons who could use the drug who do use it. The prevalence ratio is a cross-sectional measure describing the proportion of people who at one time meet the condition of drug use. It is customary to express the prevalence of drug use as the number of drug users per one thousand of the relevant population.[1] Traditionally, in drug prevalence estimation, persons counted in the numerator have largely been identified by self-reported drug use. Persons counted in the denominator might include all people in the population, all adults, or all high school students. It is also common that the numerator reflects a designated time period depending on the analytic purposes. For example, thirty-day prior use is often considered "current use" in prevalence surveys. However, when bioassays are employed, other periods may be used. For example, because of its rapid excretion from the body, a forty-eight-hour frame is typically imposed on cocaine data derived from urine-based studies.

The *incidence rate* is a measure of new cases of the condition that appear in the population. It is expressed as a number of cases per a standard time unit. Although incidence, in medical epidemiology, is

---

[1] An alternative measure is period prevalence. The period prevalence describes the ratio of people developing the condition within a specific period (e.g., over the course of one year). It is equal to the annual prevalence rate at the beginning of the year plus the annual incidence rate for that year. For example, if a prevalence rate for the prior year is .001 (one out of a thousand persons develop the disease condition), and if the annual incidence rate is .001, then the one-year period prevalence rate is .002.

typically straightforward and describes the rate of development of new cases, this is a measure more difficult to use in drug epidemiology. The complication is that the numerator of the incidence equation can include persons who may be repeatedly counted as they alternately desist and then restart using a drug.

A frequently encountered problem in modern prevalence estimations of illicit drug use is that the target population is so large that it can never be exhaustively polled. All prevalence measures are estimations. To calculate prevalence estimates for drug use, inferential methods must be employed that require the controlled enumeration of at least a portion of the population of users. If proper procedures are used in sampling the population (and identifying the population is itself often a problem), then what is known about this sample of the population can be generalized to the whole. The procedures of inferential statistics and other estimation processes are intended to provide the methods to keep this sample-to-population connection within the bounds of acceptable error.

Any such estimation must proceed from empirical data. This has its own challenges. First, a meaningful universe of users is difficult to specify. It has been popular to characterize samples by reference to frequency of use as the primary indicator of "seriousness," but there is no obvious point on which consensus is attained. Second, once the universe is identified, procedures must be employed to identify and capture an appropriate sample, to carry out the process of interviewing, and to record the relevant interview information.

Of the four major ongoing survey projects, the National Household Survey and Monitoring the Future are often called "general population self-report surveys." The Drug Abuse Warning Network and the Drug Use Forecasting System represent more selective universes. The DAWN sample is incident-based and reflects medically based drug episodes recorded by a designated observer. The DUF is based on interviews and urine screens of criminal justice arrestees.

Although this essay focuses on these four prevalence measures, a great deal of additional drug use data exists in various localities in both the public and private sectors, but its value for prevalence estimation is unknown. For example, many corporations routinely screen potential employees (and sometimes regular employees) for drug use. Local, regional, and state units of governments accumulate significant drug use data. In addition, many units of the federal government collect data on drug prevalence or relevant aspects of drug abuse. Ebener,

Feldman, and Fitzgerald (1993) have reviewed these data sources at the federal level. Twenty-nine federal data sources, including those reviewed here, were identified. However, only a few are potentially suitable for prevalence estimation or are accessible to the public. Ebener, Feldman, and Fitzgerald note that

> this lack of information about federally sponsored drug use data collections can be explained by several factors. First, at least seventeen different agencies of the federal government sponsor data series that contain indicators for monitoring different aspects of drug use among different populations in the nation, and until 1988 when the Office of National Drug Control Policy was established, no one agency had the responsibility to coordinate the various data collection activities. Second, not all of the data bases were designed with the intention of making them available for use by researchers outside the agencies that collected them. As a result, documentation was often limited to what was necessary for in-house use, and little information was published or made available to enable secondary analysis. . . . Third, because different agencies have different needs for drug data, and research has tended not to be integrated, the existing directories often contain databases related to only some aspects of drug abuse policy such as law enforcement or drug abuse services. Fourth, federal funding for a drug abuse data archive in Texas was eliminated during a period when priorities shifted away from substance abuse funding, and no institution has replaced this archive. Finally, changes and modifications in data series occur frequently, and without a central repository for all databases and current documentation, timely information about each series is difficult to obtain. [Ebener, Feldman, and Fitzgerald 1993, p. 2]

The four survey instruments discussed here are the only ones that have attained broad recognition and have high levels of accessibility. Other data sets are either important only regionally, consist of populations that have serious limitations, or remain unexplored or unavailable to the public. Hser (1993), for instance, lists six such data sources: the Uniform Crime Reports, the Client-Oriented Data Acquisition Process, the System to Retrieve Drug Evidence, the National Ambulatory Medical Care Survey, the National Hospital Discharge Survey, and the National Vital Statistics System. However, each has severe constraints on their use for drug prevalence estimation, and none has been employed in producing general prevalence estimates, although some contemporary synthetic estimation processes are theoretically capable of using them for that purpose.

In addition, various legal and administrative entities gather data that have applicability for local prevalence estimation and policy evaluation, although the nature and quality of these systems vary widely. These include data from criminal justice agencies, treatment systems, and public health departments. Localities have created ongoing organizational formats for the sharing and improvement of data exchange, primarily the Community Epidemiology Working Group and the State Epidemiology Working Group systems that function at the local and state level.

The Community Epidemiology Working Group (CEWG) network involves participants from approximately twenty metropolitan communities, and several foreign countries, who are interested in patterns and epidemiological dynamics of illegal drug use. The National Institute on Drug Abuse has published proceedings and data from these groups. The most current report (Community Epidemiology Working Group 1992) includes reports on nineteen cities, one state, and twelve foreign countries or regions. Data gathered by CEWG, affiliated governmental agencies, and other organizations have contributed to estimation procedures at times, especially in furnishing data on treatment admissions. The CEWG system is not, however, primarily involved in original research efforts. It collects data for particular municipalities: treatment admissions, DAWN data, DUF data, and law-enforcement-based information such as purity of drugs and seizure quantities by local law enforcement agencies. Many aspects of CEWG data are variable because of the system's independent and local nature. But this does mean that the data are not valuable. As Reuter (1993, p. 179) has observed, "My guess is that prevalence estimation has its most important use at the local level. Most services, whether enforcement or other, are delivered at that level. If there is some relationship between policy and prevalence estimation, that is the level at which we are likely to find it." The CEWG data are largely derivative and reflect the same basic patterns uncovered by the major surveys. Overall, cocaine use is lessening, but there is still substantial "entrenched" cocaine use. Consequently, cocaine abuse represents the single most frequent basis for admission to drug treatment programs. Drug prices in most municipalities are either stable or dropping, and deaths attributed to cocaine also appear stable or dropping.

II. Self-Report Surveys

By far the most influential and extensive studies of drug prevalence are the self-reported surveys conducted under sponsorship of the federal government. These are the NHSDA and the MTF studies.

A. *The National Household Survey on Drug Abuse*

The NHSDA has five primary objectives. First, it provides survey data on "the prevalence of use of illicit drugs, alcohol, and tobacco for a target population comprising four groups: youth (12–17), young adults (18–25), middle adults (26–34), and older adults (35 +)" (National Institute on Drug Abuse 1993*a*, p. 1). Second, it presents trend information on changes in drug use patterns since the 1970s when the survey was first conducted. Third, it examines demographic correlates of use of illicit substances. Fourth, it presents information about patterns of illicit drug use and information about perceptions of harm related to illicit drug use. In 1991, questions on criminal behavior were added. Fifth, beyond its estimates for overall national measures, the NHSDA provides prevalence estimates for six major metropolitan statistical areas: Chicago, Denver, Los Angeles, Miami, New York, and Washington, D.C.

The NHSDA was first conducted in 1971 with sponsorship and financial support from the National Institute on Drug Abuse. Responsibility for management of the survey was later transferred to the Substance Abuse and Mental Health Services Administration Office of Applied Studies. This section relies on 1991, 1992, and in a few cases 1993 data. The 1992 data represent the twelfth household survey. As of the writing of this essay, the *Main Findings 1991* have been released, as well as two other publications—the *Highlights 1991* and the *Population Estimates 1991*—that were available for some time before the release of the main findings. In addition, the *Population Estimates 1992*, the December 1993 release entitled *Race/Ethnicity/Socioeconomic Status and Drug Abuse 1991*, and several *Advanced Reports* (nos. 3, 5, and 7), which include preliminary estimates from the 1992 and 1993 data sets, were available. (Bibliographical information on these data sources is provided in the reference list; see National Institute on Drug Abuse 1992, 1993*a*, 1993*b*, 1993*c*, 1993*d*, 1993*e*, 1994*a*, 1994*b*.)

Both NHSDA and MTF use a probability sampling procedure to select participants. Because no other verification of the accuracy of response is used, such approaches have been generally called "self-report" surveys. For a variety of reasons, including respondents' lapses of memory and lack of candor, self-reported drug use does not necessarily provide a perfect image of actual patterns of drug use.

1. *NHSDA Methodology.*   The NHSDA employs a national probability sample of households. This is one of its strengths and one of its most appealing aspects. This permits the application of inferential procedures to the sample data for the purposes of generalizing to all U.S. households. The sample clusters are taken from 125 primary sampling units. Alaska and Hawaii, which were long excluded (the survey applied to the "coterminous United States"), have been included since 1991. The six major metropolitan statistical areas were designed to support separate estimates of drug use prevalence for each metropolitan statistical area independent of the national sample. The *Main Findings* volumes of the series (e.g., National Institute on Drug Abuse 1993*b*) contain detailed appendices that explain strategies of specific methodologies, data quality issues, and sampling procedures. In this section, all NHSDA data are from the 1992 official publications as released by the federal government unless otherwise noted.

One recurring criticism has been that use of a sampling procedure limited to households misses a significant population of drug users from NHSDA estimates, including those who are transient, housed in situations not defined as "households," or homeless. This criticism has been especially sharp because drug use is likely to be especially prevalent among those excluded populations. Consequently, and in a departure from previous years, the 1991 and 1992 surveys include some people living in group quarters: civilians living on military bases, people residing in college dorms, and people living in homeless shelters. Transients (defined as homeless people not in shelters) and people incarcerated in jails and prisons, however, are still not included.

There was widespread concern that including those additional groups would affect the survey's use for detecting long-term trends, but the 1991 report indicates that the distortion potentially due to the inclusion of Alaska and Hawaii and the "group quarters populations" appears to be "negligible" (National Institute on Drug Abuse 1993*a*, p. 7). The principal investigators argue that the trend data comparisons are still valid, although the sampling frame has been modified (p. 2).

To select respondents, the NHSDA identifies households and for each participating household prepares a roster recording age, race, ethnicity, and sex for all household members. Using a random sampling procedure, two, one, or no household members are selected from the roster to be interviewed. The stratification is done to assure adequate sample sizes for various ethnic and racial groups of interest. The interview process includes the use of self-administered answer sheets and "other procedures" (sealing of response sheets in envelopes, etc.) designed to assure respondents that their responses to sensitive questions are completely private.

For the 1992 data set (the twelfth), 28,832 persons twelve years or older from 118 primary sampling units were surveyed. Response rates were "95.0 percent completion rate for screening sample households, and 82.5 percent for interviewing sample individuals" (National Institute on Drug Abuse 1993c, p. 4). The survey asked respondents about use of the following substances: cannabinoids, inhalants, heroin, alcohol, cocaine, hallucinogens, psychoactives, and tobacco. Each respondent was asked to provide information regarding their use of each substance in their lifetime, the past year, and the past month.

In general, "current drug use" in NHSDA publications refers to individuals who admit to use within thirty days before the interview. However, in recent years there has been interest in weekly drug use as a marker of "hard-core addiction." Several variables that the NHSDA refers to as "demographic correlates" are also compiled for each respondent. These are age, sex, race, ethnicity, population density (community size), socioeconomic status of metropolitan area, and region (Northeast, North Central, South, West). Socioeconomic status was defined by reference to the population in the lowest one-third of either median housing value or rent.

2. *NHSDA Key Findings.* Of all 1992 respondents, 36.2 percent report use of some illicit drug or drugs in their lifetime. Approximately 11.1 percent report using some drug within the last year, and approximately 5.5 percent report use within the last month. The NHSDA population estimates for 1992 (National Institute on Drug Abuse 1993d) instruct that approximately seventy-five million Americans had used an illicit drug during their lifetimes, 22.8 million had used a drug in the preceding year, and 11.4 million in the last month. Table 1 summarizes the 1992 data, by gender and age. Table 2 shows the population estimates for illicit drug use by age and race or Hispanic ethnicity. Note that black rates of ever having used any drug are typically lower than those for whites; by contrast, arrest rates for blacks for drug offenses are far higher than for whites (Tonry 1995, chap. 3).

3. *Prevalence of Particular Drugs.* Data presented to this point concern self-reported use of any drug. The two major surveys also ask questions about particular drugs. Although the same broad pattern of

TABLE 1

NHSDA 1992 Population Estimates: Percentage of Population
Reporting Any Illicit Drug by Age and Gender

Age and Gender	Ever Used?	Past Year?	Past Month?
12–17:			
Male	16.3	11.0	5.7
Female	16.6	12.5	6.5
18–25:			
Male	53.3	30.4	16.7
Female	50.0	22.6	9.5
26–34:			
Male	66.1	22.3	12.6
Female	55.5	14.4	7.6
35 +:			
Male	34.1	6.7	3.2
Female	22.7	3.7	1.4
Total male	41.0	13.4	7.1
Total female	31.7	9.0	4.1

SOURCE.—National Institute on Drug Abuse (1993*d*).

NOTE.—Drugs include marijuana, heroin, cocaine, hallucinogens, inhalants, tranquilizers, sedatives, and stimulants.

increases in use in the 1970s and decreases thereafter characterize all drugs, the timing of the shift and the steepness of the falls vary among drugs.

a. Marijuana. Overall, marijuana is the most prevalent drug mentioned in the NHSDA. Its use is concentrated primarily among eighteen to thirty-four year olds. Approximately 33 percent of NHSDA respondents report having used it during their lifetimes. Around 4.4 percent reported using it within thirty days prior to the survey. The 1992 population estimates for the country as a whole indicate that there are nine million current users of marijuana. Table 3 details the prevalence estimations for marijuana use by age and ethnic and racial groupings. Use of marijuana among whites is far more prevalent than among other groups. About 83 percent of all lifetime users are white. Marijuana use, like use of all the major drugs, is in decline. Marijuana prevalence figures peaked in 1979. Figures 5 and 6 (which contain data on several drugs) indicate the trends in marijuana lifetime use for persons aged twelve to seventeen and eighteen to twenty-five from 1972 until 1993.

TABLE 2

NHSDA 1992 Population Estimates: Percentage of Population
Reporting Any Illicit Drug by Age and Racial/Ethnic Identification

Age and Race	Ever Used?	Past Year?	Past Month?
12–17:			
White	16.9	22.1	6.1
Black	15.1	9.9	6.1
Hispanic	17.6	12.7	7.1
18–25:			
White	56.3	28.7	13.7
Black	42.3	22.2	12.1
Hispanic	39.2	20.0	10.2
26–34:			
White	65.7	19.1	10.6
Black	51.4	18.1	10.3
Hispanic	44.3	15.1	7.8
35+:			
White	28.7	5.3	2.2
Black	28.7	5.8	3.5
Hispanic	20.7	4.1	1.3

SOURCE.—National Institute on Drug Abuse (1993*d*).

NOTE.—Drugs include marijuana, heroin, cocaine, hallucinogens, inhalants, tranquilizers, sedatives, and stimulants.

The only group that does not show this decline is persons twenty-six
and older. Lifetime prevalence for them cannot decrease over time
since they cannot reverse past exposure. Thus a better indicator is the
rate of incidence (new cases) that are reflected in the younger cohorts
entering the sampling frame. As figures 5 and 6 show, these numbers
have been falling since the late 1970s.

Figure 7 shows a plateau for older citizens as they age. This suggests
that many older persons have a high likelihood of having experimented
with drugs in their teen or early adult years but have desisted from
use as they have matured.

b. Cocaine and Crack.   About 11 percent of NHSDA respondents
reported lifetime cocaine use in any form in the *Population Estimates
1992* (National Institute on Drug Abuse 1993*d*). Approximately 2.4
percent reported using it in the preceding year, and less than 1 percent
within the preceding month. These percentages translate into population estimates of 22.6 million lifetime users, 4.9 million users in the
last year, and 1.3 million thirty-day users. The age range with the

TABLE 3

NHSDA 1992 Population Estimates: Percentage of Population Reporting Marijuana Use by Age and Racial/Ethnic Identification

Age and Race	Used Ever	Used Past Year	Used Past Month
12–17:			
White	10.8	8.4	4.1
Black	9.1	5.9	3.4
Hispanic	11.9	9.0	4.8
18–25:			
White	53.0	24.8	11.6
Black	38.9	19.8	11.2
Hispanic	35.0	15.4	8.0
26–34:			
White	63.6	14.9	8.8
Black	48.9	15.4	8.2
Hispanic	41.4	10.8	5.6
35 +:			
White	25.2	3.4	1.6
Black	27.5	4.4	2.5
Hispanic	18.2	2.2	.7

SOURCE.—National Institute on Drug Abuse (1993*d*).

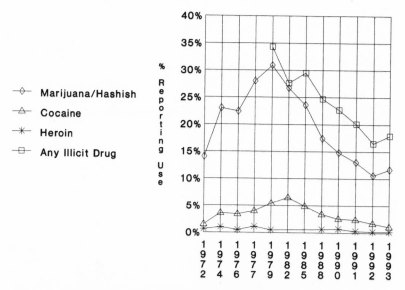

FIG. 5.—National Household Survey on Drug Abuse Trends, persons aged twelve to seventeen reporting drug use during their lifetime. Sources: National Institute on Drug Abuse (1992, 1993*a*). Note: "Any illicit drug" includes marijuana, heroin, cocaine, hallucinogens, inhalants, tranquilizers, sedatives, and stimulants.

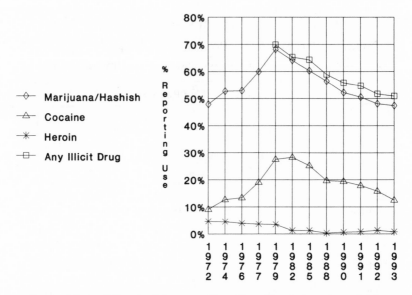

Fig. 6.—National Household Survey on Drug Abuse Trends, persons aged eighteen to twenty-five reporting drug use during their lifetime. Sources: National Institute on Drug Abuse (1992, 1993a). Note: "Any illicit drug" includes marijuana, heroin, cocaine, hallucinogens, inhalants, tranquilizers, sedatives, and stimulants.

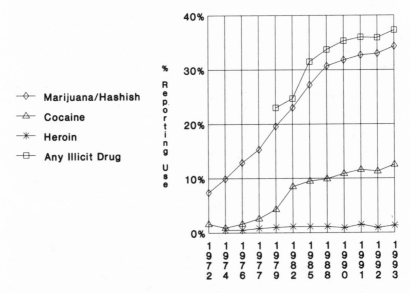

Fig. 7.—National Household Survey on Drug Abuse Trends, persons aged twenty-six and older reporting drug use during their lifetime. Sources: National Institute on Drug Abuse (1992, 1993a). Note: "Any illicit drug" includes marijuana, heroin, cocaine, hallucinogens, inhalants, tranquilizers, sedatives, and stimulants.

greatest representation, like marijuana, is between eighteen and thirty-four. Generalizations about racial and ethnic differences are complex since there is considerable covariation by age, socioeconomic status, and other variables. The NHSDA in the 1991 report on *Race/Ethnicity/ Socioeconomic Status and Drug Abuse 1991* (National Institute on Drug Abuse 1993*e*) stated that

> the relationships between race/ethnicity and drug use vary considerably according to both the type of drug and the level of use. Thus, it is difficult to make any general statements about racial/ethnic differences in drug use. For example, it is clearly impossible to say that any particular racial/ethnic groups tend to 'use drugs' more than others. . . . For both marijuana and cocaine, differences in nonfrequent use across racial/ethnic subgroups were not statistically significant. However, differences in the frequent use of these drugs were highly significant. A substantially higher proportion of blacks reported frequent use of marijuana, and both blacks and Hispanics reported higher rates of frequent cocaine use than did whites. [National Institute on Drug Abuse 1992, p. 18]

The trend is toward declining rates of cocaine use in all age groups, with current rates of use comparable to those of the early 1970s. Peak levels appear to have occurred between 1982 and 1985 for previous year and previous month use. Figures 5, 6, and 7 indicate the rates of change across age groups. The National Household Survey on Drug Abuse does not provide trend data for crack cocaine.

c. Heroin. Heroin use, while typically persistent, characterizes a very small percentage of the total NHSDA sample. Self-reported use of heroin within the preceding thirty days was so low "that reliable estimates could not be developed" (National Institute on Drug Abuse 1993*a*, p. 33). Of the six metropolitan statistical areas measured by the NHSDA, only three had a measurable level of use. Heroin is concentrated among older adults (twenty-six and older). The only significant upward change in heroin trends is among users who were thirty-five and older—an increase from .7 percent to 1.5 percent. The 1993 NHSDA *Advanced Report no. 7*, entitled *Preliminary Estimates from the 1993 Household Survey on Drug Abuse*, noted that "estimates of heroin use from the NHSDA are very conservative due to the probable under-coverage of the population of heroin users. Estimates of lifetime heroin prevalence have fluctuated from 2.0 million users in 1985 to 2.7 million users in 1991, 1.8 million users in 1992, and 2.3 million users in 1993. No significant changes in past year or past month prevalence have been detected" (National Institute on Drug Abuse 1994*b*, p. 16).

B. *Monitoring the Future: The High School Senior Survey*

The MTF project has been one of the most influential and longest-lived of all the major general population surveys. The 1992 data represent the eighteenth national survey of American high school seniors and the thirteenth national survey of college students. Although often called the "High School Senior Survey," the formal title is "Monitoring the Future—a Continuing Study of the Lifestyles and Values of Youth." Since its inception, it has been conducted under the auspices of the University of Michigan's Institute for Social Research and funded by the National Institute on Drug Abuse.

Monitoring the Future uses a nationally representative sample of all seniors in public and private high schools in the "coterminous United States." It produces cross-sectional prevalence data for each survey year. It also includes some longitudinal data. Representative samples of young adults from previous graduating classes are administered follow-up surveys by mail as part of the study. Since 1980, it has also included representative samples of American college students, one to four years past high school, who are also included in the follow-up surveys. Since 1991, annual surveys of eighth and tenth grade students have been added, and longitudinal panels will be started on this segment of the total sample. The 1992 data reported here include the first trend data on this group. Procedures and measures for these lower grades are designed to parallel the senior survey, thus facilitating cross-grade comparisons. The only distinction of consequence between the older and younger samples is that fewer questionnaire forms are used with the younger group, and therefore fewer variables are measured.

Two of the major topics covered are the prevalence of drug use among that year's school cohort and trend data that emerges when longitudinal panels from earlier cohorts are compared year-to-year. In addition, important demographic distinctions are noted in the sample population. In 1991 racial and ethnic analyses were made for the first time. Also, several new items were included, such as school grade at first drug use, intensity of drug use, attitudes and beliefs about drug use, trends in use at lower grade levels, and the sample population's perception of relevant aspects of the social environment as they may affect drug use patterns. Nine classes of drugs are covered: marijuana, cocaine, opiates, stimulants, sedatives, tranquilizers, inhalants, alcohol, and tobacco. These drug classes are used to optimize comparability to the NHSDA. Several drug subclasses are also reported in the MTF including phencyclidine (PCP), lysergic acid diethylamide (LSD), barbiturates and methaqualone, amyl and butyl nitrites, and crack. Phencyclidine and the nitrites were added in 1979, crack was added in 1986, and coverage was expanded in 1987. Methylene dioxymethyl amphetamine (MDMA) was added in 1989 (to follow-up surveys only).

The MTF project serves three purposes. The first is to develop an accurate picture of the current drug prevalence and prevalence trends among young people. The knowledge gained from the surveys is conceived as a prerequisite for rational public debate and policy making in responding to problems associated with illicit drug use. "Lacking reliable prevalence data, substantial misconceptions can develop and resources be misallocated. In the absence of reliable data on trends early detection and localization of emerging problems are more difficult, and assessments of the impact of major historical and policy-induced events are much more conjectural" (Johnston, O'Malley, and Bachman 1993, p. 4).

Second, MTF monitors factors that may help explain observed changes in drug use or offer insights into important changing patterns of drug use. Variables such as peer norms regarding drug use, beliefs about the dangers of drug use, and perceived availability of drugs can be related to fluctuations in use. The data can be used to test models regarding larger theoretical concerns about drug abuse. In the 1992 report the principal investigators noted an example of this: "Monitoring these factors has made it possible to examine a central policy issue for the country in its war on drugs—namely, the relative importance of supply reduction effects vs. demand reduction effects in bringing about some of the observed declines in drug use" (Johnston, O'Malley, and Bachman 1992, p. 4).

Third, MTF offers practical research benefits to a number of different constituencies. The data can help to determine who is at greatest risk for drug abuse problems and create a better understanding of lifestyles and values of drug users. The data can help in determining aspects of the social environment associated with drug use and in measuring the effects of major life transitions on drug use. It can help disentangle age effects (drug use patterns associated with being in a particular age group) from cohort effects (patterns associated with a particular group, whatever their ages) and history effects (patterns associated with living in periods especially receptive to drug use—e.g., the late 1960s—or living in periods especially hostile to it—e.g., the 1990s). Lastly, given that various social programs and policies have attempted to influence drug use among young people, the survey data can help in determining the effects of these programs and policies.

1. *Methodology: Monitoring the Future.*   A major strength is MTF's use of a national probability sample. Monitoring the Future employs a multistage procedure to create a nationally representative sample of its target populations. The sample is generated by a stratification process: selection of geographical areas, followed by selection of schools within areas, and finally selection of seniors within schools. Over the years the number of public and private high schools participating in a given year has ranged between 125 and 135. The survey is conducted in the spring. Each selected school is notified ten days before the survey's administration. The survey is administered to the students during a regular class period. Since there are a large number of variables and consequently many survey items, the questionnaire itself is divided into six "forms." Only demographic and drug use data are collected on all cases. For all other subdivisions of the questionnaire, data are collected from one-sixth of each school sample.

To capture trend information, a longitudinal panel design is employed of follow-up surveys for each cohort examined. These follow-up surveys are based on 2,400 randomly selected cases from each year's cohort. The 2,400 cases are randomly assigned to one of two groups, and each subgroup is polled in alternate years. Thus subgroup participants respond every other year and are surveyed by mailed questionnaires. The panel retention rates are high, more than 80 percent. The oldest panel (dating from 1976) still maintains a 65 percent response rate.

The senior year of high school is justified as an appropriate survey point for several reasons. Completion of high school forms an important "developmental marker" because it signifies the end of universal public education, and for many it means leaving the parental home and entry into full-time work. Furthermore, because of the universality of public education, polling a nationally representative sample of a particular age cohort is relatively cost-efficient and strategically feasible.

2. *MTF Key Findings.*   Like the NHSDA, the Monitoring the Future project has documented a long-term, gradual decline in the proportion

of all three measured populations (high school students, college students, and young adults) involved in the use of any illicit drug. In 1991 the annual report stated that "there have been appreciable declines in the use of a number of the illicit drugs among seniors, and even larger declines in their use among American college students and young adults more generally" (Johnston, O'Malley, and Bachman 1992, p. 17).

Because the surveys show slight upturns in drug use in the early 1990s, the 1992 report on secondary school students is more pessimistic regarding the trends. The current report states that "the trend story has become considerably more complicated to summarize this year . . . there are some reversals in the recent downward trends in use and upward trends in the perceived risk and disapproval associated with drug use" (Johnston, O'Malley, and Bachman 1993, p. 5).

The 1992 data show that only the high school senior component continues to exhibit the long-term trend of decreasing use of any illicit drug. College students and young adults showed nonsignificant increases. If marijuana is excluded, then seniors showed a decline, but not young adults or college students. Cocaine continued to "broadly decline" by amounts that do not attain statistical significance. The use of marijuana among high school seniors is at its lowest point in the history of the survey, but college students and young adults did not show any significant change. All groups showed increases in the use of LSD, but only very young students (eighth grade) showed a significant increase.

Figures 8, 9, and 10 show monthly, yearly, and lifetime prevalence for high school seniors from 1980 to 1992 for cocaine, marijuana, LSD, and "any drug." Figure 8 shows thirty days past use, which is the typical definition for "current" use of a substance. As the figure suggests, there has been substantial decline for all listed substances except LSD, which has shown a very slight upward trend. Figures 9 and 10, the annual and lifetime prevalence percentages, show consistent downward trends, again excepting LSD.

American college students appear to be following the same trend pattern as their noncollege cohort counterparts. Since 1980 there has been a general reduction in use that resembles the trend line for high school seniors. Figures 11, 12, and 13 show monthly, yearly, and lifetime prevalence percentages for college students from 1980 through 1992. The most marked declines are for thirty-day prevalence. The categories of "any drug" and marijuana show a very steep decline. Cocaine shows a decline as well, although it is more gradual. LSD

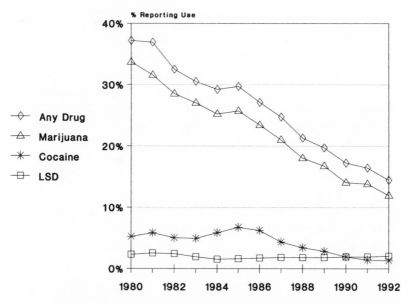

Fig. 8.—High school seniors, Monitoring the Future trends, percentage reporting thiry-day drug use. Source: Johnston, O'Malley, and Bachman (1992). Note: "Any drug" includes marijuana, heroin, cocaine, hallucinogens, inhalants, tranquilizers, sedatives, and stimulants.

appears very stable, with a slight deflection upward for the most current year. The annual (figure 12) and the lifetime (figure 13) prevalence data also show declines, but less dramatic as the time span is increased. Both LSD and marijuana show slight upward deflections for the last year in figure 12. LSD also shows an upward deflection in figure 13.

3. *Differences between Genders and Racial/Ethnic Groups.* Among secondary school students there is little difference in drug use by men and women. Trends for male and female high school students have traveled in parallel. Although there are minor differences for some drugs, overall, males and females in the MTF achieve near parity of prevalence.

That is not true of racial and ethnic differences. The 1992 MTF reports that, "while the three major racial/ethnic groups examined here—whites, blacks, and Hispanics—have quite different levels of use of some drugs, it appears that their use has trended in similar ways" (Johnston, O'Malley, and Bachman 1993, p. 127). For marijuana use, for example, all three groups have exhibited a parallel decline. However, for cocaine, use by whites and Hispanics increased compared with blacks from 1975 to the mid-1980s, when blacks began to "catch

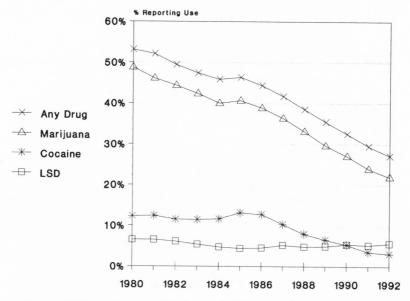

Fig. 9.—High school seniors, Monitoring the Future trends, percentage reporting annual drug use. Source: Johnston, O'Malley, and Bachman (1992). Note: "Any drug" includes marijuana, heroin, cocaine, hallucinogens, inhalants, tranquilizers, sedatives, and stimulants.

up." Blacks, however, have always had an overall lower prevalence rate. For crack cocaine, use by all three groups continues to decline. Hispanics have shown the steepest decline in crack use, and blacks the slowest rate of decline.

Regarding college students, the 1992 report notes that black seniors have consistently shown lower rates of drug use than white seniors. Of all groups, white seniors had the highest rates of use of inhalants, hallucinogens, LSD, stimulants, tranquilizers, and nonheroin opiates. Whites and Hispanics had comparable rates of use of marijuana and alcohol. Hispanics have the largest usage of cocaine, crack, heroin, and steroids. All three groups have shown declines in cocaine use, and for all of the illicit drugs the trends for all three groups have moved in parallel.

C. Critiques of the Self-Report Surveys

The National Household Survey on Drug Abuse and Monitoring the Future have been criticized by people who doubt that they can reliably estimate the prevalence of drug use. Some of these criticisms are generic and apply to both surveys. One criticism is based on skepti-

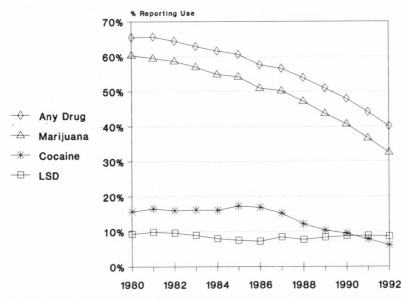

% Reporting Use

Any Drug
Marijuana
Cocaine
LSD

Fig. 10.—High school seniors, Monitoring the Future trends, percentage reporting lifetime drug use. Source: Johnston, O'Malley, and Bachman (1992). Note: "Any drug" includes marijuana, heroin, cocaine, hallucinogens, inhalants, tranquilizers, sedatives, and stimulants.

cism about the use of interviews to uncover drug use, which is stigmatized illegal behavior. Some people are likely to deny their drug use, and the proportion of such people may vary over time. The data, this criticism maintains, are inherently unreliable, and the degree of unreliability cannot be estimated. These critics cite studies that show that survey data, when compared to objective validators, consistently underestimate drug use (Fendrich and Vaughn 1994).

A second criticism is that the NHSDA and MTF surveys overrepresent stable segments of the population. Respondents must either be in a school or live in a household. Thus there is inevitably an underrepresentation of other groups, some of whom may account for a substantial proportion of the drug-using public. These general criticisms have specific relevance to each survey.

1. *Critiques of the NHSDA.*   The major criticism of the NHSDA is that its focus on households excludes groups at high risk for drug use. Critics have been especially critical of the use of survey data to estimate heroin and cocaine use. One response to this (discussed in Sect. V below) has been to create estimation procedures that would compensate for this shortcoming.

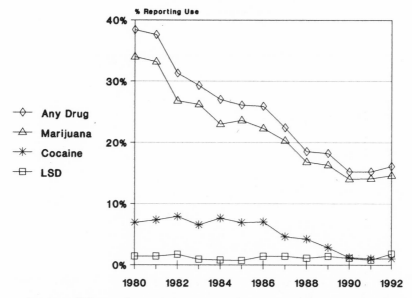

Fig. 11.—College students, Monitoring the Future trends, percentage reporting drug use in the past thirty days. Source: Johnston, O'Malley, and Bachman (1992). Note: "Any drug" includes marijuana, heroin, cocaine, hallucinogens, inhalants, tranquilizers, sedatives, and stimulants.

A 1993 report of the Committee on Government Operations of the U.S. House of Representatives, entitled *Drug Use Measurement: Strengths, Limitations, and Recommendations for Improvement* (U.S. House of Representatives, Committee on Government Operations 1993), questioned the "imputation and estimation procedures" employed by the National Institute on Drug Abuse to use NHSDA survey data to estimate national prevalence figures. The validity of these estimations is most severely criticized for heroin, but questions are raised about cocaine as well. One criticism concerns the volatility of some NHSDA data. For example, the report points out that a misclassification of fifty-three heroin users in 1991 produced a 46 percent drop in the estimated national prevalence figure for heroin users (from 701,000 to 381,000). The report notes that weighting procedures and population projections also reveal "peculiar findings" regarding heroin prevalence:

> One study, conducted for the Office of National Drug Control Policy (ONDCP) revealed two peculiar findings when the 1991 NHSDA age variable was weighted (to account for subject

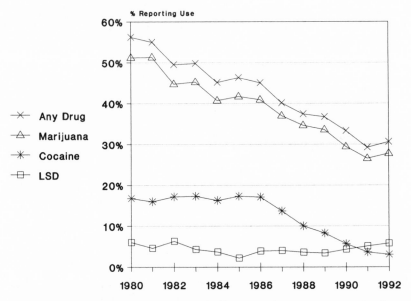

Fig. 12.—College students, Monitoring the Future trends, percentage reporting drug use in the past year. Source: Johnston, O'Malley, and Bachman (1992). Note: "Any drug" includes marijuana, heroin, cocaine, hallucinogens, inhalants, tranquilizers, sedatives, and stimulants.

sampling probabilities and nonresponse rates): 148,000 of the total 701,000 annual heroin users were age 79, and 32% of the users were older than 60.

Further detailed study showed that the 148,000 population projection figure was generated from only 2 heroin-using subjects. One 79 year old woman, when projected to the national level, accounted for an estimated 142,000 heroin users, or about 20% of all 1991 past-year heroin users. In similar fashion, 32% of the annual heroin user distribution was older than 60; this was based on population projections from only seven heroin-using subjects.

Estimation problems were also uncovered within the 1988 NHSDA annual heroin data. One weighted individual, age 64, accounted for 112,000 heroin cases when projected as a national estimate, or 21% of the total number of estimated past-year users. [U.S. House of Representatives, Committee on Government Operations 1993, p. 42]

The report also noted that similar problems exist for more frequently used drugs, most notably cocaine. For example, from 1990 to 1991,

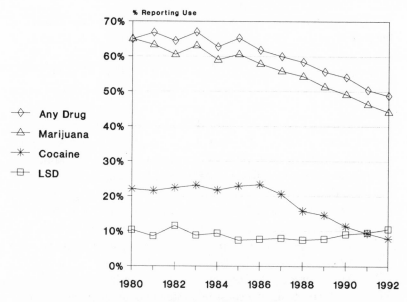

Fig. 13.—College students, Monitoring the Future trends, percentage reporting drug use during their lifetime. Source: Johnston, O'Malley, and Bachman (1992). Note: "Any drug" includes marijuana, heroin, cocaine, hallucinogens, inhalants, tranquilizers, sedatives, and stimulants.

weekly cocaine use was estimated to have increased by 193,000 cases (from 662,000 to 855,000). In 1992, NIDA revised this estimation, first to 654,000, and then to 625,000. These revisions were performed because of "problems with imputation procedures applied to the data" (U.S. House of Representatives, Committee on Government Operations 1993, p. 42). Criticisms were also raised regarding the effects of high nonresponse rates among the groups with the highest rates of cocaine use and the possibility that this effect would likely produce an underestimate.

A second criticism of NHSDA is its failure to attempt to validate the prevalence rates by use of independent measures such as bioassay techniques. A third related criticism is that the reliability of self-reported drug use may degenerate as an increasingly hostile social climate forms toward drug use. The 1980s were a period of less tolerance toward drug use than the previous two decades. As the hostility and intolerance toward drug use expanded, the accuracy of self-reports of use may have been negatively affected (Kleiman 1986).

Ideally, given these concerns regarding self-reported drug use, a survey would employ a highly reliable validation technique to estimate the degree of error in reported use versus actual use of an illicit drug. At the close of the 1970s, relatively low-cost, high-volume urinalysis procedures for detecting illicit drugs became available. The DUF system, which I examine in Section IV below, represents the first use of a chemical assay process for drug use to validate a major survey.

2. *Criticisms of the MTF.*   The MTF shares in several of these criticisms leveled at the NHSDA. It has been characterized as using a "wide array of inferential evidence" to support its current findings and substantial empirical indicators that support the internal validity of the data (Johnston, O'Malley, and Bachman 1993, p. 32). But the MTF, while using sophisticated procedures to assess its internal validity, also lacks any means of conducting external validations. Like the NHSDA, it does not use bioassay methods to assess the potential discrepancy between reported and actual use.

The MTF survey asks respondents about the honesty of their responses and has obtained a consistent rate of about 20 percent who say that they would not or are not sure they would provide honest responses. However, the inferences to be drawn from this are open to several interpretations because it lacks a logical response pattern evident in the data (Wish 1990). The self-referential nature of this question raises great difficulties. Such a question is equivalent to the paradoxical question, "Are you a liar?" Both yes and no responses to such a question are ambiguous and contradictory.

Another criticism is that students are asked to provide their names and other identifying information to the survey research staff, even though the survey is confidential. The degree to which this compromises honest responses is not known (Wish and Gropper 1990). In each year between 1979 and 1986, significant percentages of the respondents to the High School Senior Survey said that they would *not have reported* marijuana, amphetamine, or heroin use if they had ever used those substances. This may indicate that the student population surveys give conservative estimates of drug use.

A major shortcoming of the MTF survey is that it omits drop-outs. In any given year this constitutes about 15–20 percent of the national cohort. This is especially a problem since it is reasonable to assume that drug use may be very prevalent among those who quit school. Thus critics maintain that the MTF is a systematically biased measure producing undercounts compared with the age group prevalence as a whole.

The principal investigators for MTF acknowledge that this criticism is well taken, but they argue that their own analyses show that the biasing effect of losing dropouts from the sample is not significant and does not affect the accuracy of the data and the derivative estimates made from it. In the 1991 report they state that,

> while we believe that there is some underestimation of the prevalence of drug use in the cohort at large as a result of dropouts being omitted from the universe of the study, we think the degree of underestimation is rather limited for all drugs (except for heroin, crack, and PCP) and, more important, that trend estimates have been rather little affected. Short of having good trend data gathered directly from dropouts—a more expensive and technically difficult research undertaking—we cannot close the case definitively. Nevertheless, we think the available evidence argues strongly against alternative hypotheses—a conclusion which was reached by the members of the NIDA technical review on this subject held in 1982. The analyses provided in this report show that failure to include these two groups (absentees and dropouts) does not substantially affect the estimates of the incidence and prevalence of drug use. [Johnston, O'Malley, and Bachman 1993, p. 264]

The appendix to volume 1 of the 1992 report provides some examples of the changes in data outcomes under various scenarios (Johnston, O'Malley, and Bachman 1993). These hypothetical calculations show that inclusion of absentees and dropouts does not alter the findings in any substantive way, even under worst case assumptions.

There is also a possibility that schools may wish to avoid measuring the amount of drug use among its student body for fear of negative repercussions that could befall the school if the results show a high degree of drug use. While project staff have said that schools do not drop out of the process for this reason, this has never been empirically tested.

Lastly, the breakdown of MTF data by race traditionally has not been reported. The principal investigators have published some analyses of the data by racial and ethnic variables and have expanded the inclusion of ethnic and racial variables in the 1992 data (Johnston, O'Malley, and Bachman 1993, p. 16). But, as a 1993 General Accounting Office report indicated, "these results must be interpreted with caution. The smaller population size of non-whites, coupled with their clustered attendance in a limited number of schools, increases the sampling error involved in studying nonwhite drug use rates and affects the reliability of the data obtained. In addition, no safeguard procedures were adopted to ensure the representativeness of these sample groups" (U.S. House of Representatives, Committee on Government Operations 1993, p. 49).

III. Drug Abuse Warning Network (DAWN)

The Drug Abuse Warning Network has been in operation for more than twenty years and is the oldest of the four major systems reviewed in this essay. Data are reported on two types of medical events associated with drug use; one data set is based on "emergency room mentions," and the second is based on drug-involved deaths as they are known to medical examiners' offices at the participating sites. The Drug Abuse Warning Network has four major objectives: to identify substances associated with drug abuse episodes as reported by the sample institutions, to monitor drug abuse patterns and trends and to detect new abuse entities and new combinations of entities, to assess health hazards associated with abused substances, and to provide data for national, state, and local drug abuse policy and program planning.

A. Emergency Room Mentions: Annual Emergency Room Data

The DAWN emergency room data are "weighted estimates representing all drug abuse emergency room episodes in the total coterminous United States and in twenty-one metropolitan areas" (National Institute on Drug Abuse 1994f, p. 1). In 1992 the data were based on reporting by 503 hospitals of the 637 selected for the 1992 sample. The Drug Abuse Warning Network was conceived as a nationally representative sample. However, because of loss of sites and other changes over time, representativeness was lost. As of 1990, the DAWN sample was reconfigured to recapture national representation.

Since 1990 the DAWN emergency room system has employed a reconstituted and updated probability sample. The new sample was first conceptualized, and design work initiated, in 1980, and additional funding in 1986 permitted recruitment of new institutions. Since it is a representative sample, it permits inferences for each of the twenty-one metropolitan areas participating in DAWN. It also uses a "national panel" representing the balance of the coterminous United States. Thus national estimates can be made as well. The Drug Abuse Warning Network now provides good estimates for emergency room episodes and mentions for the United States as a whole and for the included metropolitan regions. The network is an "incident-based" or "episode-based" system that relies, not on self-reports, but on observers who record observations and compile records. The summary of those records forms the core of the DAWN data.

1. *Methodology.* The Drug Abuse Warning Network uses a broader conceptualization of "drug use" than do the general population surveys. The network defines "drug use" as use of prescription drugs without appropriate medical supervision and standards, use of over-the-counter drugs contrary to approved labeling, or use of *any other substance* for psychic effect, dependence, or suicide. The network characterizes people appearing in the emergency rooms of participating hospitals (or dead people examined by the medical examiner) as eligible for inclusion as a drug episode under the following conditions:

> An episode report is submitted for each drug abuse patient who visits a DAWN ER [emergency room] and for each drug abuse death encountered by a DAWN ME [medical examiner]. Each report of a drug abuse ER episode includes demographic information about the patient and information about the circumstances of the episode. Beyond drug overdoses, drug abuse ER episodes may result from the chronic effects of habitual drug usage or from unexpected reactions. Unexpected reactions reflect cases where the drug's effect was different than anticipated. Up to four different substances, in addition to alcohol-in-combination, can be specified for each ER episode. [National Institute on Drug Abuse 1994f, p. 6]

Each participating facility has a designated DAWN reporter responsible for identifying drug abuse episodes and recording and submitting data on each case, on a weekly basis, using DAWN-supplied data forms. For purposes of data quality control, DAWN administration and supervision encompasses the following activities: training of data collection personnel and reporters, provision of instruction manuals and operational manuals and guidelines, monitoring of reporting practices and site visitations and consultations for problem solving, in-house manual data editing and computer editing of data, and auditing or "reabstracting" at facilities to monitor data accuracy and integrity.

2. *Data Limitations.* Annual reports on the DAWN system include a series of delimitations on the data and interpretations that may be

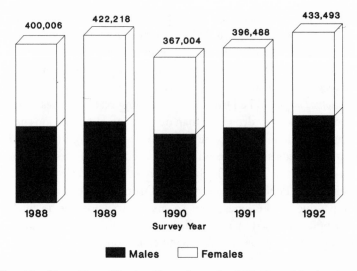

Fig. 14.—Drug Abuse Warning Network trends, 1988–92, weighted emergency room drug mentions, male and female. Source: National Institute on Drug Abuse (1994d).

made from it. Although DAWN administration exerts reasonable control over the methodology employed at each site, any analysis of the data should be tempered by the recognition that the data reflect facility-to-facility variations. The network does not use any personal identifiers; thus, the aggregate data counts may include repeat visits by the same person. Also, a *single drug abuse episode* may have *multiple drug mentions*. This does *not* mean every substance counted in a "drug mention" is necessarily the cause of the medical emergency. The mention of multiple drugs in a single episode has implications for the interpretation of data on both drug use and episode characteristics, so that it is not possible to translate them into a prevalence estimation.

3. *Key DAWN Emergency Room Findings.* The 1992 DAWN annual report estimates that, nationwide, there were 433,493 emergency room episodes (National Institute on Drug Abuse 1994f). Figure 14 shows the trend in emergency room drug mentions from 1988 to 1992. Fifty-one percent in 1992 involved males, and 49 percent were female. By race or ethnicity, 54 percent of the patients were white, 28 percent were black, and 10 percent were Hispanic. Of all these drug episodes, a suicide motive was reported in 40 percent of the cases. For episodes that were the result of nonsuicidal drug abuse, 54 percent of reports involved overdoses.

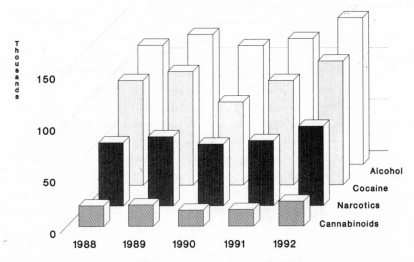

Fig. 15.—Drug Abuse Warning Network trends, 1988–92, weighted annual emergency room drug mentions by selected drug group. This is the only figure in this essay that includes alcohol and tobacco. Source: National Institute on Drug Abuse (1994*d*).

The most frequent psychoactive drugs mentioned are (in decreasing order): alcohol in combination with another drug, cocaine, heroin and other narcotics, and marijuana. If the alcohol combination cases are excluded, cocaine was the most frequently mentioned illicit drug. Figure 15 shows the trend data from 1988 through 1992 for these drugs.

Of all DAWN cocaine reports, 13 percent were from whites, 52 percent from blacks, and 27 percent from Hispanics. For blacks and Hispanics, cocaine was the most frequently occurring drug, with alcohol-in-combination as the second. For whites, alcohol-in-combination was the most frequent, and cocaine second. Heroin/morphine appears third on the list for blacks and Hispanics and sixth for whites.

In looking at the major metropolitan regions represented in DAWN, the greatest number of mentions (in decreasing order) came from the following cities: New York, Los Angeles, Philadelphia, Chicago, and Detroit. Cocaine was the most reported drug in several major cities, including Baltimore, Chicago, Dallas, Miami, New Orleans, New York, Newark, Philadelphia, and Washington, D.C.

4. *DAWN Emergency Room Trends.*   Network data, when trends are examined, stand in contrast to the general population surveys previously reviewed. Emergency room episodes *increased* 10 percent over the 1991–92 period. Statistically significant increases were seen for

males, for all racial and ethnic categories, and were concentrated in the age groups between nineteen and fifty-five years of age. Cocaine mentions increased 18 percent. The degree and significance of the DAWN cocaine increases vary from site to site. However, in several major cities there were dramatic increases: Boston (42.6 percent), Chicago (47.3 percent), Atlanta (57.6 percent), and New York (26.8 percent). While alcohol was the most frequently reported substance (33 percent of emergency room mentions), cocaine ranked second at 28 percent. Overall, statistically significant increases were seen for eight groups of drugs. Amphetamines increased 62 percent, and PCP was up 52 percent. Heroin, at 34 percent, and cocaine, at 18 percent, were both statistically significant increases.

B. Medical Examiners' Reports

The second component of the DAWN data are medical reports. Those collected for the 1992 report come from 137 medical examiners in thirty-eight different metropolitan areas in the United States. Medical examiners are responsible for establishing the legal cause of death for any citizen when death occurs under "suspicious circumstances" or while the person is involved or may have been involved in criminal activity. For example, a young individual found dead by the police would normally constitute a "suspicious circumstance," and the body would be examined by the medical examiner to assign a cause of death. Drug overdose deaths, criminals killed during the course of a crime, and similar cases are also typically reviewed by the medical examiner.

1. *Methodology.* A report is filed for each drug abuse death encountered by a DAWN medical examiner. In each of the thirty-eight cooperating sites, a designated reporter records data by reviewing the appropriate record and transfers the information to a DAWN medical examiner report. In addition to identification, demographic data, and cause of death data, the reporter can list up to six substances found to be involved in the episode. The determination of the presence of the substance is based on seven categories, including a review of the death certificate, toxicological report, autopsy, death scene investigation, physical signs on the deceased, and statements made by family, friends, or hospital staff who attended the deceased. The seventh category is a residual category. Training and quality control procedures are administered by DAWN staff that are comparable to those described in the section on the DAWN emergency room episode reports.

2. *DAWN Medical Examiner Data Limitations.* The DAWN report

series lists the following cautions regarding review and interpretation of the data: only drug abuse resulting in death is counted, and only those at DAWN sites; AIDS deaths are excluded, and cases are excluded when the drug is listed as "unknown"; and if multiple drug mentions are included in the report, *each* drug mentioned is reported as a "manner of death." As a consequence of the third condition, a particular cause of death can not be attributed to a particular drug mention since that causal link cannot be established. This represents a serious limit on the use of DAWN data to draw inferences about links between a particular drug and morbidity.

3. *Key Findings.* In the 1992 report (National Institute on Drug Abuse 1994*d*), the DAWN medical examiner data listed 7,562 drug-related deaths. In approximately 66 percent of these cases, drugs were a direct cause of death, and in 34 percent of the cases, they were a contributory factor. Of the deceased, 75 percent were male, and 25 percent were female. In 23 percent of these cases the medical examiner determined that the overdoses were intentional and classified the deaths as suicides.

The most frequently mentioned drugs on the medical examiner reports were cocaine in 46 percent of the cases, alcohol in combination with some other drug in 39 percent of the cases, and heroin in 33.6 percent of the cases. Cocaine was the top-ranking drug reported for both sexes and was mentioned in connection with half of the male deaths and 35 percent of the female deaths. Approximately 75 percent of the cases involved a single drug, while the balance were multidrug episodes.

Whites accounted for 56 percent of the deaths, blacks 29 percent, and Hispanics 13 percent. Drug-related deaths of blacks were more likely to involve cocaine (69 percent) than were those of whites (32 percent) or Hispanics (56 percent).

4. *Trends.* Like the DAWN emergency room data, the medical examiner data also show an increase in the number of deaths over the last three reporting years. Figure 16 shows the trend in deaths from 1988 to 1992. From 1991 to 1992, deaths increased by approximately 7 percent (from 6,204 to 6,724). In general, the trends from 1990 to 1992 reflect increases; the 1990–92 transformations should be emphasized, rather than longer time comparisons, because of the reconstitution of the DAWN sample frame. It should be borne in mind that, of the four systems reviewed in this essay, the DAWN medical examiner data constitutes a relatively small sample. Annual percentage changes

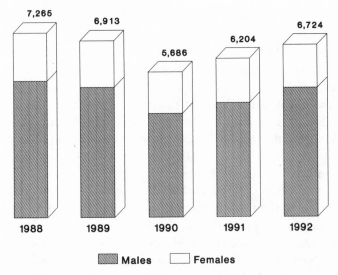

FIG. 16.—Drug Abuse Warning Network trends, 1988–92, weighted emergency room drug deaths, male and female. Source: National Institute on Drug Abuse (1994*f*).

are more volatile. Small absolute changes in numbers can account for substantial percentage changes.

Between 1991 and 1992 there was a 9 percent increase in drug-related deaths. Over this period cocaine mentions increased 11 percent, and heroin mentions were up 21 percent. In examining the changes by major metropolitan area, the largest percentage increases were in Norfolk, Virginia (120 percent), Buffalo (60 percent), Cleveland (50 percent), and San Francisco (44 percent).

5. *Criticisms of DAWN.* The DAWN system has provoked the fewest public or published criticisms. Network data are highly specialized. They are primarily used as indicators of the changing prevalence of various drugs that result in death or medically threatening intoxication (e.g., heroin, barbiturates). Those drugs, when abused, have consequences that are severe and are particularly likely to result in an appearance by an abuser in an emergency room. The difficulty with these data is that it is almost impossible to know with any precision how these numbers relate to general population prevalence estimations, although it is widely assumed that they move in parallel. That is, if increasing proportions of the general population use heroin, more persons might be expected to appear in emergency rooms seeking help for heroin-related problems or to show up as suspicious deaths to be

investigated by a medical examiner. The Drug Abuse Warning Network has thus been relied on to document or corroborate prevalence changes observed by other surveys or to show a link to certain key indicators. Thus, for example, if the police begin to seize large quantities of heroin, indicating more heroin use, corresponding effects in the DAWN medical examiner data and emergency room frequencies would be expected.

However, DAWN has distinct limitations that are detailed in the DAWN annual reports (National Institute on Drug Abuse 1994*f*). As noted, the DAWN sample went through a long period of degradation. Thus, for several years, both the generalizability of the data and the trend value of the data are open to some question.

IV. The Drug Use Forecasting System
The Drug Abuse Warning Network is the oldest of the four major systems. The Drug Use Forecasting System is the youngest.

The Drug Use Forecasting System was established in 1987 by the National Institute of Justice, the research agency of the Department of Justice. The primary rationale was to gather drug prevalence data on people under arrest, a population not normally sampled by the general population surveys (NHSDA and MTF). Beyond compiling self-reported drug use and other information from respondents, the DUF became the first large-scale prevalence study to use a chemical assay procedure to measure drug prevalence independent of self-report.

Given the legitimate concerns regarding the validity of self-reports of drug use, a survey should employ a reliable validation technique to estimate the degree of error in *reported* versus *actual* use. Late in the 1970s, low-cost, high-volume urinalysis procedures for detecting illicit drugs became available (Wish and Gropper 1990). The Drug Use Forecasting System uses urine screening for all respondents included in the sample and thus represents the first use of a chemical assay process for drug use to validate a major survey. However, unlike NHSDA and MTF, DUF is not a national probability sample of arrestees. However, while DUF cannot be used to generate a national figure for arrestees, for a given DUF site, the quarterly data probably provide a "good representation" of arrestees for that locality (Chaiken and Chaiken 1992). Chaiken and Chaiken reported three main findings. First, DUF arrestees "provide a good representation of the arrestees who are booked in the particular locations where DUF operates . . . however, booked arrestees are not representative of the totality of arrestees in the city or county" (p. 1). Second, there was no observed change in drug use prevalence when controlling for types of arrest, and, third, the prevalence of drug use does not seem to vary with offense seriousness.

The Drug Use Forecasting System was developed to produce quantitative data on the drug prevalence among arrestees not only for its own informational sake but because these data could be used to forecast general population drug use trends as well. This was premised on the belief that, relative to the general population, trends in a criminally deviant subpopulation may function as a leading indicator for general drug use. "One might expect that, as an illicit drug becomes available in a community, those more deviant persons who are committing crimes might be the first to use it. The urine-test results for heroin from arrestees in the District of Columbia showed evidence of the growing heroin epidemic in Washington in the 1970's one to one-and-a-half years before other indicators such as new treatment admissions, overdose deaths, and emergency room admissions" (Wish and Gropper 1990, p. 332).

The DUF system started with eight sites in 1987. By 1992 the system included twenty-four sites. Twenty-one sites collected data on both males and females, and three on males only. Twelve DUF sites also collect data from juvenile arrestees. The system conducts more than 25,000 urinalyses annually on its total sample group.

A. The Drug Use Forecasting System Methodology

At each site DUF staff interview volunteer arrestees who appear at that site's central booking facility. The staff also collect urine specimens from the interviewees. On a quarterly basis, 225–50 arrestees, solicited over approximately ten to fourteen days, are asked to participate, on a voluntary and confidential basis. They are asked, among other things, about their current drug use. Respondents are selected so that they primarily represent arrestees charged with serious, nondrug offenses. Each site has a cap on the number of drug-charged cases it will interview, and some categories of arrestees (such as traffic offenses) are excluded.

The DUF samples are not random samples, and the generalizability of the findings has been the chief focus of critics of DUF data (Harrison 1992a; U.S. House of Representatives, Committee on Government Operations 1993). However, as Wish notes, "while the sampling scheme for the DUF cities does not permit the computation of combined national estimates of drug use in arrestees, it does yield accurate estimates of recent drug use in arrestees in each participating city" (Wish 1990, p. 385). A report of the General Accounting Office (U.S. House of Representatives, Committee on Government Operations 1993, p. 53) takes issue with this, arguing that the "DUF recognizes that this procedure might result in a charge distribution of arrestees in the DUF sample that differs from the charge distribution of all arrestees of a given city."

B. The Drug Use Forecasting System Findings Based on Urinalysis Outcomes

The DUF annual reports emphasize the outcomes of the urine assays as its major finding, and little information is provided in recent reports on self-reported drug use. For example, the 1992 DUF annual report contains no self-report data (National Institute of Justice 1993). The 1992 report principally provides findings on the urinalysis outcomes for prominent drugs, by gender (race, ethnicity) and site. It also provides data on arrest charges as determined from official records (i.e., not "self-reported" charges). The report also provides data on the urinalysis outcomes and charges for sites that test juveniles, and it provides trend information for various drugs as measured by the urinalysis outcomes. But there is no presentation of data regarding the degree of the self-reported drug use of the subjects, or how this level of use compares to the findings of the urine assays.

The report does not explain why it does not include information on self-reported drug use, but it should be noted that, compared to both NHSDA and MTF, the DUF annual report is a relatively small document, in 1992 composed of thirty-two pages. The other three systems' annual reports run hundreds of pages. The primary architect of the DUF system, Dr. Eric Wish, has said in public forums that DUF originally focused on gathering urine specimens for purposes of drug screening. He has characterized the original process of interviewing as primarily a device to establish rapport with subjects to enhance the probability that they would voluntarily produce urine specimens for analysis.

The National Institute of Justice has made the complete data files for all DUF sites available to the public on computer diskette, so anyone wanting to analyze the self-report data has access to it. The DUF self-report data have been analyzed by several researchers, several of whom (Harrison 1989, 1992a; Mieczkowski 1990; and Rosenfeld and

Decker 1993) have compared outcomes of urine tests and self-reported drug use.

Harrison (1992*b*) analyzed 1989 DUF data from all sites, a total of 21,991 cases, and concluded that "surprisingly, the data show a high amount of congruence between self-report and urinalysis" (Harrison 1992*a*, p. 3). This conclusion rests on considering all cases arrayed in a 2 × 2 table in which the positive and negative outcomes for self-report and urine test constitute the table's matrix. Harrison emphasized, in her analysis, that the largest percentage of cases was concordant (i.e., urine and self-report were in agreement). However, Rosenfeld and Decker (1993), in surveying DUF data from thirteen cities for 1989, reached the opposite conclusion. They state that

> perhaps the most compelling challenge to the validity of offenders' accounts of illegal drug use comes from the Drug Use Forecasting (DUF) program operated by the National Institute of Justice (NIJ), which records arrestees' drug use through confidential self-reports and, for recent use, voluntary urine tests. The DUF data show higher levels of drug use among arrestees when measured by urine tests than when measured by self-report. The discrepancy between tested and self-reported use is particularly large for cocaine. . . . Cocaine use is underreported by a sizable margin in all cities, in most cases by more than 50%. [Rosenfeld and Decker 1993, p. 3]

These seemingly incompatible conclusions from the same data may occur because the accuracy of self-report varies by response category and drug type. Arrested abstainers from drugs are highly accurate in reporting their abstinence. But arrested users of drugs (with perhaps the exception of marijuana) are very likely to misreport their drug use. Harrison (1992*a*, p. 3) notes this when she states, "One of the common misinterpretations of the congruence of urinalysis and self-report occurs when focusing only on those with positive urinalysis. Negative urinalysis must be considered as well. Failure to consider the full range of response may be what led the DUF researchers to conclude that drug use is not accurately self-reported. It is true, however, that if you only consider those who test positive, only about one third to one half admit their drug use."

Mieczkowski analyzed DUF data from Detroit comparing 454 cases of self-reported use and the associated urinalysis outcomes, controlling for appropriate time differentials and examining the effects of use intensity and drug type, and concluded that "there is more concordance in every category of drug and at each level of use than can be accounted for by random chance." He notes that "substance type appears to be related to the probability of a non-concordant or invalid response. Cocaine users have a quite distinctly higher rate of non-valid denial when compared to users of the other tested substances" (Mieczkowski 1990, p. 295). Self-reported drug use is likely to be accurate for those who are drug abstainers—they rarely falsely claim to have used a drug when they have not. However, a substantial number of users falsely deny drug use. For cocaine, based on DUF results, this difference is roughly two to one: twice as many persons who test positive for cocaine deny any cocaine use when compared with those who admit using it.

The DUF experience offers an important critique of the reliability of the general population surveys that rely on self-reported drug use to estimate prevalence. The DUF findings imply that surveys used in populations with potentially high levels of drug use probably underestimate drug use prevalence, perhaps quite significantly.

C. Key Findings from the 1992 Annual Report

The Drug Use Forecasting System has had a substantial effect for several reasons. It has shown that bioassay-based validations of surveys are possible, even in a relatively adversarial setting. It has also demonstrated that there is a very large percentage of drug-positive cases at criminal justice intake. And it has shown, at least within its own context, that self-reported use of drugs generates severe underestimates when compared to prevalence as indicated by bioassay. And this third point is precisely what critics of the general population surveys have argued for years.

The DUF system showed that for arrestees the number of positive urine test results as a percentage of all arrestees tested was very large. The system continues to report drug prevalence at much greater levels than the general population surveys. The percentage of booked male arrestees positive for any drug measured by DUF in 1992 ranged from 47 percent (Phoenix) to 78 percent (Philadelphia); female arrestees ranged from 44 percent (San Antonio) to 85 percent (New York/Manhattan). In twenty-one of the twenty-four DUF sites, more than one-half of all arrestees were drug-positive. Multiple-drug-positive urines were common, especially in San Diego, Chicago, Los Angeles, New York (Manhattan), and Philadelphia. The DUF prevalence values are

TABLE 4

The Five Highest Ranking Drug Use Forecast Cities in 1992:
Percentage of Arrestees Testing Positive by Urinalysis

City and Gender	Percent Testing Positive for Any Drug	Percent Testing Positive for Cocaine
New York:		
Male	77	62
Female	85	72
Philadelphia:		
Male	78	63
Female	78	67
San Diego:		
Male	77	45
Female	72	37
Cleveland:		
Male	64	53
Female	74	66
St. Louis:		
Male	64	50
Female	70	62

SOURCE.—National Institute of Justice (1993).

NOTE.—Drugs include Cannabinoids, Opiates, Cocaine, Amphetamines, Barbiturates, Tranquilizers, Diazepam, Methaqualone, PCP, and Darvon.

high by comparison with any previous survey data on illicit drug use. Table 4 lists the percentages of arrestees positive for any drug and positive for cocaine, by gender, of the five-highest ranking cities for 1992.

Cocaine is the most prevalent drug among DUF arrestees. The percent of male arrestees testing positive for cocaine ranged from 16 percent (Omaha) to 62 percent (Manhattan and Philadelphia). Female arrestees ranged from 25 percent (San Antonio) to 76 percent (Cleveland). Marijuana was the second most prevalent drug, ranging from 11 percent to 33 percent for males and from 4 percent to 28 percent for females. Opiates (primarily heroin) ranged from 1 percent (Fort Lauderdale and Kansas) to 21 percent (males in Chicago, females in Manhattan and San Diego). Overall, other drugs were only modestly represented, with some local exceptions for amphetamine (primarily western sites).

In the 1992 DUF report, trends for "urine positive at arrest for any illicit drug" are examined over the 1988–92 collection years (National

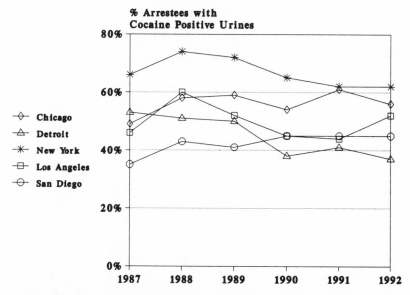

Fig. 17.—Trends in cocaine prevalence: percentage of arrestees testing positive for cocaine by urinalysis for five major Drug Use Forecast cities. Source: National Institute of Justice (1993).

Institute of Justice 1993). At most DUF sites, positive results for any drug fluctuated but, overall, remained high. Figure 17 displays the trends for cocaine for five major cities. These trends vary when considering specific drugs. For example, marijuana declined at most DUF sites from 1988 to 1991. But the 1992 data show some slight increases for marijuana use (as indicated by urinalysis). Cocaine use peaked in 1988 and 1989, but the decreases since then have been slight and variable across sites. Opiate use, like cocaine, either remained stable or decreased only slightly. The DUF data are not aggregated into single national numbers since sites do vary in their methodologies and conditions.

D. Urinalysis Data and Self-Reported Drug Use

The DUF experience has implicitly raised issues regarding the appropriateness of relying on self-reported drug use to measure the prevalence of drug use. In effect the DUF system has shown that self-reports, at least in this group, are very likely substantially underreported. For example, DUF data reported by Harrison (1989) suggest that twice as many persons tested positive for cocaine by urinalysis as reported cocaine use. Harrison in discussing the DUF data noted that "the bottom line is that our estimates of drug use based solely on self-report would be about half to two-thirds of what they are based on urinalysis for the drugs arrestees are most likely to test positive for—cocaine, marijuana, and the opiates. . . . Overall, we conclude that arrestees are unlikely to reveal the true pattern of their recent drug use in personal interviews, even when assured of the anonymity and confidentiality of their responses" (Harrison 1989, p. 6).

One final development should be noted regarding the use of drug assay procedures and their role in drug prevalence determinations. Over the last several years researchers have begun to use hair-based drug assays to evaluate use in various populations, including arrestees. Hair analysis permits a relatively long retrospective window (several weeks or months) for detecting drug exposure. Early work by Mieczkowski et al. (1991) and Feucht, Stephens, and Walker (1992) indicates that urine-based counts of drug exposure may themselves be undercounts, at least for cocaine. Mieczkowski et al. (1991), for example, doing a DUF emulation study found twice as many cocaine exposed arrestees in Pinellas County, Florida, when comparing hair to urine assays. Feucht, Stephens, and Walker (1992) used hair assays to evaluate prevalence in a DUF juvenile population in Cleveland. Of eighty-eight subjects tested, seven tested positive for cocaine in their urine, and fifty tested positive for cocaine by hair analysis. Of the thirty-eight subjects who tested negative for cocaine by hair assay, all tested negative by urinalysis as well. Others have reported the effectiveness of hair analysis in detecting drug exposure in ways that could alter current prevalence estimations (Ostrea, Parks, and Brady 1989; Callahan et al. 1992). If these findings continue to be sustained, the implication is that even urine-based estimates of cocaine prevalence may be too conservative (Mieczkowski et al. 1993).

V. Estimations: Synthetic, Multiple Capture, and System Dynamics

It is an axiom of drug epidemiology that exhaustive enumeration of the target population is impossible. Consequently, "when a population cannot be observed directly, its size must be inferred from other information about the population. Measurable quantities must stand in for unmeasurable ones" (Wickens 1993, p. 187). The problems noted for the systems discussed in this essay also provide a motivation for sophisticated approaches to combine the measures in a type of meta-analysis and to approximate an estimation for the nation as a whole.

This section examines three such meta-estimations. The first is an exercise by Eric Wish, who suggested that DUF data showed that the number of cocaine users who were arrested could account for all the cocaine users the NHSDA suggested in the entire country. This was followed by a more detailed examination of synthetic approaches by the U.S. Senate Judiciary Committee, directed primarily by Mark Kleiman. Last, the most sophisticated meta-analysis focusing on "heavy" cocaine users was done by William Rhodes.

Three methods have been proposed to make more accurate and complete national estimations of the illicit-drug-using population: synthetic estimations, multiple capture methods, and system dynamics models. What they all share in common is an approach that coherently *integrates multiple sources of information*. Thus, these procedures have the potential to use the different survey data sets and combine them into a more accurate national prevalence estimate.

Multiple capture, system dynamic, and synthetic estimation models all have benefits and disadvantages that need to be considered in examining a specific problem. All estimation approaches are based on idealized models that are inevitably violated in real world settings. To make a reasonable and meaningful interpretation of the estimation outcome, various aspects of the data not included in the estimation model must be considered and understood. Lastly, researchers should use multiple methods. This is desirable because estimates can then be compared for consistency.

Each technique is based on a different strategy. Multiple capture methods use two or more samples taken from a target population. Based on values calculated from the samples, the analyst estimates a parametric value for a population. That estimate, in turn, is based on a probability distribution assumption for key variable values, typically either a Poisson distribution or a log-linear model.

System dynamics models, such as Markov chain analysis, which are particularly apt for open populations (populations whose model elements actively enter and exit the population pool) have not been used to estimate drug prevalence. But they have been used in limited ways to describe drug market dynamics and large-scale systems integration of drug behavior (Levin, Roberts, and Hirsch 1975; Kennedy, Reuter, and Riley 1993). A system dynamic model consists of "an interconnected set of algebraic and difference equations representing the continuous ebb and flow of people, materials, and information. After being assigned initial conditions consistent with historical data, the set of equations is used to generate output over time" (Homer 1993, p. 252).

These models are based primarily on feedback structures that characterize relevant variable relationships in the target population. They are typically dependent on historical conditions to establish their start-up state, but once initiated they are driven by internal relationships. The major use of these models has been in understanding change and describing potential outcomes of a system under different conditions. Policy gaming and drug market analysis have used this approach (DiNardo 1993; Kennedy, Reuter, and Riley 1993).

Synthetic estimates are attempts to evaluate prevalence in a population for which total enumeration is not feasible. The technique is particularly useful for establishing drug prevalence measures. It is a procedure that permits the derivation from a particular sample (the calibration sample) of estimated values. The procedure uses statistical mechanisms applied to a calibration sample and, through mathematical manipulation, allows those calibrations to be applied to an entire population. Thus it appears particularly attractive in grappling with prevalence data for drug users. Wickens (1993) discusses various methods by which drug prevalence and related estimations can be made. For unobserved populations (populations from which no data are drawn) synthetic estimation is particularly appropriate and can be applied in a cross-sectional method (closed population) or a longitudinal method (open population). "When the size of an unobserved population is to be estimated, it is necessary to construct the estimate from some other observable characteristic. In effect, one creates an artificial image of the population, hence these techniques are known as synthetic estimates" (Wickens 1993, p. 187).

However, Wickens considers drug prevalence estimations to be "hybrid cases" that are driven by a mixture of indicators and represent "the best (or only) way to proceed when the population is large or composite. Synthetic estimations for complex populations necessarily have an ad hoc quality" (Wickens 1993, p. 187). Because of different conceptual bases for approaching the problem of drug prevalence, there is no single best estimation procedure.

Synthetic estimations allow more complex considerations and integrations of empirical data than simple projections or extrapolations from single data sets. But they involve very large assumptions about the data and its setting. In reflecting on these assumptions Rhodes has pointed out that, "in practice, the application of synthetic estimation to drug use prevalence appears to be more art than science. The data from the calibration sample are sparse, biased, and otherwise inaccurate. All three conditions mitigate against making probability based confidence intervals" (Rhodes 1993, p. 313). However, and in spite of these caveats, synthetic estimations have played an important role in the controversy surrounding the usefulness and accuracy of survey-based drug prevalence data, especially the NHSDA.

1. *Wish's Estimation of Cocaine Users in Sixty-two Cities.*   Wish (1990) is an important example of synthetic prevalence estimation. Wish, critical of the undercounting in NHSDA and the MTF data, observed that while these surveys show in recent years a "dramatic drop in middle class and casual drug use . . . there remains a stubborn hard core of lower-class drug use that is intense and, perhaps, still growing" (p. 395). Wish noted dramatic differences in user estimates from the general population surveys and DUF. For example, "current use" of cocaine (within the past month) is from eight to twelve times higher among DUF respondents, and cocaine use within the last three days (based on the outcomes of urinalysis) is seventeen to twenty-five times higher. For marijuana and heroin, prevalence in the DUF sample was also greater by significant amounts.

Using data compiled from twenty-one DUF sites, Wish synthesized a "rough estimate" of the prevalence of cocaine use in the arrestee population in the largest American cities in 1988. Wish obtained the number of arrests for each DUF city, basing the arrest data on the Uniform Crime Report rate. He then multiplied this number of arrests by the percentage of male arrestees testing positive for cocaine for the 1988 DUF year. This operation was then carried out for each DUF city, and each city's values were summed. Using this method Wish estimated that there were 1.1 million cocaine-positive arrestees in these DUF sites.

In order to apply these DUF estimates to non-DUF cities of similar size, Wish identified forty-one such cities in the United States with populations greater than 250,000 (a total of sixty-one cities, minus twenty cities that were already DUF sites, equaling forty-one non-DUF cities). Again, estimating—from the Federal Bureau of Investigation's Uniform Crime Report—the total number of arrests in these cities, Wish calculated that there were 1.36 million such arrests (17.2 million population at 7,901 arrests per 100,000 population). He then estimated a high and low value for those arrestees who tested positive for cocaine. To estimate the low value, he took the DUF city with the lowest incidence of cocaine-positive arrestees (Indianapolis, 15 percent), and, for the high, he took the average cocaine-positive rate of 41 percent for the (then-operating) twenty-one DUF sites. His calculations yielded values ranging from 203,000 to 637,000 cocaine-positive arrestees. Last, to estimate the total number of cocaine-positive arrestees, he added the DUF value to the non-DUF value, correcting for rearrests. His estimation is that 1.3–1.7 million arrestees in the sixty-one largest cities would have tested positive for cocaine at arrest. To allow for rearrests, Wish multipled this estimate by .75. He concludes that a conservative estimate is that 978,000–1.3 million persons were cocaine-positive at arrest in 1988.

The difference between these estimates and those derived from NHSDA is stark. As Wish notes, "To put the estimate of cocaine use among arrestees in perspective, we compared them to the estimates of the number of weekly cocaine users in the U.S. household population in 1988. The arrestee population in the 61 largest cities contains about as many weekly cocaine users (937,000 to 1.3 million) as is estimated to exist in the entire U.S. household population (620,000 to 1.1 million)" (Wish 1990, p. 390).

2. *The Senate Judiciary Committee.* Wish's work resulted in efforts by others to evaluate current prevalence estimations of "hard-core" drug users, with a special emphasis on cocaine. One influential examination was detailed in a series of reports and papers generated by the staff of the Senate Judiciary Committee under the chairmanship of Senator Joseph Biden of Delaware. These efforts and their implications are contained in three documents: reports from the Majority Staffs of the Senate Judiciary Committee and the International Narcotics Control Caucus (U.S. Senate, Committee on the Judiciary 1992a, 1992b) and the Staff Report of the Committee on the Judiciary, United States Senate (U.S. Senate, Committee on the Judiciary 1990). Biden, writing in May 1990, observed that "other researchers have previously shown that the Household Survey [NHSDA] count is incomplete in many respects. Most significantly, in a path-breaking study, Dr. Eric Wish, a fellow at the National Institute of Justice, recently offered data suggesting that the criminal justice system encounters over one million hard-core addicts in a given year. If this is true, Dr. Wish observes, then the Household Survey is at least short by half" (U.S. Senate, Committee on the Judiciary 1990, p. IV).

The Senate staff reports argue that there are many more "hard-core" drug users in the United States than are currently documented through the major general population surveys. There are "at least 2.2 million hard core cocaine addicts in America—almost triple the number revealed by the NIDA Survey" (U.S. Senate, Committee on the Judiciary 1990, p. 1). In some cities the number of these users is described as being extraordinarily high—for example, in New York City, one out of every forty persons is a hard-core cocaine user. Weekly users are highly unlikely to receive treatment and especially likely to be involved in crime.

The 1990 staff report focuses on the prevalence of "hard-core" cocaine users (i.e., those who use once a week or more often) and includes a synthetic estimation. Later staff reports (U.S. Senate, Committee on the Judiciary 1992a, 1992b) are more expansive and include other drugs. Here I focus on cocaine estimation since it has been dealt with in detail and is consistent with the conclusions reached for the other major drugs. The estimation was done by the committee staff (U.S. Senate, Committee on the Judiary 1990) under the direction of Mark Kleiman of Harvard University. The major findings regarding cocaine prevalence were that there were many more serious cocaine users than were documented by the NHSDA (roughly twice as many) and that this population was increasing, with a projection then of three million hard-core users by the end of 1991. This estimation process extended Wish's work by including homeless persons, school dropouts, and other populations not included in NHSDA or MTF.

The estimation procedure employed four data sources: individuals in drug treatment (based on data from individual states), the number of the homeless, those under detention by the criminal justice system (based largely on DUF data), and the NHSDA. The estimation process consisted of a summation of the populations of each group, with adjustment made to eliminate duplicate counting of people who may fall into several categories. Using arrest reports and drug treatment admissions data for each state, every state was "allocated" a proportion of the total estimate, and each state was also assigned a per capita concentration value (addicts/thousand population).

The estimation strategy was to supplement the NHSDA data with counts from populations that are not included in the survey. Treatment admissions for cocaine were established by requesting information about admissions to publicly run or supported drug treatment programs from members of the National Association of State Alcohol and Drug Abuse Directors. The treatment counts included all programs that had received some level of federal funding. The number of "hard-core" cocaine admissions nationwide approximated 208,000 (of 700,000 total admissions). Using estimations based on Treatment Outcome Prospective Study data, and eliminating noncocaine clients, this figure was reduced to 197,000 in order to account for duplicate admissions (Hubbard et al. 1989). This figure is conservative since it does not include individuals who were in private treatment settings. The committee staff reports note that the treatment admissions population does not contribute substantially to the total number of cocaine addicts, although cocaine users do place a large demand on treatment services nationwide.

The homeless are a second "missed" population. Estimates of the number of homeless people in the United States range between one and three million (approximately seven to eleven homeless persons for every thousand Americans). For the purposes of estimation, the committee assumed that there were 2,100,000 homeless people. A more difficult estimation was determining a reasonable formula for calculating the number of homeless who were drug-addicted, in general, and cocaine-addicted, specifically. Using data available from selected cities that had estimated the relative difference in likelihood of addiction between homeless and nonhomeless people, the committee used a multiplication factor of five. That is, five times the estimated NHSDA rate of cocaine addiction would yield an approximate and conservative value for homeless cocaine addicts. This yielded an actual value of 2.5 percent. Thus, 2.5 percent of the nation's homeless (2,100,000 persons) yields 55,000 homeless cocaine addicts. Homeless addicts constitute, therefore, only a small fraction of the total estimation for the nation. However, the committee strongly notes that these persons, although small in absolute number, "present one of the most desperate aspects of our Nation's drug problem" (U.S. Senate, Committee on the Judiciary 1990, p. 13).

The third NHSDA-deficient population, and the major contributing group, are persons in the criminal justice system—persons under arrest, in detention, or under penal supervision. In addition, the committee argued that those under scrutiny by criminal justice agencies—those on probation, parole, conditional release, and the like—are very unlikely to admit to any drug use when polled. In order to estimate this population, the committee emulated the work of Wish but modified it substantially by using different assumptions for base calculations and including different populations. Estimation procedures used DUF site averages for cocaine-positive arrestees and extrapolated those values to large cities (250,000+ populations) that are not DUF sites. For small cities, the committee used a conservative 15 percent estimation and, for rural and suburban populations, an even lower rate of 7.5 percent. The Judiciary Committee arrived at the following estimations of hard-core cocaine addicted arrestees: 1.07 million in large cities, 113,000 for small cities, and 348,000 for rural and suburban communities, for a total of 1,529,000.

The total number of cocaine addicts then can be calculated from these four sources: the homeless, those in treatment, those under the control of the criminal justice system, and those in households. Of the 197,000 treatment cases (based on Treatment Outcome Prospective Study data), 40 percent would be counted as arrestees, thus the net 120,000 should be added to any national estimate. Of the 55,000 homeless, the committee includes only 5,000 since "most homeless addicts are either arrested, admitted to treatment, or both" (U.S. Senate, Committee on the Judiciary 1992b, p. 42). Since arrest status is used to eliminate the treatment and homeless overlaps, the 1.5 million DUF estimate constitutes a third unique group. To estimate the degree of overlap between arrestees and the NHSDA population, the committee uses percentages of the NHSDA group that admit to having been arrested (30 percent) or in treatment (10 percent) to reduce the NHSDA fraction accordingly. Thus, of the 862,000 NHSDA cases, 345,000 are included in other populations of arrestees, clients in treatment, or the homeless. The "unique" component for the NHSDA then is 517,000. Summing these yields a total of approximately 2.2 million. "All told, the sum of our four surveys, less any addicts included in more than one of the surveys, indicates a national total of approximately 2,200,000 hard-core cocaine addicts. Even this figure—an astounding 2 times the official Government estimate—is probably too low. In each of the three surveys original to this report, as well as in generating the national total, this report employed only the most conservative estimates" (U.S. Senate, Committee on the Judiciary 1990, p. 21). Thus the Judiciary Committee report increases the numbers of Wish's estimate by approximately one million. These additional cases came largely by including several populations Wish did not consider (he restricted his estimation to criminal justice populations) and by extending the criminal justice estimations to include suburban and rural areas and smaller cities.

3. *Rhodes' Estimations of Cocaine and Heroin Prevalence.* At the end of

1989, the Office of National Drug Control Policy sought advice on prevalence data for the major illicit drugs of abuse. Abt Associates of Cambridge, Massachusetts, prepared a synthetic prevalence estimation for the organization (Rhodes 1993). Rhodes attempted to estimate weekly cocaine and heroin use by criminal-justice-involved adults.

Rhodes sought to estimate the number of persons arrested and booked from Uniform Crime Report data for urban, suburban, and rural areas. This figure was estimated at 8.8 million adult bookings for 1990. He then developed weighted rates of cocaine-positive arrestees by deriving them from DUF data for the twenty-two sites in operation in 1990. To do this Rhodes used a regression estimation procedure to weight and reconstitute DUF rates of drug-positive individuals for site geography, gender, and offense category. Based on this, he estimated that 2.7 million arrests would result in positive urinalysis assays for cocaine. Rhodes then argued that several adjustments must be made to the 2.7 million figure. Only a fraction of this group is involved in weekly use. Some fraction is also rearrested, thus appearing in the population of arrestees more than once in a year. Alternately, another fraction is involved with the justice system but avoids arrest during a given calendar year. To make an estimation of users who are arrested in a given year, Rhodes assumed that the probability could be represented as a homogeneous Poisson process. This resulted in an estimation that 3.2 million persons in contact with the justice system were cocaine users. Using a variety of sources, Rhodes estimated that 56 percent are "heavy" (i.e., weekly) users. This is equivalent to 1.8 million persons. Of these 1.8 million, approximately 214,000 are incarcerated at any given time.

No factor is added to the estimation for the homeless. It is believed that the homeless, who are heavily involved in cocaine use, are at high probability to be involved with the justice system. Thus, they are largely accounted for in that estimation fraction. For high school students, detained juvenile offenders, and school dropouts, Rhodes estimated approximately 41,000 are heavily involved in cocaine use. The number for college students is estimated to be 15,000. The number of heavy cocaine users in the military is assumed to be insignificant. These groups, relative to the criminal justice system, do not make a major contribution to the final prevalence number.

Last, Rhodes accepts that the self-reported data from the NHSDA represents the general population of cocaine users. There is overlap, however, between the prior categories and those persons represented in the NHSDA. Rhodes estimates the nonoverlap population to be 205,000 (out of 662,000 self-reported weekly cocaine users in the NHSDA). Summing all components of the estimation, Rhodes concludes that there were approximately two million heavy cocaine users for the year 1990, a number he says "is reasonable, but we do not believe it is precise" (Rhodes 1993, p. 311). Repeating this approach for heroin, Rhodes estimated 658,000 heavy users of heroin for 1990.

The driving population behind the estimation is users involved in the justice system. Assumptions used for other contributing populations (e.g., students, etc.), even if relatively inaccurate, would not produce serious distortions in the estimate. Of more concern are the assumptions used in generating the criminal justice numbers. Rhodes notes, for example, that the estimation settled on an assumption of a 30 percent cocaine-positive rate for all booked arrestees. However, varying that number from 25 percent to 40 percent would produce a fluctuation in the estimation of nearly a million cases (1.7–2.6 million). A similar problem is encountered in estimating the number of weekly users. Rhodes derived a figure of 56 percent for estimating the number of cocaine positive users who are weekly users. However, if the number is varied between 50 percent and 80 percent (80 percent is the estimate used by the Judiciary Committee), the fluctuation is again a million cases (from 1.8 to 2.8 million).

The significance of these biasing factors is impossible to know. It is possible that these factors could compound one another (i.e., the biases run in similar directions). A more plausible assumption is that to some degree these biasing sources mitigate each other. Rhodes estimates that a range of 1.5 to 2.5 million "hard-core" cocaine users is reasonable and generally consistent with other research.

VI. Conclusions

There is substantial disagreement on the current best estimates of drug use prevalence. That should come as no surprise. Arguments about prevalence, potently coupled with a sense of urgency and fear about drug use, are long-lived in American society. Drug use, its consequences, and its extent have seldom been uncontroversial. There is no reason to expect them to be so now. The major feature of this controversy is to what degree the estimations derived from the major surveys on drug abuse are conservative, and this implicates a series of issues discussed in this essay.

The only unique addition to prevalence studies in this century is the development of bioassays that are cost-effective, quick, and accurate. And, given that development, it is surprising how little use has been made of biological testing to validate survey responses. Only the DUF system employs bioassays on a large scale, and DUF does not investigate representative samples of the population. And while hair assays are sufficiently reliable for certain important categories of drugs, they have yet to be used even in pilot studies to see how they would affect the interpretation of survey-based estimations of past drug use.

Prevalence estimation never takes place in a political vacuum, and, since these estimates are seldom (as yet) extremely precise or exact, they are inevitably manipulated in the politics that surround drug policy. While concerns and complaints about the selective interpretation or molding of drug use data are understandable and merit attention, it is hard to imagine that such data will ever be immune from manipulation and misrepresentation.

Even those who have been most critical of the current survey research do not assail the professionalism, integrity, and effort of the investigators who have conducted this work. The current survey-based prevalence estimations are characterized by all sides as well done. However, their results are, at least according to some views, misleading and perhaps wildly misleading. And there is a consensus that the official surveys are underestimates; some might prefer to call them "conservative." No one argues that any of the general population surveys overestimates drug use.

Multiple source methods or "triangulation" approaches to estimation inevitably produce higher numbers than the NHSDA or MTF, but these estimations are not free from controversy. Ranges of these estimations vary widely, sometimes by millions of estimated users. Furthermore, there is no comfortable fit between drug prevalence estimations for the general population, drug importation data, drug data based on criminal justice populations, and medically based public health and treatment data. Haaga and Reuter (1991, p. 20) observe,

A major weakness of the current system of data collection,
both from a scientific and policy perspective, is the lack of
dissemination of data sets for secondary analysis. For example,
NHSDA, DAWN, the System to Retrieve Drug Evidence, and
NDATUS [the National Drug Abuse Treatment Utilization
Survey] have not been made available as public-use tapes, nor
have agencies generally been willing to make data sets available

to researchers who sought them. Consequently the published research based on these data is meager. Only the annual high school senior surveys of Monitoring the Future have been made available for secondary analysis.

The lack of thorough analysis of existing data suggests that there is no general agreement as to whether the major problem is measurement itself or intrinsic differences in data targets. A lack of attention to analysis has resulted in fragmentation because only the most basic findings are reported for some data sets. The NHSDA, for example, collects data on employment and income, but the data have never been published. Similar criticisms were raised by the General Accounting Office report (U.S. House of Representatives, Committee on Government Operations 1993) regarding race and ethnicity in the MTF, although the MTF has moved to make up for this to some degree.

The collection of drug prevalence data can be improved by advancing the comparability of surveys between different populations, by making data sets publicly available for secondary analysis, and by supporting such activity both logistically and financially. Prevalence estimators, for their part, should continue to develop rigorous estimation procedures, like synthetic estimation, in order to integrate data from disparate sources.

Current data, while imperfect, is a net asset for the study of drug prevalence and related issues and can usefully inform policy makers, even if that information must be treated gingerly. It is incumbent on policy makers to consider the use of this data in formulating policy when the data are well founded. Policy formulators and advocates must similarly recognize that using data selectively to prop up a priori ideological claims will only alienate the analytic community and reduce the quality of information that good scholarship can extract from good data.

Survey research will continue as the prime method for measuring drug use. Substantial energy and resources have been expended in developing such surveys, and they are a reliable and familiar mechanism for cost-effective monitoring of drug use. But meeting the current pressures to enhance validation of the findings is critical if the confidence of those who we expect to be influenced by the research is to be maintained and enhanced.

Prevalence estimations based on multiple data sources will be the hallmark of future work. To be accomplished effectively, three conditions must be satisfied. First, to the extent possible, the "political stakes" invested in the outcome of drug data need to be eliminated or minimized. Second, agencies need to cooperate in reducing barriers to maximize the comparability of research and data collection. There needs to be a concomitant commitment to providing ready access to researchers to complete data sets for the purposes of secondary analysis. Third, synthesizing methodologies need further elaboration. If agencies are successful in producing broadly comparable data sets, then analytic techniques must be developed to make effective use of them. Synthetic estimation procedures offer the brightest and most cost-effective way to enhance the accuracy of prevalence estimations.

APPENDIX

In looking at attempts to estimate the prevalence of drug use in earlier eras, there are five major sources of statistical data: surveys of physicians, pharmacists, and allied medical professions; the records of narcotics maintenance clinics; military and draft records on rejections from service due to drug addiction; revenue data indicating the amounts of legally imported narcotics entering the United States; and prevalence estimates generated by units of government and private research in the early twentieth century.

I. The Earliest Prevalence Surveys

Americans have long worried about the dimensions and effects of addictive and habituating drugs. Drug use has been linked historically to the general notion of "intemperance." While primarily tied to the "spiritous liquors," the nineteenth-century idea of intemperance was also identified with the use of other drugs, especially opiates.

Appendix table A1 identifies several early historical efforts to estimate prevalence rates for drug addiction. The earliest is a 1741 article in the *Connecticut Courant* on "The Use of Opium." The column decried the addicting power of opiate use, seeing it as an extension of the general vices of drinking and gambling. The use of intoxicating substances—because of their induction of "idleness, improvidence, and intemperance"—resulted in impoverishment and social "dependence." Impoverishment and the failure of citizens to discharge their civic responsibilities arose as a consequence of "drunkenness, idleness, and vice of all kind" (p. 56). The *Courant* article gave a high prevalence figure of ten to sixteen opiate addicts for every 1,000 citizens in New York.

Early drug prevalence estimates were primarily focused on opiates, with less emphasis on other psychoactive substances in use by physicians of the time. However, "drug use" did include, besides various opiate preparations, cocaine, marijuana, chloral hydrate, and other substances typically offered to the public as tonics and medicinals.

Courtwright (1982) considers the Marshall survey of 1877, carried out in Michigan, to be the first "systematic" estimate of the prevalence of opiate use.

TABLE A1

Early Drug Prevalence Estimations

Source	Prevalence Estimation	By Location
Connecticut Courant 1741	10–16/1,000	New York
Stevens 1850	3–4/1,000	National
Marshall 1878	5.8/1,000	Rural Michigan
Earle 1880	4–5/drugstore	Chicago
Hull 1885	2/drugstore	Iowa
Wright 1910	Rates of importation	. . .
DuMez et al. 1919	.5–1 million	National
Hynson 1920	2/1,000	New York, Philadelphia
Kolb and DuMez 1924	1/1,000	National
Terry and Pellens 1928	237,000	National, 1919

Orville Marshall (1878) surveyed 200 physicians in 96 small towns in Michigan (omitting Detroit, Grand Rapids, and Saginaw). The responding physicians reported 1,313 addicted persons, which led Marshall to conclude that there were 5.8 opiate addicts per 1,000 members of the population. Terry and Pellens (1928), extrapolating from the Marshall survey data a half-century later, estimated that in 1877 there were slightly more than one quarter of a million (251,936) addicts in the United States (Brodsky 1985).

Another early observer of addiction epidemiology, Enos Stevens (1850), wrote on opium use in the *Boston Medical and Surgical Journal*. He estimated that there were three to four addicts per 1,000 citizens "nationwide" during the decade 1840–50. This number, while lower than the Marshall estimate, is not wildly inconsistent with it. Projecting Stevens's estimates by simple multiplication produces a national estimate of 81,414 addicts in 1850.

Indirect indicators of drug use have been employed since the nineteenth century to estimate drug prevalence. Charles Earle (1880) surveyed fifty drugstore pharmacists in Chicago and reported that these pharmacies served 235 "addict-customers." Thus, each store serviced between four and five addicts. Justin Hull (1885) attempted to survey a sample of Iowa druggists. Reporting in the *Biennial Report of the Iowa State Board of Health*, Hull (1885) noted that the responding drugstores reported 235 opium addicts, suggesting an average of about two addicts for each retail druggist. Terry and Pellens (1928) extrapolated from this to estimate 182,215 opiate addicts in the United States in 1884.

In 1920 the American Pharmaceutical Association, under the direction of Henry Hynson, surveyed cities on the East Coast, including New York, Baltimore, Brooklyn, and Philadelphia (Hynson 1920). The survey targeted persons with "drug habits" and thus included all abused drugs, not just opiates. The report observed that there was reason to believe the survey totals and estimations represented undercounts. This is the first critical reference to the issue of undercounting in prevalence estimations. Hynson and his colleagues found that there were four to five drug abusers per drugstore within the surveyed cities. Considering the data by locale, they estimated an addict-to-population ratio of approximately two per thousand citizens in larger cities and towns. Hynson's committee also sent questionnaires out to one hundred physicians in Baltimore and to physicians in Philadelphia. The physicians reported, on average, six "addicted patients." The committee concluded that there were about 200,000 drug "habitués" in the United States (Musto 1973). Counting the actual number of practicing physicians and estimating the number of addicted patients per physician, Courtwright (1982) estimates a total number of 718,494 addicts in the United States at the turn of the century.

II. Evaluating the Records of Narcotic Maintenance Programs

Before the Harrison Act of 1914, a number of legal narcotics maintenance clinics operated in the United States. Records from these clinics have been used to reconstruct prevalence estimates for cocaine and opiate abusers. The work of Lawrence Kolb and Andrew DuMez (1924) suggested that there were approximately one to two opiate addicts for every thousand citizens in the thirty-four cities that contained narcotics clinics. This would yield an estimate of approximately 105,000 opiate addicts nationwide. However, the addict-to-population ratios varied widely by locale. Charles Terry, who operated a city-funded narcotics clinic in Jacksonville, estimated an 8:1,000 ratio for his city, four times the number estimated by Kolb and DuMez. This dramatic difference is an early indication of the differences that may exist between national prevalence data and the data that characterize a local region or metropolitan area.

Terry and Pellens (1928), extrapolating from data gathered at a New York City clinic during 1919, projected that the number of opiate addicts in the United States was slightly more than 140,000. However, at that time many opiate users were maintained in private settings by physicians, so the public clinic data are likely to have been an underestimate. Using federal survey data derived from questionnaires directed to more than 3,000 public health officers, Terry and Pellens (1928) estimated that in 1918 there were 237,655 opiate addicts.

III. Military Records

An alternative source for drug prevalence data are records that contain some indicator of opiate or other drug consumption. Military draft records for men inducted into the armed services are one example. World War I data show that the ratio of draftees rejected because of addiction compared to those inducted was quite low, at least if those ratios are compared to various estimates of opiate addicts per 1,000 population. These figures, according to Courtwright (1982), suggest that one of every one thousand inductees was likely to be excluded because of drug addiction (the actual ratio was four rejectees per 5,000 inductees).

IV. Legal Imports

The importation of opium, which prior to the development of purely synthetic narcotics was the sole source for opiate-based preparations, has also been used indirectly to estimate the prevalence of opiate users. According to the U.S. Public Health Service, between 1860 and 1900 approximately 7,000 tons of crude opium and 800 tons of smoking opium were legally imported into the United States (Kolb and DuMez 1924). Because of smuggling and other factors (such as variations in tariff rates), trend analysis based on changes in the amount of opium imported is probably reliable, but absolute numbers are not. Based on this data, Courtwright (1982) estimated that there were approximately 220,000 opiate addicts around the turn of the century, a number within the range suggested by many other observers (Musto 1973).

V. Early Official Estimates of Drug Prevalence

At the beginning of the twentieth century the federal government began to publish the first official estimations of opiate-addicted populations in the United States. Two influential reports of this era were the work of Hamilton Wright's (1910) "Report on the International Opium Commission" (done for the United States Senate), and the United States Treasury Department report of 1919 entitled *Traffic in Narcotic Drugs* (DuMez et al. 1919). Wright did not estimate the absolute number of addicts but dwelled on the relative increase in the population of addicts. He was primarily interested in arguing that the increase in opium importation was more rapid than the absolute increase in the population. This, Wright argued, proved a serious increase in the number of opiate addicts. DuMez estimated that in 1918 there were "conservatively" 750,000 addicts and perhaps as many as 1.5 million nationwide. Around this period the Treasury Department estimated that the number of drug addicts probably "exceeded 1,000,000" at the time of the report. DuMez's data were based on a physician survey of 136,745 medical doctors, 52,693 of whom responded.

Historically, these data are generally characterized as wildly inaccurate. They were made in a context of intense political lobbying and struggle regarding both domestic policies toward drugs and international negotiations regarding narcotics control treaties: "During the decade 1910 to 1920, the crucial period for the formulation of American drug policy, public opinion concerning opiate addiction was profoundly influenced by inaccurate and even falsified data" (Courtwright 1982, p. 33).

* * *

Fifty years later things appear not to have changed much. Inciardi (1986, p. 118), commenting on the early 1970s when American drug control policy became a highly visible aspect of federal politics, observes that "[President] Nixon's description of the drug problem and its relation to crime often went beyond the parameters of reasonable estimate . . . the billions of dollars of losses from thefts and robberies that Nixon claimed addicts were committing to buy their heroin supplies was actually over 25 times greater than the value of all property stolen and unrecovered throughout the United States in 1971."

REFERENCES

Anglin, M. D., J. Caulkins, and Y. Hser. 1993. "Prevalence Estimation: Policy Needs, Current Capacity, and Future Potential." *Journal of Drug Issues* 23(3): 345–59.

Brodsky, Marc. 1985. "History of Heroin Prevalence Estimation Techniques." In *Self-Report Methods of Estimating Drug Use*, edited by Beatrice Rouse, Nicholas Kozel, and Louise Richards. NIDA Research Monograph no. 57. Washington, D.C.: U.S. Government Printing Office.

Callahan, C., T. Grant, P. Phipps, G. Clark, A. Novack, A. Streissguth, and V. Raisys. 1992. "Measurement of Gestational Cocaine Exposure: Sensitivity of Infant's Hair, Meconium, and Urine." *Journal of Pediatrics* 120(5): 763–68.

Chaiken, J., and M. Chaiken. 1992. "Analysis of the Drug Use Forecasting (DUF) Sample of Adult Arrestees." Draft Report to the National Institute of Justice, Washington, D.C. Cambridge, Mass.: Abt Associates.

Community Epidemiology Working Group. 1992. *Epidemiological Trends in Drug Abuse—Proceedings*. Washington, D.C.: U.S. Government Printing Office.

Connecticut Courant. 1741. "The Use of Opium." 6(suppl.):56.

Courtwright, David. 1982. *Dark Paradise: Opiate Addiction in America before 1940*. Cambridge, Mass.: Harvard University Press.

Courtwright, D., H. Joseph, and D. Des Jarlais. 1989. *Addicts Who Survived: An Oral History of Narcotics Use in America, 1923–65*. Knoxville: University of Tennessee Press.

DiNardo, John. 1993. "Law Enforcement, The Price of Cocaine, and Cocaine Use." *Mathematical and Computer Modelling* 17(2):53–64.

DuMez, A., H. Rainey, R. Hunt, and B. Rhees. 1919. *Traffic in Narcotic Drugs*. United States Treasury Department, Special Narcotics Committee. Washington, D.C.: U.S. Goverment Printing Office.

Earle, Charles. 1880. "The Opium Habit: A Statistical and Clinical Lecture." *Chicago Medical Review* 2:442–46.

Ebener, P., E. Feldman, and N. Fitzgerald. 1993. *Federal Databases for Use in Drug Policy Research: A Catalog for Data Users*. Santa Monica, Calif.: RAND.

Fendrich, M., and C. Vaughn. 1994. "Diminished Lifetime Substance Use over Time: An Inquiry into Differential Underreporting." *Public Opinion Quarterly* 58:96–123.

Feucht, T., R. Stephens, and M. Walker. 1992. "Cocaine Use among Juvenile Arrestees: A Comparison of Self-Report, Urinalysis, and Hair Assay." *Journal of Drug Issues* 24(1/2):99–116.

Frauenthal, J. C. 1980. *Mathematical Modeling in Epidemiology*. New York: Springer-Verlag.

Haaga, J., and P. Reuter. 1991. *Improving Data for Federal Drug Policy Decisions*. Santa Monica, Calif.: RAND.

Harrison, L. 1989. "The Validity of Self-Reported Drug Use among Arrestees." Paper presented at the annual meeting of the American Society of Criminology, Reno, Nevada, November.

———. 1992a. "The Validity of Self-Reported Drug Use." Paper presented at the European Social Science Research Group on Drug Issues, third annual conference, London, September.

———. 1992b. "Trends in Illicit Drug Use in the United States: Conflicting Results from National Surveys." *International Journal of the Addictions* 27(7): 817–47.

Homer, J. 1993. "A System Dynamics Model for Cocaine Prevalence Estimation and Trend Projection." *Journal of Drug Issues* 23(2):251–79.

Hser, Y. 1993. "Data Sources: Problems and Issues." *Journal of Drug Issues* 23(2):217–28.

Hubbard, R., M. Marsden, R. Valley, H. Harwood, E. Cavanaugh, and H. Ginzberg. 1989. *Drug Abuse Treatment: A National Study of Effectiveness*. Chapel Hill: University of North Carolina Press.

Hull, J. M. 1885. "The Opium Habit." In *Iowa State Board of Health: Third Biennial Report*. Des Moines, Iowa: George E. Roberts. Reproduced in *Yesterday's Addicts*, edited by H. W. Morgan, pp. 39–42. Norman: University of Oklahoma Press, 1974.

Hynson, H. P. 1920. "Report of the Committee on Acquirement of the Drug Habit." *American Journal of Pharmacy* 74(November):551.

Inciardi, J. 1986. *The War on Drugs*. Mountain View, Calif.: Mayfield Publishing.

Johnston, Lloyd D., Patrick M. O'Malley, and Jerald G. Bachman. 1992. *Smoking, Drinking, and Illicit Drug Use among American Secondary School Students, College Students, and Young Adults, 1975–1991*, vol. 1, *Secondary School Students;* vol. 2, *College Students and Young Adults*. Washington, D.C.: U.S. Government Printing Office.

———. 1993. *National Survey Results on Drug Use from Monitoring the Future Study, 1975–1992*, vol. 1, *Secondary School Students;* vol. 2, *College Students and Young Adults*. Washington, D.C.: U.S. Government Printing Office.

Kennedy, M., P. Reuter, and J. Riley. 1993. "A Simple Economic Model of Cocaine Production." *Mathematical and Computer Modeling* 17(2):19–36.

Kleiman, M. 1986. "Data Analysis Requirements for Policy toward Drug Enforcement and Organized Crime." In *America's Habit*, edited by the President's Commission on Organized Crime. Washington, D.C.: U.S. Government Printing Office.

———. 1992. *Against Excess: Drug Policy for Results*. New York: Basic Books.

Kolb, L., and A. DuMez. 1924. "The Prevalence and Trend of Drug Addictions in the United States and the Factors Influencing It." *Public Health Reports* 39(May):1179–1204.

Latimer, D., and J. Goldberg. 1981. *Flowers in the Blood: The Story of Opium*. New York: Franklin Watts.

Levin, G., E. Roberts, and G. Hirsch. 1975. *The Persistent Poppy*. Cambridge, Mass.: Ballinger.

Marshall, O. 1878. "The Opium Habit in Michigan." *Annual Report to the Michigan State Board of Health* 6:61–73.

Mieczkowski, T. 1990. "The Accuracy of Self-Reported Drug Use: An Evaluation and Analysis of New Data." In *Drugs, Crime, and the Criminal Justice System*, edited by R. Weisheit. Cincinnati: Anderson.

Mieczkowski, T., M. D. Anglin, S. Coletti, B. Johnson, E. Nadelmann, and E. Wish. 1992. "Responding to America's Drug Problems: Strategies for the 1990's." *Journal of Urban Affairs* 14(3/4):337–57.

Mieczkowski, T., D. Barzelay, B. Gropper, and E. Wish. 1991. "Concordance of Three Measures of Cocaine Use in an Arrestee Population: Hair, Urine, and Self-Report." *Journal of Psychoactive Drugs* 23(3):241–49.

Mieczkowski, T., H. Landress, R. Newel, and S. Coletti. 1993. "Testing Hair for Illicit Drug Use." National Institute of Justice Research in Brief no. NCJ 138539. Washington, D.C.: National Institute of Justice.

Morgan, H. 1974. *Yesterday's Addicts: American Society and Drug Abuse, 1865–1920*. Norman: University of Oklahoma Press.

Musto, David. 1973. *The American Disease: Origins of Narcotic Control*. New Haven, Conn.: Yale University Press.

National Institute of Justice. 1993. *Drug Use Forecasting—1992 Annual Report*. Washington, D.C.: National Institute of Justice.

National Institute on Drug Abuse. 1992. *National Household Survey on Drug Abuse: Population Estimates 1991*. U.S. Department of Health and Human Services. Washington, D.C.: U.S. Government Printing Office.

———. 1993a. *National Household Survey on Drug Abuse: Highlights 1991*. U.S. Department of Health and Human Services. Washington, D.C.: U.S. Government Printing Office.

———. 1993b. *National Household Survey on Drug Abuse: Main Findings, 1991*. U.S. Department of Health and Human Services. Washington, D.C.: U.S. Government Printing Office.

———. 1993c. *National Household Survey on Drug Abuse Advanced Report no. 3. Preliminary Estimates from the 1992 Household Survey on Drug Abuse*. Washington, D.C.: U.S. Government Printing Office.

———. 1993d. *National Household Survey on Drug Abuse: Population Estimates 1992*. U.S. Department of Health and Human Services. Washington, D.C.: U.S. Government Printing Office.

———. 1993e. *National Household Survey on Drug Abuse: Race/Ethnicity/Socioeconomic Status and Drug Abuse 1991*. Washington, D.C.: U.S. Government Printing Office.

———. 1994a. *National Household Survey on Drug Abuse Advanced Report no. 5. Perceived Availability and Risk of Harm of Drugs. Estimates from the 1993 Household Survey on Drug Abuse*. Washington, D.C.: U.S. Government Printing Office.

———. 1994b. *National Household Survey on Drug Abuse Advanced Report no. 7*.

Preliminary Estimates from the 1993 Household Survey on Drug Abuse. Washington, D.C.: U.S. Government Printing Office.

———. 1994c. *Drug Abuse Warning Network (DAWN). Annual Emergency Room Data—1991*. Ser. 1, no. 11-A. Rockville, Md.: U.S. Department of Health and Human Services, National Institute on Drug Abuse.

———. 1994d. *Drug Abuse Warning Network (DAWN). Annual Emergency Room Data—1992*. Ser. 1, no. 12-A. Rockville, Md.: U.S. Department of Health and Human Services, National Institute on Drug Abuse.

———. 1994e. *Drug Abuse Warning Network (DAWN). Annual Medical Examiner Data—1991*. Ser. 1, no. 11-B. Rockville, Md.: U.S. Department of Health and Human Services, National Institute on Drug Abuse.

———. 1994f. *Drug Abuse Warning Network (DAWN). Annual Medical Examiner Data—1992*. Ser. 1, no. 12-B. Rockville, Md.: U.S. Department of Health and Human Services, National Institute on Drug Abuse.

Ostrea, E., P. Parks, and M. Brady. 1989. "The Detection of Heroin, Cocaine, and Cannabinoid Metabolites in Meconium of Infants of Drug Dependent Mothers." *Pediatric Research* 25:225a.

Reuter, P. 1993. "Prevalence Estimation and Policy Formulation." *Journal of Drug Issues* 23(3):167–84.

Rhodes, William. 1993. "Synthetic Estimation Applied to the Prevalence of Drug Use." *Journal of Drug Issues* 23(3):297–322.

Rosenfeld, Richard, and Scott Decker. 1993. "Discrepant Values, Correlated Measures: Cross-City and Longitudinal Comparisons of Self-Reports and Urine Tests of Cocaine Use Among Arrestees." *Journal of Criminal Justice* 21:223–31.

Stevens, Enos. 1850. *Boston Medical and Surgical Journal* 41:119–21.

Terry, C. E., and M. Pellens. 1928. *The Opium Problem*. New York: Bureau of Social Hygiene.

Tonry, Michael. 1995. *Malign Neglect: Race, Crime, and Punishment in America*. New York: Oxford University Press.

U.S. House of Representatives, Committee on Government Operations. 1993. *Drug Use Measurement: Strengths, Limitations, and Recommendations for Improvement*. Gaithersburg, Md.: U.S. General Accounting Office.

U.S. Senate, Committee on the Judiciary. 1990. *Hard-Core Cocaine Addicts: Measuring and Fighting the Epidemic*. 101st Congress, 2d Sess. Washington, D.C.: U.S. Government Printing Office.

U.S. Senate, Committee on the Judiciary. The Majority Staffs of the Senate Judiciary Committee and the International Narcotics Control Caucus. 1992a. *The President's Drug Strategy: Has It Worked?* Washington, D.C.: U.S. Government Printing Office.

———. 1992b. *Fighting Drug Abuse: Tough Decisions for Our National Strategy*. Washington, D.C.: U.S. Senate Judiciary Committee.

Weil, Andrew. 1986. *The Natural Mind: An Investigation of Drugs and the Higher Consciousness*. Boston, Mass.: Houghton Mifflin.

Wickens, Thomas. 1993. "Quantitative Methods for Estimating the Size of a Drug-Using Population." *Journal of Drug Issues* 23(2):185–216.

Wish, E. 1990. "U.S. Drug Policy in the 1990s: Insights from New Data from Arrestees." *International Journal of the Addictions* 25(3A):377–409.

————. 1993. "From the Acting Director." *CESAR Reports* 3(1):4.

Wish, E., and B. Gropper. 1990. "Drug Testing by the Criminal Justice System." In *Drugs and Crime*, edited by M. Tonry and J. Wilson. Vol. 13 of *Crime and Justice: A Review of Research*, edited by Michael Tonry and Norval Morris. Chicago: University of Chicago Press.

Wright, H. 1910. "Report from the United States of America." *Report on the International Opium Commission, 1909*, vol. 2. Shanghai: *North China Daily News and Herald*.

Author Index—Volumes 1–20*

* The number in parentheses indicates the volume in which the author's essay is published.

415

Subject Index—Volumes 1–20*

British gas suicide story, (10):79

Bullying, (17):381

Burglary, (14):73

Cartage industry in New York, (18):149

Child maltreatment, incidence and prevalence of, (11):219

Classification (*see also* Prediction): for control in jails and prisons, (9):323; for risk, (9):249; for treatment, (9):293; selected methodological issues, (9):201

Community: and crime prevention, (19):21; dynamics of, and crime prevention, (8):387; importance of in understanding crime, (8):1; organizations and crime, (10):39; service orders, (6):51

Community crime careers, (8):67; in Britain, (8):101

Community policing (*see also* police and policing): elements of and impediments to, (10):1; and problem solving, (15):99; workability of, (8):343

Court (*see also* Juvenile court): eyewitness testimony in, (3):105; hypnosis in, (3):61; insanity defense in, (6):221

Crime (*see also* Police and policing): and age, (7):189; and approaches to

family violence, 1640–1980, (11):19; and biology, (2):85; causation of, (1):203; in cities, (8):271; and criminal juries, (2):269; and delinquency, (1):289; deterrence of, (2):211; fear of, and neighborhood change, (8):203; and gender, (4):91; and justice in eighteenth- and nineteenth-century England, (2):45; and mental disorder, (4):145; opportunities for, (7):1; organizational, (18):1; placement, displacement, and deflection of, (12):277; and public opinion, (16):99; research on drugs and, (13):1; and rights and utility, (3):247; and the savings and loan crisis, (18):247; strategic prevention of, (19):1; and urban economic and neighborhood conditions, (8):231; and women, (14):307

Crime prevention: and auto theft, (16):1; and bullying, (17):381; and city-center street crimes, (19):429; developmental, (19):151; evaluation of, (19):585; implemention of, (19):535; public health and criminal justice approaches to, (19):237; and repeat victimization, (19):469; and retail-sector crimes, (19):263; situational, (19):91, (4):225; strategic approaches to, (19):1; and substance abuse, (19):343

* The number in parentheses indicates the volume in which the essay is published.

Title Index—Volumes 1–20*

* The number in parentheses indicates the volume in which the essay is published.

Volume Index—Volumes 1–20

Crime and Justice: An Annual Review of Research, edited by Michael Tonry and
Norval Morris
Volume 3 (1981):